# The United States and Latin America

# The United States and Latin America

## An Historical Analysis of Inter-American Relations

GORDON CONNELL-SMITH

A HALSTED PRESS BOOK

JOHN WILEY & SONS
New York

Library of Congress Catalog Card No 74-11911
ISBN 0 470 16856 0

Published in the U.S.A. by Halstead Press
a Division of John Wiley & Sons, Inc., New York
Printed in Great Britain

# Preface

In an earlier work I recorded my appreciation of the very considerable help I had received from several distinguished scholars. Over the years my debt to them has grown immeasurably. I welcome the opportunity of acknowledging this and of renewing my warmest thanks. I would like to mention particularly Professor Robin Humphreys, whose retirement from the Directorship of the University of London Institute of Latin American Studies coincides with the publication of this book. There can be few indeed among the very many colleagues and former pupils honouring the occasion who owe so much to his help and encouragement.

Professor Lewis Hanke, who likewise did a great deal to launch my research in the field of inter-American relations, has never ceased to allow me to draw upon his expertise and kindness. I have also been extremely fortunate in enjoying the friendship of Dr. Bryce Wood, whose outstanding contributions in my field (manifest in this book) have been augmented by fruitful discussion and many helpful suggestions. I would like to express again my warm thanks to Professor Martín Quirarte, the Director, for all his help during my visits to the archives of the Ministry of External Relations in Mexico City; and to Miss Helen Kaufmann of the Columbus Memorial Library in Washington for the bibliographical support I have received over the years. I must thank also Mr. Paul Richardson, my publisher, for all he has done during the preparation of the book. Nearer to home, I am greatly indebted to my friend and colleague, Dr. Howell A. Lloyd, who read my manuscript with all his usual care and acute perception—to my great advantage. A specialist in the early modern period, his wide range of historical interests and knowledge—happily for me—includes contemporary international history. I must, of course, dissociate Dr. Lloyd, and the others whom I have named, from the judgements I have expressed in the book and whatever errors the latter may contain.

I gratefully acknowledge the funds I have received in support of my research in the United States and Latin America from the Rockefeller Foundation, the William Waldorf Astor Foundation, the Royal Institute of International Affairs, the University Grants Committee and my own University of Hull.

Finally, there has been the indispensable contribution of my family, to whom I would like to dedicate this book. In addition to displaying their customary tolerance, they have in various ways, including proof checking and offering numerous stylistic improvements, taken a most positive part in the enterprise.

Kirk Ella                                                              July, 1974


For Wendy,
Sarah and Nicholas

# Contents

Preface                                                                    v

Introduction                                                              ix

1 The Background                                                           1

2 The Beginnings to the Formulation of the Monroe Doctrine              41

3 Latin America and the Manifest Destiny of the United States          71

4 Pan Americanism and the Intervention Issue                          107

5 Good Neighbours and Wartime Partners                                146

6 The United States and Latin America in the Post-War
  World I: Up to the Cuban Revolution                                  187

7 The United States and Latin America in the Post-War
  World II: Since the Cuban Revolution                                 226

8 Conclusion                                                          267

  Index                                                               289

# Introduction

This book follows upon my earlier work, *The Inter-American System*,[1] and its enlarged Spanish-language edition.[2] I was then concerned with the international organisation through which relations between the United States and Latin America are in part conducted. It is those relations that are now my subject; the inter-American system itself is only one— albeit a not insignificant—aspect of them. Moreover, my present historical analysis begins long before the inter-American system was established in 1890; and it includes an examination of important developments which have occurred since my earlier books were published.

Inevitably, because of its scope, this book is largely a work of synthesis. Yet it contains a sizeable nucleus of original research, developed in the course of my earlier investigations into the history of the inter-American system, and subsequently enlarged to cover further sources of information. Those sources include fresh visits to the United States and countries of Latin America, during which I was able to discuss my subject anew with leading scholars and men prominent in public life. They also include documentary materials, principally relating to recent developments in the Organization of American States, and in particular to Mexico's participation in the inter-American system, as recorded in the archives of the Mexican Ministry of External Relations.

Mexico occupies a very important place in the history of United States relations with Latin America, primarily because of her geographical position: her northern boundary is the frontier between the two Americas. Because of her contiguity with the United States, Mexico has had the longest and most unhappy experience of the latter's power and policies. In addition to having been dispossessed of more

---

[1] Gordon Connell-Smith, *The Inter-American System* (London, Oxford University Press for the Royal Institute of International Affairs, 1966).

[2] *Id.*, *El Sistema Interamericano* (México, D.F., Fondo de Cultura Económica, 1971).

than half of her national territory, she has suffered United States intervention in all its main forms: military, economic and political. Nor
has the issue of race been insignificant in United States attitudes towards Mexicans (to whom the highly offensive term 'greasers' has only
too often been applied by unthinking North Americans), as towards
Latin Americans generally. The proximity of Mexico has also meant
that relations with her have often furnished issues in United States
domestic politics. Revolutionary nationalism in Mexico offered the
first serious challenge to United States hegemony from within Latin
America, and the (Franklin) Roosevelt administration's adjustment to
it was an important element in the formulation and application of its
Good Neighbour policy. In short, United States relations with Mexico
have highlighted major aspects of her relations with Latin America as a
whole, of which they have been described as providing something of a
barometer. Interestingly, Mexico is often cited as the Latin American
country with whom the United States enjoys the best relations
today.[3]

In view of the enormous amount of material available—and the fact
that I cannot myself claim to have examined more than a proportion of
it—I have not attempted to construct a comprehensive bibliographical
apparatus for this book. My footnote references may be supplemented
from the select bibliographies contained in my earlier works. On this
occasion I have confined my references to published materials in the
English language, though I have included in my selection works by
Latin American historians and social scientists. Many of the works
cited contain substantial bibliographical references. Among general
bibliographies an outstanding, though now dated, compilation is
S. F. Bemis and G. G. Griffin, *Guide to the Diplomatic History of the
United States, 1775–1921* (Library of Congress, Washington,
United States Government Printing Office, 1935: Reprint, Gloucester,
Mass., 1959). A year after this first appeared publication began of the
annual— and indispensable— *Handbook of Latin American Studies*
(Cambridge, Mass., Harvard University Press, 1936–51; Gainesville,
University of Florida Press, 1951– ). A valuable specialist bibliography
was published in 1968: David F. Trask, Michael C. Meyer and Roger
R. Trask, *A Bibliography of United States-Latin American Relations*

---

[3] See, for example, United States Senate, 91st Congress, 1st Session. *Survey of the
Alliance for Progress. Compilation of Studies and Hearings of the Subcommittee on American
Republics Affairs of the Committee on Foreign Relations, United States Senate* (U.S. Govern-
ment Printing Office, Washington, 1969), p. 20.

*since 1810: A Selected List of Eleven Thousand Published References* (Lincoln, University of Nebraska Press). All these bibliographies contain materials in languages other than English.

Most of my sources, including the secondary works I have consulted, originate in the United States. This circumstance is explicable basically in terms of availability and accessibility of documents[4] and the very much greater amount written on my subject by North than by Latin Americans. It also reflects the fact that a study of United States relations with Latin America is largely a critique of United States Latin American policies: in other words, it reflects the power situation in the western hemisphere. Thus a key source is the series *Papers relating to the Foreign Relations of the United States*, published by the State Department from 1861. For earlier years there are W. R. Manning (ed.), *Diplomatic Correspondence of the United States concerning the Independence of the Latin-American Nations* (3 vols., New York, 1925); and *Diplomatic Correspondence of the United States: Inter-American Affairs, 1831–1860* (12 vols., Washington, Carnegie Endowment for International Peace, 1932–9). Messages and speeches of United States Presidents (and sometimes speeches by Secretaries of State) often have been of considerable significance in inter-American relations. The Monroe Doctrine itself, of course, derives from such a source. Hearings of congressional committees—and especially of subcommittees concerned with United States relations with Latin America—can also be valuable; so, for background information—and knowledge of the kind of information available to members of the United States Congress—are studies especially compiled for them by university professors and other consultants.[5] Incidentally, such university professors sometimes have had experience of inter-American affairs in government positions.

Memoirs provide another useful source, especially for the historian of the contemporary period. Such an historian has available many other forms of evidence as potential checks on these essentially personal statements. But the personal dimension is invaluable, for diplomatic correspondence, by contrast, is not calculated to reveal the *attitudes* of those conducting international relations. Memoirs often disclose how little attention Latin America has received from most United States administrations, as well as the assumptions and prejudices of the people

---

[4] The records of the Organization of American States are housed in the General Secretariat (the former Pan American Union) in Washington, D.C.

[5] See, for example, above, p. x, n. 3.

concerned. Newspapers, and books written by journalists about particular events and issues, can also be extremely valuable as sources. For newspapers not only reflect the climate in which political decisions are made; they also help to form it. This is especially true in the case of the United States. My study demonstrates the significance of journalism at key points in the history of United States relations with Latin America.

My research into inter-American relations has been enriched by the opportunities for personal discussion afforded me by distinguished men directly involved in conducting them. In my previous books I have acknowledged their kindness. Since then I have had very many more interviews, including some with leading participants in certain major events. Many of these discussions were 'off-the-record' and non-attributable, and I have therefore decided not to make individual acknowledgement of any of them. During my travels in Latin America and the United States I have had countless conversations with all manner of people interested in my subject. But this book still rests principally upon a foundation of documents and other written materials, primary and secondary, only a selection from which is included in my footnote references.

The text of this book likewise comprises a selection: what I judge to be the most important aspects of relations between the United States and Latin America, and those issues, events, institutions and persons which have shaped them in the past and influence them in the present. My selection does not differ radically from those of others who have written about inter-American relations, but I would claim that my approach is more critical—and realistic—than that customarily adopted by United States historians towards their country's policies. These historians have helped to project what I have called the 'self-image' of the United States. This self-image represents inter-American relations as having differed fundamentally from those normally obtaining between great powers and weak ones, because of the unique benevolence of United States policies. It derives, of course, from that propensity for identifying morality with power so characteristic of great nations— and reflected by their historians. In this case, the most influential such historian has been Professor S. F. Bemis. Bemis's study, *The Latin American Policy of the United States: An Historical Interpretation*, although published over thirty years ago, is still used as a basic textbook on inter-American relations, and is widely regarded as a 'classic' on its subject. 'Tendentious and didactic', in the words of a younger

North American historian, 'the work has never been completely sup-
planted by more recent books on the same topic'.[6] This study contains
an embarrassingly large number of quotations from Bemis; they could
have been multiplied. But the self-image of the United States in her
relations with Latin America can be sustained only by ignoring or
glossing over unpleasant realities. This book contains many examples
of United States historians doing both.

A corollary to the United States self-image is an assumption that
there exists an essential harmony of interests between the two Americas.
Good inter-American relations may, therefore, be assured by enlightened
leadership on both sides. Historians warmly sympathetic to United
States policies have tended to attribute admitted difficulties to irrational
and 'ultranationalistic' attitudes on the part of Latin Americans. More
objective historians freely admit that United States policies have not
always been enlightened. Indeed, in recent years, many North American scholars—social scientists ominously more prominent among them
than historians—have written very critically on various particular
aspects of inter-American relations and on United States policies in
Latin America. I have quoted extensively from their work in this book.
But, in my judgement, United States historians analysing inter-
American relations have shown a marked disinclination to draw the
general conclusions to which their own often searching criticisms of
particular policies so clearly point. For the most part, they have been
unable to dissociate themselves from the United States self-image; and
so they cling to a conviction that, in spite of many—even serious—
mistakes, their country's intentions have been good.

The basic assumptions which influence the judgement of even the
more critical United States historians of inter-American relations are,
significantly, shared by Senator William Fulbright and well illustrated
by his book, *The Arrogance of Power*.[7] Fulbright has been an outstanding critic of United States foreign policy in recent years—which
makes his views of considerable importance in an analysis of North
American attitudes towards Latin America. In his book, which deals
only in part with the region, the senator repeatedly affirms the 'good'
and even 'noble' intentions of the United States in Latin America,
although he himself describes 'good intentions' as 'a highly subjective

6 Lester D. Langley, 'The Diplomatic Historians : Bailey and Bemis', *The History
Teacher*, vol. vi (November 1972), p. 65.
7 J. William Fulbright, *The Arrogance of Power* (paperback edn., Harmondsworth,
1970).

criterion of national behaviour'.[8] High on the list of United States good intentions—for Senator Fulbright as for United States historians—is dedication to the promotion of democracy in Latin America (although the evidence of United States preference for co-operative dictators is overwhelming).[9] One sentence from *The Arrogance of Power* epitomises the muted criticism I have been discussing: 'Most [Latin Americans] ... think they need protection from the United States and the history of the Monroe Doctrine and the "Roosevelt Corollary" *suggests that their fears are not entirely without foundation.*'[10] To contrast the complacency of even liberal North Americans with the depth of Latin American feeling about United States policies is to realise how irreconcilable is the United States self-image with the image of her that prevails south of the Rio Grande.

Thus there exists a need for a critical, scholarly historical analysis of United States relations with Latin America. Even so, in endeavouring to meet this need I have incurred a very considerable debt to the United States historians whom I quote, very often critically, in this book. The starting point of all historical writing is the work of others, and whatever merit my book may be deemed to possess owes a very great deal to the stimulus of their ideas as well as to the corpus of factual knowledge they accumulated and the bibliographical tools they fashioned.

However, I reject the assumptions upon which most of these earlier studies were based and I am much more critical of United States policies towards Latin America than the vast majority of my predecessors have been. This does not imply, of course, acceptance on my part of what might be called the Latin American interpretation of those policies. In international affairs, policies are indissociable from power, and if power is not to be equated with morality, neither is there moral virtue in weakness. But it is because of the immense margin of power which she has enjoyed over her weaker neighbours, and the use to which she has put it, that the United States must accept the major responsibility for the condition of her relations with Latin America. Several years ago I wrote:

> The United States is bound to use her power to promote her interests as her government and people interpret these. It would be surprising if there were a true community of interests between the most industrially advanced

[8] *Ibid.*, pp. 24, 28, 98.
[9] I discuss this point below, pp. 277 ff.　　　[10] *Op. cit.*, p. 98. My italics.

and militarily powerful nation in the world and the twenty mainly under-developed, militarily weak republics to the south. The record shows unmistakably that there does not exist a community of interests between the United States and Latin America in the field of peace and security. On the contrary, as the record again indicates, the promotion of United States peace and security appears, in the last analysis, to be incompatible with the exercise of sovereignty by the Latin American countries.[11]

The essay in which these words appeared was concerned with the question of peace and security in the western hemisphere. But the divergence of interests between the United States and Latin America was even more marked in the economic field. Since then (1968) it has become increasingly evident that the fulfilment of Latin American aspirations in economic development and social progress is incom-patible with the region's present degree of dependence upon the United States.

I have employed in this book what I have called elsewhere 'a con-temporary approach'.[12] The book is an essay in contemporary history, in several senses of that much debated term. The whole period my study embraces falls within what some historians consider to be con-temporary history: the last two hundred years. A very significant seg-ment falls within my own lifetime. And my study covers events which were occurring even as the manuscript was being completed (the end of 1973). No less importantly, as I have indicated, I have employed the materials and techniques of contemporary history, including journalism, interviews with participants in significant events and attendance at international conferences— as well as the study of relevant original documents, printed sources and secondary works. However, a con-temporary approach involves more than the techniques of studying and writing contemporary history.

An important characteristic of such an approach is the historian's awareness of his own circumstances, and therefore of the essentially subjective character of all historical writing: of the latter's primary concern with judgement and not with supposedly objective facts. I began to study the history of inter-American relations following the

---

[11] Gordon Connell-Smith, 'The Inter-American System : Problems of Peace and Security in the Western Hemisphere', in Robert W. Gregg (ed.), *International Organiza-tion in the Western Hemisphere* (Syracuse, N.Y., Syracuse University Press, 1968), p.90.
[12] Gordon Connell-Smith and Howell A. Lloyd, *The Relevance of History* (London, 1972), ch. 3.

Cuban revolution, which caused a great upsurge of interest in Latin America among members of the academic community as well as government in the United States. In the event, the nineteen-sixties and early nineteen-seventies have proved a critical period in the history of United States relations with Latin America. I have tried to view the events of these years in a wider historical perspective, and at the same time—as a complementary part of my historical analysis—to view earlier events in the light of the new perspectives which more recent developments have induced. Unremitting comparison between historical phenomena occurring at different points in time is an essential feature of a contemporary approach. The impact of the Cuban revolution upon inter-American relations well illustrates this point. For while that revolution must be evaluated in the light of United States policies towards the island from early in the nineteenth century, the challenge posed to the United States by Cuba's alignment with the Soviet Union adds a new perspective to the history of the Monroe Doctrine (central to any study of inter-American relations).

Analysing contemporary events reminds the historian of certain realities which he might otherwise overlook. One such is that history is at least as much concerned with myths as with 'facts'. People have always been motivated by what they believe to be true much more than by what scholars may later judge to have been 'the actual truth'. And their beliefs have stemmed more from assumptions and prejudices than from reliable information (often not available to them in making decisions). This book illustrates the importance of myths in shaping the history of inter-American relations. Again, a contemporary approach emphasises history's concern with people—a necessary corrective to the professional historian's chronic addiction to 'documents'. It is particularly important for scholars, so ready to pass judgement upon politicians, to realise the complexity of, and the difficulties inherent in, the decision-making process. A contemporary historian should be more sympathetic towards the decision maker because, conscious of his own place on the moving frontier of time, he knows that he himself is making only interim judgements upon situations which are always in the process of change. Yet how much easier it is for him to arrive at his judgements in the quiet of his study than it is for the decision maker to arrive at his, under great and generally conflicting pressures, in rapidly changing situations where real people are immediately, urgently, involved!

In such a spirit I present my study. I have stressed that it is essentially a critical appraisal of United States policy towards Latin America. It has been written during a period when the assumptions upon which United States foreign policy traditionally have been based have been increasingly called into question. As Dr. Henry Kissinger said shortly after becoming Secretary of State, '. . . now we are in a situation where we have to conduct foreign policy the way many other nations have had to conduct it throughout their history. We no longer have overwhelming margins of safety and we no longer have overwhelming margins of resources.'[13] The United States has for some years been seeking a rapprochment with the Soviet Union. Along with her withdrawal from Vietnam she has been moving to normalise her relations with China. She is trying to come to terms with an increasingly assertive Western Europe. And, against the background of the energy crisis, she has been re-examining her commitment to Israel. Even in Latin America, where the United States still enjoys an immense margin of power, this is no longer 'overwhelming', and she faces a growing challenge. The need is apparent for a reappraisal of her Latin American policy. To such a reappraisal I would like this study to contribute, in however modest a degree. For it is addressed not merely to fellow scholars and general readers, but also to those concerned with formulating and executing policy. I have been encouraged in this last respect by the interest shown in my previous books and articles on the subject by men in public life in both the United States and Latin America.

I develop my analysis in eight chapters. The first chapter contains background information showing the basis of relations between the United States and Latin America and how these relations are conducted. Chapter II examines the origins of United States interest in Latin America; the establishment of diplomatic relations between the two Americas; and the background to the formulation of the Monroe Doctrine. Chapter III demonstrates the consequences for Latin America of the fulfilment of 'Manifest Destiny', including the war with Mexico and the establishment of protectorates over Cuba and Panama. In chapter IV Pan Americanism is examined and its relationship to the growing United States hegemony over Latin America analysed. The motives and consequences of United States interventions in the Caribbean region are discussed. The Good Neighbour policy in peace and during the Second World War is critically examined in chapter V.

---

[13] Quoted in *Horizons USA*, 74/1 (United States Information Agency, Washington, D.C.), p. 33.

Chapters VI and VII are devoted to the period since the end of the Second World War, with the Cuban revolution marking the division between them. The final chapter offers some interim conclusions in the light of the preceding analysis.

# 1　The Background

This book is an historical analysis of relations between two Americas: the United States and Latin America. The subject at once raises a fundamental question. Since there must be two such entities before relations can be said to exist between them, can 'Latin America' be said to exist as an entity at all? Obviously, the United States exists in the sense that its member-states, despite their often considerable differences, all recognise the sovereignty of the federal government and the authority of its central institutions, particularly in the sphere of foreign policy. But the term 'Latin America', like the terms 'Indo-America' and 'Ibero-America' that are sometimes used, refers to twenty distinct republics. Between these republics there are differences of very great significance. Although eighteen of them were formerly parts of the Spanish American Empire, the contrasts between them are extremely marked in such important respects as size, natural resources, population, racial composition and the degree of political and economic maturity each has achieved. There are further differences between these countries and the largest Latin American country of all: the former Portuguese American Empire, Brazil. Haiti, once a French colony, is different again.

However, the diversity of 'Latin America', the heterogeneousness of its constituent parts, is compatible with my argument. For it is my contention that the term 'Latin America' is meaningful above all *within the context of my subject.* On the one hand, what the peoples of Latin America do have in common above all else is a broadly similar attitude towards the United States: an attitude that expresses so many of those peoples' aspirations and problems. On the other, the United States does have a distinctive Latin American policy: a policy which both is influenced by and itself influences United States relations with individual Latin American countries, as well as relations among the latter themselves. This book will analyse the inter-action of attitude and policy that gives the term 'Latin America' its validity and so distinguishes the twenty republics collectively from their northern neighbour. In the unflattering words of the eminent Mexican scholar, Daniel Cosío Villegas, Latin America is 'a formless mass tied to the coattails of the United States'.[1]

Others have employed more flattering, and more affectionate, words and images to identify Latin America. The phrase 'Our America' has been used by, among others, the Mexican philosopher Leopoldo Zea,[2] and the Argentine revolutionary Che Guevara.[3] The phrase carries overtones of reaction against United States domination. So, too, does the mythological image of 'Ariel', popularised by the Uruguayan writer José Enrique Rodó, which contrasts Latin Americans with the United States 'Calibans', and provides them with 'the justification of their racial characteristics, the compensation for their practical backwardness, the claim to spiritual superiority over the Titan of the North'.[4] For what above all distinguishes Latin America from the United States is the disparity of power between them. The United States has always been significantly more powerful than the other American countries. In the twentieth century she has enjoyed an increasingly wide margin of superiority in economic, military and political power over any or all of the Twenty Republics, so that by now the imbalance of power in the western hemisphere is vast indeed. This dominant position of the United States, crudely portrayed in Juan José Arévalo's famous polemic, *The Shark and the Sardines*,[5] is the determining factor in inter-American relations.

Latin America is, in fact, the immediate zone of interest of the United States, as it was even before the Latin American countries became independent. President Monroe's pronouncement of 2 December 1823, which later became the Monroe Doctrine, adumbrated United States hegemony in the western hemisphere a clear year before the Battle of Ayacucho, which virtually ended the wars of Spanish American independence. Already United States leaders were referring to 'their own hemisphere'. They had a clear intention to establish an

---

[1] *American Extremes* (Austin, University of Texas Press, 1964), p. 179.
[2] *Latin America and the World* (Norman, University of Oklahoma Press, 1969), pp. 30, 77, 92 ff., etc.
[3] E.g., John Gerassi (ed.), *Venceremos!: The Speeches and Writings of Ernesto Che Guevara* (New York, 1968), pp. 416, 419–21. Fidel Castro has also used the phrase.
[4] Stephen Clissold, *Latin America: A Cultural Outline* (London, 1965), p. 108.
[5] New York, 1961.

imbalance of power in the Americas by keeping the countries of Latin America outside the European balance of power system. The United States was to be the only great power in the western hemisphere, and the Latin American countries would be part of an American system in which she would be paramount. In the words of Professor Van Alstyne, 'The Monroe Doctrine is really an official declaration fencing in the "western hemisphere" as a United States sphere of influence'.[6]

Linked with her ambition to achieve hegemony in the Americas has been a conviction, associated with the concept of 'Manifest Destiny',[7] that the United States possesses a natural right to it. This right derives not only from her obvious superiority over Latin America in such vital areas as political organisation and economic dynamism, but also from an assumed moral superiority over both Latin America and the European powers whom she has sought to exclude from effective influence in the western hemisphere. Latin American weakness has invited intervention by great powers. Against the designs—real and imagined —of such powers from outside the hemisphere the United States has been Latin America's self-appointed protector. Her protection has sometimes involved armed intervention and occupation. For the United States has assumed that Latin America must be under either her control or that of her potential enemies. This assumption tends to be self-fulfilling, and it may equally be argued that the Latin American countries 'can find protection against the northern neighbor only by using his enemies across the oceans as a balance against him'.[8] The case of Cuba since the revolution may be cited to support both propositions.

Thus has the United States adopted an attitude of superiority towards Latin America and Latin Americans: a 'tutelary style' which, moreover, 'has tended to reinforce United States tendencies to think of and deal with Latin America as a whole'.[9] In the judgement of one North American historian:

It is widely assumed in the United States that the nations of Latin America are an inferior species of states that belong rightfully in the sphere of

---

[6] R. W. Van Alstyne, *The Rising American Empire* (Oxford, 1960), p. 99.

[7] See below, pp. 71 ff.

[8] Nicholas J. Spykman, *America's Strategy in World Politics: the United States and the Balance of Power* (New York, 1942), p. 360.

[9] Herbert Goldhamer, *The Foreign Powers in Latin America* (Princeton, N.J., Princeton University Press, 1972), p. 208.

influence of the United States, existing primarily for the purpose of implementing its foreign policy, contributing to its defense, and servicing its economy.[10]

Another has declared the treatment of Latin Americans as inferiors to be the most serious source of United States difficulties in Latin America.[11] United States arrogance towards Latin America reflects the vast disparity of power between them, which encourages North Americans to pay scant regard to the sensibilities of Latin Americans. Such arrogance is of long-standing: Anglo-Saxon attitudes of superiority towards the Spanish and Portuguese elements in Latin America date from the colonial period, as do racist attitudes towards people of Indian and Negro origin.

When the United States asserted her hegemony over Latin America at the end of the nineteenth century, her leaders openly proclaimed her civilising mission and seldom hid their belief that Latin Americans generally were unfit to govern themselves. Race has been an important factor in United States relations with Mexico, the acquisition of more than one half of whose territory may be viewed as an extension of the despoliation of the North American Indians. But racial discrimination has been particularly acute in the sensitive Caribbean region,[12] where a very large proportion of the population is non-European and the Negro strain is strong. It is here that most United States armed interventions have taken place. Panama has been a flashpoint of racial friction, linked with nationalism directed against the United States. The outlook of United States citizens in the Canal Zone (the 'Zonians') resembles the traditional attitude of white settlers in Africa and elsewhere towards the 'natives'. But these are only particular examples of a general attitude of superiority with its ominous racial overtones. Theodore Roosevelt's Corollary to the Monroe Doctrine of 1904 was based upon the wider premise: the inferiority of Latin Americans and their unfitness to manage their own affairs. The Monroe Doctrine has

---

[10] Robert N. Burr, *Our Troubled Hemisphere : Perspectives on United States–Latin American Relations* (Washington, D.C., The Brookings Institution, 1967), p. 48.

[11] Frank Tannenbaum, 'The United States and Latin America', *Political Science Quarterly*, vol. lxxvi, no. 2 (June 1961), p. 163.

[12] I use this term to include the countries of Central America and Panama as well as the island republics. During the last few years the former British dependencies in this region have become more closely linked with the United States and Latin America. This has important implications in respect of the question of race in inter-American relations. See below, pp. 284–5.

always implied that Latin Americans are among the backward peoples of the world who, but for United States protection, would have been colonised as Asians and Africans had been.[13] Woodrow Wilson's reported desire to 'teach them to elect good men' reflected similar views. Even Franklin Roosevelt's concession, 'They think they are just as good as we are and many of them are',[14] betrays an innate sense of superiority which has shown itself from the beginning in United States attitudes towards Latin America. The sentiments expressed by these three famous Presidents, each of whom played an outstanding role in the history of United States relations with Latin America, have been shared by their fellow countrymen generally: most importantly by those, like themselves, involved in the formulation and execution of policy towards the region.

For the United States does have a distinctive policy towards Latin America as a whole. Sometimes it has been called a 'Pan American policy'.[15] As we shall see, it is within what used to be termed the 'Pan American system'—subsequently the inter-American system— that this policy may be most clearly seen in operation. There is an Assistant Secretary of State for Inter-American Affairs and the State Department has a Latin American Division. The main unifying ingredient in United States policy towards the countries of Latin America has been furnished by the Monroe Doctrine. The Latin American writer who said that 'the story of the Monroe Doctrine is the story of inter-American relations' was guilty of little exaggeration.[16] Moreover, the United States has pursued special policies towards Latin America as a whole in response to particular situations. Outstanding among these have been the Good Neighbour policy associated with President Franklin Roosevelt, and the Alliance for Progress launched by President Kennedy. In addition, within the broader framework of her Latin American policy, the United States has pursued a 'Panama policy': she is especially concerned with both the internal and external affairs of the small countries lying close to the Panama Canal. As we have already noted, it is in this region—the Caribbean region—that by far the

---

[13] It is ironical that over the last decade or so the countries of Latin America have increasingly associated themselves with the 'Third World'. See below, p. 284.

[14] See below, p. 175.

[15] See below, p. 14.

[16] Gaston Nerval, *Autopsy of the Monroe Doctrine: the Strange Story of Inter-American Relations* (New York, 1934), p. v. 'Gaston Nerval' is the pseudonym of the Bolivian diplomatist Raúl Díez de Medina.

majority of her overt interventions have taken place. But, as the repercussions of these interventions illustrate, her Panama policy has importantly affected her relations with Latin America as a whole. Professor Lloyd Mecham has gone so far as to assert: 'American diplomacy has been so much concerned with the countries of the [Caribbean[17]] area that it is hardly an exaggeration to say that most of its major policy decisions and actions relating to Latin America originated in this region.'[18]

The overall objective of United States Latin American policy has been to safeguard and enhance her considerable interests in the region. In practice, this has meant the establishment and subsequent maintenance of her hegemony through the exclusion of extra-continental power capable of challenging it; in the absence of such power she has faced no serious challenge from Latin America itself. United States interests in Latin America are strategic (involving her security), economic and political. These are, of course, closely related to each other. She also has an important moral and psychological stake in the region.

The United States has always maintained that her security would be threatened by the intervention of extra-continental powers in Latin America. President Monroe declared that 'we should consider any attempt on their part to extend their system to any portion of this hemisphere as dangerous to our peace and safety'. In 1823 the Doctrine was directed principally at the members of the Holy Alliance; in the twentieth century it has been challenged first by the Axis powers and, more recently, by the Soviet Union and China.[19] United States strategic interests in Latin America were greatly increased early in this century by her acquisition of the Panama Canal. She has important military installations in and around the Canal Zone, where the headquarters of her Southern Command are located. She has, among other bases on the approaches to the Canal, those at Roosevelt Roads in Puerto Rico and Guantánamo Bay in Cuba. Moreover, the National Aeronautic and

---

[17] For Mecham, 'Caribbean' means 'not only the island republics, but also the republics of Central America, including Panama, and Colombia and Venezuela'.

[18] J. Lloyd Mecham, *A Survey of United States–Latin American Relations* (Boston, Mass., 1965), p. 239.

[19] The United States has generally referred to a threat from 'international communism' or 'the Sino-Soviet powers', even though it has long been recognised that the Soviet Union and China have seldom acted in unison and, indeed, have been in open dispute for some years.

Space Administration (NASA) has some dozen missile tracking stations in Latin America.[20]

The military contribution of Latin America to the security of the United States is mainly the provision of such facilities. Thus, although there has been a collective security pact covering the western hemisphere since 1947 (the Inter-American Treaty of Reciprocal Assistance[21]) there exist no military arrangements comparable, for example, with the North Atlantic Treaty Organization (NATO). The countries of Latin America have been neither able nor willing to make a substantial contribution to the defence of the hemisphere against external aggression. United States motives for associating them with the defence of the continent have been primarily political. It is a question not merely of providing her with military facilities, but of denying such facilities to her potential enemies. And while the strategic importance of the Caribbean region has been diminished by the development of long-range missiles, the United States has demonstrated her continuing concern lest bases should be established there under the control of a hostile power. Meanwhile, for the last decade or so, internal security in Latin America has been the United States chief preoccupation. She has been an active promoter of counter-insurgency programmes and has co-operated closely with the Latin American military in this field.[22]

The United States has very considerable economic interests in Latin America in terms of her foreign trade, private investment and public investment in economic aid programmes. According to President Nixon in his report on foreign policy to Congress in May 1973, for example, the book value of United States investments in Latin America had risen to over $16,000 millions. But the importance of the United States economic stake in Latin America is not to be measured in terms of such figures alone. It is significant—the more so in the light of the growing energy crisis of the nineteen-seventies—that a high proportion of United States private investment in Latin America traditionally has been in petroleum and mining enterprises.[23] This has linked her

---

[20] For further details of these bases see, for example, Edwin Lieuwen, *The United States and the Challenge to Security in Latin America* (Columbus, Ohio, Ohio State University Press, 1966), pp. 10 ff.     [21] See below, pp. 196–7.

[22] See below, p. 21. It is noteworthy that President Kennedy had a particular interest in counter-insurgency: what Arthur M. Schlesinger, Jr., *A Thousand Days: John F. Kennedy in the White House* (paperback edn., London 1967), p. 287, describes as 'an old preoccupation from Senate days'.

[23] United States manufacturing investment in Latin America grew more rapidly in the nineteen-sixties, however.

economic and security interests, for the region is an important source of strategic raw materials. Yet it is in order to supply her industries generally, and not only those specifically concerned with defence, that the United States has sought to *control* the economies of Latin America. She has achieved a high degree of success in this regard: key resources in the region are owned by her citizens. Latin America is heavily dependent upon the United States as a market and as a source of investment capital; United States aid has substantially increased this dependence. She dominates Latin America economically as she does militarily. Although some of them have sizeable industrial sectors, the countries of the region generally have colonial-type economies, as they had during the period of European imperial rule. It is not surprising that the United States is widely regarded as an imperial power in her relationship with Latin America, and has even been described as 'our new mother country'.[24] Latin America's economic independence would mean the end of United States control: a revolutionary change from its historical condition of subordination. Latin American nationalism is basically anti-(North) American.

It follows that the United States has very considerable political interests in Latin America. These are concerned fundamentally with maintaining in power governments representative of those groups whose interests are furthered by co-operating with her, and preventing the coming to power of those groups who seek to bring about revolutionary change. In short, the United States seeks to promote stability based upon the *status quo*. She is a counter-revolutionary power in Latin America. This accords with her overall foreign policy and especially *vis-à-vis* the Soviet Union and China. Incidentally, Latin American support for her policies in other regions of the world has been of value to the United States; for example, in the General Assembly of the United Nations.

In addition to her strategic, economic and political interests in Latin America, the United States has a significant moral and psychological stake in the region.[25] What is involved here is first what may be termed her self-image, and secondly her posture in world affairs. All powers, of course, protest the virtue of their motives in dealing

---

[24] Leopoldo Zea, quoted in Clissold, *op. cit.*, p. 108. The case of Cuba well illustrates this point, for she passed at once from colonial status to that of a United States satellite. Since the revolution Cuba has once again changed her 'mother country'.

[25] Cf. the observations of Governor Rockefeller in his report to President Nixon (1969). See below, p. 257.

with others; usually the great majority of their peoples believe their leaders and—perhaps to a greater degree than critics would concede—political leaders are inclined to believe their own virtuous protestations.[26] And great nations readily equate morality with power. It has often been argued—by Americans as well as others—that the United States has been at greater pains to proclaim her own virtue than most powers have been theirs, and more prone to self-deception in this respect. One American historian, for example, has affirmed:

> that American foreign policy has a vocabulary all its own, consciously—even ostentatiously—side-stepping the use of terms that would even hint at aggression or imperial domination, and taking refuge in abstract formulae, stereotyped phrases, and idealistic clichés that really explain nothing. Phrases like 'Monroe Doctrine', 'no entangling alliances', 'freedom of the seas', 'open door', 'good neighbour policy', 'Truman doctrine', 'Eisenhower doctrine', strew the pages of American history but throw little light on the dynamics of American foreign policy. Parrot-like repetition of these abstractions and other generalities produces an emotional reflex which assumes that American diplomacy is 'different', purer, morally better than the diplomacy of other powers. There is a strong pharisaical flavour about American diplomacy, easily detected abroad but generally unrecognized at home.[27]

But regardless of its wider relevance, the self-image of the United States and its projection into the region is a significant element in her relations with Latin America.

The vocabulary of her policy towards Latin America suggests that the United States treats the region on a basis of equality. The image is fostered of a family or a good neighbourhood. The Latin American countries are 'our sister republics', 'the good neighbours', 'our southern partners' and so on. Given her overwhelming power, this suggests no little benevolence on the part of the United States. In the latter's self-image this benevolence is in marked contrast to the traditionally malevolent designs of the European powers upon Latin America. Policies of economic control and even armed occupation have been different (and therefore justifiable[28]) when carried out by the

---

[26] My personal experience of political leaders in the field of inter-American relations has inclined me increasingly to this view.

[27] Van Alstyne, *op. cit.*, p.7.

[28] The United States has claimed that the wars by which she secured so much Mexican territory and deprived Spain of Puerto Rico and Cuba, as well as the Philippines, were 'just wars'. See below, pp. 112, 200. Theodore Roosevelt pronounced the war against

United States. Thus did Woodrow Wilson strongly condemn 'foreign' economic and financial exploitation of the Caribbean region and preside over a considerable tightening of United States economic control there. And thus did Professor Bemis feel able to describe Wilson, who ordered more armed interventions in Latin America than any other United States President, as 'that great noninterventionist'.[29] A generation later, when United States economic penetration of Latin America —and the establishment of her hegemony over the region—had gone very much further than in Wilson's time, Secretary of State Cordell Hull still warned of the dangers from extra-continental powers: 'lawless nations, hungry as wolves for vast territory with rich undeveloped natural resources such as South America possesses'.[30] Friendship with the United States was the surest safeguard against such dangers.

The United States self-image, in which she has not been an imperialist power in relation to Latin America, has been sustained by reference to her own anti-imperial origins and by a particular interpretation of imperialism. Unlike her critics, she interprets imperialism as direct political rule rather than the economic exploitation of supposedly inferior peoples. Of course, even by her own interpretation, the forcible occupation of countries in the Caribbean region during the early decades of this century must be considered imperialism. But this was a temporary phase and in any case well intentioned. Its main justification was to prevent more sinister European interventions. Bemis described United States interventions in Cuba, for example, as 'occasional interventions, abundantly supported by treaty right', and as 'reluctant and temporary. . . . This forbearance shows lack of a fundamental advancing urge like that of the imperialist powers of the Old World in Asia and Africa'.[31] For Professor Mecham 'United States imperialism protected the hemisphere against Old World imperialistic powers. It was a

Spain 'the most absolutely righteous foreign war' of the nineteenth century (Howard K. Beale, *Theodore Roosevelt and the Rise of America to World Power* (paperback edn., New York, 1962), p. 40.

[29] Samuel Flagg Bemis, *The Latin American Policy of the United States: An Historical Interpretation* (New York, 1943), p. 389.

[30] Quoted in Bryce Wood, *The Making of the Good Neighbor Policy* (New York, Columbia University Press, 1961), p. 182. The circumstance which gave rise to this warning was a move by the Bolivian government in 1937 to assert its economic independence by expropriating a United States-owned oil company. See below, p. 171.

[31] Bemis, *op. cit.*, pp. 278-9. 'A fundamental advancing urge' is, in my judgement, an apt description of 'Manifest Destiny'. See below, pp. 71 ff.

case of our imperialism against their imperialism. But it was a benevolent imperialism that disappeared as soon as the European danger vanished after World War I.'[32] Moreover, time and again we find the assertion being made by those both formulating and executing United States Latin American policy that the 'best elements' in the occupied countries welcomed United States intervention. Those actively opposing United States action have been denounced as either 'the ignorant masses' or 'bandits', 'communists' and so on.[33] As for economic imperialism, Bemis dismisses it as a myth:

> Any dispassionate study of the economic relations between the United States and Latin America, particularly those concerning investments, shows that, far from there having been any exploitation of the Latin American republics by economic imperialism, it has been the other way around: it is the Latin American governments which have exploited the capital of United States nationals indiscreet enough to have allowed their property to be trapped within the sovereign authority of those nations.[34]

It is very widely believed in the United States that Latin America has been the recipient of considerable generosity on her part, and that, in the last decade or so especially, very large amounts of economic aid have been given to the region without return. This belief, incidentally, has bred resentment at apparent Latin American ingratitude.

The self-image of the United States as a benevolent paramount power in the Americas furnishes the basic justification for her policy of excluding extra-continental powers from effective influence in the region. It derives from the assumption of moral superiority over the European great powers which was a vital ingredient in the Monroe Doctrine. It has become increasingly important to her world posture, especially within the context of the Cold War. As one American writer has put it, 'of course there is no comparison between American patience and forbearance with unruly states in the Western Hemisphere and corresponding Russian policies in Eastern Europe'.[35] Thus Latin America should provide something of a showcase for United States foreign policy generally. No less important for her self-image and for her world posture is the claim that she has tried, albeit with limited

---

[32] *A Survey of United States–Latin American Relations, op. cit.*, p. 462. It did not so disappear. See below, p. 146.  [33] See below, pp. 140, 151, 161.

[34] *Op. cit.*, p. 350.

[35] John Lukacs, *A History of the Cold War* (New York, 1961), p. 230, n. 12. But such a comparison is made below, pp. 270 ff.

success, to promote representative democracy in Latin America: a claim made, incidentally, in the face of widespread criticism in the region that she has consistently supported (and even promoted) dictatorships favourable to her interests. This claim is advanced by United States scholars as well as by political leaders and publicists. We shall consider it later.[36]

An historical analysis of United States Latin American policy must always keep in mind the fact that 'the United States', like 'Latin America', is by no means a monolithic entity. And although the historian can identify United States interests consistently pursued in broad terms over a period of time, these have not always been pursued rationally and single-mindedly in particular situations; nor have those concerned always been agreed upon either the specific interests to be safeguarded or the means to be adopted to safeguard them. All this is evident from an examination of how United States Latin American policy is formulated and executed. Chief executive power under the United States constitution is, of course, vested in the President who, in the field of foreign policy, draws advice from various quarters—individuals and agencies—amongst whose number the Secretary of State and the State Department constitute but one, and not always the most influential.[37] Other government departments and agencies are importantly involved in making United States foreign policy, and their influence has increased during and since the Second World War. Prominent among these today are the Agency for International Development (AID), the Central Intelligence Agency (CIA) and the military establishment ('the Pentagon'), The influence of the latter, for example, may be seen in United States increased co-operation with—and therefore strengthening of—the military in Latin America. The role of the Central Intelligence Agency was most conspicuous in two of the major crises which have occurred in inter-American relations since the end of the Second World War: that over Guatemala in 1954 and the Bay of Pigs invasion of 1961. Its hand has been seen in other instances where governments following policies disapproved by the United States have been overthrown by coups. The case of President Goulart of Brazil is a

---

[36] See below, pp. 277 ff.

[37] Cf., for example, R. Harrison Wagner, *United States Policy Toward Latin America: A Study in Domestic and International Politics* (Stanford, Stanford University Press, 1970), p. 77: 'The Defense Department . . . by distributing its spending among key congressional constituencies and by developing reserve officer and veterans organizations to support the demands of the services for funds, has become a much more secure government department.'

notable example.[38] These departments and agencies compete for influence over the President in the formulation and execution of policy. An outstanding case of a policy bedevilled by rivalries between different government departments and agencies, as well as conflict between the Executive and the Congress, is the Alliance for Progress.[39] In a given situation there may be conflict between economic and political interests; and between strategic interests and either or both of these. Different groups with conflicting economic interests may be involved in particular situations, as were, for example, the oil companies and the owners of silver mines in Mexico in the late nineteen-thirties.[40]

In the field, the situation obtaining in Washington may be paralleled by rivalries among the representatives of the government agencies and between different private interests. On this point Robert Kennedy wrote:

> In some countries of the world, the most powerful single voice is that of the AID administrator, with the Ambassador—even though he is representing the State Department and is ostensibly the chief spokesman for the United States and its President—having relatively little power. In some countries that I visited the dominant United States figure was the representative of the CIA; in several of the Latin American countries it was the head of our military mission. In all these countries an important role was played by the USIA[41] and, to a lesser degree, the Peace Corps, the Export-Import Bank, the American business community in general, and, in certain countries, particular businessmen.[42]

In addition to government departments and agencies, the President may employ 'special advisers' to whom he entrusts missions to foreign countries. There have been notable instances of such missions in the case of Latin America as we shall see in due course. Sometimes an individual ambassador enjoys a special relationship with the President which gives him unusual influence in particular situations: the case of

---

[38] See below, p. 29.

[39] The Alliance for Progress has been described as 'merely a pawn in the interdepartmental competition for power and favor within the United States government'. Jerome Levinson and Juan de Onís, *The Alliance That Lost Its Way: A Critical Report on the Alliance for Progress* (Chicago, A Twentieth Century Fund Study, 1970), p. 112.

[40] See below, p. 174, n. 60.

[41] The United States Information Agency.

[42] *13 Days: The Cuban Missile Crisis October 1962* (London, 1969), pp. 112–13.

Josephus Daniels in Mexico during Franklin Roosevelt's presidency is an outstanding example.[43]

Although he turned out to be a very sympathetic ambassador, Daniels was appointed through the spoils system,[44] which historically has contributed in no small measure to the prevalence of low-calibre men in United States diplomatic posts in Latin America. But such appointments also reflect the vast imbalance of power in the western hemisphere. For although the United States has a distinctive Latin American policy, and although their relations with their powerful northern neighbour are of the first importance for the countries of Latin America, nevertheless the latter generally has been a low priority area for the United States government. Some United States Presidents have had personal experience of the region before attaining to the presidency (Theodore Roosevelt and William Howard Taft in Cuba, for example), but few have had to devote much time as chief executive to Latin American problems. The involvement of President Wilson with the Mexican revolution and President Kennedy with the Cuban revolution are notable exceptions. Very seldom indeed has Latin America been, in the latter's words, 'the most critical area'.

Diplomatic posts in Latin America have not been greatly sought after by career foreign service officers[45] in spite of the assertion which used to be made in the instructions given to her delegates to the international conferences of American states that 'Among the foreign relations of the United States as they fall into categories, the Pan American policy takes first place in our diplomacy'.[46] Sumner Welles, an outstanding figure among United States diplomats dealing with Latin America, wrote on this point:

> Three years after I entered the foreign service of the United States I asked to be transferred to a post in Latin America. It was not difficult to secure compliance with my request, but it was hard to prevent my superiors from

---

[43] See below, pp. 173 ff.

[44] Not only was Daniels Franklin Roosevelt's former chief as Secretary of the Navy in Woodrow Wilson's cabinet (Roosevelt had been his Assistant Secretary), but he also had claims to office as an influential Democratic politician who had campaigned for Roosevelt in the 1932 presidential election.

[45] For criticism of the poor quality of United States diplomats in Latin America by men who were themselves foreign service officers in the region, see, for example, D. G. Munro, *Intervention and Dollar Diplomacy in the Caribbean, 1900–1921* (Princeton, N.J., Princeton University Press, 1964), p. 544; and W. F. Sands, *Our Jungle Diplomacy* (Chapel Hill, University of North Carolina Press, 1944), pp. 192–4.

[46] E.g. U.S. Dept. of State, *Foreign Relations of the United States, Diplomatic Papers*, 1938, vol. v (U.S.G.P.O., Washington, 1956), p. 54.

entering a notation upon my efficiency record that my judgment and mental stability should receive especial scrutiny. In those remote days assignment to Latin-American posts was usually reserved for those who required disciplinary action, or for those who had proved themselves misfits or incapable.[47]

While undoubtedly there have been improvements in the quality of United States diplomats in Latin America since Welles began his foreign service career, the region normally (that is in the absence of a significant crisis) has remained a low priority area for United States diplomacy. With a limited general interest in the region, special interests have been unduly influential in shaping United States Latin American policy, especially those interests related to overseas trade and investment, and, more recently, to national security. United States business interests have been particularly well represented not only in the embassies in Latin America, but also among the policy makers in Washington.[48] This is hardly surprising since the promotion and safeguarding of her economic interests for long comprised the major task of United States diplomacy in Latin America. But, whether connected with business or not, those who formulate and execute United States Latin American policies share the same ethos of capitalism and democracy. As preoccupation with security questions in the hemisphere has grown, the role of the United States military in policy making has increased.[49]

The United States Congress has certain specific powers in the field of foreign policy, notably that of making appropriations to finance it and, in the case of the Senate, of giving its 'advice and consent' to treaties with foreign powers and appointments in the foreign service. Both Houses have Foreign Relations Committees, that of the Senate being the more prestigious and influential; these in turn have subcommittees concerned with Latin America. On occasions the President has been forced to abandon a policy because of congressional opposition. A notable example in the case of Latin America was the rejection by the Senate of President Grant's treaty to annex the Dominican Republic in 1870.[50] But such occasions have been exceptional. The

---

[47] *Where Are We Heading?* (New York, 1946), p. 182.

[48] This book contains some prominent examples, such as Adolf Berle and Spruille Braden.

[49] Cf. President Eisenhower's warning about the 'military–industrial complex'. See below, p. 24, n. 74.

[50] See below, p. 94.

B

President has become increasingly powerful in the field of foreign policy and the Congress less so. Even the congressional prerogative of declaring war is now largely academic, for as Commander-in-Chief the President is able to deploy the armed forces and commit the United States to hostilities without a formal declaration of war. Korea and Vietnam are outstanding instances in recent times. Sending the marines into small Latin American countries seldom has incurred substantial Congressional opposition.

Nevertheless Congress has importantly influenced United States Latin American policy. Its influence generally reflects its character; it is composed of representatives of sectional interests, whereas the President represents the country as a whole. These interests, understandably, have been concerned to obtain concessions from Latin American governments and not to make them for the sake of what the President might judge to be the national interest. This may clearly be seen, for example, in the implementation of the Good Neighbour policy which, in Bryce Wood's judgement, was more effective in those areas subject to the executive branch alone. Specifically, as Dr. Wood points out, Roosevelt was unable to overcome the opposition of domestic interests to the relaxation of sanitary regulations in favour of meat imports from Argentina: a measure which might well have improved relations with the latter at a time when these were difficult.[51] Restrictions imposed by Congress upon Latin American imports into the United States have aroused great resentment in Latin America, which manifested itself, for example, in the hostile reception accorded to Vice-President Nixon during his 1958 tour.[52] Another cause of resentment at that time was United States support of dictators, some of the most notorious of whom had powerful friends (and lobbyists) in the United States Congress. One such was Rafael Trujillo of the Dominican Republic, as was made clear when the House of Representatives rejected an attempt by one of its members (Charles O. Porter) to have aid withdrawn from the Dominican dictator.[53] There have been other liberal critics of United States Latin American policy in Congress:

---

[51] Bryce Wood, 'The Department of State and the Non-National Interest: The Cases of Argentine Meat and Paraguayan Tea', *Inter-American Economic Affairs*, vol. xv, no. 2 (Autumn, 1961), pp. 3–32. But, as Wood points out, Roosevelt would not risk alienating those whose support he needed for important domestic legislative proposals over 'this relatively minor issue of foreign policy.' (*Ibid.*, pp. 22–3.)

[52] See below, pp. 223–4.

[53] John Gerassi, *The Great Fear in Latin America* (revised paperback ed., New York, 1965), pp. 244–5. See below, pp. 277–8.

prominent among them recently have been William Fulbright, chairman of the Senate Foreign Relations Committee, who opposed both the Bay of Pigs invasion and the Dominican intervention of 1965, and Frank Church, chairman of that committee's subcommittee on Western Hemisphere Affairs. But the influence of such men upon policy has been very limited. Much more influential have been those advocating a more assertive, even aggressive Latin American policy. Incidentally, uninhibited discussions in the United States Congress on the affairs of Latin American countries are not calculated to improve inter-American relations.

With the development of aid programmes Congress has gained new opportunities of influencing United States Latin American policy. It has generally exerted this influence to use such programmes as a stimulus to United States trade and investment, and to secure concessions from Latin American governments in return for aid. Congress has strongly opposed any significant relaxation of restrictions upon Latin American imports into the United States. In Senator Church's words: 'Not only did the pressures of domestic politics change our aid to loans, but concern over our chronically adverse balance-of-payments led the Congress to insist upon tying these loans to the purchase of goods and services in the United States. Thus our aid—so-called— became an ill-disguised subsidy for American exports. ... But the worst political consequence of all has been the inability of Congress to resist temptation to use the aid program as both carrot and stick to reward or punish recipient governments, depending on how we may regard their behavior. Since 1961, the punitive sections of the Foreign Assistance Act have increased from four to 21.'[54] The best known of these punitive measures is the Hickenlooper Amendment, providing for mandatory suspension of aid to any country that nationalised, expropriated or seized United States-owned property and failed to provide equitable and speedy compensation. The Congress also passed similar measures to support United States fishing rights against attempts by Latin American governments to extend the limits of their territorial waters.

The influence of special interests has been enhanced by the general tenor of public opinion in the United States towards Latin America and its affairs. It is a self-flattering myth that in democracies public

---

[54] Frank Church, 'Toward a New Policy for Latin America', in Richard B. Gray (ed.), *Latin America and the United States in the 1970's* (Itasca, Illinois, 1971), p. 344.

opinion is a moderating—even liberalising—element in the field of foreign policy. In no other democracy is this myth given more credence than in the United States. In the words of Secretary of State Charles Evans Hughes speaking in 1928: 'The policy of the United States is in the control of the American people, acting through representative institutions. Executive and Congress must bow to public opinion. The dominant spirit of the American people is generous, liberal, instinct with love of independence and respect for it.'[55] In Professor Bemis's judgement, writing of United States policy towards Cuba, 'The urge to annex was there, no doubt, for a century, but it was bridled, curbed, and halted by a great and historic self-denial, checked by the common people of the United States and their opposition to imperialism.'[56] The overall record supports neither of these assertions. United States public opinion has been characterised by a general lack of interest in Latin America, coupled with a vague but deeply held conviction that the United States possesses the right to direct the region's affairs. It is important to note that the most revered policy of the United States in the whole field of foreign affairs is the Monroe Doctrine. The latter has enjoyed the very strong support of public opinion in the United States, especially perhaps among the many Americans who have a far from clear idea of what it entails. Crudely interpreted, the Monroe Doctrine affirms that Latin America is 'our part of the world'[57] in which non-American powers have no right to challenge the United States.

In the light of Bemis's assertion it is interesting to note that Cuba, whose revolution has posed the most serious challenge ever offered to the Monroe Doctrine, furnishes a good example of links between domestic politics and public opinion in the United States, and the latter's Latin American policy. For much of the nineteenth century the slavery issue in United States domestic politics curbed a very strong desire to annex Cuba; in 1898 public opinion was aroused to demand war

[55] Quoted in Arnold J. Toynbee, *Survey of International Affairs, 1927* (London, Oxford University Press for the Royal Institute of International Affairs, 1929), p. 404.

[56] *The Latin American Policy of the United States, op. cit.*, p. 279.

[57] Robert Kennedy (*13 Days, op. cit.*, p. 69) quotes the President himself using this phrase at the time of the missile crisis. Interestingly, Theodore Sorensen, the President's Special Counsel, in his account of the crisis, quotes another occasion when John F. Kennedy used such a phrase: ' "We cannot tell anyone to keep out of our hemisphere,' young Jack Kennedy had prophetically written twenty-two years earlier in *Why England Slept*, 'unless our armaments and the people behind these armaments are prepared to back up the command, even to the ultimate point of going to war." ' (Theodore C. Sorensen, *Kennedy*, paperback edn., London, 1966, p. 782.)

with Spain over the island. Much more recently President Kennedy, who had tried to make political capital out of the Cuban situation during his election campaign,[58] found himself under strong domestic pressure 'to do something about Castro'. To many Americans this meant military action to overthrow the Cuban leader. But while an invasion of Cuba almost certainly would have been immediately popular,[59] Kennedy no less certainly would have been censured had it proved a prolonged operation involving loss of *American* life on any scale. Opposition to the Vietnam war has shown all too clearly how such loss can arouse public opinion in the United States. But President Coolidge's experience in Nicaragua in the nineteen-twenties already showed how a protracted operation in a small Latin American republic could arouse domestic opposition.[60]

Over the last few pages I have been concerned to stress that the United States is not a monolithic entity and that United States Latin American policy is the end product of what is always a complex and sometimes a confused process of decision making at different levels. In his recent review of an important book by Abraham Lowenthal on the Dominican intervention of 1965, Dana G. Munro, an outstanding example of a North American scholar with considerable diplomatic experience, observed:

> the actions of a government are not always the result of conscious decisions made after a rational consideration of objectives and alternatives; they are shaped by the prejudices and assumptions of the policy makers, and often the options open to the president or the secretary of state are limited by what lesser officials have done or failed to do. These facts, long apparent to people who have had to deal with such matters, are often overlooked by students who conceive of foreign policy as the result of 'conscious, optimizing choice by a single actor ('the state') picking among alternative ways to affect a foreign situation.'[61]

This is a salutary reminder. Yet, for all the diffusion of power, and the confusions which sometimes arise as a consequence, there does emerge

---

[58] See below, p. 231.

[59] This judgement is based partly upon my own impressions from being in Washington and other parts of the United States in 1961 and 1962.

[60] See below, p. 152. It is possible that Kennedy was actually influenced by Coolidge's experience.

[61] Review of Abraham F. Lowenthal, *The Dominican Intervention* (Cambridge, Mass., Harvard University Press, 1972), in *The Hispanic American Historical Review*, vol. 53, no. 2 (May 1973), pp. 320–1.

a Latin American policy having certain clear, consistent objectives. This is generally so even in the short term. Professor Munro praises his author for 'a thoughtful discussion of the Dominican intervention as an illustration of how foreign policy is made'. The praise is not undeserved, and the story of the Dominican intervention of 1965 is indeed a confused one.[62] But not only is it evident from the author's own account that throughout the affair United States policy makers at different levels had one clear objective: to prevent the establishment of 'a second Cuba' in Latin America. Lowenthal specifically goes further: 'The aim of preventing a "second Cuba" shaped American policy toward the Dominican Republic at every stage after Trujillo's death in May 1961.'[63] The truth is that United States policy makers not merely subscribe to a number of broad objectives (such as the maintenance of United States security, the promotion of her foreign trade and investments, and so on); as I have been at pains to show, they also share certain fundamental 'prejudices and assumptions' in respect of Latin America.

Let us now consider the main instruments United States governments have employed in implementing their Latin American policy. These are all manifestations of the United States' immense power, evident in the main fields of inter-American relations. Although they are inter-related we will consider them in terms of military, political, economic and cultural instruments. In pursuing her objectives in Latin America the United States sometimes has resorted to the use of armed force. The fulfilment of her 'Manifest Destiny' to become a 'continental republic' led her to make war upon Mexico and deprive her nearest Latin American neighbour of more than a half of her national territory. As a result of conflict with Spain in 1898, the United States acquired Puerto Rico and the lease, in perpetuity, of a naval base in Cuba as well as effective control of that island. Her naval forces ensured the success of the Panamanian revolt against Colombia in 1903, and thus gained her quasi-sovereignty—again in perpetuity—over the Canal Zone. On numerous occasions—the last as recently as 1965— the United States has landed her marines on the territory of the small countries of the Caribbean region to secure her objectives. She did so in Mexico during the Revolution, when she also sent in an overland expeditionary force. For almost three decades she claimed under the Roosevelt Corollary to the Monroe Doctrine the right—and even the

---

[62] See below, pp. 241 ff.      [63] *The Dominican Intervention, op. cit.*, p. 26.

duty—to take such military action. The threat of resort to military force has also been an important instrument of United States Latin American policy as, for example, in the cases of Chile in 1892;[64] Cuba in 1933;[65] and the Dominican Republic in 1961.[66] During the nineteenth century it was mooted on a number of occasions that the United States should try to purchase Cuba under threat of seizing the island in the event of a Spanish refusal to sell;[67] and in 1916 President Wilson purchased the Danish West Indies (Virgin Islands) under just such a threat.[68]

The military power of the United States is also influential in Latin America through the supply of weapons and training facilities. Over a half of the Latin American countries have concluded Mutual Defense Agreements with the United States, and all of them have received military equipment from her. Since the early nineteen-sixties emphasis in inter-American military co-operation has been on internal security, so that training and weapons have been directed towards counter-insurgency. Closer relations between the United States and Latin American military establishments have been encouraged through the Inter-American Defense Board, the Inter-American Defense College and counter-insurgency training both in the Canal Zone and through teams sent into Latin American countries. The Bolivian troops who eventually defeated and killed Che Guevara, for example, were United States trained and 'advised'. At the same time, the United States has encouraged the Latin American military to undertake 'civic action': in other words, to engage in social projects such as building roads, schools and so on. Such engagement, it was hoped, would improve the military's image among the population and so assist in the task of counter-insurgency.[69] Both counter-insurgency and civic action programmes have enabled the military to expand its already considerable role in Latin American politics. They have also increased the political leverage of the United States in the region.[70]

---

[64] See below, p. 96.

[65] See below, pp. 161–2.          [66] See below, p. 235.

[67] E.g. the notorious 'Ostend Manifesto'. See below, p. 82.

[68] Arthur S. Link, *Wilson: Campaigns for Progressivism and Peace, 1916–1917* (Princeton, N.J., Princeton University Press, 1965), p. 81.

[69] For a discussion of the subject, see Willard F. Barber and C. Neale Ronning, *Internal Security and Military Power: Counterinsurgency and Civic Action in Latin America* (Ohio State University Press, 1966).

[70] The United States traditionally has justified her military assistance on the grounds that it would encourage the Latin American military to develop a greater professionalism: to respect civilian government and eschew politics. However, since the onset of the Cold

The fact is that the internal weakness of most countries of Latin America is such as to make them very vulnerable to United States political penetration. The United States has a number of political instruments at her disposal in attaining her objectives in the region: one such has been her recognition policy, regarded by Latin Americans as a major form of intervention in their internal affairs. In the Caribbean region, in particular, recognition by the United States often has been crucial to the survival of a government. And the latter has used this instrument both to subvert governments of which she has not approved, and to force acceptance of certain commitments from others as the price of recognition. The case of President Grau San Martín of Cuba in 1933 is a notable example of the first;[71] that of President Alvaro Obregón in Mexico a decade earlier illustrates the second.[72] The withholding of recognition by the United States often has been a positive encouragement to the opponents of certain regimes to overthrow them, even when the United States has not been directly involved in subversive operations. Only governments commanding broad-based support can withstand such pressure. Weak governments have little choice but to co-operate with the United States.

Another significant political instrument wielded by the United States is the invocation of international law. For the latter has been created in the main by the great powers, who alone can in practice enjoy many of the rights in theory possessed by all nations. Hence the United States stresses the international obligations of Latin American governments and the sanctity of treaties. The 'perpetual' treaties under which she maintains the base at Guantánamo in Cuba and exercises quasi-sovereignty over the Panama Canal Zone are outstanding examples of international law favouring the United States. Neither treaty can be modified without the consent of both parties to it: in other words unless the United States decides it is in her interests to make concessions. But she has invoked international law most often in support of claims by her citizens against Latin American governments. In the nineteenth century and the early part of the twentieth such claims have been concerned mainly with default on debts and damages suffered by civil disorder, denial of justice and so on. More recently, their main concern has been the expropriation of American companies with what the latter consider to be inadequate compensation. Inciden-

---

War, United States military advisers have encouraged their Latin American counterparts to adopt a strongly anti-communist political position.

   [71] See below, p. 162.          [72] See below, p. 148.

tally the United States government (like European governments in similar circumstances) generally has supported the often grossly inflated claims of its companies and even shared their indignation when the valuation made by the Latin American governments for compensation purposes has been based upon those same companies' tax returns!

Another important political instrument is furnished by the United States economic aid programmes in Latin America. The granting or withholding of aid can be as significant as in the case of recognition. We have already noted attempts made by the United States Congress to use this instrument in order to reward or punish Latin American governments according to their treatment of American interests. The aid programmes themselves increase United States political penetration of Latin America in various ways in addition to their influence upon the military there. For example, the Agency for International Development maintains a training programme for Latin America's police forces. According to Professor Edwin Lieuwen:

> The program involves training for handling mob demonstrations and conducting counterintelligence work. Also, the U.S. government vigorously supports, via the Inter-American Security Committee, a hemisphere-wide program to curtail the travel of Latin American subversives and guerrillas to and from Cuba, as well as the flow of arms and propaganda from that island.[73]

Thus her aid is used to increase United States influence in key areas of Latin American internal affairs. And, in the last analysis, the United States makes the vital decisions regarding aid and not the Latin American governments which receive it.

The aid programmes constitute an important exercise of United States economic power in her Latin American policy. At the same time they have the effect of augmenting that power. For whatever benefits Latin America receives from them (and these are not to be dismissed as negligible) receipt of aid increases the region's dependence upon the United States. 'Aid' in this context is, in fact, an ambiguous if not misleading term, for most of it today takes the form of loans which have to be spent in the United States. In other words, the programmes have

---

[73] *The United States and the Challenge to Security in Latin America, op. cit.,* p. 16. This type of aid, and the resentment it can arouse, were highlighted when a United States security adviser was assassinated by Uruguayan urban guerrillas (*Tupamaros*) in August 1970.

the theoretical and ostensibly altruistic purpose of promoting the economic development of Latin America, but the practical consequence of assisting United States economic prosperity and increasing her economic control of the recipient nations. United States economic power largely determines the pattern of Latin American development. Often her vast business concerns in the region are much more powerful than the host governments. Even the larger countries of Latin America find it hard to curb the power of the giant United States companies[74]— leaving aside the threat of losing economic aid (often vital to a government in the short term) should they seriously try to do so.

In addition to her military, political and economic penetration of Latin America the United States has promoted cultural penetration as an instrument of her foreign policy. We noted Senator Robert Kennedy's reference to the important role played by the United States Information Agency in all the countries of the region. The basic task of the USIA is to project the most favourable image of the United States and the 'American way of life'. It also helps to promote the idea of an essential harmony of interests between the United States and Latin America. Together with considerable private United States interests in Latin American publishing and broadcasting media, the USIA has worked to enhance American influence in the region. Considerable impetus was given to this process by the Second World War when, in the words of Professor Dozer, 'the United States assiduously cultivated the Latin American peoples by means of an extensive information and cultural program'.[75] But such programmes were not initiated during the Second World War, nor was it then that the United States began to foster the idea of a community of interests shared by her and the Latin American countries. Almost half a century earlier the Pan American movement was launched and the inter-American system established.

The inter-American system is an important instrument through which the United States has organised Latin American support for her own policy of limiting extra-continental influence in the Americas, and

---

[74] Indeed, the power of the great corporations poses problems even for the United States government. Shortly before leaving office, President Eisenhower warned against 'the acquisition of unwarranted influence, whether sought or unsought, by the military–industrial complex'. Quoted in Schlesinger, *A Thousand Days, op. cit.*, p. 264. The link with the Pentagon, Schlesinger's point here, adds a further dimension to the problems.

[75] Donald M. Dozer, *Are We Good Neighbors? Three Decades of Inter-American Relations, 1930–1960* (Gainesville, University of Florida Press, 1959), p. 81.

has sought to counter the growth of 'Latin Americanism' directed against herself. It has been of greater significance since the end of the Second World War as the United States has challenged the Soviet Union and China in what they consider to be their spheres of influence, while endeavouring at the same time to keep these powers— and, incidentally, the United Nations—out of 'her hemisphere'. The United States self-image, and her world posture, are significantly involved in the inter-American system. For she claims the latter is a unique association of a great power and small powers in self-flattering contrast to the imperialism practised in the past by the western European great powers and, more recently, by the Soviet Union in eastern Europe. Professor Mecham has described it as 'an arrangement without parallel in the history of Great Power and small-states relations'.[76] Another American scholar has asserted that 'Pan-Americanism was the choice of the United States rather than imperialism'.[77] Pan Americanism and the inter-American system based upon it derive from what has been called 'The Western Hemisphere Idea': that the peoples of the western hemisphere stand in a special relationship to one another setting them apart from the rest of the world.[78] It is claimed that bonds of unity have been forged between the United States and Latin America by historical experience, geographical propinquity and the sharing of common political ideals and institutions. The most significant historical experience they shared was that of being at one time dependencies of European powers and (with the virtual exception of Brazil) of fighting for independence. Geographically, the Americas are said to form a continental unit distinct and separate from the rest of the world. In political terms, the American states subscribe to the ideal of representative democracy and practise the republican form of government.

These claims are open to strong challenge. The historical experience of the United States has differed in many crucial respects from that of Latin America.[79] The colonisation of the two regions, for example,

---

[76] J. Lloyd Mecham, *The United States and Inter-American Security, 1889–1960* (Austin, University of Texas Press, 1961), p. viii. However, I do draw such a parallel. See below, p. 268.

[77] J. B. Lockey, *Essays in Pan-Americanism* (Berkeley, University of California Press 1939), p. 158.

[78] Arthur P. Whitaker, *The Western Hemisphere Idea: its Rise and Decline* (Ithaca Cornell University Press, 1954), p. 1.

[79] For a discussion by 'historians of the Americas' of the question its title poses, see Lewis Hanke (ed.) *Do the Americas have a Common History?: A Critique of the Bolton Theory* (New York, 1964).

was very different in terms of both time and the character of the colonising powers who 'reproduced themselves' in the Americas: 'the England so reproduced was the England of the Stuarts and the Commonwealth, whereas the Spain so reproduced was that of the Catholic sovereigns and of Charles V. . . . Thus the two movements differed in the world which they brought with them; they differed still more in the world which they found: the English found no Mexico, no Peru, no Bogota.'[80] An analysis of the colonial period itself, and of what might be called the colonial heritage of the Americas, would reveal further significant differences. Following independence the historical experience of the two Americas diverged still further. In the words of one distinguished Latin American, 'An empire was destroyed in the south, while one was built in the United States. A process of integration made the United States; a process of disintegration divided the twenty nations to the south.'[81] Moreover, while the economies of both the Americas were greatly affected by Europe's expanding capitalist–industrial system during the nineteenth century, the consequences were fundamentally different in the two regions. In the case of Latin America there was an intensification of its colonial economy. The region became 'more and more a producer of foodstuffs and raw materials for the great industrial states and more and more a debtor to financial interests in those states, whose growing investments were giving them an ever-tighter hold over its means of production and distribution.' But the United States copied and even improved upon the European system, so that by 1900 'the mature, expanding economy of the United States had given it an international position and outlook which was becoming more and more like that of the great powers of Western Europe and less and less like that of the economically backward debtor nations of Latin America'.[82] And in the twentieth century, as we shall

---

[80] F. A. Kirkpatrick, *The Spanish Conquistadores* (London, 1946), pp. 345–6.

[81] Carlos Dávila, *We of the Americas* (Chicago and New York, 1949), p. 17. Dr. Dávila was Provisional President of Chile and later Secretary General of the OAS. The view he expressed here has been challenged by his fellow Chilean, Felipe Herrera, the first President of the Inter-American Development Bank, in Claudio Véliz (ed), *Obstacles to Change in Latin America* (London, Oxford University Press for the Royal Institute of International Affairs, 1965), p. 231: 'According to one interpretation of Latin American history, the winning of emancipation in the nineteenth century meant the breaking up and dispersal of the great colonial empire of Spain. However, a more thorough scrutiny of the political, cultural, economic, and social characteristics of the colonial period shows that, despite its outward semblance of unity, Latin American society in reality lacked underlying geographical and structural cohesion.'

[82] Whitaker, *op. cit.*, pp. 89–90.

see, the United States eventually took over the position of those European powers in Latin America.

Again, the idea that the Americas form a continental unit distinct and separate from the rest of the world is an illusion. Although the western hemisphere is a continental island, and North and South America are connected by land, normal communications between them are not overland. And by air Washington is closer to Moscow than to Buenos Aires, while Rio de Janeiro is further from the centre of the North American continent than any European capital except Athens.[83] Nevertheless, the concept of the countries of the western hemisphere as neighbours has been a persistent one, though it has a political rather than a geographical validity. The concept of common political ideals and institutions likewise is a mixture of fact and myth. In spite of such aberrations as the short-lived Mexican monarchies of Iturbide and Maximilian, and the more durable Empire of Brazil, the general adoption of republican forms of government in Latin America (with constitutions often roughly modelled on that of the United States) gave the appearance of common political systems. A strong tendency to identify the republican form of government with freedom and democracy has been general in the Americas, where this freedom has been contrasted with the tyranny of extra-continental systems such as monarchy, fascism and international communism. But the gap between ideal and actuality in the matter of representative democracy (to which all the American states subscribe in principle) remains very wide and shows (in the early nineteen-seventies) signs of widening rather than of narrowing.

Thus the premises upon which Pan Americanism is based contain a very large element of myth. But the inter-American system is a reality and has been so for over eighty years: ever since 'The International Union of American Republics' was established in 1890. It includes certain treaties and agreements between the American nations; numerous inter-American institutions created to further common objectives and the observance of agreed principles; and a form of multilateral diplomacy through which the American states conduct a part of their international relations. Although representing only a small part of inter-American diplomacy, the inter-American system affects—at times significantly—bilateral relations between the American States. It has

---

[83] Robin A. Humphreys, *The Evolution of Modern Latin America* (Oxford, 1946), p. 161.

frequently provided a convenient, sometimes even necessary, framework within which bilateral agreements (mainly between the United States and individual Latin American countries) have been concluded, notably in the field of defence. Since the end of the Second World War the inter-American system has included a collective security pact (the Inter-American Treaty of Reciprocal Assistance) and, as its centrepiece, the Charter of the Organization of American States (OAS). There has been increased international co-operation between the American states, especially in the economic and social fields; and new institutions have been created to further such co-operation. Prominent among such institutions have been the Inter-American Development Bank and the Inter-American Committee on the Alliance for Progress. In 1970 an amended OAS Charter came into effect, reflecting these and other developments. The role of the inter-American system in relations between the United States and Latin America will be described and analysed at various points in this book, and evaluated in the conclusion. For the moment we may remark that its establishment—and durability—reflect the dominant part played by United States policy in shaping her relations with Latin America; for the system is not a natural grouping, but the creation of that policy.

Let us now turn to the Latin American side of inter-American relations, noting that it is within the inter-American system that the United States is in continuous multilateral diplomatic contact with the other republics of the hemisphere. We cannot, of course, talk of a Latin American 'United States policy' comparable with a United States Latin American policy. If the United States is not a monolithic entity, Latin America, by comparison, is not an entity at all. Nevertheless it was asserted at the outset that the United States does have relations with 'Latin America'. There is a distinct division within the inter-American system between the 'One' and the 'Twenty'.[84] We have noted differences between the United States and Latin America in such areas as culture, economic development and race; but, above all, in power. The most important common factor shared by the Latin American countries in distinction from the United States is their weakness in the face of her immense strength.

Latin American weakness has two, inter-related aspects: the weakness of the countries themselves (in terms of resources, internal organisation

---

[84] The admission of three Commonwealth countries to the inter-American system (see below, p. 247, n. 42) and the exclusion of Castro's Cuba change the second figure but not the 'distinct division'.

and so on) and that of their governments. The Latin American countries are all to an important extent what have been called 'penetrated systems': 'in which non-members of a national society participate directly and authoritatively through actions taken jointly with the society's members, in either the allocation of its values or the mobilization of support on behalf of its goals.'[85] We have noted extensive United States penetration in key areas of Latin American society. This is to be seen most obviously in the case of the small countries of the Caribbean region. The United States Ambassador who declared the holder of his post to be the second most important man in Cuba, for example, perhaps erred more on the side of modesty than on that of arrogance.[86] That was before the Cuban revolution. But even the largest country of Latin America, Brazil, has shared to a significant extent the characteristic weaknesses of the region. This was highlighted by the unsuccessful attempt to follow an 'independent' foreign policy in the early nineteen-sixties. There can be no doubt that the Brazilian officers who overthrew President Goulart in April 1964 were encouraged to do so by the knowledge that their action would be warmly approved by the United States government—as indeed it was.[87] There has been considerable suspicion that United States involvement was more direct. The new president, 'a close friend' of the United States military attaché in Brazil, 'was clearly the candidate most preferred by the United States Embassy'.[88] Some years later the military attaché in question was revealed as being 'one of the most senior officers in the CIA'.[89] At all events, the new military rulers of Brazil closely indentified themselves with the interests of the United States, especially on the issue of Cuba and international communism in the hemisphere. They were also much more favourably disposed than the Goulart administration had been

---

[85] James N. Rosenau, quoted in Carlos A. Astiz (ed.), *Latin American International Politics: Ambitions, Capabilities, and the National Interest of Mexico, Brazil, and Argentina* (Notre Dame, University of Notre Dame Press, 1969), p. 10.

[86] Earl Smith. For President Kennedy's reportedly critical reaction to Smith's remark, see Schlesinger, *A Thousand Days, op. cit.*, p. 192.

[87] See below, p. 240.

[88] Ronald M. Schneider, *The Political System of Brazil: Emergence of a 'Modernizing' Authoritarian Regime, 1964–1970* (New York and London, Columbia University Press, 1971), p. 124, n. 30.

[89] It was revealed in the Watergate Hearings into the 'bugging' of the Democratic party headquarters during the United States presidential election campaign of 1972: Peter Flynn, 'The Brazilian development model: the political dimension', *The World Today*, vol. 29, no. 11 (November 1973), p. 485. General Vernon Walters gave evidence to the Senate Select Committee in his capacity as Deputy Director of the CIA.

towards North American investments. The AID mission in Brazil, which had been greatly reduced in size during the last months of the Goulart administration, was substantially increased after the military coup. Three years later, when a reduction of United States personnel in Latin America was under way, a spokesman of the United States embassy in Brazil is reported to have said: 'We are not concerned with numbers alone. What concerns us is that the United States is exercising too direct a role here over too broad a spectrum. We have taken what might be called the Mother Hen approach. . . .'[90]

The case of Mexico is more subtle. Although more stable and better integrated than most countries of the region, Mexico is extensively penetrated by United States capital[91] and heavily dependent upon American tourism and markets. Yet, on the surface, she has successfully followed an 'independent' foreign policy, especially on the issue of Cuba. But although she has consistently refused to support sanctions against the island and has continued to maintain diplomatic relations with the Castro government, those relations have been cool and thus by no means provocative to the United States. Indeed, relations with the latter have steadily improved as Mexican governments have tended to become increasingly conservative. But such governments, for domestic reasons, have had to maintain the idea that the Mexican revolution is still proceeding; and it is in the United States interest to help them do so by accepting Mexico's 'revolutionary sympathy' for Cuba. Moreover, the United States derives two further advantages from Mexico's Cuban policy. In the first place, Mexico's apparent defiance bolsters her self-image: it supports her claim that the inter-American system is very different from the Soviet system in the degree of freedom it allows to the weaker members. Secondly, all travellers between Mexico and Cuba are identified and the information is passed to—or perhaps is actually obtained by—United States security agencies. Mexico thus provides what has been called a United States 'window' looking into Cuba.[92] At the same time, Mexico has been most circumspect in her criticism of United States policies in Latin America, invariably justifying her own position on juridical grounds. There are thus strict limits to the independence of even the largest and the most internally stable of the Latin American countries.

---

[90] Quoted in Goldhamer, *The Foreign Powers in Latin America*, *op. cit.*, p. 209.
[91] Mexican laws to limit such penetration clearly are being circumvented.
[92] See below, pp. 240–1.

Co-operation, then, is the hallmark for Latin America in its relations with the United States. Of course there are groups in all the
Latin American countries who positively gain from such co-operation,
and they are generally in or near the centres of power. The unrepresentative character of so many Latin American governments has made
United States support of great, sometimes crucial importance to them.
A corollary to this is the widespread resentment of United States
domination throughout the region. Latin American nationalism is
directed primarily at the United States. To some extent the Latin American ruling groups share this feeling even while pursuing policies of
co-operation with her. In addition to such factors as cultural antipathy,
the interests of the landowning oligarchies do not always coincide
with those of the United States; and pressure by the latter to carry out
some measure of reform (in order to forestall revolution), for example,
has aroused opposition. And even the most unrepresentative Latin
American governments do not want to appear subservient to the United
States. Indeed, they often make political capital out of the anti-
Americanism rife among their peoples. It can be a useful diversion
from discontent with their own policies; and the expropriation of a
United States company, for example, as well as being a popular move,
is more congenial to Latin American landowners than are serious
agrarian reforms. It has been observed of the situation in Panama,
where anti-United States nationalism is particulary strong: 'The
oligarchy . . . utilizes United States occupation of Panama's territory
as an outlet through which is directed popular dissatisfaction. Con-
veniently the blame for any inequities perpetrated by the rulers is
shifted to the United States via the Canal and the Zone. The oligarchy is deceitful; to the people of Panama it expresses Yankeephobia
while simultaneously courting the favor of the United States,'[93]

In addition to widespread anti-Americanism common to the whole
region—though more marked in some countries than in others and
affecting policies in differing degrees—there are a number of issues
upon which a substantial measure of common ground exists among the
Latin American governments. Traditionally, the issue which has produced the strongest common front *vis-à-vis* the United States has been

---

[93] Sheldon B. Liss, *The Canal: Aspects of United States–Panamanian Relations* (Notre
Dame University Press, 1967), p. 8  Víctor Alba also singles out the Panamanian oligarchy
in making the same point in his polemical *Alliance Without Allies: The Mythology of
Progress in Latin America* (New York, 1965), pp. 61–2.

that of intervention. There has been a 'Latin American position' on a number of aspects of international law, though relating to what are essentially economic and political issues. The United States has for long found it difficult to obtain the support of the other Latin American governments when involved in a serious dispute with one of them. And in recent years there has been a growing Latin American consensus on the broad front of economic relations with the United States.

The intervention issue has been the most emotive in the history of relations between the United States and Latin America, and the central issue for a great part of the twentieth century. It is linked with the Monroe Doctrine because the United States has always sought to justify her interventions on the grounds that they were necessary in order to forestall interventions by 'foreign' (that is, non-American) powers. Given her overwhelming power, whatever policy the United States pursues in Latin America may be interpreted as intervention in some form: the question basically is how Latin Americans regard her motives in specific situations. There have been occasions when the United States has been accused of supporting dictatorial governments by not intervening to bring about their downfall. There have been groups soliciting United States intervention to assist them to gain or regain power, especially in the Caribbean region. In recent years anti-Castro Cuban exiles have been the outstanding example of such groups.

But complex though the question undoubtedly is, some aspects of it are clear enough. Unilateral armed action by the United States, such as she practised in the Caribbean region during the first three decades of the twentieth century—and again in 1965—has aroused the greatest resentment in Latin America and constitutes intervention in its most obvious form. When the United States eventually accepted the principle of 'non-intervention' in the nineteen-thirties, her leaders understood that it was unilateral armed intervention they were renouncing. But it soon became evident that the Latin Americans interpreted intervention more broadly. Diplomatic pressure by the United States on behalf of her nationals in dispute with Latin American governments was regarded as intervention; as was non-recognition of governments unless they gave certain undertakings. Later the granting or withholding of economic aid was also viewed in the same way, especially when this was obviously used to further United States economic or political objectives. Moreover, there has been strong feeling in Latin America against 'collective intervention in multilateral guise'. Thus widely—even unrealistically—interpreted,[94] the principle of 'non-intervention' is regarded in Latin America as the cornerstone of the inter-American system. The Mexican diplomatist, Jorge Castañeda, has declared: 'The principle of non-intervention perhaps represents the greatest conquest of Pan Americanism. No other international principle has had such deep roots in the juridical conscience of the American states or had greater importance in the life of the hemisphere.'[95]

We have already noted the invocation of international law as an instrument of United States Latin American policy. From the Latin American viewpoint, international law only too often has supported on juridical grounds essentially inequitable treaties and concessions. The treaties were imposed upon Latin American countries because of their weakness and the concessions granted for the same reason and, most frequently, by dictatorial regimes. The United States often has made a commitment to honour these 'international obligations' a condition of recognition and has vigorously opposed efforts by Latin American governments to free themselves from them. The greatest such efforts have been made by 'national revolutionary' governments, which have sought to regain for their countries ownership, or at least control, of their own resources, alienated by previous governments because of weakness and venality.

Mexico furnished the precedent for what has since become a more common issue in Latin America's relations with the United States. The Mexican revolution began effectively in 1911 when Porfirio Díaz, who had first become President in 1876, was overthrown.[96] By the end of the Díaz dictatorship nearly one half of Mexico's total national wealth was owned by foreigners. In addition to the alienation of vast amounts of Mexican land, Díaz, contrary to traditional Spanish law followed by his predecessors, had granted ownership of subsoil minerals to foreign (including, importantly, United States) interests. Such grants were nevertheless 'legal', though, in Professor Ronning's words, 'it was "law" created by Díaz, enforced by his army and police and used in the interest of a tiny minority.'[97] Not surprisingly, Díaz was highly re-

---

[94] The 'non-intervention' clauses of the OAS Charter are thus interpreted. See below, pp. 200–1.

[95] *Mexico and the United Nations* (New York, 1958), p. 179.

[96] It began officially on 20 November 1910, when Francisco Madero called for a mass uprising against Díaz.

[97] C. Neale Ronning, *Law and Politics in Inter-American Diplomacy* (New York, 1963), p. 37.

garded by the United States and other beneficiary governments.[98] After
the fall of Díaz the revolutionary government sought to regain her
alienated resources for Mexico. Articles to this end were included in the
new Mexican constitution promulgated in 1917 which vested ownership of lands and all minerals in the nation. The United States pressed
for assurances that the constitution would not be applied retroactively
to her oil companies in Mexico and made the matter a condition of
recognising President Alvaro Obregón in 1923. When Mexico
eventually expropriated American (and other foreign) oil companies in
1938 the United States demanded prompt, effective and adequate compensation as required under international law. Mexico denied it was an
international question, and insisted that the matter of compensation
should be decided under her own constitution and laws. She therefore
refused to submit the dispute to international arbitration.[99] Since the
end of the Second World War United States companies have been
expropriated in more Latin American countries, with the matter of
'prompt, effective and adequate compensation' always at the centre of
the disputes between the expropriating governments and the companies. The United States has by no means given up the right to support her citizens in such disputes, nor have the Latin American governments in her view ceased to have obligations under international law in
these cases. But in practice she has invoked international law less and
relied more upon economic sanctions or the threat of them.

An increasingly significant issue where the United States has invoked international law and which illustrates the efforts of Latin
American governments to 'change the rules' is that of territorial waters
and fishing rights. Chile, Ecuador and Peru on the Pacific coast of
South America have been the countries most directly involved in disputes with the United States (and other maritime powers) on this issue,
but there is wide support in the rest of Latin America for their position.
Argentina and Brazil are among other Latin American countries also
claiming jurisdiction over an expanse of sea up to two hundred
nautical miles from their coasts. The Pacific coast countries have been
especially anxious to conserve their fishing resources against exploitation by greater maritime powers. The latter have taken their stand upon
the narrower limits generally recognised under international law.[100]

---

[98] See Elihu Root's eulogy, below, p. 134.
[99] For details of this dispute and the eventual settlement, see below, pp. 173–5.
[100] An international conference on the law of the sea was due to open at Caracas in
June 1974.

But Latin Americans have not failed to note that the United States has not always abided by international law in cases where this has conflicted with her own interests. When she pressed Mexico to accept international arbitration over the expropriation of the oil companies, for example, Mexicans recalled the Chamizal question. This issue arose from the shifting course of the Rio Grande, raising the question of whether the Chamizal area was part of the Mexican town of Ciudad Juárez or of El Paso in Texas. In 1911 a Canadian arbiter ruled that two-thirds of the Chamizal was Mexican and only one-third belonged to the United States. The latter refused to accept the judgement.[101] A few years later, when the Central American Court of Justice upheld claims from Costa Rica and El Salvador that their rights had been violated by a treaty empowering the United States to construct a canal through Nicaragua, the Wilson administration supported the Nicaraguan government in refusing to accept the court's decision—an action which was the main cause of the court's demise.[102] Nor did the United States accept Colombia's request to have the circumstances of her loss of Panama referred to arbitration.[103] It is also of interest, in the light of the claim of many Latin American countries to extend their territorial waters, that in 1945 the United States government asserted that it regarded 'the natural resources and subsoil of the continental shelf beneath the high seas but contiguous to the coast of the United States as appertaining to the United States, subject to its jurisdiction and control' and that it would be 'proper to establish conservation zones in those areas of the high seas contiguous to the coasts of the United States wherein fishing activities have been or in the future may be developed and maintained by its nationals alone'.[104] An expert witness, in a statement to a United States congressional subcommittee in 1969, declared that 'the seeds of the present fishing rights dispute with Peru can be traced to President Truman's Proclamation of 1945 on the continental shelf'.[105]

Expropriation of American companies exploiting major resources

---

[101] The Chamizal dispute was not resolved until more than half a century later. See below, p. 241.

[102] See below, pp. 141–2. The treaty in question was terminated in 1971 (*ibid*).

[103] See below, p. 105, n. 64.

[104] Ronning, *Law and Politics in Inter-American Diplomacy, op. cit.*, pp. 109–10.

[105] *United States Relations with Peru. Hearings before the Subcommittee on Western Hemisphere Affairs of the Committee on Foreign Relations, United States Senate, Ninety-First Congress, First Session, April 14, 16, and 17, 1969* (U.S.G.P.O., Washington, 1969), p. 64.

and the claim to extended territorial waters are attempts by Latin America to change its position of economic subordination to the United States (and, to a lesser degree, to other highly industrialised powers). Dissatisfaction with this position has been mounting since the end of the Second World War and has found expression within the inter-American system where the division between the two Americas has been greatly sharpened. The Latin Americans have felt that, in view of their special relationship with the United States, they are entitled to substantial assistance in tackling their economic and social problems. But they believed themselves neglected in favour of other regions in the immediate post-war years. In particular, the countries of Latin America complained about both the form and amount of United States aid they received, and demanded better terms of trade with her. Hopes raised by the Alliance for Progress in 1961 were soon disillusioned. In the wake of that disappointment they began to co-operate more closely with one another to present a common front to the United States on fundamental economic issues. In 1969 they reached the 'Consensus of Viña del Mar' after a meeting of a Special Commission for Latin American Coordination (CECLA) held at that Chilean resort. President Nixon was informed that henceforth the United States would have to recognise 'the distinctive personality of Latin America'.[106] The Consensus reflected the urgent need for unity in confrontation with the United States, even though it represented only a modest step towards it.

The achievement of unity is one of the two principal courses open to the Latin American countries through which to lessen their dependence upon the United States and redress in some measure the vast imbalance of power in the western hemisphere. Although even the combined strength of all the Latin American countries would still not compare with that of the United States in the foreseeable future, a united Latin America would possess greater bargaining power on significant issues, especially economic ones. Latin Americans have always been conscious of their weakness, and the concept of Latin American unity —or at least Spanish American unity—is an old one. It is associated with some of the great heroes of Spanish American independence, above all with Simón Bolívar. But the hopes of the Liberator and others were in vain for, as we noted earlier, independence brought fragmentation to Spain's empire in America, in ominous contrast to the subsequent expansion of the thirteen British colonies in North America to

---

[106] See below, pp. 255–6.

become eventually the most powerful nation in the world.[107] Yet the idea of Latin American integration—or, as some would say, 'reintegration'—has never lacked advocates.

The story of efforts to give practical expression to this idea has been predominately one of failure, both among the Latin American countries as a whole and in Central America, where attempts at integration in some form have been more persistent. Since the end of the Second World War more serious endeavours have been made to promote *economic* integration, but progress has been disappointing. Only a small proportion of the foreign trade of the individual Latin American countries is within the region, and political as well as economic factors work against their achieving the proclaimed goal of a Latin American Common Market. Political problems are formidable. Generally speaking, the Latin American countries have not completed the process of national and social integration; they are still striving to create their national personalities in the face of regional and often racial differences, as well as tensions between social classes. Until a greater degree of unity has been achieved within the individual countries, Latin American civilian governments will lack sufficient authority to establish effective supranational institutions of integration in the face of opposition from powerful domestic interest groups. This would be so even if Latin American governments, a large proportion of which are dominated by the military, possessed the will to bring about integration. There is little evidence that such is the case.

Traditionally, relations among the Latin American countries have been neither intimate nor particularly friendly. Geography has imposed formidable obstacles to the development of a feeling of unity, while historical circumstances have linked the Latin American countries more closely intellectually and economically with Europe than with one another. In the present century the power of the United States has made relations with her generally more important than those among the individual republics themselves. Meanwhile, the development of closer relations between the Latin American countries has been hindered by rivalries among them. Their differing size and strength, ill-defined and frequently disputed frontiers, and the combination of internal strife and external ambition—these have all helped to foster discord. Rivalries and frontier disputes have persisted to the present day. The traditional rivalry between Argentina and Brazil is related to

[107] See above, p. 26.

the fundamental division of Latin America between the former Spanish and Portuguese empires. This brings to mind the distinctive position of Brazil, accounting for over a third of Latin America's population. Brazil's policy towards integration, as the largest and most powerful of the twenty republics, is crucial. Historically, she has held aloof from efforts at closer co-operation initiated by Spanish American governments, and has been particularly friendly towards the United States. Although Brazil helped to form the Latin American Free Trade Association (LAFTA) and in the early nineteen-sixties followed a 'Latin American' rather than an 'inter-American' policy, the military coup of 1964 brought a resumption of her customary role in this century of co-operation with the United States.

The second main course open, in principle, to Latin America for redressing the vast imbalance of power in the western hemisphere so disadvantageous to it is to develop closer relations with extra-continental powers. As we have seen, the policy of the United States has focused upon limiting such relations, which might lead to 'intervention' in 'her hemisphere'. United States ability to secure respect for the Monroe Doctrine from both non-American powers and international organisations has greatly limited opportunities for Latin America of finding a counterpoise to her domination. Britain, the most influential non-American power in Latin America during the nineteenth century, was the first to accept the Monroe Doctrine. The challenges to United States hegemony in the twentieth century, from the Axis powers in the nineteen-thirties and early nineteen-forties and from the communist countries since the end of the Second World War, have not secured wide support in Latin America, though the twenty republics have been less than wholehearted in opposing them. Yet the Latin American countries have been anxious to develop closer relations with other regions of the world. They welcomed the establishment of the League of Nations, of which, in marked contrast to the United States, they all became members at one time or another. Later they all became founder members of the United Nations and participated increasingly in the affairs of other parts of the world. But the League was chary of taking action upon 'American questions', and the United Nations has been only relatively less so.[108]

---

[108] But in recent years Latin American countries have been more successful in getting grievances against the United States discussed in the United Nations. In March 1973 an extraordinary meeting of the Security Council was held in Panama. See below, p. 262.

Thus, given such factors as their individual weakness, their inability hitherto to form a strong grouping among themselves, and their economic dependence upon the United States, virtually the only course open to the countries of Latin America has been to join with their powerful neighbour in the inter-American system. In so doing they might hope both to safeguard themselves against any extra-continental threats and to exert collective pressure upon the United States to exercise her enormous power with restraint. It may well be 'reasonable to suppose that the Latin Americans are able to exert a good deal more leverage over a United States tied to the inter-American system than a United States outside it'. At all events, as the same writer asserts, 'the power imbalance in the hemisphere is so great that in no case could a United States determined on expansionism be deterred by Latin America'.[109] But, given United States power and her policy objective of organising them in a system under her hegemony, the countries of Latin America have had no real option but to participate. To regard their continued membership of that organisation as proof of the high value they attach to it is to ignore the realities of power.

As we have seen, the inter-American system is based upon the Western Hemisphere Idea, postulating a separation of the Americas from other continents. But the American states have never been isolated from the rest of the world. Since the end of the Second World War relations between the United States and Latin America have been increasingly influenced by developments in other parts of the world. In the first place, all the American states joined the United Nations and thus became involved with the problems of other regions. Then the Cold War increased United States commitments in Europe and Asia, and Latin American political support for her position became important to her. Eventually, the challenge from international communism reached Latin America, bringing new strains to inter-American relations. The emergence of the 'Third World', whose members rejected the Cold War concept of a division of the nations into 'Free' and 'Communist' in favour of one between 'developed' and 'developing', was of great significance. For the countries of Latin America came to identify themselves with the Third World, in spite of close ties with the United States. This trend has accelerated in recent years. Latin American governments, whatever their political complexion, have tried to increase

---

[109] Jerome Slater, *A Revaluation of Collective Security: The OAS in Action* (Ohio State University Press, 1965), p. 37, n. 62.

their trade with the Soviet Union and other communist countries in order to lessen their dependence upon the United States. There has also been a notable increase in West European and Japanese trade and investment in Latin America.

Clearly, there have been very significant developments in relations between the United States and Latin America during recent years. The ability of Cuba to leave the inter-American system and join that of the Soviet Union is sufficient in itself to suggest that a dramatic change in the hemisphere situation has taken place. The election of a Marxist president in Chile in 1970 may yet prove a comparably significant landmark in the erosion of the United States position in Latin America, in spite—or even because—of Salvador Allende's overthrow and death three years later. Yet the United States has never been more powerful in absolute terms, and Latin America is as dependent upon her in crucial ways as ever before. In the concluding chapter we will consider this apparent paradox by analysing the present situation and discussing future prospects. But let us first embark upon the historical analysis of relations between the two Americas which is the core of this study.

# 2 The Beginnings to the Formulation of the Monroe Doctrine

Diplomatic relations between the United States and Latin America date from the year 1822, when President Monroe's administration recognised the governments of Gran Colombia[1] and Mexico. But the foundations of United States policy towards her southern neighbours were laid even before any single independent state existed in the western hemisphere. The major objectives of this policy as it developed after the United States herself achieved independence were territorial expansion and the aggresive promotion of trade. These objectives were already discernible in the colonial period. As subjects of the British Empire, the colonists were involved in the wars for control of North America and in efforts to break Spain's monopoly of trade with her New World territories. American territorial questions were significant issues in European wars between 1689 and 1763, and the North American colonists were active in contraband trade and privateering which British subjects conducted in Spanish America. One prominent American colonist who strongly supported expansion, both commercial and territorial, at the expense of other European powers was Benjamin Franklin. Franklin and other American leaders regarded themselves as the natural and rightful heirs to Britain's position in the western hemisphere.[2] They already possessed British attitudes towards Spain and Spanish Americans.

The limitations and restrictions which, in her own interests, Britain placed upon their territorial and commercial ambitions rank high among the causes of the colonists' revolt against her. However, by 1776, in spite of British restrictions and the Spanish monopoly, North Americans had managed to build up a sizeable trade with Spanish possessions in the Caribbean region as well as with the Iberian

---

[1] Comprising, until its dissolution in 1830, present-day Colombia, Ecuador and Venezuela.
[2] Van Alstyne, *The Rising American Empire, op. cit.,* pp. 20, 147–8.

peninsula.[3] In time of peace they had developed a contraband trade, especially in logwood and slaves; in time of war they turned to privateering. During the war of North American independence which was, of course, also a European war, Spain as well as France was eventually involved, though not as an ally of the United States. Nevertheless, North American ships were allowed to put into Spanish American ports to take on supplies, provided they paid for them in cash, bills of exchange, or Negro slaves. The North Americans contrived to send agents to Spanish American ports to facilitate this trade, though Spain did not recognise them and they had to leave with the coming of peace.

During the period between the achievement of United States independence and the revolt of Spanish America, inter-American trade increased considerably. Spain's intermittent involvement in European wars compelled her to tolerate neutral trade with her colonies, and the United States, as the most important neutral maritime power, was the chief beneficiary of the concessions she made. North American commerce with Chile, for example, grew very rapidly during this period, though trade with the Pacific coast of South America was still theoretically forbidden by Spain. It has been estimated that during the decade from 1796 to 1806 United States trade with Spanish America increased from three per cent to twelve per cent of her total export trade, providing 'employment for scores of ships and important markets for the products of both farm and factory'.[4] In 1797, when the Spanish government opened its colonial ports to neutrals, the United States appointed agents in a number of them—though again they were not recognised as such by Spain. Circumstances had therefore forced the Madrid government to open the door to United States trade with its American possessions well before the independence movements there provided the North American republic with new opportunities.

As Spain nevertheless limited the promotion of United States trade with her American possessions so did she thwart United States territorial expansion. Spanish North American possessions hemmed in the United States to the west (Louisiana) and to the south (the Floridas). Moreover, Spain was not a signatory to the peace treaty of 1783 which had agreed the boundaries of the United States. She recognised neither these boundaries, nor the right of United States citizens freely to

---

[3] Harry Bernstein, *Origins of Inter-American Interest, 1700–1812* (University of Pennsylvania Press, 1945: Reissued, New York, 1966), pp. 15 ff.

[4] Arthur P. Whitaker, *The United States and the Independence of Latin America, 1800–1830* (The Johns Hopkins Press, 1941: paperback edn., New York, 1964), p. 38.

navigate the Mississippi river as was also written into the treaty with Britain. Spanish policy appeared not only to thwart, but even to threaten the United States. But however sincere the latter's concern for her security, Spanish fears of United States aggression were much more soundly based. Louisiana and the Floridas were sparsely populated and inadequately defended. The expansionist ambitions of the American frontiersmen posed a growing menace not only to Louisiana and the Floridas, but to Texas and to other parts of Mexico as well. To help offset it the Spanish government resorted to the desperate expedient—later to be followed by the Mexicans with such unhappy consequences for themselves—of seeking to wean the frontiersmen from their allegiance to the United States with grants of land and commercial privileges.

But the European situation, which had been so advantageous to the United States in securing her independence with most generous boundaries, continued to develop to her advantage. Spain became involved in the wars following the French Revolution in 1793, sometimes allied with and at others against Britain. This involvement eventually decided her (in 1795) to sign a treaty recognising both the United States boundaries as conceded by Britain in 1783 and the right of Americans to navigate the Mississippi from its source to the sea. The Pinckney Treaty (named after the United States Minister in Madrid) also granted United States citizens the 'right of deposit' of their goods for transshipment at New Orleans or some other place near the mouth of the Mississippi. Soon a much greater opportunity was afforded the United States for profiting from the European situation. Spain had come to realise how difficult was the task of retaining her North American possessions in the face of the growing strength of the United States. She therefore proposed to cede Louisiana to France, under whose rule it would constitute a more formidable obstacle to United States expansion and thus afford stronger protection for her more valuable territories to the west. News reaching the United States of negotiations between the French and Spanish governments to this end was followed by the suspension in 1802 of the right of deposit at New Orleans, with no alternative facilities being offered as stipulated in the Pinckney Treaty. This was a substantial blow, especially to western interests in the United States. But it proved only temporary. A revolt of the Negro slaves in Saint Domingue and the difficulties experienced by the French in subduing it (mainly because of the outbreak of yellow fever among their forces) helped to convince Napoleon it would be better to dispose of Louisiana to his own best advantage. The French ruler was also importantly influenced in this decision by his plans in Europe. Thus the United States, whose leaders were attempting to purchase New Orleans and both the Floridas, was able to buy the territory of Louisiana for the sum of $15 millions. Whether it was Napoleon's to sell is open to argument, but Spain—whom Napoleon had thus betrayed—had no choice but to acquiesce in the sale. The Spanish government did not, however, accept the United States contention that the territory she had purchased included Texas, and West Florida as far as the Perdido river.

But Spain's already weakening position in America was soon to be undermined by Napoleon's invasion of the Iberian peninsula (in 1807–8). President Jefferson was quick to see the possibilities this opened up for the United States. Immediately, it appeared to offer the opportunity of securing the boundaries of the Louisiana Purchase according to the United States interpretation, and of seizing the Floridas. But there were even more far-reaching prospects emerging from the growing movement for independence in Spanish America. Jefferson and his cabinet decided in October 1808 to authorise United States agents in Cuba and Mexico to let it be known to 'influential persons' there—unofficially—that the United States government, while unable to commit itself to support action on their part to declare their independence from Spain, would adopt a friendly posture. The United States leaders would be influenced by 'a firm feeling that our interests are intimately connected, and by the strongest repugnance to see you under subordination to either France or England, either politically or commercially'. Shortly afterwards Jefferson made his policy quite clear in instructions he sent to the governor of Louisiana. He said that the United States would be 'well satisfied' to see Cuba and Mexico remain in their present dependence upon Spain, 'but very unwilling to see them in that of France or England, politically or commercially'. However, he went on to declare that the interests of those advocating independence in these territories, and—by implication—the rest of Spanish America, and the interests of the United States were the same, 'and that the object of both must be to exclude all European influence from this hemisphere'.[5]

Thus were the long-term and the short-term objectives of United

[5] Whitaker, *The United States and the Independence of Latin America, 1800–1830. op. cit.*, pp. 42–3.

States policy towards Spanish America clearly enunciated. The ultimate objective was to exclude all European influence from the Americas. The short-term objectives were to fulfil immediate territorial ambitions where practicable—the Floridas and perhaps Texas—and to oppose the transfer from Spain to some stronger European power of those territories whose acquisition was a distinct possibility in the future. We have already noted Spanish fears for the future of Mexico as a major consideration in her transfer of Louisiana to Napoleon: fears which were greatly increased by the outcome of that event. More immediate was United States interest in Cuba, which Jefferson greatly coveted and which many Americans regarded as an appendage to the Floridas. Clearly the island was both strategically important and economically valuable. In Jefferson's view Cuba was 'the most interesting addition which would ever be made to our system'. In 1808 he sent an envoy to Cuba to explain to the Spanish Captain-General there that, while preferring the island to remain in Spanish hands rather than pass into British or French control, the United States was ready to buy it from Spain if the latter could not maintain herself there. Jefferson even toyed with the idea of making a deal with Napoleon under which he might secure Cuba. There were elements in the island willing to consider annexation by the United States—primarily in order to preserve slavery in view of its possible abolition by Spain— but American leaders did not feel strong enough to challenge Britain so openly. For the British government, too, was exercised over the future of Cuba.

Meanwhile Jefferson had been applying pressure upon Spain to cede the Floridas. He contended that West Florida was a part of the Louisiana Purchase, and tried to obtain East Florida in settlement of claims made by American citizens for various injuries allegedly suffered at the hands of Spain since the beginning of the European wars. Spain's capacity for resisting this pressure was greatly reduced in 1808. There were a number of insurrections assisted by immigrants from the United States, first in West and later in East Florida. In October 1810, following a revolt in the Baton Rouge district of West Florida, President James Madison, who had succeeded Jefferson the previous year, ordered the occupation of part of West Florida (up to the Perdido river), though asserting that this was a temporary occupation subject to later negotiation. It was justified mainly on the grounds that Spanish authority in the area had collapsed, and that it was taken in order to forestall a 'foreign' occupation.

This argument for the partial occupation of West Florida was elevated into a principle of policy by the prompt passage of a joint resolution of the two Houses of the United States Congress:

> Taking into view the peculiar situation of Spain and her American provinces; and considering the influence which the destiny of the territory adjoining the southern border of the United States may have upon their security, tranquillity, and commerce: Therefore,
>
> Resolved, by the Senate and House of Representatives of the United States of America in Congress assembled, that the United States, under the peculiar circumstances of the existing crisis, cannot without serious inquietude see any part of the said territory pass into the hands of any foreign Power; and that a due regard to their own safety compels them to provide under certain contingencies, for the temporary occupation of the said territory; they, at the same time, declare that the said territory shall, in their hands, remain subject to a future negotiation.

The No-Transfer Resolution of 1811 has been described as 'the first significant landmark in the evolution of ... [United States] Latin American policy'.[6] It reflects both the immediate and long-term aims. It foreshadows the main argument traditionally advanced to justify United States interventions in Latin America: that these were necessary to forestall interventions by 'foreign' (that is to say, non-American) powers. In her own self-image, as we have seen, the United States is not a 'foreign' power in her relations with the countries of Latin America. Immediately, this resolution empowered President Madison to occupy East Florida should there arise a danger of 'foreign' occupation, and meanwhile, if possible, he was to make arrangements to this end with the 'local authorities'. In fact, one of the commissioners sent to the Florida frontier for this purpose began—with Madison's tacit assent—to stir up revolution among the immigrants from the United States living there. Although Madison repudiated this action, the United States remained in possession of the territory occupied following the commissioner's action, and Congress passed acts for annexing the whole of West Florida.

A few weeks later war broke out with Great Britain, a major cause of which was the desire of the 'war hawks' in Washington to annex Canada as well as the whole of the Floridas and, if possible, Texas.

---

[6] Bemis, *The Latin American Policy of the United States: An Historical Interpretation, op. cit.*, p. 30.

Failure to attain these objectives by war (1812–14) caused the United States leaders to turn to diplomacy. They now adopted formally a policy of neutrality in the struggle taking place in Spanish America, but held over Spain the threat of recognising the independence of the revolutionary governments and of occupying the rest of the Floridas should she not negotiate the territorial questions to their satisfaction. A very eloquent argument was the invasion of East Florida by General (later President) Andrew Jackson in 1818. Jackson's immediate objective was to deal with Indians who had been attacking United States citizens from across the frontier. But the future President cherished a well-known ambition—shared by many of his fellow citizens—to conquer Spanish territory. In these circumstances, and with no effective support forthcoming from Britain (two of whose subjects were executed by Jackson after conviction for having conspired with the Indians), Spain agreed to the Adams–Onís[7] Treaty of 1819. By the terms of this treaty, the United States received the whole of the Floridas, but not Texas, and a new boundary in the west, giving cartographical form to the territory secured by the Louisiana Purchase. The United States government assumed payment of all claims made by her citizens against Spain up to the sum of five million dollars.[8] In Professor Merk's words, the Adams–Onís Treaty had been obtained 'By means of thinly veiled threats—threats to seize East Florida (already seized in part by Andrew Jackson), threats to seize Texas by right of a shadowy American claim and to recognize the revolted colonies of Spain in Latin America, and threats to have a showdown on the claims for damages suffered by American citizens at the hands of Spain'.[9]

Thus had Napoleon's invasion of the Iberian peninsula and the subsequent revolt of the Spanish American colonies enabled the United States to achieve some of her immediate territorial ambitions. New opportunities were also afforded her for commercial expansion, although Jefferson's trade embargo in 1808 and the war of 1812 with Britain caused temporary setbacks. After the restoration of peace in 1815 United States trade with Spanish America greatly increased. Although never allowed to enjoy general freedom of commerce with

---

[7] Luis de Onís was the Spanish Minister to the United States.

[8] It is often erroneously asserted that the United States purchased the Floridas for this sum.

[9] Frederick Merk, *Manifest Destiny and Mission in American History : A Reinterpretation* (New York, 1963), p. 15.

the colonies Spain still controlled, the United States managed to conduct some trade with all of them, though under different conditions in
different ports. In the first place, while maintaining its monopoly in
principle, the Spanish government itself was compelled by circumstances to make exceptions: licenses were granted to foreigners, including United States citizens, to take not only essential goods such as
munitions and foodstuffs but even general merchandise to loyal ports.
Secondly, local colonial officials often authorised United States commerce on the grounds of urgent necessity. And there was also considerable contraband trade. With those colonies which Spain no longer
controlled the United States enjoyed general freedom to trade, though
faced with varying tariffs and port regulations, and sometimes trading
on less favourable terms than those accorded to Britain. It is significant that by far the most important part of her trade with Latin
America at this time was with Cuba, which remained in Spain's possession for most of the remainder of the century. In 1821 more than
two-thirds of the total value of United States exports to Spanish
America went to Cuba alone.[10] On the other hand, trade with Mexico,
like Cuba a special object of United States ambition, was on a much
smaller scale. Spain maintained tighter control of Mexico than of
Cuba (whose needs were more dependent upon United States merchants)
and Britain was the main beneficiary of such relaxations as she made in
the case of the former. United States interest in Mexico was more
territorial than commercial.

We noted that even as early as the war of North American independence the United States (as she was to become) sought to establish
agents in Spanish America to protect her commerce and assist her
traders there. After the outbreak of revolt in Spanish America such
'agents for commerce and seamen' were sent further afield than hitherto.
However, the first formal diplomatic agent of the United States to reside in Latin America was sent not to Spanish America but to Rio de
Janeiro (in 1809). Brazil was, in fact, the only Latin American country
in which the United States had regular diplomatic and consular representation during most of the following decade. The situation in Brazil
was very different from that in Spanish America. When Napoleon's
army invaded Portugal in 1807 the Prince Regent fled to America under
British naval protection. The Portuguese court and government were

---

[10] Whitaker, *The United States and the Independence of Latin America, 1800–1830*
*op. cit.*, p. 130.

transferred to Rio de Janeiro, which now became the capital. Almost immediately Brazil was thrown open to trade with all friendly nations, thus ending the former well-enforced Portuguese monopoly. In 1815 Brazil was raised to the status of a kingdom on terms of equality with Portugal under the common crown. The United States government, which had maintained a legation in Lisbon until President Jefferson suspended it on grounds of economy, sent a Minister to the new capital in Brazil. But United States influence there was for the time being much less than that of Britain.

Such were the short-term territorial and commercial gains the United States derived from the situation created by Napoleon's invasion of the Iberian peninsula. But what of Jefferson's contention that the object of both the United States and those advocating independence in Spanish America must be to exclude all European influence from the western hemisphere? This was a very remote prospect indeed when Jefferson voiced it. Events in Spanish America were confused, and little reliable information about them was available in the United States. It was some time before the Spanish American leaders themselves progressed from an indignant rejection of Joseph Bonaparte (Napoleon's brother) as their ruler to demands for independence; and the likelihood of their achieving it was for a long time in doubt. Jefferson left the presidency in the spring of 1809, and his successor, James Madison, moved cautiously in formulating a policy on the question of Spanish American independence.

Madison's caution was understandable. Although there were liberals in the United States stirred by the spectacle of 'fellow Americans' struggling for liberty as they themselves had done a generation earlier, they were comparatively few in number. There was widespread ignorance of Spanish America and Spanish Americans, and not inconsiderable Anglo-Saxon prejudice against them. Moreover, this prejudice often was shared by United States leaders, including James Monroe and John Quincy Adams, neither of whom initially showed much interest in the Spanish Americans. Moreover, the situation in Spanish America was confused, and fortunes in the struggle there fluctuated in time and place. United States policy towards the independence movements was inevitably affected by their prospects of success. Intimately linked with these were the European situation and the policies of the great powers towards events in the Americas: above all, their ability and willingness to assist Spain in the struggle to hold her American empire. The most important of these powers was

Britain. At the same time there were conflicting views within the
United States about the policy to be pursued. There was at first a
divergence among commercial interests between those with a bigger
involvement in trade with the Iberian peninsula and those anxious to
press advantages from Spain's weakness in America. On territorial
questions there were advocates of a more aggressive policy than that
favoured by the administration, especially those desiring war with
Britain in order to seize Canada. The immediate policy of the Madison
administration was to convince the Spanish American insurgents of
United States goodwill—and to derive benefits from so doing—while
at the same time maintaining diplomatic relations with Spain in order
to achieve by negotiation important territorial and commercial objectives which we have already noted.

In practice, the United States followed for several years a policy
which purported to be impartial but actually favoured the Spanish
American insurgents. Soon after the independence movements began
the Madison administration increased the numbers of its agents and
observers in Latin America. In addition to the 'agents for seamen and
commerce', special agents were sent on particular missions to the region,
and regular consular agents appointed in some cases. Perhaps the best
known of these agents—later to play a notorious role in early diplomatic relations between the United States and Mexico—was Joel
Poinsett.[11] Poinsett was sent to Buenos Aires in 1810 and in the following year was appointed consul general for the provinces of Buenos
Aires, Chile and Peru. In his original instructions, he was ordered not
only to promote commerce, but also 'to diffuse the impression that the
United States cherish the sincerest good will towards the people of
Spanish America as neighbors'. Moreover:

> ... in the event of a political separation from the parent country, and of
> the establishment of an independent system of National Government, it
> will coincide with the sentiments and policy of the United States to pro-
> mote the most friendly relations, and the most liberal intercourse, between
> the inhabitants of this hemisphere, as having all a common interest, and as
> lying under a common obligation to maintain that system of peace, justice,
> and good will, which is the only source of happiness for nations.[12]

---

[11] See below, pp. 74–5.

[12] William R. Manning (ed.), *Diplomatic correspondence of the United States concerning
the Independence of the Latin-American Nations* (3 vols., New York, 1925), vol. 1, pp.
6–7.

In short, Poinsett and the others were to act as both political observers and promoters of commerce while at the same time assuring the insurgents of their government's sympathy towards their aspirations. Poinsett did more. He not only gave military aid to the insurgents but even became involved in their internal factional quarrels.

In his annual Message to Congress in November 1811 President Madison referred sympathetically to the Spanish colonies struggling for independence; and there followed a resolution in the House of Representatives expressing 'a friendly solicitude in the welfare of these communities, and a readiness, when they should become nations by the exercise of their just rights, to unite with the Executive in establishing such relations with them as might be necessary'. But the government offered the Spanish insurgents more than expressions of sympathy. Madison allowed revolutionary agents to reside in the United States and facilitated their purchases and shipments of arms. He even corresponded with them unofficially. United States citizens were engaged in privateering and other hostile activities against the Spanish authorities. And, as we have seen, Madison was in the process of taking over West Florida. Naturally, Spain protested against such a travesty of impartiality; but to little effect.

Spanish protests were somewhat more effective after the war of 1812–14. It had been the confident expectation of the 'war hawks' of 1812 that the involvement of Britain and her ally Spain in war against Napoleon would enable the United States to make easy territorial conquests. The expectation was disappointed; and in the event the United States was fortunate herself not to lose territory. She failed to take Canada, and the Florida question was settled by diplomacy, with Texas renounced for the time being. At the peace negotiations the United States delegates represented, in the words of one historian, 'a country properly fearful now that their associate Napoleon had been overthrown'.[13] In September 1815 the United States government issued a proclamation of neutrality in the war between Spain and her rebellious colonies. But its neutrality laws, even when somewhat revised in 1817 and 1818 to close loopholes, proved less than adequate—especially when support for the insurgents grew in the United States. After James Monroe (who had been Secretary of State under Madison) became President in 1817 he was under increasing pressure to change

---

[13] W. H. Callcott, *The Western Hemisphere: Its Influence on United States Policies to the End of World War II* (Austin, University of Texas Press, 1968), p. 11.

United States policy in favour of the insurgents. The latter's agents in Washington became increasingly importunate in their demands for recognition; particularly so was the representative of the United Provinces of the Rio de la Plata,[14] which declared their independence in 1816. Outstanding among United States advocates of recognition was Henry Clay, Speaker of the House of Representatives.

Clay had been a leading war hawk in 1812 and he was a strong political rival of John Quincy Adams, now Monroe's Secretary of State and therefore his presumed successor. This rivalry involved conflict between Congress and the Executive over policy towards Spanish America. In 1818 Clay tried to engineer recognition of the United Provinces of the Rio de la Plata by means of a Congressional appropriation for the salary of a minister to them. He claimed that Congress could effect recognition through the exercise of its power to regulate foreign commerce. In the course of making his proposal Clay declared to the House of Representatives that whatever forms of government the new nations of Spanish America established, 'these governments will be animated by an American feeling, and guided by an American policy. They will obey the laws of the system of the New World, of which they will compose a part, in contradistinction to that of Europe'.[15] Two years later Clay proposed the creation of a 'system of which we shall be the centre, and in which all South America will act with us' in promoting inter-American commerce and at the same time establishing 'the rallying point of human wisdom against all the despotism of the Old World'.[16] Clay's motion was lost, however. It was widely held that the power of recognition belong rightfully to the Executive, and there was still a great deal of uncertainty about the situation in Spanish America.

Adams, as we have noted, had a poor opinion of the Spanish Americans and their ability to govern themselves. He rejected Clay's concept of a 'system' embracing the United States and Latin America: 'As to an American system', he declared, 'we [the United States] have it—we constitute the whole of it ... there is no community of interests between North and South America ... no basis for any such system.'[17]

---

[14] Subsequently Argentina.

[15] Quoted in Dexter Perkins, *A History of the Monroe Doctrine* (Boston, Mass., 1955), p. 4.

[16] Whitaker, *The Western Hemisphere Idea, op. cit.*, p. 32.

[17] *Ibid.*, p. 35.

Although an 'imperialist' in the matter of expansion in North America,[18] and even described by Professor Weinberg as 'so ardent an advocate of Indian dispossession',[19] Adams was not at first interested in South America nor in extending United States influence there. In March 1821 he told Clay:

> ... I have not yet seen and do not now see any prospect that they will establish free or liberal institutions of government ... They have not the first elements of good or free government. Arbitrary power, military and ecclesiastical, is stamped upon their education, upon their habits, and upon all their institutions ... I have little expectation of any beneficial result to this country from any future connection with them, political or commercial.[20]

At all events, Monroe and Adams were not ready to grant recognition to the Spanish Americans; still less to accept the existence of a common American 'system'. In 1817 the President had sent a number of special commissioners on a fact-finding mission to South America. Since they gave conflicting reports of the situation there the administration was confirmed in its decision not to grant recognition. Monroe and Adams were, of course, importantly influenced by the negotiations being conducted with Spain over the Floridas, and found the demands of Clay and others an embarrassment. The Spanish American leaders were very disappointed by the Monroe administration's policy, and angered when the Adams–Onís Treaty was concluded. They felt their interests had been sacrificed to the territorial ambitions of the United States, and believed the treaty contained a secret undertaking by Monroe not to grant them recognition. This last was not so; the United States had refused to make such a commitment. In fact, prospects of recognition were enhanced by the conclusion of the treaty. But not until 1821 was it finally ratified; Spain's delay in ratifying had been due partly to the United States refusal to agree not to recognise the insurgents.

In May 1820 Henry Clay, who had criticised the treaty because it did not include the annexation of Texas, succeeded in carrying through the House of Representatives a motion resolving:

---

[18] Merk, *Manifest Destiny and Mission in American History: A Reinterpretation, op. cit.,* p. 14.

[19] Albert K. Weinberg, *Manifest Destiny: A Study of Nationalist Expansionism in American History* (Baltimore, The Johns Hopkins Press, 1935: paperback edn., Chicago, 1963), p. 86.

[20] S. F. Bemis, *John Quincy Adams and the Foundations of American Foreign Policy* (New York, 1949), p. 354.

that it is expedient to provide by law a suitable outfit and salary for such Minister or Ministers *as the President, by and with the advice and consent of the Senate,* may send to any of the Governments of South America, which have established, and are maintaining, their independence on [*sic*] Spain.[21]

But this did not affect the policy being pursued by the administration. Nor did another resolution, adopted on the eve of the arrival in Washington of Spain's ratification of the Adams–Onís Treaty. This stated 'That the House of Representatives participates with the people of the United States in the deep interest which they feel for the success of the Spanish provinces of South America which are struggling to establish their liberty and independence'; and declared 'that it will give its Constitutional *support* to the President of the United States, *whenever he may deem it expedient* to recognize the sovereignty and independence of any of the said provinces'.[22] Monroe and Adams were not to be hurried. The military situation early in 1821 was unpromising and in some of the provinces controlled by the insurgents conditions were unstable and confused. Privateers commissioned by the insurgents were plundering neutral ships, including those of the United States. This issue specifically held up recognition of the government in Buenos Aires. But by the end of the year Spain's hold over her colonies had greatly weakened, and the Buenos Aires authorities had satisfied United States complaints about the depredations of privateers.

It was now that President Monroe decided the time had come to recognise the new states and to foster their goodwill by so doing. In a special message to Congress (on 8 March 1822) he declared that Chile, the United Provinces of the Rio de la Plata, Peru, Colombia and Mexico were fully independent and certain to remain so. The President contended that the United States was recognising an established fact, and not committing an act of hostility towards Spain. Her policy of neutrality was unaffected. Spain protested but did not break off relations with the United States. Congress made an appropriation of $100,000 to meet the expenses of 'such missions to the independent nations on the American continent as the President might deem proper'. On 19 June 1822 Monroe began the process of recognition by formally receiving as *chargé d'affaires* the accredited diplomatic agent in Washington of Gran Colombia. Before the end of the year the United States

---

[21] Bemis, *John Quincy Adams and the Foundations of American Foreign Policy, op. cit.,* p. 352. Bemis's italics.         [22] *Ibid.,* p. 353. Bemis's italics.

recognised the Empire of Mexico.[23] In the following year Buenos Aires and Chile, and in 1824 the Empire of Brazil[24] and the United Provinces of Central America[25] were accorded recognition. Peru, the last stronghold of Spanish power in South America (where the final battle was held at Ayacucho in 1824), was recognised in 1826. Other Spanish American states were recognised as they emerged and established their sovereignty. Although the first country of all to become independent, Haiti was not recognised by the United States until 1862 because of opposition from slave-holding states. Recognition of the Dominican Republic, who was under Haitian rule from 1822 until 1844, took place in 1866.

But by 1822 the attitude of Monroe and Adams had evolved beyond a simple willingness to recognise the facts of sovereignty in Latin America. They had come to adopt a policy very much along the lines advocated by Clay. This is well illustrated by the instructions given by Secretary Adams to United States Ministers appointed to two of the new nations in the following year: the United Provinces of the Rio de la Plata and Gran Colombia. The success of the Spanish American revolutions was now declared to have stemmed from the principles and example of the United States own revolution. The independence of the new nations ranked among the most important events in history. It was asserted that, although her national obligations prescribed neutrality, the United States had exercised all her moral influence in favour of Spanish American independence until the time was actually ripe for recognition. Her policy towards the new nations was to uphold the principle of republicanism against any Latin American tendencies towards monarchy, and to support an American system separated from the monarchical and tyrannical system of Europe. But Adams was cautious in the matter of United States participation in a congress under consideration by Colombia which might lead to proposals for close political co-operation among American states. In his instructions to the minister appointed to Buenos Aires he said:

---

[23] The short-lived empire of Iturbide. See below, p. 73.

[24] Dom Pedro, left in Brazil as regent when his father returned to Portugal in 1821, declared for independence the following year with himself as emperor.

[25] The countries of Central America did not emerge as separate states until 1838. In the colonial period they formed the Captaincy–General of Guatemala under the Viceroyalty of New Spain (Mexico) and subsequently joined Iturbide's Mexican empire. They became independent as the United Provinces of Central America until the latter's dissolution in 1838. The reunion of the Central American states has been a recurring theme in their history.

To any confederation of Spanish American provinces for that end [republicanism and independence of Europe], the United States would yield their approbation and cordial good wishes. If more should be asked of them, the proposition will be received and considered in a friendly spirit, and with a due sense of its importance.[26]

The United States favoured promoting commerce with the new nations on the basis of the most-favoured nation, and wanted them to be commercially as well as politically independent of Europe. The United States was the first country outside their own number to recognise the independence of the new nations. In Bemis's enthusiastic judgement, 'This recognition was the greatest assistance rendered by any foreign power to the independence of Latin America.'[27]

The United States naturally was anxious to impress upon the new states the value of her recognition and the evidence it offered of her goodwill towards them. Her leaders were particularly concerned to counter the very considerable influence Great Britain enjoyed with the countries of Latin America. British and United States policies towards the revolt of Spain's American colonies had some common features. Both countries were officially neutral, while each contained a growing body of liberal and commercial opinion strongly supporting the rebels; they therefore had difficulty in enforcing their neutrality legislation. Each maintained the right to trade freely with any part of Spanish America, and, except for Britain's special privileges in Brazil (deriving from the position she had enjoyed in Portugal before escorting the Portuguese royal family to America), neither sought exclusive commercial rights in Latin America. Both the United States and Britain opposed intervention in Spanish America by the European powers whether on Spain's behalf or their own.

But the United States and Britain basically were rivals in Latin America. Their interests in the region conflicted—or appeared to do so—at every turn. Politically, Britain would have liked to see monarchies established in the new nations of Spanish America and she set great store by the preservation of the principle of monarchy in Brazil. The United States strongly desired republics for Latin America and her leaders came to embrace the idea of an American system separate from Europe. Britain, in Canning's words, was not prepared to contemplate 'a division of the world into European and American,

---

[26] Quoted in Whitaker, *The United States and the Independence of Latin America, 1800–1830, op. cit.*, p. 418.　　　[27] *John Quincy Adams, op. cit.*, pp. 361–2.

Republican and Monarchical'.[28] Commercially, there was fear on each side that the other would obtain advantages at its expense, though there was less direct competition between their trading interests than they imagined. Each also feared the other's territorial ambitions, and the rivalry of their respective agents in Spanish America often was acrimonious.

In the long term, it was the ambition of the United States to replace Britain as the most influential power in Latin America. A separate 'system' for the hemisphere (under her leadership) meant the exclusion of European influence, and this again meant, above all, that of Britain. John Quincy Adams, now the most important figure shaping United States Latin American policy, was fully convinced that his country's inherent superiority would one day bring her a commanding position in world affairs. But he was fully aware of Britain's present power and the limits it set upon the immediate fulfilment of United States ambitions. Thus, in Sir Charles Webster's words, he:

> ... was anxious to avoid all risk of immediate conflict, and at the same time not to give up anything which would be of importance to the great United States of the future. He wished to preserve the Americas as a separate system, but he was also conscious that a considerable share of the Spanish heritage would fall to the United States unless she tried to grasp it too soon.[29]

George Canning, the British Foreign Minister, was likewise aware of the enormous potential of the United States and therefore anxious to limit the opportunities for her to expand her territory or influence.

In the short term, then, a common interest in opposing intervention in Spanish America by other powers and United States awareness of Britain's present power provided the basis for a possible understanding between them. It is noteworthy that the Monroe administration had been reluctant to recognise the new Spanish American states without Britain's taking similar action; and, indeed, after eventually recognising them unilaterally, it proceeded slowly with the appointment of ministers to them. As early as 1818 the United States had approached Britain about joint recognition of the government in Buenos Aires, but

---

[28] R. A. Humphreys, 'Anglo-American Rivalries and Spanish American Emancipation', *Transactions of the Royal Historical Society, Fifth Series*, vol. 16 (1966), p. 141.
[29] C. K. Webster (ed.), *Britain and the Independence of Latin America, 1812–1830 Select Documents from the Foreign Office Archives* (London, 1938), vol. 1, p. 42.

had met with an unfavourable response. Significantly, the Monroe administration had deemed it wiser not to proceed at that stage without British co-operation, though Adams claimed later that the United States initiative (by raising the possibility of Anglo-American co-operation) had helped to deter a policy of intervention by the Holy Alliance on Spain's behalf being adopted at the Congress of Aix-la-Chapelle later that year.

In 1823 the initiative came from the British side. Britain had become increasingly estranged from the Holy Alliance over the congress system and its interventions to uphold legitimacy in Europe. The French invasion of Spain in March 1823 in support of the Spanish monarchy drew from Canning a demand for assurances that there would be no intervention against what he ominously described as 'the *late* Spanish possessions in America'.³⁰ Britain received no such assurances. It is difficult to judge how seriously Canning viewed the threat of European intervention in Spanish America at this stage. Clearly it was to Britain's advantage that both the United States and the Spanish Americans should believe the threat a real one against which only her own policies and power provided an adequate defence. At all events, it appears that Canning's policy towards the European powers on the question of the Spanish American colonies impressed Adams favourably, and the British Foreign Minister had reason to believe that a proposal for Anglo-American co-operation would be well received in Washington. Canning judged that his position *vis-à-vis* the Holy Alliance would be strengthened by a joint declaration with the United States on the subject of the Spanish American colonies.

And so, in August 1823, Canning made his famous overtures to Richard Rush, the United States Minister in London. The British Foreign Secretary proposed a joint declaration of policy embodying five points: that recovery of the colonies by Spain was hopeless; that the question of recognition was one of time amd circumstance; that no obstacle was to be put in the way of an understanding between Spain and her colonies; that neither of the signatories aimed at possession of any portion of the colonies for themselves; and finally, that neither could view with indifference the transfer of any such portion to another power. Canning affirmed the urgency of the matter, for he expected the French following their action in Spain, to propose 'a Congress, or some less formal concert and consultation, specially upon the affairs of

---

³⁰ *Britain and the Independence of Latin America, op. cit.*, vol. 2, p. 112. My italics.

Spanish America'. But Rush, although doubtless flattered by Canning's overtures, was not prepared to respond immediately. He pointed to a most important difference in their respective countries' policies. The United States had recognised the new states; Britain had not done so. Canning could not agree to accord recognition yet, and Rush referred the whole matter to Washington.

Before submitting Canning's proposal to his cabinet President Monroe sought the advice of his two predecessors, former Presidents Jefferson and Madison. Both favoured United States acceptance. Jefferson supported the idea of a separate American system, but believed that this could best be assured by co-operation with Britain because of her great power: 'Great Britain is the nation which can do us the most harm of any one, or all on earth; and with her on our side we need not fear the whole world.' Madison concurred, but wanted a pronouncement expressing disapproval of the French invasion of Spain and of any intervention against the Greeks, then in revolt against Turkey. President Monroe appears to have favoured Madison's proposed declaration against the intervention of great powers in the affairs of weak states in any part of the world.

In the cabinet discussion which followed only Adams opposed collaboration with Britain. The Secretary of State was less convinced than the others of the danger of European intervention in Spanish America, and strongly of the opinion that Britain was already committed to preventing any such eventuality. He believed there was no need for the United States to play the role of 'a cock-boat in the wake of the British man-of-war'. She had the opportunity, presented her by Canning's offer, of making her own declaration rather than allowing Britain to take the main credit for protecting the new states. Moreover, Adams strongly suspected that Canning had another motive: to limit the territorial expansion of the United States by securing from her a pledge not to acquire Spanish American territory for herself. In Adams's mind especially was Cuba, which in important ways epitomised the whole position.

We have noted the view that Cuba formed an appendage to the Floridas, the whole of which the United States had acquired by this time. We saw that Jefferson coveted the island and how United States trade with it had grown enormously. Cuba, clearly, was one part of Spain's heritage in America to which the United States seemed the destined heir. President Monroe confided to Jefferson: 'I have always concurred . . . that too much importance could not be attached to that

Island ... we ought, if possible, to incorporate it'.[31] In Adams's judgement:

> (Cuba) almost in sight of our shores ... has become an object of trans-
> cendent importance to the commercial and political interests of our Union.
> Its commanding position ... the character of its population ... its safe and
> capacious harbor of the Havana ... the nature of its productions and of its
> wants ... give it an importance in the sum of our national interests with
> which that of no other foreign territory can be compared, and little in-
> ferior to that which binds the different members of this Union together ...
> it is scarcely possible to resist the conviction that the annexation of Cuba
> to our Federal Republic will be indispensable to the continuance and
> integrity of the Union itself ... there are laws of political as well as of physi-
> cal gravitation; and if an apple, severed by the tempest from its native tree,
> can not choose but fall to the ground, Cuba, forcibly disjoined from its
> own unnatural connection with Spain, and incapable of self-support, can
> gravitate only towards the North American Union, which, by the same
> law of nature, can not cast her off from its bosom ...[32]

What exercised Adams and other United States leaders was that
Britain or some other European power might intervene to seize Cuba
before this natural 'gravitation' could take place. Their policy had
always been to oppose the transfer of the island from Spain to a
stronger European power and to avoid any action themselves which
might provoke intervention by Britain or France. They were also
opposed to any attempt by the new Spanish American states to liberate
Cuba. Unquestionably, Canning feared United States ambition to
acquire the island, and this was an important element in his proposal to
Rush.[33]

Adams's view prevailed, and it was decided that the United States
should make a unilateral declaration of policy. Moreover, the Secretary
of State dissuaded Monroe from making any references to interventions
in Europe as Madison had suggested: '... if an issue must be made
up between us and the Holy Alliance it ought to be upon grounds

---

[31] Quoted in Hugh Thomas, *Cuba or The Pursuit of Freedom* (London, 1971), p. 101,
n. 35.

[32] James W. Gantenbein (ed.), *The Evolution of Our Latin-American Policy: A Documentary Record* (New York, Columbia University Press, 1950), pp. 425–6.

[33] But it was secondary to his main aim of scoring a diplomatic victory over the
European powers, which, in spite of his failure to obtain a joint declaration, he later
claimed in his famous boast: 'I called the New World into existence to redress the balance
of the Old'.

exclusively American; that we should separate it from all European concerns, disclaim all intention of interfering with these, and make the stand altogether for an American cause'.[34] Adams was also largely responsible for another part of the President's eventual declaration. This was occasioned by a controversy with Russia over the latter's colonial claims on the north-west coast of America, which the Tsar had been endeavouring to extend. By his own account, Adams informed the Russian Minister in Washington in July 1823 that 'we should contest the right of Russia to any territorial establishment on this continent, and that we should assume distinctly the principle that the American continents are no longer subjects for any new European colonial establishments'.[35] The particular controversy was settled by compromise, and Russia retained territory in America until the United States bought Alaska from her in 1867. But the non-colonisation principle had been affirmed and was embodied in the Message to Congress which Monroe preferred as the vehicle for his declaration to the diplomatic channels advocated by Adams. This early and outstanding example of 'open diplomacy', involving an appeal to public opinion, calls for comment. And Professor Perkins declares, '. . . how much more effective the declaration to Congress than an unostentatious diplomatic protest, how much more gratifying to the national pride, how much more productive of prestige in South America, how much more disconcerting to Europe!'[36]

What later came to be called the Monroe Doctrine consisted of two widely separated passages in the President's Message to the United States Congress of 2 December 1823.[37] In the first of these, Monroe referred to the discussions with Russia over their clash of interests in north-west America. He said:

> . . . In the discussions to which this interest has given rise and in the arrangements by which they may terminate the occasion has been judged proper for asserting, as a principle in which the rights and interests of the United States are involved, that the American continents, by the free and

---

[34] Allan Nevins (ed.), *The Diary of John Quincy Adams, 1794–1845: American Political, Social and Intellectual Life from Washington to Polk* (New York and London, 1928), p. 310.

[35] *Ibid.*, p. 298.

[36] Dexter Perkins, *The Monroe Doctrine, 1823–1826* (Cambridge, Mass., Harvard University Press, 1927: Reprint, Gloucester, Mass., 1966), p. 260.

[37] They are reproduced, for example, under the heading 'The Original Monroe Doctrine', in Perkins, *A History of the Monroe Doctrine, op. cit.*, pp. 394–6.

independent condition which they have assumed and maintain, are henceforth not to be considered as subjects for future colonization by any European powers.

In the second passage, the President declared that the political system of the 'allied' (that is, European) powers was essentially different from that of 'America':

> ... We owe it, therefore, to candor and to the amicable relations existing between the United States and those powers to declare that we should consider any attempt on their part to extend their system to any portion of this hemisphere as dangerous to our peace and safety. With the existing colonies or dependencies of any European power we have not interfered and shall not interfere. But with the Governments who have declared their independence and maintained it, and whose independence we have, on great consideration and on just principles, acknowledged, we could not view any interposition for the purpose of oppressing them, or controlling in any other manner their destiny, by any European power in any other light than as the manifestation of an unfriendly disposition toward the United States.

United States policy in regard to Europe, Monroe affirmed was 'not to interfere in the internal concerns of any of its powers'. But in regard to the Americas:

> ... It is impossible that the allied powers should extend their political system to any portion of either continent without endangering our peace and happiness; nor can anyone believe that our southern brethren, if left to themselves, would adopt it of their own accord.

The second passage ended: 'It is still the true policy of the United States to leave the parties to themselves, in the hope that other powers will pursue the same course.' In other words, Monroe reaffirmed United States neutrality in the wars of Spanish American independence.

The Monroe Doctrine is vastly more important for what it was to become than for what Monroe actually said in 1823. Yet, owing to the inferences which may be drawn from them—and have been over the years—the words themselves require further examination. The relevant passages of the Message contain several references to United States rights and interests (above all, her security), which Monroe declared would be threatened by any extension of the European political system to any part of the western hemisphere. On these grounds the

United States claimed the right to forbid any further European colonisation in the hemisphere as well as intervention against the new states of Latin America. As a corollary to this assumption of the right to be vitally concerned in the affairs of Latin America the United States affirmed that her policy was not to interfere in the internal concerns of any of the European powers. From this it could be inferred—and, as we shall see, subsequently was—that 'American affairs' in the continental sense were to be considered the 'internal concern' of the United States. President Monroe's words make it clear that in the United States view the other American countries stood in a special relationship to her as distinct from the European powers, whose influence in the western hemisphere (specifically further to colonise it or to extend their system to any part of it) she openly aimed to curtail. In the light of the known ambitions of her leaders, as well as the weakness of the new nations of Latin America, the United States evidently was to be the great power which would determine the destinies of the American continent.

But what of the President's assertion that 'with the existing colonies or dependencies of any European power we have not interfered and shall not interfere' and that 'it is still the true policy of the United States to leave the parties [that is, Spain and the new states] to themselves'? Previous events and the well-known ambitions of the United States belied both. She had interfered in the Floridas in order to acquire them and had unsuccessfully attempted to seize Canada by force. Her ambition was eventually to exclude all European influence from the continent, and she was pursuing vigorous policies to increase her own. Of great future interest is Monroe's assertion that the Latin Americans ('our southern brethren') would not adopt the European political system of their own accord. From this it could be assumed that were a Latin American country to adopt such a system or to seek to align itself with a non-American state this must have come about through intervention by the extra-continental power. Such an assumption has been extremely important in the development of the Monroe Doctrine, which was to become increasingly associated with United States interventions in Latin America, often justified on the grounds that they were necessary to prevent interventions by 'foreign' (that is, non-American) powers.[38]

---

[38] As we have seen, the occupation of part West Florida in 1810 had been justified mainly on the grounds of forestalling a 'foreign' occupation. See above, p. 45.

It has been argued that the Monroe Doctrine involves a departure from the national policy of isolationism associated with Washington's Farewell Address and Jefferson's warning against 'entangling alliances'. There were those in the United States Congress who voiced such fears at the time, and especially a little later when the Executive proposed to send delegates to the Congress of Panama. Yet the Doctrine could well be considered as an application of the United States national policy of isolationism to the hemisphere as a whole. For isolationism involved keeping the United States separate from the European balance of power, while the Doctrine applied this policy to Latin America as well. And, far from involving 'entangling alliances', it was essentially a unilateral policy of the United States—and has always remained so. The Latin Americans were not invited to co-operate in establishing an American system; on the contrary Monroe affirmed that such a system, essentially different and separate from the European, already existed and that they were part of it. Therefore, while the Monroe Doctrine generally received enthusiastic support within the United States, it had no comparable reception in Latin America. Moreover, those Latin Americans welcoming it were disillusioned when its unilateral character was confirmed by United States refusal to make it the basis of an alliance or even to give the new states a firm commitment to their defence against possible European intervention. Between 1824 and 1826 five Latin American states made unsuccessful overtures to Washington for either an alliance (in the cases of Chile, Colombia and Brazil) or an assurance of contingent aid (in the cases of Mexico and the United Provinces of the Rio de la Plata).

On the question of the United States giving a firm pledge of assistance to other American states threatened by the intervention of European powers, the Colombian Minister in Washington, José Maria Salazar, was told this would be given only in case of 'a deliberate and concerted system of the Allied Powers to exercise force', and, moreover, would be dependent upon 'a previous understanding with those European Powers, whose interests and whose principles would secure from them an active and efficient coöperation in the cause'. On this response to Colombia's enquiry Dexter Perkins comments:

> Put in plain and blunt terms this means that the United States, in spite of its brave words, would not act unless Great Britain did, and, to all appearances, would not act except in the event of a general European intervention. Was not this a good deal like coming in as a cock-boat in the wake

of the British man-of-war? If the Adams note to Salazar was not the abandonment of the Doctrine, it was, I think it must be conceded, a distinct retreat. It put American policy toward the South American republics on a footing considerably less audacious than did the message of 1823.[39]

It must be remembered (as Perkins himself noted) that the approval of the Congress would have been required for an alliance. Monroe's Message was merely a pronouncement of the Executive.

Meanwhile Canning had fully recovered from the diplomatic set-back he had received at Adams's hands. The British Foreign Minister bent every effort to undermine the position of the United States in Latin America, while maintaining cordial relations on the surface. His first major move after the abortive overtures to Rush was to secure from France a pledge that force would not be used against the new Spanish American states. Since Britain made clear her determination to prevent it in any case, the French gave way. In a memorandum which is named after him, the French Minister in London, the Prince de Polignac, declared: 'That his Government believed it to be utterly hopeless to reduce Spanish America to the State of its former relation to Spain. That France disclaimed, on her part, any intention or desire to avail herself of the present state of the Colonies, or of the present situation of France toward Spain, to appropriate to herself any part of the Spanish possessions in America. . . . That she abjured, in any case, any design of acting against the Colonies by force of arms.'[40] The Polignac Memorandum was signed before President Monroe's Message was issued, though the United States did not receive news of it until afterwards. 'From then on', in Professor Bemis's words, 'the Monroe Doctrine and the Polignac Memorandum were rival placards over Latin America competing for the diplomatic allegiance of the new states—and for their commerce.'[41] But there was no doubt which seemed the more impressive in Latin American eyes. Nor was the Monroe Doctrine given a great deal of importance in Europe. European leaders, like the Latin American, paid more regard to London than to Washington at this time. In the following year (1824) Britain began the process of recognition with Buenos Aires, Mexico and Colombia. This further increased British influence in the region.

Another occasion for Britain to demonstrate her influence with the new states—and for the United States to underline her position—was

---

[39] *The Monroe Doctrine, 1823–1826, op. cit.*, p. 192.
[40] Quoted in *ibid.*, pp. 117–18.    [41] *John Quincy Adams, op. cit.*, pp. 401–2.

provided in 1826 by the Congress of Panama, then in Colombia. This, the first and most famous of the Spanish American conferences held during the nineteenth century before the establishment of the inter-American system,[42] had been proposed by Simón Bolívar—the greatest figure among the Spanish American leaders—with the object of forming a confederation of Spanish American states. It is significant that Bolívar did not invite the United States to attend the Panama Congress. The Colombian government, which did so during his absence in Peru, referred in its invitation to President Monroe's Message. Mexico and Central America also invited the United States to be represented at Panama. John Quincy Adams had succeeded Monroe as President in 1825 and had appointed his old rival Henry Clay as Secretary of State.[43] Both Adams and Clay favoured United States participation in the Panama Congress. In his Message to the House of Representatives explaining why he did so, Adams pointed to the important interest the United States had in the matters to be discussed there. He mentioned specifically the future of Cuba and Puerto Rico, still in the hands of Spain:

> The invasion of both those islands by the united forces of Mexico and Colombia is avowedly among the objects to be matured by the belligerent States at Panama. The convulsions to which, from the peculiar composition of their population, they would be liable in the event of such an invasion, and the danger therefrom resulting of their falling ultimately into the hands of some European power other than Spain, will not admit of our looking at the consequences to which the Congress at Panama may lead with indifference. . . .[44]

When he sent the Senate his nominations for the Panama mission President Adams made clear that they were 'neither to contract alliances, nor to engage in any undertaking or project importing hostility to any other nation'.[45] In spite of these assurances, however, Adams met with strong opposition in the Congress, which took so long to vote the necessary finance that neither of the two delegates nominated arrived in Panama in time to take part in the deliberations.

It is quite evident from the instructions given to the United States

---

[42] The relationship between these conferences and the inter-American system is discussed below, pp. 108–10.                                   [43] See below, p. 74.

[44] Gantenbein, *The Evolution of Our Latin-American Policy: A Documentary Record op. cit.*, p. 39.

[45] Perkins, *The Monroe Doctrine, 1823–1826, op. cit.*, p. 207.

delegates that, had they taken part in the discussions at Panama, their main task would have been strongly to reiterate their government's opposition to any projects for liberating Cuba and Puerto Rico.[46] We have already noted Adams's own view that Cuba would eventually fall to the United States by the process of 'political gravitation'; and that, for the time being, United States leaders wanted the island to remain in the hands of Spain from whom it could be acquired in due course. Therefore, the United States not only endeavoured herself to persuade the Spanish government to recognise the independence of the new states as the necessary price of retaining Cuba and Puerto Rico, but even approached other European powers, such as Russia, to use their influence with Spain to the same end. In December 1825 Secretary Clay had asked both Mexico and Colombia to suspend expeditions they were planning against Cuba and Puerto Rico. In his instructions to the United States delegates to the Panama Congress Clay also voiced fears of a possible uprising of the African slaves in Cuba should there be an invasion of the island. Clearly, he had the Haitian experience in mind. United States opposition to attempts to liberate Cuba at this time (however seriously these were contemplated by Mexican and Colombian leaders) give further point to the contention of Cuban nationalists that the United States has never wanted their country to be truly independent. Even Bemis has said: 'the United States never manifested any particular eagerness for Cuban independence, because the people of the island might remain content with that, whereas if they stayed under the misgovernment of Spain they might someday prefer annexation'.[47]

In contrast to the United States, Britain still maintained her readiness to enter into a self-denying ordinance regarding the island. She, too, was invited to the Panama Congress. Bolívar believed that any league of Spanish American states needed Britain's support against Europe or even the United States. 'All America combined', he wrote in July 1825, 'is not worth as much as a British fleet.'[48] Canning was determined to prevent the United States from assuming the leadership of any confederation of American states which might emerge at Panama in 1826.

---

[46] International American Conference, *Reports of Committees and Discussions Thereon, Vol. IV, Historical Appendix: The Congress of 1826, at Panama, and Subsequent Movements toward a Conference of American Nations* (Washington, 1890), pp. 113–50.

[47] *The Latin American Policy of the United States, op. cit.,* p. 94.

[48] Humphreys, 'Anglo–American Rivalries and Spanish American Emancipation' *op. cit.,* p. 154.

'You will understand', he instructed Edward Dawkins, whom he sent
to the Congress, 'that to a league among the States lately Colonies of
Spain, limited to objects growing out of their common relation to
Spain, His Majesty's Government would not object. But any project
for putting the United States of North America at the head of an
American Confederacy as against Europe would be highly displeasing
to your Government.'[49] But Canning's fears on this score, as we have
seen, were unjustified, for the United States government would not
have undertaken such a commitment even had she been represented at
Panama and invited to do so. Dawkins was able to reassure him: 'The
general influence of the United States is not, in my opinion, to be
feared.' Then he added, 'It certainly exists in Columbia, but it has been
very much weakened even there by their protests against an attack on
Cuba. . . .'[50] In this matter Britain had been very careful not to associate
herself with the United States. Canning had stressed this in his instructions to Dawkins:

> The British Government, indeed, are so far from denying the right of the
> New States of America to make a hostile attack upon Cuba, whether con-
> sidered simply as a possession of a Power with whom they are at war, or
> as an arsenal from which expeditions are fitted out against them, that we
> have uniformly refused to join with the United States in remonstrating
> with Mexico and Columbia against the supposed intention, or in intimating
> that we should feel displeasure at the execution of it. We should indeed
> regret it, but we arrogate to ourselves no right to control the military
> operations of one belligerent against another.[51]

Thus, on an important issue, Britain had appeared in a better light
than the United States in the eyes of Latin Americans.

Britain's policy here was, of course, opportunistic. She was concerned to enhance her position as the most influential external power in
Latin America and to undermine the influence of the United States,
which at this stage was very much less than hers. We have seen how
United States leaders were anxious earlier not to pursue policies in
respect of Spanish America too far out of line with those of Britain;

---

[49] Webster, *op. cit.*, vol. 1, p. 404.                    [50] *Ibid.*, p 423
[51] *Ibid.*, p. 408. Earlier, Canning had expressly forbidden Charles Vaughan, the
British Minister in Washington, to discuss this question further with Secretary of State
Henry Clay (*Ibid.*, vol. 2, pp. 542–3). Canning had been much put out by Vaughan's
report of a discussion he had with Clay about the United States intention to dissuade
Mexico and Colombia from undertaking operations against Cuba. (*Ibid*, pp. 536–7.)

notably in the question of recognising the new states. Britain's known opposition to any attempt on the part of the Holy Alliance to help restore Spanish rule over her American colonies was an important factor in making feasible President Monroe's unilateral declaration in 1823. The admission that she could not give a firm pledge to aid the new states should there be intervention against them, without Britain's support, underlined this point. Moreover, Britain herself carried out a number of interventions in Latin America which clearly challenged Monroe's pronouncements in this regard.

In 1828 Britain demonstrated her influence by intervening in the conflict between Argentina (as the United Provinces of the Rio de la Plata were later to become) and Brazil, and forcing them to accept Uruguay as an independent buffer state between them. In 1833 she occupied the Falkland Islands and in 1839 Ruatan Island off Honduras: both violations of the United States non-colonisation principle. In 1841 she occupied the port of San Juan at the mouth of the river of the same name in Nicaragua. The United States did not feel able to protest. Nor was Britain the only European power to intervene in Latin America at this time. In 1838, for example, France occupied Vera Cruz in Mexico, and the island of Martín García in the River Plate. Britain and France conducted a joint blockade of the Rio de la Plata in 1845.

Each of these interventions by European powers was an obvious 'manifestation of an unfriendly disposition toward the United States' in the words of President Monroe's Message. But the latter itself could equally be regarded as unfriendly towards the European powers. For Monroe's proposition denied them what they regarded as rights in respect of territories which were in no special relationship to the United States beyond being part of the same continent. Lord Salisbury's assertion in 1895 at the time of the Venezuelan crisis was equally relevant[52] to the original Message: 'The Government of the United States is not entitled to affirm as a universal proposition, with reference to a number of independent States for whose conduct it assumes no responsibility, that its interests are necessarily concerned in whatever may befall those States, simply because they are situated in the Western Hemisphere.'[53] The crucial difference lay in the vast increase of United States power in the meantime.

For the day of the United States was to come, as her leaders had

---

[52] Perhaps more so, since by 1895 the inter-American system had been established.
[53] See below, p. 98.

been confident in 1823, although fully aware of her presently limited power. We have looked at the words of the Message within the context of their time and in the light of the known ambitions of the men concerned in its formulation. We must now turn to the development of the Message into a powerful 'Doctrine'. In this development a key factor is the link with 'Manifest Destiny' which, as we have seen, had its roots in the colonial period. This too was a major determining factor in the development of United States Latin American policy. We shall therefore examine the concept of Manifest Destiny and consider how its fulfilment in the nineteenth century helped to shape relations between the United States and Latin America.

# 3 Latin America and the Manifest Destiny of the United States

We noted at the end of the previous chapter how on a number of occasions in the years following Mr. Monroe's Message of 1823 Britain and France intervened in Latin America in clear disregard of the main principle the President had affirmed. These years constituted for the Message what Dexter Perkins has called 'the period of quiescence'.[1] Not until the eighteen-forties did the United States begin to elevate the famous passages of the Message into a 'Doctrine' and to apply and extend them as the central theme of her Latin American policy. During the same decade, the phrase 'Manifest Destiny' came into popular use to describe and justify ambitions having a significant affinity with the Monroe Doctrine. The many aspects of Manifest Destiny have been analysed in Albert Weinberg's classic work to which reference has already been made.[2] In this chapter we shall consider the main aspects relevant to United States policy towards Latin America during the remainder of the nineteenth century. Manifest Destiny was particularly significant for United States relations with Mexico and for her policy in the Caribbean; above all in respect of Cuba. It was also of importance in the matter of an isthmian canal. In all these aspects rivalry with Britain was a major factor.

The main elements in Manifest Destiny—as we have noted—were present even in the colonial period: above all, the urge to expand territorially and belief in an inherent right to do so. This 'right' contained a number of elements capable of development and extension with circumstances. They included the superiority of the white ('civilised') man over the ('savage') Indians whom he dispossessed and often exterminated; the better use to which he would put the land he was seizing (what Weinberg has described as 'the destined use of the soil'); and the

---

[1] *The Monroe Doctrine, 1826–1867* (Baltimore, The Johns Hopkins Press, 1933: Reprint, Gloucester, Mass., 1966), chapter 1.
[2] See above, p. 53, n. 19.

superiority of his institutions ('the extension of freedom'—an argument for taking over territory from European 'tyrannies' and allegedly incompetent and despotic Latin American governments). Arguments used to justify a policy of despoliation towards the Indians could be developed to justify aggressive policies towards other coloured peoples whose territory or resources were the object of United States ambition, or even 'to peoples who, though largely white in population, were considered inferior in civilization and economic efficiency'.[3] Mexico and the Caribbean were soon to provide opportunities for the application of the ideas of Manifest Destiny.

We have already remarked how Mexico and Cuba were particular objects of United States concern and ambition when the future of the Spanish American empire was threatened by Napoleon's invasion of the Iberian peninsula. Both figured prominently in the concept of Manifest Destiny: Mexican territory had to be acquired if the United States was to become a truly continental republic, while Cuba was widely regarded as an appendage to the Floridas which must some day become a part of the Union. As we have seen, the United States recognised Mexico's independence in December 1822—the first nation outside the new Spanish American states to do so, as she frequently reminded the Mexicans; Cuba she wished to remain Spanish for the time being, and among various moves she made to prevent the island's liberation was the discouragement of Mexican and Colombian plans to that end. The future of Cuba, in which Mexico had considerable interest, was only one issue which rendered relations between the latter and the United States delicate from the outset.

Mexico inherited from Spain the Adams–Onís Treaty of 1819 which was not ratified until 1821 and whose provisions in respect of marking boundaries had not yet been implemented. In the United States there were influential people, such as Henry Clay, soon to be Adams's Secretary of State, and Andrew Jackson, later Adams's successor as President, who had strongly criticised the Adams–Onís Treaty for its renunciation of the claim to Texas. Mexico had every reason to fear for the future not only of Texas but others of her northern provinces such as California and New Mexico which were sparsely populated and inadequately policed, and already the object of penetration by North American frontiersmen. The internal situation in Mexico greatly

---

[3] Weinberg, *op. cit.*, p. 95. It is, of course, one of the classic arguments advanced by imperialistic peoples that they can utilise to better advantage the lands and resources they are seizing from supposedly inferior peoples.

weakened her prospects of resisting the Manifest Destiny of her already much stronger neighbour. The empire of Iturbide was overthrown in March 1823 (less than a year after it had been established), and Mexico entered the era of Santa Anna, so unhappy for the dictator's own country but correspondingly felicitous for the United States in the furtherance of her ambitions at Mexico's expense.

Mexico, fully aware of these ambitions, wanted to secure confirmation through a 'treaty of limits' of the Adams–Onís provision under which the Sabine River was designated as the eastern boundary between the two countries. The United States, on the other hand, sought 'rectification' of this boundary: hopefully, as far eastward as the Rio Grande, but at least to the line of the Colorado River.[4] The Adams administration was prepared to pay one million dollars for the boundary of the Rio Grande, half that sum for the Colorado.[5] Another immediate objective of the United States, linked with the question of boundaries, concerned the opening of the Santa Fé trail. This involved surveying, marking out and protecting a road leading from the frontier settlements of the United States on the Missouri River to the nearest settlements in New Mexico. Trade in the region concerned had increased enormously in the years following the collapse of Spanish power, and weak Mexican governments were unable effectively to regulate it. Growing numbers of North Americans were moving across unmarked boundaries and coming into conflict with Indians. The United States Congress was taking measures to protect its citizens in the region—measures which the Mexican government not surprisingly believed were connected with eventual acquisition of the territory. Mexico therefore wanted to delay agreement on marking out the road until a treaty of limits had been concluded.

Although the United States recognised Mexico in December 1822, it was not until May 1825 that she had a Minister in Mexico City. This delay stemmed partly from the unstable political situation in Mexico during the intervening years, but also from politics in Washington. The choice of Minister to Mexico was importantly linked with the presidential election of 1824. At one stage Andrew Jackson was invited

---

[4] The Colorado River which flows through Texas.

[5] Bemis declares (*The Latin American Policy of the United States, op. cit.*, p. 76): 'If Mexico had been willing to sell she would have avoided the whole later Texas question, and the Mexican War that resulted from it, and the ensuing great territorial cession of 1848.' This judgement is strangely at variance with his general analysis of Manifest Destiny and the establishment of the continental republic.

to fill the post: an invitation which he declined. Secretary Adams and
the General were rivals for the presidency, which accounts for both the
invitation and the refusal. Finally, Joel Poinsett, who had entertained
hopes of becoming Adams's Secretary of State, was offered and accepted
the post of Minister to Mexico when the new President appointed his
old rival, Henry Clay, to the first post in his cabinet. Jackson had
gained most votes in the presidential election, but not the required
majority in the electoral college. In the House of Representatives,
which now had to make the decision, Clay (also a candidate) had thrown
his support to Adams. Poinsett had already represented the United
States in both South America[6] and Mexico. He was well qualified by
experience for the post, but proved to be an unhappy choice.[7]

By the time Poinsett arrived in Mexico he found the British (whom
he had vigorously opposed during his stay in South America) strongly
entrenched there. Although Britain's recognition of Mexican independence had come later than had that of the United States, it was
valued more highly. The Polignac Memorandum seemed more impressive than the Monroe Doctrine in Mexico as elsewhere in Latin America
at this stage. Nor was it difficult for Britain to convince Mexico of her
greater disinterestedness. Of course she was pursuing her own interests,
as was the United States hers. But, unlike the latter, Britain had no
territorial ambitions which threatened Mexico's national territory; nor
did she desire to acquire Cuba and thus need to involve herself with
the Mexican government over the island's future. Doubtless the British
Minister let it be known that in 1823 his country had proposed a joint
declaration with the United States to warn off European intervention
and to disclaim any ambition for Spanish American territory themselves. He may even have suggested the main reason why the United
States had declined her proposal.

Poinsett therefore faced a difficult task. The Mexican government
firmly resisted his demands for rectification of the boundaries in favour
of the United States. Moreover, it was unwilling to conclude a commercial treaty on the basis of complete reciprocity, which would have
been so much to the advantage of the United States in view of her
greatly superior economic and maritime strength. Negotiations for
treaties of commerce and 'limits' were therefore protracted. Meanwhile

---

[6] See above, pp. 50–1.

[7] But not, interestingly, in the judgement of Josephus Daniels, who described Poinsett
as 'the most versatile, dynamic, and able of all American diplomats to Mexico': *Shirt-
Sleeve Diplomat* (Chapel Hill, The University of North Carolina Press, 1947), p. 437.

there were continual disputes over the rights and privileges of United States traders and their property in Mexico. United States merchants complained of maltreatment at the hands of Mexican officials; the latter complained of violations of Mexican laws by North Americans. Poinsett was frequently presenting claims against the Mexican government for losses suffered by United States citizens at the hands of robbers and bandits. It is significant that for a long time Poinsett pressed for an article to be inserted in the proposed commerical treaty under which Mexico would be obliged to return runaway slaves to their owners in the United States. The treaty of limits signed in 1828 confirmed the boundary provisions of the Adams–Onís Treaty. Not until after Poinsett had left his Mexican post was a commercial treaty between the United States and Mexico concluded. Poinsett's proposed article on the return of fugitive slaves was omitted; an article was inserted to regulate and protect commerce between Missouri and Mexico —the Santa Fé route; and 'perfect reciprocity' would be established between the signatories after six years. In his vigorous pursuit of United States interests Poinsett had been in prolonged conflict with the British Minister; and this led him to meddle in Mexican politics on behalf of pro-United States as opposed to pro-British elements. In the end the Mexican government demanded his recall: a request to which the United States government agreed in 1829. However, the choice of successor, made by the new President, Andrew Jackson, was not calculated to make a favourable impression in Mexico. He was one Anthony Butler, of whom it has been said that his sole qualifications for the post were 'an acquaintance with Texas and a strong desire to see the United States obtain it'.[8]

Butler had, in fact, been instructed by Jackson to try to buy Texas from the Mexican government, as had Poinsett earlier by Adams. Already the situation in Texas was looking ominous for Mexico. In 1821 the Spanish authorities had embarked upon a desperate course of encouraging immigration into that sparsely populated province. They had hoped to attract immigrants of various nationalities, but in the event the vast majority were North American frontiersmen in search of cheap land. Some brought slaves with them. Slavery was abolished in Mexico in 1829, but the government in Mexico City had little control over the situation in Texas. Its efforts to regulate immigration and

---

[8] Justin H. Smith, *The War with Mexico* (2 vols., New York, 1919: Reprint, Gloucester, Mass., 1963), vol 1, p. 62.

commerce between Texas and the United States met with little success. In Bemis's words, 'All the elements of friction were present and none of effective control'.[9] By 1830 the Mexican government realised that the situation in Texas bore ominous resemblance to the one in the Floridas earlier. American frontiersmen were employing the same techniques: ostensibly carrying out lawful commerce or forming colonies loyal to the host government, but covertly undermining the latter's position. Clashes with the Indians they were dispossessing and with the Mexican authorities trying to control them brought about conditions in which the United States government claimed to be an interested party. The roles of the frontiersmen and those of the United States government were complementary in this 'old frontier process of state making at the expense of a foreign government'.[10] As claims of its citizens against the Mexican government mounted, the United States government hoped Mexico would realise that her best policy would be be to sell Texas before she lost it anyway. But the Mexican government would not oblige. In 1835, after the adoption of a new, centralist constitution which threatened their virtual autonomy, the Texan Americans revolted against the Mexican government. Texan independence was declared the following year.

The Texans defeated the Mexican forces under Santa Anna, whom they captured and sent to Washington. In captivity, the Mexican dictator promised to confirm Texan independence: a promise he promptly repudiated when released. But Texas effectively had been lost. Relations between the United States and Mexico were embittered by these events. The United States government had declared itself neutral in the conflict, though it had occupied the Nacogdoches region of Texas as a protective measure, it said, against the incursions of Indians. But in Mexican eyes the United States had been the chief instigator of the Texan rebellion. Nor was Mexico alone in holding this view. John Quincy Adams, now strongly opposed to the acquisition of Texas because of the slavery issue in United States domestic politics, accused the Jackson administration of being a party to a Southern conspiracy to extend slavery. Yet it was the slavery issue—the admission of more slaveholding states into the Union—that delayed the annexation of Texas. Just before leaving office, in March 1837, Jackson recog-

---

[9] *The Latin American Policy of the United States, op. cit,* p. 77.
[10] Merk, *Manifest Destiny and Mission in American History: A Reinterpretation, op. cit.,* p. 22.

nised Texan independence, anxious to anticipate Britain, who also was much interested in the territory's future. For eight years Texas was to remain an independent state, recognised as such by European powers including Britain and France. These two nations were eager to promote a treaty between Mexico and Texas on the basis of a pledge by the latter not to annex herself to the United States: in other words, to have an independent Texas as a buffer against further United States expansion. Britain's influence over Texas in this project was weakened by her anti-slavery policy. Finally, the United States Congress, by joint resolution of both Houses, voted for annexation in March 1845—just as the then President John Tyler was about to relinquish office. The situation created by this vote faced a new President, James K. Polk.

Polk had been elected the previous year with strong support to implement 'Manifest Destiny': a concept which embraced not only the acquisition of Texas, but also that of California (into which North American pioneers had been moving over the years) and the territory in between them. At this time the United States was in dispute with Britain over the Oregon country, and was suspicious of British designs on California as of her negotiations with the Texan government. These negotiations were proceeding when the annexation resolution was passed by the United States Congress. The Texans now decided for annexation rather than continued independence. At the end of December 1845 Texas was formally admitted into the Union. Meanwhile, Polk had been trying to negotiate with the Mexican government for the purchase of California and New Mexico as well—along with the settlement of the claims of United States citizens against Mexico. No Mexican government could possibly have agreed to such a sale of national territory: it strains credulity to imagine that the United States government could have conceived it possible. Mexico had already declared that the annexation of Texas by the United States would be regarded as equivalent to a declaration of war. Before war broke out, however, President Polk issued a Message to Congress which involved the reaffirmation and extension of the principles enunciated by President Monroe exactly twenty-two years earlier.

In the judgement of Dexter Perkins, 'Second only in importance to the message of December 2, 1823, in the history of the Monroe Doctrine, stands the message of President Polk of December 2, 1845.' Moreover, he goes on, 'This important pronouncement gave new life to the principles which had been promulgated twenty-two years before;

and from the time when it was enunciated there begins a new period in the history of the Doctrine itself.'[11] Polk's declaration was to a large extent a response to the efforts of Britain and France to maintain an independent Texas in order to restrict United States power. In Britain's view, expressed by Lord Aberdeen, her Foreign Secretary:

> the continuance of Texas as an Independent Power, under its own Laws and institutions, must conduce to a more even, and therefore a more permanent, balance of interests in the North American continent. . . .

Guizot, the French Prime Minister asserted:

> In America, as in Europe, by the very fact that we have political and commercial interests, we need independent states, a balance of power. This is the essential idea which ought to dominate France's American policy.[12]

But a balance of power was precisely what the United States would not permit in the Americas. She was determined to maintain an imbalance which was so markedly—and increasingly—in her own interests. So President Polk declared in his Message:

> The American system of government is entirely different from that of Europe. Jealousy among the different sovereigns of Europe, lest any one of them might become too powerful for the rest, has caused them anxiously to desire the establishment of what they term the balance of power. It can not be permitted to have any application on the North American continent, and especially to the United States. We must ever maintain the principle, that the people of this continent alone have the right to decide their own destiny. Should any portion of them, constituting an independent state, propose to unite themselves with our confederacy, this will be a question for them and us to determine, without any foreign interposition. We can never consent that European powers shall interfere to prevent such a union, because it might disturb the balance of power which they may desire to maintain upon this continent.[13]

After referring with warm approval to President Monroe's original Message and reiterating its non-colonisation principle, Polk said:

---

11 *The Monroe Doctrine, 1826–1867, op. cit.,* p. 62.
12 *Ibid.,* p. 71 (both quotations).
13 Gantenbein, *The Evolution of Our Latin-American Policy, op. cit.,* pp. 328–9.

'... it should be distinctly announced to the world as our settled policy, that no future European colony or dominion shall, with our consent, be planted or established on any part of the North American continent'. Polk appeared to contract the scope of the Doctrine by his reference to 'North America';[14] but he importantly extended it by the limits he placed upon diplomatic interposition by European powers in America. By implication this placed limitations upon other American states in their relations with European powers: they could not put themselves under the 'dominion' of such powers even should they wish to do so. Polk was to make this plainer in 1848. Meanwhile, the United States was moving towards war with Mexico.

Nearly four weeks after Polk's message to Congress Texas was formally admitted to the Union. In view of the position Mexico had taken on annexation the President sent troops into Texas as a protective measure. But he made another attempt to purchase California and New Mexico, and also instructed his commissioner to offer United States assumption of the payment of claims due to her citizens in return for Mexican recognition of the Rio Grande as the western boundary of Texas. Mexico refused to treat on any of these matters. Following the failure of this initiative Polk ordered General Zachary Taylor to advance to the Rio Grande. This was a provocative step, for the Rio Grande had never been the boundary of Texas and the recent United States offer in respect of it confirmed that at least it was in dispute. But Polk needed war in order to seize California. Shortly after United States forces arrived at the Rio Grande (in March 1846) Mexican troops crossed the river and attacked them. This was all Polk required to recommend Congress to declare war. Mexico 'has passed the boundary of the United States, has invaded our territory and shed American blood upon American soil'. War had come, and 'notwithstanding all our efforts to avoid it, exists by the act of Mexico herself'. Representative Abraham Lincoln accused Polk of 'the sheerest deception'.[15] As a result of victory in the war that followed the United States received by the Treaty of Guadalupe Hidalgo confirmation of her title to Texas and the cession of New Mexico and Upper California. She agreed to pay $15 millions to Mexico and to assume payment of her own citizens' claims up to $3,250,000. Polk's negotiator was instructed to try to purchase Lower California and the right of transit

---

[14] However, Polk gave his unqualified support to the original pronouncement.
[15] Van Alstyne, *The Rising American Empire, op. cit.*, p. 143.

D

across the Isthmus of Tehuantepec. But these were not obtained in the treaty. Thus had Manifest Destiny been partially fulfilled through conquest—but, the United States has always maintained, by conquest *following a just war*. Mexico had been the aggressor![16]

The Treaty of Guadalupe Hidalgo did not fully satisfy the United States appetite for Mexican territory. There was a demand by some expansionists for the acquisition of all Mexico. A major obstacle to the achievement of this desirable objective was the fact that, while the northern provinces already acquired were sparsely populated, the southern parts of the country contained large numbers of Mexicans. In short, the expansionists wanted Mexico's land, not her people. In this situation, a new aspect of Manifest Destiny was advanced: the mission of regenerating backward (that is, coloured) peoples. The Mexicans were not yet fitted to enjoy the liberty whose extension had hitherto been a main justification of territorial expansion. But in truth what was involved here was the extension not of freedom, but of slavery. However, while the war with Mexico had been good politics, 'All Mexico' proved not to be. The United States made further efforts to purchase Lower California and the northern parts of the states of Coahuila, Chihuahua and Sonora. She succeeded only in obtaining, through the Gadsden Purchase of 1853 (named after the United States Minister to Mexico), the southern parts of New Mexico and Arizona. The United States wanted this territory for a projected transcontinental railroad: the Mexican dictator Santa Anna needed the purchase money.

Mexican territory figured also in President Polk's second extension of President Monroe's principles, which came in a special message to Congress on 29 April 1848. It was occasioned by a situation which had arisen in the Mexican state of Yucatán following an Indian rebellion there. The white authorities offered 'dominion and sovereignty' over the state in exchange for assistance not only to the United States but also to Britain and to Spain. Polk was much exercised over the possibility of Britain acquiring Yucatán. Therefore, reiterating Monroe's words that 'we should consider any attempt on their part to extend their system to any portion of this hemisphere as dangerous to our peace and safety', Polk declared that if Yucatán should fall into the hands of a European power it would be 'dangerous to our security'. The relevance of President Monroe's pronouncement to the Yucatán situation was challenged in the United States Congress, notably by John C. Calhoun; thus demon-

---

[16] See below, p. 112.

strating that the Message had not yet acquired the status of a 'Doctrine', nor the almost blind support it was later to enjoy in American politics. The Yucatán offer was withdrawn and that ended the affair. But Polk had made an assertion, implicit in Monroe's unilateral declaration of policy, which clearly limited the sovereign rights of other American states in their relations with non-American powers. For the United States was opposed to any voluntary transfer of their sovereignty to such powers. And this has become a central feature of United States Latin American policy: a logical extension of President Monroe's Message of 1823 and not—it must be stressed—a perversion of it.

The eighteen-forties, then, witnessed the popularisation—and fulfilment in large measure—of Manifest Destiny, and the reiteration and extension of President Monroe's famous pronouncement in relation to United States Latin American policy. In these developments Mexico, as we have seen, was the principal focus of United States ambition and achievement. What of Cuba, importantly linked with Mexico in the concept of Manifest Destiny? Significantly, John L. O'Sullivan, editor of the *Democratic Review*, who is credited with having coined the phrase 'Manifest Destiny', had interests in Cuba and was once arrested and tried for filibustering adventures in the island. As we have noted, the acquisition of Cuba had been an eventual goal of United States leaders virtually from the beginning of the Union, and, although Spain's rule continued—with United States blessing and support—after the loss of all her mainland colonies in America, the island was economically much more closely linked with the United States. In the eighteen-forties demands for obtaining Cuba were greatly stimulated by the Mexican war and its aftermath. The island was especially attractive to the Southern states:

> In Cuba whites were a minority. Colored and mixed elements formed well over half the population. Most of them, however, were, happily, slaves. These would not become American citizens if Cuba were annexed. Whites would, of course, become citizens. They would increase the power of the South in Congress. The slaves would add their bit, too, under the three-fifths provision of the Constitution.[17]

The idea gained ground that in order to guarantee slavery in the United States Cuba must be acquired. Moreover, fears were expressed that

---

[17] Merk, *op. cit.*, p. 209.

under British influence Spain would emancipate the slaves and Cuba would be 'Africanised'.

Such fears were shared by slave-owning sugar planters in the island, some of whom favoured annexation by the United States to prevent possible emancipation. O'Sullivan asserted that these Cubans would furnish the money to buy the island from Spain. This in turn would stimulate the also desirable demand of the North to obtain Canada in order to offset the addition of Cuba to the Union as a slave state. President Polk was persuaded to try secretly to purchase Cuba from Spain; interestingly, the sum involved was far larger than the one offered Mexico for California. But Spain indignantly refused to sell. Franklin Pierce, who became President in 1853, also tried vainly to buy Cuba. In 1854 there was published the so-called 'Ostend Manifesto', a document drawn up by the United States Ministers to Spain, France and Britain in which they declared that should Cuba become a menace (through 'Africanisation') and should Spain refuse to sell her to the United States 'then, by every law, human and divine, we shall be justified in wresting it from Spain if we possess the power'. The minister in London was James Buchanan, Secretary of State under Polk and later to succeed Pierce as President. As Secretary of State, Buchanan had been closely concerned with Polk's offer for Cuba. Now he was responsible for the Manifesto's becoming public knowledge. President Pierce, though an expansionist and in general sympathy with the sentiments expressed by the three Ministers, could not openly support them. As President, Buchanan, too, tried to buy the island, having declared in his inauguration speech that if he could 'settle' slavery and then add Cuba to the Union he would be 'willing to give up the ghost and let the vice-president succeed'.[18] But, in Hugh Thomas's words, 'The U.S. slid into civil war at a time when the South still hoped that the acquisition of Cuba would enable them to perpetuate slavery inside or outside the Union.'[19] This hope vanished when in 1861, in order to win friends in Europe and to secure diplomatic recognition, the leaders of the Confederate states disavowed all plans for annexing Cuba.

By the outbreak of the Civil War, then, Cuba still had not been annexed. Nevertheless, the march of Manifest Destiny had drawn the United States south of Mexico into Central America. This was a region

---

[18] Thomas, *Cuba or The Pursuit of Freedom, op. cit.*, p. 228.
[19] *Ibid.*, p. 230.

in which hitherto the United States had shown little concern and where Britain was dominant. Britain's interests centred on the settlement of Belize on the westerly shore of the Bay of Honduras; the Bay Islands, of which Ruatan is far the largest and was the most important; and the 'Mosquito Shore' on the east coast of what are now the republics of Honduras and Nicaragua. British involvement in Central America dated back to the colonial period and was the subject of dispute and certain agreements with Spain. Spanish rule over the region (the Captaincy-General of Guatemala as it then was) ended with the establishment of the United Provinces of Central America—after a brief period as part of Iturbide's Mexican empire.[20] This lasted until 1838 when Central America dissolved into the five separate states of today. At this stage Britain did not claim sovereignty over Belize, which was a 'settlement' and not a colony. The status of the settlement remained anomalous after the United Provinces of Central America came into being. Naturally the latter, though unrecognised by Spain, regarded themselves as heir to Spanish rights in Central America and therefore to Belize: Britain denied that this was so, and proceeded to extend her interests in the region. In 1839 Britain seized Ruatan, which was regarded as the 'key to command' both Belize itself and the Mosquito shore; and in 1841 she occupied San Juan port at the mouth of the San Juan River in the name of the Mosquito king. Further encroachments were made by British representatives in the area, which brought the British government into disputes with the Central American states, especially over the boundaries of the Mosquito kingdom.

The Central American republics were not alone in their concern over Britain's policy. The government of New Granada (as Colombia was then called) also disputed the Mosquito king's claims which Britain sponsored. This matter now became linked with the question of an isthmian canal, for which there had been various projects over the years. The question of such a canal was not regarded by either the United States or New Granada as an essentially 'American' matter, and European support was sought for the enterprise. In 1842 New Granada proposed that the British, French and United States governments should participate. All three would guarantee the neutrality of the canal and of the territory through which it would pass, and the

---

[20] The Captaincy-General of Guatemala had come under the Vice-royalty of New Spain (Mexico) during the colonial period.

fulfilment of the privileges granted to the company undertaking its construction. Britain did not favour the proposal; France supported the canal project generally, but had reservations about the guarantee of the territory of New Granada when this was discussed. In 1846, encouraged by the concern expressed by President Polk in the previous December over European intervention in America,[21] New Granada turned to the United States, whose Minister in Bogotá, Benjamin Bidlack, was then negotiating commercial matters. Bidlack was offered a satisfactory treaty of commerce and navigation in return for a United States guarantee of New Granada's sovereignty over the Isthmus of Panama. Bidlack accepted and signed the treaty since named after him, though he had no instructions other than those concerning commerce and navigation.

The Bidlack Treaty guaranteed to the United States and her citizens the right of way or transit across the Isthmus of Panama by any means of communication then existing, or that might subsequently be constructed, for lawful commerce and paying tolls no higher than those charged to citizens of New Granada. In Article XXXV the United States made the following pledges of great significance:

> And, in order to secure to themselves the tranquil and constant enjoyment of these advantages, and as an especial compensation for the said advantages, and for the favours they have acquired by the 4th, 5th, and 6th articles [regulating tariff duties] of this Treaty, *the United States guarantee positively and efficaciously to New Granada, by the present stipulation, the perfect neutrality of the before mentioned Isthmus,* with the view that the free transit from the one to the other sea, may not be interrupted or embarrassed in any future time while this Treaty exists; and in consequence, *the United States also guarantee, in the same manner, the rights of sovereignty and of property which New Granada has and possesses over the said territory.*[**]

This was the only occasion during the nineteenth century on which the United States agreed to defend the territory of a Latin American state. But it must be noted that the United States and New Granada both expressed confidence that Britain and France, in the light of the treaty, would give similar guarantees. In the event neither did so.

President Polk favoured the Bidlack Treaty, and, in his message to the Senate recommending ratification, declared:

---

[21] See above, pp. 77–9.
[22] Quoted (and italics added) by Bemis, *The Latin American Policy of the United States, op. cit.,* p. 105.

The importance of this concession to the commercial and political interests of the United States cannot easily be overrated. The route by the Isthmus of Panama is the shortest between the two oceans, and from the information herewith communicated it would seem to be the most practicable for a railroad or canal.

In the Senate there was at first considerable misgiving over the commitment contained in the treaty. But the mood of Manifest Destiny and growing awareness of the new interests arising from the recent acquisitions from Mexico helped secure ratification in June 1848. United States concern with the situation in Central America now grew rapidly, and dispute with Britain followed. Despite her territorial encroachments Britain's interests in Central America were basically commercial; the United States had a new and growing strategic interest in the region. When in 1848 Britain moved to take permanent possession of San Juan port, nominally on behalf of the Mosquito king, the United States was readier to heed Nicaraguan protests. For the port of San Juan (renamed Greytown by the British) was regarded as vital to a possible route for an inter-oceanic canal. Moreover, following the discoveries of gold in California, transit routes across Central America became of far greater importance since they were easier and safer than routes across the United States, and very much faster than the long sea voyage round Cape Horn. United States and British representatives in the region became involved in bitter rivalry in their pursuit of rights and concessions.[23] In particular, concessions sought by United States interests for transit projects in Nicaragua conflicted with British claims on behalf of the Mosquito kingdom. However, compromise was possible between the governments since neither country at this stage aimed at monopolising the San Juan River nor at controlling a transisthmian canal.

Thus came about the Clayton–Bulwer Treaty of 1850, named after the then United States Secretary of State and the British Minister in Washington. Under its terms, the two countries bound themselves not to seek exclusive control over an isthmian canal; nor to fortify such a canal or its vicinity; nor to colonise or exercise dominion over any part of Central America. The neutrality of the canal was guaranteed, and transit charges would be equal for citizens or subjects of the two countries. In general terms, the Clayton–Bulwer Treaty reflected the

---

[23] See R. A. Humphreys, 'Anglo-American Rivalries in Central America' *Transactions of the Royal Historical Society, Fifth Series*, Vol. 18 (1968), pp. 174–208.

interests and power of the signatories in Central America in the middle of the nineteenth century. But it could not remain acceptable to the United States as her power and interests in the region grew. Even at the time of its signature the treaty was criticised as violating the Monroe Doctrine and placing limitations upon the United States' own expansion in Central America.[24] Meanwhile there were disputes over interpreting its terms. Britain declared that the references to colonisation and alliances in the region applied only to the future, thus affecting neither Belize nor her protectorate over the Mosquito Indians. The United States asserted that the treaty had present application in these respects.

Tension between the two countries mounted as it became clear that Britain was not proposing to end her protectorate over the Mosquito Indians, still less to give up Belize; though she was willing to cede Greytown. The situation was exacerbated in 1852 when Britain established the Colony of the Bay Islands, and a change of administration in the United States brought the opponents of the Clayton–Bulwer Treaty to power. When James Buchanan, former Secretary of State and future expansionist President,[25] was appointed Minister to Britain he was instructed:

> to induce Great Britain to withdraw from all control over the Territories and Islands of Central America, and, if possible, over the Balize also, and to abstain from intermeddling with the political affairs of the Governments and people in that region of the world.[26]

In the region itself there were numerous incidents. In 1854 a particularly serious one developed at Greytown, where a United States warship had been sent to protect an American company in dispute with the town authorities, who were trying to curb the aggressive expansion of its

---

[24] James Buchanan, for example, declared that the Clayton–Bulwer Treaty 'reversed the Monroe Doctrine' and applied it 'against the United States'. As Dexter Perkins observes (*The Monroe Doctrine, 1826–1867, op. cit.*, p. 212): 'According to this viewpoint, the object of the famous declaration was to reserve to the United States the sole privilege of conquest or acquisition in the New World, and to clear the path of European rivalries.' Cf. R. W. Van Alstyne's references to the Monroe Doctrine's 'hidden positives to the effect that the United States shall be the only colonizing power and the sole directing power in both North and South America. This is imperialism preached in the grand manner . . .' (*The Rising American Empire, op. cit.*, p. 99).

[25] And co-author of the 'Ostend Manifesto'. See above, p. 82.

[26] William R. Manning (ed.), *Diplomatic Correspondence of the United States: Inter-American Affairs, 1831–1860* (Washington, D.C., 12 vols., 1932–9), vol. vii—*Great Britain* (1936), pp. 86–7.

activities.[27] The incident culminated in the bombardment of Greytown by the warship and its commander afterwards ordering what remained of the town to be set on fire and destroyed. This outrage had been perpetrated 'to teach the inhabitants a lesson'. It was widely condemned in the United States, but the government refused either to disavow what had happened or to compensate those British subjects whose property had been destroyed. The British government did not feel able to take a firm line with the United States over the incident. It was involved in the Crimean War and British public opinion would not have supported conflict with the United States over such remote and insignificant imperial interests as the Bay Islands and the Mosquito kingdom. In 1860, having failed to obtain an agreement with the United States over revising the Clayton–Bulwer Treaty, Britain concluded separate treaties with individual Central American republics. Under the terms of these treaties she relinquished her claims to all territories except Belize, which, with its extended boundaries, became in 1862 the colony of British Honduras.[28] These arrangements had meanwhile proved to be acceptable to President Buchanan.

In the eighteen-fifties a new element had entered the Central American situation: United States filibusters, linked with Manifest Destiny and Southern expansionism. The most notorious of these filibusters was a certain William Walker, who had already made a name for himself by leading an expedition into Lower California in an attempt to add it and another Mexican state, Sonora, to the territory of the United States. Taking advantage of civil conflict then raging in Nicaragua, Walker led an expedition to that country in 1855 and allied himself with one of the conflicting parties. He received financial backing from a group of United States interests seeking transit concessions in Nicaragua and this incurred the bitter enmity of the powerful Vanderbilt Company already operating there, whose charter Walker caused to be revoked. The Pierce administration was less than wholehearted in its efforts to prevent recruitment of filibusters in the United States. In the event it was Vanderbilt who was mainly responsible for Walker's downfall. However, this was not the end of Walker's career, which came in 1860

---

[27] This incident is described in Mary W. Williams, *Anglo–American Isthmian Diplomacy, 1815–1915* (Washington, The American Historical Association, 1916: Reprint, New York, 1965), pp. 171 ff.

[28] It is still a matter of dispute between Britain and Guatemala. See below, pp. 177, n. 67, 222, n. 83.

in Honduras, when the failure of a further adventure brought about his death by firing squad.

By 1860 the United States clearly was replacing Britain as the most influential power in the Central American region. The filibusters were but one manifestation of an increasingly aggressive policy which boded ill for the independence of the Central American republics and for New Granada's hold on Panama. North Americans crossing the isthmus on their way to the California gold-fields and the influx of foreign labour to build the Panama railroad added to existing unrest in that area. Riots in Panama in 1856 led to United States naval vessels landing men, who occupied the railway station: the forerunner of many such landings in the general region during the coming years. Not surprisingly, Central Americans now feared not Britain, but the United States. In 1855 Guatemala suggested that Britain and France should either secretly or openly take her under their protection; Costa Rica, in the following year, asked for both arms and for the protection of the great European maritime powers; and a similar request was made by the former Nicaraguan Minister in Washington. 'The United States, at the end of the fifties', according to Dexter Perkins, 'was feared and hated by those whom it assumed at times to protect.'[29] Nor was this growing fear confined to the Central American region. New Granada, who had been friendly towards the United States during most of the preceding period, was now much cooler, partly because of the aggressive attitude of the United States at the time of the Panama rioting in 1856. Mexico was given new reasons to fear further United States aggression against her. And even in South America anti-United States feeling was growing. In Perkins's judgement, 'The prestige of the United States, despite the development of the Monroe Doctrine, was, perhaps, never lower in the republics of the South than it was in the decade of the fifties.'[30]

At the end of the eighteen-fifties James Buchanan was President. We have already noted his pro-slavery and strongly expansionist senti-ments; especially his role in the notorious 'Ostend Manifesto'. Buchanan strongly disliked the Clayton–Bulwer Treaty, and predicted that Cen-tral America would eventually become part of the United States. Meanwhile, he pursued what Professor Bemis has described as 'The

---

[29] *The Monroe Doctrine, 1826–1867, op. cit.*, p. 248.

[30] *Ibid.*, p. 252. It would be truer to say 'because of' rather than 'despite' the develop-ment of the Monroe Doctrine. For as it developed so did the Doctrine tend to become associated with United States intervention.

unscrupulous expansionist designs on Mexican territory of the pro-slavery Democratic administrations in the United States'.[31] In December 1858 in his Annual Message to Congress President Buchanan declared that United States claims against Mexico had once again accumulated to a sum exceeding $10 millions, and drew attention to unstable conditions in that country, especially along the northern border. He requested congressional authority for establishing a 'temporary protectorate' over northern Chihuahua and Sonora. He did not receive it. In his Annual Message the following year Buchanan sought approval for the use of military force for the purpose of 'obtaining indemnity for the past and security for the future'. But this, too, he failed to receive. Nevertheless, in December 1859, taking advantage of the straits to which the Mexican government of Benito Juárez was reduced at that time, Buchanan succeeded in obtaining the McLane–Ocampo Treaty. Under the terms of this agreement, the United States would have acquired, in return for a loan of $4 millions, a perpetual right of way across the Isthmus of Tehuantepec; two railroad routes across northern Mexico to the Gulf of California; the right to defend these transit routes with troops; and the right to intervene in Mexico, in case of great danger, without Mexican consent. A separate convention gave the United States a general police power over her southern neighbour. These agreements were rejected in the Senate by twenty-seven votes to eighteen: fourteen southern and two northern senators voted for them, twenty-three northerners voted against. Bemis has described Buchanan's Mexican policy in 1859 as 'a design first and foremost to advance slavery' which 'might well have served as a model for Japan's Twenty-One Demands on China in 1915'. But, he went on, 'it cannot be affirmed too strongly that the United States as a nation refused to follow the banner of this Pennsylvania President's black imperialism'.[32]

As we have seen, the most extravagant projects for expansion in these years were advocated by southerners, who were even more concerned to safeguard the institution of slavery than to fulfil their country's Manifest Destiny. This objective, many of them believed—with good reason—required the addition of more slave states to the Union. Hence the sparsely populated northern territories remaining to Mexico were particularly attractive to these expansionists, as was Cuba. As the slavery issue in United States politics became crucial, zeal for

---

[31] *The Latin American Policy of the United States, op. cit.*, p. 109.
[32] *Ibid.*, p. 110.

Manifest Destiny among Northerners was significantly tempered by fears of southern expansionism. Thus Buchanan's policy was rejected. By now the United States was moving towards the Civil War, which brought to an end the first phase of Manifest Destiny. At each stage of her territorial expansion and of the reassertion and extension of the Monroe Doctrine, arguments of Manifest Destiny had been importantly complemented by the fears expressed for United States security. There were fears of British and French intrigues in Texas, for example, and of British designs on California. Although often exaggerated, these fears were by no means groundless: certainly the European powers concerned wanted to curb United States territorial expansion. During the period of the Civil War United States claims that the European powers entertained aggressive plans against Latin America were given new substance, especially by interventions which took place in the Dominican Republic and Mexico.

The Dominican Republic did not win her independence from Haiti until 1844, and after that the Dominicans continued to fear the reassertion of Haitian control. As a consequence efforts were made at various times to secure protection from the United States and from certain European powers: Britain, France and Spain. In 1854, at a time when the United States had not yet recognised the independence of the Dominican Republic, recognition was offered in exchange for the cession of territory on Samaná Bay for a naval base. In the face of British and French protests, however, negotiations were broken off. On this episode, Perkins has commented:

> The diplomacy of the Pierce administration had been thoroughly out-manœuvered; a more thoroughgoing assertion of diplomatic influence and diplomatic pressure by European powers in the affairs of an American state is not to be recorded.[33]

Spain, still of course in possession of Cuba, continued to be interested in the Dominican Republic and the latter's fears of Haiti encouraged hopes of reannexation. The Spanish government was aware that the United States would regard such a move as a violation of the Monroe Doctrine. But when the Dominican President, Pedro Santana, in order to maintain himself in power, offered—and, indeed, eventually proclaimed—the reannexation of his country to Spain, the Spanish govern-

---

[33] *The Monroe Doctrine, 1826–1867, op. cit.*, pp. 271–2.

ment (on 19 May 1861) declared it to be once again part of the Spanish Empire. By that time Spanish troops had already been sent to the Dominican Republic.

In spite of the deteriorating domestic situation in the United States as these events unfolded, and the outbreak of the Civil War in April 1861, Abraham Lincoln's Secretary of State, William Seward, protested in the most vigorous terms to the Spanish government. Seward made veiled threats of retaliatory action against Cuba and Puerto Rico towards which (though they were 'on many accounts very attractive to the American people') the United States hitherto had acted with forbearance on the assumption that Spain would not be 'an inquiet or aggressive neighbor'.[34] But Seward was unable to follow his blustering words with effective action; the Spanish government continued to defy the Monroe Doctrine. It was not long, however, before Spain ran into difficulties in the Dominican Republic. The reimposition of Spanish rule proved unacceptable to the people and widespread insurrection necessitated large-scale reinforcement of Spanish troops. An outbreak of yellow fever decimated the Spanish forces and the whole enterprise became extremely costly. Thus in the end Spain decided it was not worthwhile and withdrew her troops in 1865. Meanwhile she had become involved in another pathetic attempt to recapture something of her former empire. After a diplomatic controversy with Peru, whose independence she still had not recognised, Spanish troops seized the Chincha Islands. Chile, Bolivia and Ecuador also became involved in hostilities with Spain. Secretary of State Seward took the occasion to warn Spain against attempting to reannex Peru. But such a warning was unnecessary. Spain had no intention of making any such attempt, and gave up the islands in 1865.

Much more serious was the intervention in Mexico during the period of the Civil War in the United States. We have seen how Mexico's weakness had made possible the extensive United States territorial expansion during what has been called the era of Santa Anna, and how instability in Mexico continued to be a temptation to further expansion. Following the overthrow of the dictator in 1855 Mexico entered the period of 'The Reform', in which the Liberals, whose eventual leader was Benito Juárez, and the Conservatives, who opposed 'The Reform', were soon engaged in bitter civil war. This was the situation which had proved so tempting to Southern expansionists in the United States in

---

[34] *Ibid.*, p. 288.

the late eighteen-fifties. In the prevailing conditions in Mexico, United States citizens often suffered damage to their persons and property—which stimulated demands for intervention and retribution. European powers likewise claimed extensive damages against Mexico, generally, like those of the United States, grossly exaggerated. When in July 1861 Juárez was forced to suspend all service on Mexico's foreign debt Britain, France and Spain agreed to take punitive action: they sent forces to the Mexican port of Vera Cruz. They disclaimed any intention of attacking Mexico's sovereignty or territorial integrity. But Napoleon III of France had more ambitious plans: to establish a monarchy of his choosing (the Archduke Maximilian of Austria) in Mexico. The French Emperor convinced himself that this would be to liberate and regenerate the Mexican people; and that the best elements in the country would welcome a monarchy. In important respects, such arguments were comparable with those advanced by President Buchanan in favour of intervening in Mexico in 1859, and have commonly been used to justify interventions by both the United States and the European powers. But neither Britain nor Spain was prepared to support Napoleon's scheme when they finally discovered its full implications. The British government was unwilling to provoke the United States even though that country was engaged in civil war. In the words of the British Foreign Secretary at the outset:

> Without at all yielding to the extravagant pretensions implied by what is called the Monroe Doctrine, it would as a matter of expediency be unwise to provoke the ill feeling of North America, unless some paramount object were in prospect and tolerably sure of attainment.[35]

Thus the French Emperor mounted without his original partners what has generally been regarded as the most serious challenge to the Monroe Doctrine before 1960.

As Britain desired, the plan of punitive action against Mexico was made known to the United States, and her participation invited. Seward responded by affirming that the United States did not challenge the right of European powers, either singly or collectively, to wage war upon an American state. This was in line with traditional United States policy which, as we have seen, ignored a number of armed interventions undertaken by European powers in Latin America to secure

---

[35] Perkins, *The Monroe Doctrine, 1826–1867, op. cit.*, p. 371.

redress of grievances. However, Seward declined the invitation to be a participant in the proposed action against Mexico. As doubts arose about the aims of the intervention Seward made clear United States opposition to any subversion of President Juárez's government. The Secretary of State was much more guarded in his pronouncements than he had been in the case of Spain and the Dominican Republic. But there was a growing demand in the United States for the enforcement of the Monroe Doctrine, and in April 1864 the House of Representatives passed a unanimous resolution condemning what was happening in Mexico. As the Civil War in the United States drew to a close so did Secretary Seward's protests grow firmer. At the same time Napoleon III's difficulties in Mexico grew greater and he faced other pressing problems in France and Europe. He had been misled by Mexican conservatives about the acceptability of a European monarch. French armed force alone could maintain Maximilian as Emperor in Mexico, and this could not be provided for much longer. Napoleon, like the Spanish government in the case of the Dominican Republic, found his adventure too expensive and wanted to withdraw from it. When the Civil War ended the United States government increased its diplomatic pressure for the withdrawal of all French troops from Mexico. Twenty-five thousand United States troops were concentrated on the frontier of the Rio Grande. The French withdrawal began in the autumn of 1866 and ended in the spring of 1867. Maximilian was left to his fate: execution by firing squad at Querétaro in June 1867. Whatever the force of other factors in bringing about Napoleon III's retreat from Mexico, the outcome was seen in the United States—and not without justification—as a resounding vindication of the Monroe Doctrine. Although Seward tactfully refrained from alluding to it in the diplomatic correspondence, in the words of Dexter Perkins, it 'had become a true national dogma, endorsed by all parties, and awakening an instantaneous response in the breasts of patriotic Americans'.[36]

In the quarter of a century following the Civil War enormous changes occurred in the United States. There was Reconstruction in the South; the settlement of the Far West; and the great industrial revolution in the North. The United States was less concerned with foreign affairs, including relations with Latin America. Nevertheless, during these years a number of significant developments helped to pave the

---

[36] *The Monroe Doctrine, 1867–1907* (Baltimore, The Johns Hopkins Press, 1937 Reprint, Gloucester, Mass., 1966), p. 2.

way for the new phase of expansionism which was to take place in the eighteen-nineties. The first was an extension of the Monroe Doctrine by the Grant administration: General Grant had long been an ardent supporter of the Doctrine. In 1869 he proposed to annex the Dominican Republic—with the agreement of that country's government—as a preventive measure, he said, against possible European intervention. In recommending the treaty of annexation to the Senate in May 1870 (unsuccessfully in the event), President Grant declared that 'The doctrine promulgated by President Monroe has been adhered to by all political parties, and I now deem it proper to assert this equally important principle that hereafter *no territory* on this continent (European or American) shall be regarded as subject to transfer to a European power'. Henceforth the no-transfer principle[37] was considered to be part of the Monroe Doctrine. This interpretation was reinforced shortly afterwards by a memorandum to Congress from Grant's Secretary of State, Hamilton Fish.

The next important development concerned the question of an isthmian canal. We noted that when the Clayton–Bulwer Treaty was signed in 1850, providing for joint Anglo-American control of such a canal, there were those in the United States who opposed this agreement on the grounds that it violated the Monroe Doctrine; and that almost immediately there was dispute between the signatories over interpreting its terms.[38] It was inevitable that as the United States became more powerful she should become correspondingly less satisfied with an agreement she had entered into when she was comparatively weaker. When in 1879 the French engineer, Ferdinand de Lesseps, proposed to build a canal with private capital President Rutherford Hayes reacted unfavourably. De Lesseps's proposal was fully in accordance with the terms of the Clayton–Bulwer Treaty: a canal constructed and financed by private enterprise with government encouragement. But Hayes declared that 'The policy of this country is a canal under American control'. Such a canal, he said, 'would be the great ocean thoroughfare between our Atlantic and our Pacific shores, and virtually a part of the coast line of the United States'. In 1881 James G. Blaine, the Secretary of State, openly attacked the Clayton–Bulwer treaty which, he said, favoured Britain because of her preponderant naval power. But more than that:

---

[37] See above., p. 46.
[38] See above, pp. 85–6.

Its provisions embody a misconception of the relative positions of Great Britain and the United States with respect to the interests of each government in questions pertaining to this continent. The Government of the United States has no occasion to disavow an aggressive disposition. . . . At the same time, this government, with respect to European states, will not consent to perpetuate any treaty that impeaches our right and long-established claim to priority on the American continent. . . .[39]

Blaine went on to assert that 'The military power of the United States, as shown by the recent civil war, is without limit, and in any conflict on the American continent altogether irresistible'. The British government did not agree, affirming that since the United States had openly declared that any canal built would be 'part of her coastline', the Latin American states in the vicinity of the canal could not 'retain as independent a position as that which they now enjoy'.[40] But the United States was beginning to construct a new navy and Alfred Thayer Mahan, the apostle of United States sea-power and one of the expansionists of 1898, was soon to come to prominence. The United States would be seeking coaling stations in the Caribbean.

Blaine, whom we shall see in the next chapter as a great advocate of Pan Americanism as an instrument for increasing United States influence in Latin America, was much concerned over the extent to which European powers, and especially Britain, dominated the commerce of Latin America. 'Never had the flow of British capital to Latin America been so great as in the decade of the 'eighties', declares Professor Robin Humphreys, 'and never had European economic penetration, led by Britain, been so extensive'.[41] But meanwhile United States industry had developed to the point where it needed foreign markets, and United States capital was looking abroad. Blaine believed that Latin America was his country's rightful domain: 'while the great powers of Europe are steadily enlarging their colonial domination in Asia and Africa it is the especial province of this country to improve and expand its trade with the nations of America'.[42] In 1882 Blaine was greatly perturbed by what he described as 'an English war on Peru, with Chile as the instrument'; the War of the Pacific (1879–83). He declared

---

[39] Quoted in Van Alstyne, *The Rising American Empire*, op. cit., p. 163.
[40] *Ibid.*, p. 164.
[41] 'Anglo-American Rivalries and the Venezuela Crisis of 1895', *Transactions of the Royal Historical Society*, Fifth Series, vol. 17 (1967), p. 146.
[42] *Ibid.*, loc. cit.

before the House Committee on Foreign Affairs during its investigation of United States efforts to end that war:

> I think it will be demonstrated in the very near future that the United
> States will have to assume a much more decided tone in South America ...
> or else it will have to back out of it, and say that it is a domain that does
> not belong to us, and we surrender it to Europe.[43]

United States attempts to mediate in the War of the Pacific, in which Chile defeated Peru and Bolivia and gained territory from each, had been anything but successful. Her relations with Chile were worsened during the Chilean civil war, which broke out in 1891 between President José Balmaceda and the Congress. The United States favoured the President, who was defeated. A number of incidents caused friction in relations between the two countries, but the most serious occurred after Balmaceda's defeat: the *Baltimore* affair in October 1891. The captain of the U.S.S. *Baltimore* allowed a large number of his crew to go ashore at Valparaiso, in spite of the known animosity of the Chileans towards the United States. Violence ensued: two sailors died, others were injured, and some imprisoned. Not surprisingly, the Chilean and United States versions of what had happened were greatly at variance with each other. After lengthy enquiries and an exchange of notes the United States demanded a suitable apology and adequate reparations. Dissatisfied with Chile's response, President Harrison and Secretary Blaine eventually (in January 1892) threatened to suspend diplomatic relations, and asked Congress to authorise the use of force to obtain satisfaction of their demands. In the face of this threat of war Chile capitulated. Not only had Chile been humiliated, but Latin America as a whole was given a foretaste of the coming assertion of United States hegemony over the hemisphere.[44]

A very significant step towards the establishment of that hegemony was taken by the United States in the Venezuelan crisis of 1895. This crisis derived from a long-standing dispute between Great Britain and Venezuela over the boundary of British Guiana. For some years the Venezuelan government had been endeavouring to enlist United States support of its cause, often invoking the Monroe Doctrine. It had

---

[43] Quoted in Lockey, *Essays in Pan-Americanism, op. cit.,* pp. 52–3.
[44] Ominously, Harrison's humiliation of Chile was warmly applauded by Theodore Roosevelt: to an extent which earned him the nickname of 'the Chilean volunteer'. See for example, Thomas, *Cuba or The Pursuit of Freedom, op. cit.,* p. 312.

virtually no success until it secured the services as special agent in the United States of a certain William Lindsay Scruggs, a former United States minister in Colombia and Venezuela, who had been dismissed for misconduct. Scruggs's pamphlet, *British Aggressions in Venezuela or the Monroe Doctrine on Trial*, was widely distributed in the right circles and proved extremely influential as propaganda in the Venezuelan cause. Scruggs even discussed the question with President Cleveland, of whom it has been written: 'At no moment during his eight years as President could Grover Cleveland have used a diplomatic diversion to better advantage than in 1895.'[45] Cleveland was convinced that the Venezuelan cause was good domestic politics. Britain was unpopular in the United States. In the previous year she had been involved in a limited intervention in Nicaragua which had aroused public concern and criticism of the President for not taking a firm line then. Cleveland and his recently appointed Secretary of State, Richard Olney, decided that United States interests were involved in the Anglo-Venezuelan dispute and that they should adopt a more aggressive policy towards Britain: hence Olney's famous despatch of 20 July 1895 in which he invoked the Monroe Doctrine, and maintained that Britain should submit the dispute to arbitration. Moreover, Olney declared:

Today the United States is practically sovereign on this continent, and its fiat is law upon the subjects to which it confines its interposition. Why? . . . It is because, in addition to all other grounds, its infinite resources combined with its isolated position render it master of the situation and practically invulnerable as against any and all other powers.

All the advantages of this superiority are at once imperilled if the principle be admitted that European powers may convert American states into colonies or provinces of their own.

Commenting on the first sentence quote above, Professor Van Alstyne declares: 'Thus in 1895 Olney bared the hidden purpose of the Monroe Doctrine, the assertion of a right of unlimited intervention in any issue concerning the two American continents.'[46] In the last sentence Olney was saying in effect that the United States must not allow the present favourable imbalance of power to be upset by European intervention.

Not until November did the British Prime Minister reply to Olney's

---

[45] J. A. S. Grenville and G. B. Young, *Politics, Strategy, and American Diplomacy: Studies in Foreign Policy, 1873–1917* (New Haven and London, Yale University Press, 1966), p. 158. The role of Scruggs is discussed in chapter five.

[46] *The Rising American Empire, op. cit.*, p. 164.

despatch. In studiously courteous terms, Lord Salisbury chided Olney for his interference in the dispute between Britain and Venezuela, corrected various errors of fact in the despatch, and rejected the Secretary of State's proposals for arbitration. Moreover, Salisbury also rejected Olney's interpretation of the Monroe Doctrine:

> Mr Olney's principle that American questions are for American decision, even if it receive any countenance from the language of President Monroe (which it does not), cannot be sustained by any reasoning drawn from the law of nations. The Government of the United States is not entitled to affirm as a universal proposition, with reference to a number of independent States for whose conduct it assumes no responsiblity, that its interests are necessarily concerned in whatever may befall those States, simply because they are situated in the Western Hemisphere.[47]

The British Prime Minister had the better of the verbal exchange. But that was all.

On 17 December 1895, in a special Message to Congress, President Cleveland strongly reaffirmed the Monroe Doctrine and its application to the Anglo-Venezuelan dispute. Congress was requested to make an appropriation for a commission which would determine the boundary; and the President declared that, when the commission's report had been submitted and accepted, the United States would be in duty bound 'to resist by every means in its power as a willful aggression upon its rights and interests the appropriation by Great Britain of any lands or the exercise of governmental jurisdiction over any territory which after investigation' the United States had 'determined of right' belonged to Venezuela.[48] Cleveland's ultimatum—as it appeared to be—came as a shock to Britain, where the idea of war with the United States was virtually unthinkable. Britain's indignation at this time was directed principally at the German Kaiser for his telegram of congratulations to President Kruger on the defeat of the Jameson raid. As Cleveland's advisers had judged, Britain was much too preoccupied with South Africa and other questions to embroil herself with the United States over Venezuela. So Britain agreed to arbitration as the United States had demanded, and thereby she went a long way towards accepting the Monroe Doctrine as interpreted in Washington at this time. It is beside the point that Britain was still much stronger overall in military and

---

[47] Quoted in Humphreys, 'Anglo-American Rivalries and the Venezuela Crisis of 1895', *op. cit.*, p. 153.        [48] *Ibid.*, pp. 154–5.

naval terms than the United States. She was not prepared to challenge the Monroe Doctrine by force.

The outcome of these events was far from reassuring for Latin Americans. Venezuela was not only disappointed by the result of the arbitration, which generally was favourable to Britain. She was humiliated by the way it was carried out. Her case was conducted by the United States, and she was consulted only at the very end of the negotiations—and then only perfunctorily. Olney is reported to have told one British emissary that 'Venezuela has got to do exactly as we tell her'.[49] Once Britain had conceded that the dispute had legitimately involved the United States and the Monroe Doctrine the Secretary of State had achieved his objective, and became conciliatory towards her. Olney showed little concern for Venezuelan rights or sensibilities. As for Latin America as a whole, the claims of the United States asserted by Olney in his despatch of 20 July 1895 could only fill the region with misgiving. Events were beginning to demonstrate that as United States power and pretensions grew so would the effective sovereignty of the Latin American countries tend to diminish. As Britain retreated from Latin America in the face of United States pressure, so did Latin America lose whatever advantages it had been able to derive from the rivalry between these powers.

The year 1895, which witnessed the crucial early stages of the Venezuelan crisis, saw also the death of John L. O'Sullivan, who had popularised the phrase 'Manifest Destiny' in the eighteen-forties and who, as editor of the *Democratic Review* and by more personal effort, had promoted the policy of expansion it embodied.[50] O'Sullivan died in obscurity, but even before his death the United States was moving into another phase of Manifest Destiny. Its main protagonists were now in the Republican party while in the previous phase they had been mainly among the Democrats. Like the earlier phase, the new Manifest Destiny was also linked to the Monroe Doctrine; but it contained another significant element. Whereas in the middle of the century the expansionists were bent on fulfilling United States ambitions in the American continent, their counterparts at the end of the century—the 'Expansionists of 1898'[51]—were consciously furthering the emergence of the United States as a world power. And, as a result of

[49] Grenville and Young, *op. cit.*, p. 175.　　　　[50] See above, p. 81.

[51] See Julius W. Pratt, *Expansionists of 1898: The Acquisition of Hawaii and the Spanish Islands* (Baltimore, The Johns Hopkins Press, 1936: paperback edn., Chicago, 1964).

events in 1898, the United States did take her place in the ranks of the imperial powers. In this connection, the links between her expansion in the Caribbean and her acquisitions in the Pacific are significant.

Thus along with newly voiced ambitions for status as a world power there were older objectives to be attained. Of these the longest standing was the acquisition of Cuba; more recent was the demand for an isthmian canal under the sole control of the United States; and, most recently, the need for coaling stations for an expanding navy. Together the achievement of these goals would go far to giving the United States control of the Caribbean. The centrepiece was Cuba, where in 1895 a new revolt against Spain had begun. Now the situation was more propitious for United States intervention than it had been during the previous insurrection, which had lasted from 1868 until 1878. Leading expansionists in the Republican party, such as Theodore Roosevelt and Henry Cabot Lodge, saw in the Cuban situation an opportunity to achieve wider imperialist aims, in the Pacific as well as the Caribbean. Their party included in its platform for the 1896 presidential election a promise to secure the independence of Cuba from Spain. Its candidate, William McKinley, was elected. There has been a great deal of debate over McKinley's role in the Spanish-American War: especially over his alleged desire for peace but weakness in the face of strong demands for war—from the Congress, the new, popular press and his expansionist colleagues. The circumstances surrounding the sinking of *The Maine* in Havana harbour have never been adequately determined. An examination of such matters regrettably lies outside the scope of this study. Nor can we dwell upon the background to the war and United States motives for intervening. United States intervention was the culmination of many decades of determination one day to wrest the island from Spain; and Cuba was specifically the focal point of expansionist ambitions in 1898. However, this is not to dismiss as irrelevant the humanitarian feelings aroused by accounts—real and fabricated—of the sufferings of the Cubans at the hands of Spain.

On 20 April 1898, in a joint resolution, the United States Congress declared: '... it is the duty of the United States to demand, and the Government of the United States does hereby demand, that the Government of Spain at once relinquish its authority and government in the island of Cuba and withdraw its land and naval forces from Cuba and Cuban waters'. The President was directed and empowered to use whatever military force might be required to obtain Spain's compliance. The Spanish government regarded this resolution as 'equivalent to a declaration of war', and broke off relations on 21 April. The same day the United States opened hostilities. In measured under-statement, George Kennan has commented:

> Thus our government, to the accompaniment of great congressional and popular acclaim, inaugurated hostilities against another country in a situation of which it can only be said that the possibilities of settlement by measures short of war had by no means been exhausted.[52]

But much more important than the background to the Spanish-American war, for relations between the United States and Latin America, were—and continue to be—its consequences. Widely different views have been taken of these by North Americans, on the one hand, and Cubans—and Latin Americans generally—on the other.

In her self-image, the United States fought to liberate Cuba, and, after a short period of occupation, granted the island its independence: an act of unparalleled generosity on the part of a great power, especially in view of Cuba's strategic importance to her and a long-standing ambition to annex the island. In Professor Bemis's words: 'If ever there were an emblem of pride on the escutcheon of American idealism, it is the attitude in our century of the Continental Republic toward Cuba.'[53] The congressional resolution of 20 April had declared that 'the people of Cuba are, and of right ought to be, free and independent'. 'Impulsively, without debate or roll call',[54] there was added to this resolution an amendment proposed by Senator Teller of Colorado, 'an apostle of the New Manifest Destiny—*that dictum of self-determination as well as of peaceful expansion*'.[55] The Teller Amendment declared: 'That the United States hereby disclaims any disposition or intention to exercise sovereignty, jurisdiction, or control over the said island except for the pacification thereof, and asserts its determination, when that is accomplished, to leave the government and control of the island to its people.' 'These words', declared Bemis, 'sounded hollow to a cynical Europe and Asia hardened to a contrary practice. They have been made good.'[56]

---

[52] George F. Kennan, *American Diplomacy, 1900–1950* (paperback edn., New York, 1952), p. 16.

[53] *The Latin American Policy of the United States, op. cit.*, p. 279.

[54] Henry Wriston, 'A Historical Perspective', in John Plank (ed.), *Cuba and the United States: Long-Range Perspectives* (Washington, D.C., The Brookings Institution, 1967), p. 10.

[55] Bemis, *The Latin American Policy of the United States, op. cit.*, p. 138. My italics.

[56] *Ibid., loc. cit.*

This is not the case. The fine words of the Teller Amendment were belied both by the terms of the later Platt Amendment and by United States policy towards Cuba both before and after those terms were imposed upon the Cubans. The independence granted by the United States to Cuba is comparable—to take a particularly apposite example —with that granted by Britain to Egypt in 1922: in other words, conditions were imposed which rendered the recipient a client or satellite of the donor.[57] Cuban sovereignty was limited in various crucial ways, including the occupation in perpetuity of part of the island's territory; nor did the United States 'leave the government and control of the island to its people'. United States requirements were set out in an amendment to an army appropriation bill, formally proposed by Senator Orville Platt, chairman of the Senate Foreign Relations Committee, but written by the Secretary of War (later Secretary of State) Elihu Root. Under its terms Cuba was required to sell or lease lands to the United States for coaling or naval stations; Cuba's power to make treaties and her capacity to contract debts were both limited; and the United States was given the right to intervene in order to preserve Cuban independence and to maintain law and order. 'Nowhere', as Bemis himself observed, 'is the real purpose of the United States in the War of 1898 with Spain stated more frankly and concisely than in the Platt Amendment reserving to the United States the right to intervene in Cuba to protect life, property, and individual liberty, to preserve the independence of the island, *and to facilitate the defense of the United States*, including naval bases.'[58]

The imposition of the Platt Amendment—for the Cubans had no choice but to accept its terms as a part of their constitution—and of a *permanent* treaty with the United States merely underlined the true situation which had obtained from the outset. The United States intervened not to back up the Cubans struggling for independence, but to wrest control of the island and its future from Spain. The fears expressed by José Martí, the apostle of independence who was killed early in the war, that the United States would take over the struggle and rob them of their independence, seemed to Cuban nationalists to have been justified. The United States refused to recognise a Cuban government and the client status of the island was underlined by the fact that no Cuban signed the peace treaty at the end of the war. Under

---

[57] There is an interesting parallel between United States policy in the Caribbean and British in the Middle East. See below, p. 269.

[58] *The Latin American Policy of the United States, op. cit.*, pp. 138–9. Bemis's italics.

the terms of the Treaty of Paris, signed on 10 December 1898, the 'civil rights and political status' of Cuba were to 'be determined by the Congress' of the United States. During the fighting North Americans had shown little but contempt for the Cubans: an attitude that persisted into the occupation. Theodore Roosevelt, who became President of the United States before the military occupation ended, shared this contempt. He 'wanted to teach the "cheating, mañana lot" to behave decently'.[59]

Roosevelt soon was given—and seized—another opportunity to further United States expansionist ambitions, and to demonstrate his attitude towards 'dagoes' as he and many of those around him referred to Latin Americans. The Spanish–American war had underlined the importance to the United States of an isthmian canal and had reinforced her determination that such a waterway should be under her complete control. Even before the Treaty of Paris had been signed President McKinley made this point in his Annual Message to Congress. Such control would require the abrogation of the Clayton–Bulwer Treaty which, as we have noted, had grown increasingly irksome to United States leaders. Britain, whose government alone among the major European powers had been sympathetic towards the United States in the Spanish–American war, was prepared to agree, at first with some reservations. After an initial treaty which still placed some restrictions upon the United States, a second was signed in 1901 leaving her free to acquire sovereignty over a site and to fortify the canal when built. This was the second Hay–Pauncefote Treaty, named after the United States Secretary of State (John Hay) and the British Minister in Washington (Lord Pauncefote). It marked the final acceptance by Britain of the predominant position of the United States in the Caribbean region. By the time the treaty was proclaimed Theodore Roosevelt was President. The question that remained was one of choosing a site for the canal. There were two main possibilities: a route through Nicaragua and one through the Isthmus of Panama, a province of Colombia. In 1867 the United States had concluded a treaty with Nicaragua under which she obtained transit rights comparable with those she acquired from Colombia under the Bidlack Treaty.[60] We have seen how the proposal of the French engineer De Lesseps to form a canal company had aroused the concern of President Hayes.[61] De Lesseps did, in fact,

---

[59] Wriston, 'A Historical Perspective', *op. cit.*, p. 13.
[60] See above, p. 84.           [61] See above, p. 94.

go ahead with his project, but the French company had long since run out of funds. A commission was appointed to investigate both routes. It eventually recommended the Nicaraguan, and this was accepted by the House of Representatives. But, before the recommendation was considered by the Senate, vigorous lobbying on behalf of the French company prevented a firm commitment to it. The President eventually was authorised to negotiate with the French company and the Colombian government; if a satisfactory arrangement could not be made with them, he should proceed with the construction of a canal through Nicaraguan territory.

So the United States, working closely with representatives of the French company, entered into negotiations with Colombia. A treaty was signed with the Colombian Minister in Washington, Tomás Herrán, upon whom a great deal of pressure had been applied. But the Colombian government was extremely reluctant to ratify the Hay–Herrán Treaty both because of the cession of sovereignty involved and of what it regarded as the inadequate compensation offered. Colombian public opinion was strongly against the treaty and the Colombian Senate rejected it unanimously. Two men were especially disconcerted by Colombia's non-co-operation with their scheme: President Roosevelt and one Philippe Bunau-Varilla, former engineer and self-proclaimed chief shareholder in the French company. Bunau-Varilla urged Roosevelt to proceed with the project regardless of Colombia, and even asserted that such action was legally possible under the Bidlack Treaty by which the United States had guaranteed Colombian sovereignty over the isthmus! Roosevelt had little difficulty in convincing himself that the Colombians were blackmailing the United States and that to deprive them of the isthmus in order to construct a canal would be a great benefit for civilisation. As he wrote to John Hay, 'I do not think that the Bogota lot of jack rabbits should be allowed permanently to bar one of the future highways of civilization.'[62]

Thus the United States intervened in Colombia to bring about the creation of the Republic of Panama: conduct acknowledged by Bemis to be 'the one really black mark in the Latin American policy of the United States, and a great big black mark, too'.[63] Bunau-Varilla made his contribution by instigating, financing and directing a revolt of the

[62] Elting E. Morison (ed.), *The Letters of Theodore Roosevelt, vol. III, The Square Deal, 1901–1903* (Cambridge, Mass., Harvard University Press, 1951), p. 567.
[63] *The Latin American Policy of the United States, op. cit.*, p. 151.

Panamanians. Roosevelt did his part by preventing Colombia from landing troops on the isthmus to stop the secession. By such means did the United States, who, under the terms of the Bidlack Treaty, had guaranteed the sovereignty of Colombia, despoil her of the province of Panama.[64] Roosevelt was proud of his role in the affair and even exaggerated it—'I took the Canal': until his death he vigorously opposed any action or even statement by United States representatives which might suggest regret. A mere three days after the start of the uprising the Roosevelt administration recognised the independence of Panama; the President was anxious to present Congress with a *fait accompli* and forestall any move in favour of the Nicaraguan route.

Nor was there delay in negotiating a treaty with the new republic. Not surprisingly, the Panamanian delegate by whom the treaty was signed was Bunau-Varilla. The Hay–Bunau-Varilla Treaty was signed on 18 November 1903. Under its terms, the United States was granted *in perpetuity* a strip of Panamanian territory, ten miles wide, through which the canal would be cut: the Panama Canal Zone. She was also granted in perpetuity the use of other lands and waters outside the zone which might be needed 'for the construction, maintenance, operation, sanitation and protection of the said enterprise'. Over all this territory the United States received quasi-sovereignty:

> ... all the rights, power and authority within the zone ... and within the limits of all auxiliary lands and waters ... which the United States would possess and exercise if it were the sovereign of the territory within which said lands and waters are located, to the entire exclusion of the exercise by the Republic of Panama of any such sovereign rights, power and authority.

The United States could employ whatever troops and construct whatever fortifications it might consider necessary for the defence of the canal. Panama could use the canal free of charges and the United States had privileges within the zone in respect of such things as taxes and import duties. The United States guaranteed the independence of Panama and assumed the right of intervention to maintain it if necessary. Panama was to receive the sum of $10 millions upon ratification of the treaty and $250,000 annually beginning nine years after that. The Hay–Bunau-Varilla Treaty bears a significant resemblance to the

---

[64] The United States subsequently refused Colombia's request that the matter be referred to arbitration.

permanent treaty with Cuba signed in the same year. In each case the United States was to exercise sovereign rights over part of the smaller country's territory; in each case she had obtained the right of intervention under circumstances which she would determine.

Thus at the beginning of the twentieth century the United States had become the paramount power in the western hemisphere. To a very considerable extent the promise of the Monroe Doctrine had been fulfilled. The European power whose influence in Latin America provided the most serious obstacle to United States hegemony over the region had given way on every major dispute with her. In the year the treaties were signed with Cuba and Panama Britain openly made a virtue of necessity. In February 1903 her Prime Minister declared that 'We welcome any increase of the influence of the United States of America in the great Western Hemisphere'. Another spokesman for the British government went even further when he affirmed: 'The principle of the Monroe Doctrine has always received the unwavering support of successive Ministries in this country, and no temporary inconvenience will cause us to waver in our adhesion to the policy established by the American people.'[65] Goodwill—flavoured by a strong ingredient of imagination—could hardly have gone further. The United States had long proclaimed the existence in the Americas of a 'system' separate from that of Europe. Even before the end of the century he had taken the first steps towards giving some such system institutional form. In the first chapter we looked briefly at Pan Americanism and the Western Hemisphere Idea.[66] In the following chapter we shall examine the beginnings of the inter-American system and the effect upon it of the intervention issue.

---

[65] Perkins, *The Monroe Doctrine, 1867–1907, op. cit.*, pp. 360–1.
[66] See above, pp. 24 ff.

# 4 Pan Americanism and the Intervention Issue

The promotion of Pan Americanism by the United States in the late eighteen-eighties was closely linked with her emergence as a world power and, specifically, with her determination to establish hegemony over Latin America. This is well illustrated by the fact that the most influential advocate of Pan Americanism in the United States was James G. Blaine, Secretary of State in the short-lived Garfield administration and again under Benjamin Harrison. As we saw in the previous chapter,[1] Blaine was a firm believer in United States pre-eminence in Latin America. His policy had two particular aims: greatly to increase United States trade with Latin America, and to provide for the peaceful settlement of disputes between American states. These aims were importantly linked, for both involved curbing European influence and intervention in Latin America, British above all. Moreover, conditions of peace and stability were essential for the great increase in trade which Blaine sought to bring about.

In November 1881 invitations were issued to all the other American governments to take part a year later in a congress at Washington 'for the purpose of considering and discussing the methods of preventing war between the nations of America'. The War of the Pacific was then taking place, but Blaine hoped it would have ended by the time the congress met. But the congress did not meet. Garfield's assassination brought Blaine's political rival, Chester Arthur, to the presidency and, three months later, Frederick T. Frelinghuysen to the State Department. In the following August Frelinghuysen withdrew the invitations (which some nations had already accepted), ostensibly on the grounds that the War of the Pacific had not ended, but clearly as part of a general reversal of Blaine's Latin American policy. Between 1881 and Blaine's return to office under Harrison in 1889, however,

---

[1] See above, pp. 94–6.

other influences were at work promoting the Pan American movement in the United States. In Congress, among others, was future President William McKinley; and there were influential publicists outside it. In May 1888 an Act of Congress authorised the United States President to arrange what was to be the First International Conference of American States. Although the invitations were issued under the Democractic administration of Grover Cleveland (who did not himself favour the Act), by the time the conference met the Republicans were back in office and Blaine, as Secretary of State once more, presided over it.

It has been a sedulously cultivated myth that the inter-American system, which was formally established as a result of the Washington conference, is based upon the ideals of Simón Bolívar: that Bolívar is the father of Pan Americanism. Such a myth clearly serves the interests of those in the United States—and Latin America—anxious to promote Pan Americanism. It has no basis in reality—except that myths create their own reality. We have seen how Bolívar himself was concerned with Spanish American unity and how, far from favouring a 'system' embracing the United States and Latin America to the exclusion of Europe, he wanted British support for his Spanish American League.[2]

In addition to the Congress of Panama to which we have already referred,[3] there were three other comparable conferences: the First Congress of Lima (11 December 1847–1 March 1848); the 'Continental Congress', held at Santiago de Chile (September 1856); and the Second Congress of Lima (14 November 1864–13 March 1865). These conferences had several important features. First, they represented efforts by the participating countries to unite in the face of external threats to their independence. These threats came first from Spain and her potential allies; this was the case in 1826 and 1847.[4] Then, fear of United States expansionist policies, manifested by the Mexican War and the filibustering activities of William Walker in Central America, became an important factor in bringing about the Continental Congress. Finally, threats from Europe again during the period of the United States Civil War stimulated the holding of the Second Congress of

---

[2] See above, p. 67.

[3] See above, pp. 66 ff.

[4] The First Congress of Lima had been called mainly because of a threatened invasion of Ecuador by a former President of that country, General Juan José Flores, who was trying to raise an armed expedition in Spain and England. The United States was invited informally to attend by the President of Peru, but did not send a delegate. She was not invited to the other conferences.

Lima. The background to the last of these 'political conferences'[5] illustrates the dilemma facing the countries of Latin America at that time: if the United States was strong enough to enforce the Monroe Doctrine, her power could be a threat to their independence, while if she was too weak to do so, they were likely to be threatened from Europe.

A second important feature of these conferences was the limited number of participants; they were attended by only a few Spanish American countries, with some extra-continental representation at the Congress of Panama. The most notable absentee—and this, above all, sets them apart from the International Conferences of American States—was, of course, the United States. But she was by no means the only one. Neither of the other two non-Spanish American countries attended any of them. Haiti was ignored, but Brazil was invited to the Congress of Panama, though (like the United States) not by Bolívar. Argentina likewise took no part in these gatherings, thus beginning a long tradition of opposition to closer international ties within the hemisphere. Of the remaining Spanish American countries only some were represented at each of the conferences. The achievements of these conferences would therefore have been limited in scope even had all the various treaties and agreements adopted at them been ratified. In fact, none of them came into effect.

A third important feature of these conferences, then, is the enormous gap they reveal between the ideal of Latin (or at least Spanish) American unity long held by some Latin Americans and the meagre results of their efforts to achieve it. Inability to unite to meet threats from external aggression was complemented by failure to create machinery for solving disputes among themselves. The latter was an even harder task for, as external threats receded, nationalism proved a stronger force than internationalism. So, although the importance of establishing the principle of arbitration of disputes between them was fully realised, no arbitration agreement was put into effect; and no international conferences were called to solve the bitter boundary disputes or to end conflicts such as the Paraguayan War (1864–70) and the War of the Pacific (1879–83). These conferences did not augur well for the future of international co-operation among the Latin American countries. But they did provide something of a precedent for the United States

---

[5] A number of technical and juridical conferences were held between the Second Lima Congress and the First International Conference of American States.

when she came to promote her quite different concept of Pan Americanism.

The First International Conference of American States was held in Washington from 2 October 1889 until 19 April 1890. All the Latin American countries except the Dominican Republic were represented.[6] The agenda for the conference, approved by the United States Congress and contained in the invitations, consisted mainly of commerical matters, including a proposal for a customs union. But a plan would be considered for the arbitration of all disputes between the American states. United States concern to increase her trade with Latin America was shown also in the composition of her delegation and the provision of a '6,000-mile, "de luxe" railroad excursion, conducted by the United States government for the benefit of the visiting delegates, and with the apparent object of casting considerable light on the industrial might of the United States on display in all the great cities east of the Mississippi'.[7] This tour, which took place before the delegates got down to serious business, was ostentatiously boycotted by the Argentine representatives, whose opposition was in no small measure responsible for the failure of the United States to attain her major commercial objectives. Indeed, the Washington conference took litte effective action on any of the chief items on the agenda. In particular, the proposal for a customs union was rejected and no firm arbitration treaty was adopted. The only tangible result of significance was the establishment of institutions. The conference created an international association named 'The International Union of American Republics' for the prompt collection and distribution of commercial information. This association was to be represented in Washington by an agency called 'The Commercial Bureau of the American Republics' under the supervision of the United States Secretary of State. Both institutions were to continue in existence for ten years in the first instance, but would be renewed for further such periods unless a majority of members of the Union decided otherwise. Such were the modest beginnings of the inter-American system.

Some of the issues discussed at the Washington conference underlined the difficulties in the way of harmonious relations in the western hemisphere. The divergence of interests between the United States as a

---

[6] The Dominican Republic declined to attend because the United States had not ratified a treaty of arbitration and commercial reciprocity signed in 1884.

[7] T. F. McGann, 'Argentina at the First Pan American Conference', *Inter-American Economic Affairs*, vol. 1, no. 2 (September 1947), p. 27.

great power and the Latin American countries as small ones was well brought out in the debate on 'Claims and Diplomatic Intervention'. The conference voted to recommend that the governments represented there should recognise the following as principles of American international law:

1. Foreigners are entitled to enjoy all the civil rights enjoyed by natives, and they shall be accorded all the benefits of said rights in all that is essential as well as in the form or procedure, and the legal remedies incident thereto, absolutely in like manner as said natives.
2. A nation has not, nor recognizes in favor of foreigners, any other obligations or responsibilities than those which in favor of the natives are established in like cases by the constitution and the laws.

This recommendation followed what was called the 'Calvo Doctrine', after the Argentine jurist, Carlos Calvo. Latin American countries had long included in their constitutions a provision that aliens should be guaranteed equal treatment with their own citizens but could not claim special privileges. Often a 'Calvo clause' was included in contracts with foreign investors under which the latter renounced the right to appeal to their governments for diplomatic assistance. Great powers, including the United States, rejected the Latin American position in this matter. They argued that the Calvo Doctrine ran contrary to international law, which required states to maintain a certain minimum standard of conduct in their treatment of foreigners irrespective of how they treated their own citizens. Moreover, they claimed that the right to intervene on behalf of their citizens could not be affected by any renunciation on the latter's part.

So, while the Latin American countries[8] supported the resolution on 'Claims and Diplomatic Intervention', the United States voted against it, taking her stand on international law and denying, incidentally, the existence of an 'American international law'. This division on the question of diplomatic intervention was essentially a conflict of interests between the great power, seeking to expand economically, and the small powers fearful that such expansion would lead to intervention when disputes arose between them and the great power's business

---

[8] Except Haiti, who abstained on the grounds that, while agreeing with the second paragraph of the recommendation, her constitution did not allow full property rights to foreigners. During the United States occupation, however, a new constitution was imposed upon Haiti, in which these restrictions were removed. See below ,p. 142.

E

concerns. Thus was posed at the very first international conference of American states the intervention issue which has overshadowed United States relations with Latin America ever since.

There was a similar conflict of views on a resolution to condemn 'the right of conquest'. The United States objected to this on the grounds that it would apply in cases where a country had acquired territory as indemnification for an aggression committed against it. She obviously was thinking of her past acquisitions: had she not maintained that Mexico had been the aggressor in the war which brought her so much Mexican territory? She may even have had future possibilities in mind. At all events, this was another significant issue upon which the United States took one stand and all the Latin American countries— except, in this case, Chile—the other. Chile abstained because of her own recent conquests at the expense of Bolivia and Peru resulting from the War of the Pacific.[9] Eventually a compromise recommendation on the right of conquest was linked with what proved to be an abortive arbitration treaty. A Plan of Arbitration was adopted by the conference 'as a principle of American international law for the settlement of the differences, disputes or controversies that may arise between two or more of them'. But the treaty subsequently signed by eleven of the states never came into effect: not one of the signatories ratified it by the agreed date. In this respect the First International Conference of American States followed the unhappy precedent of the earlier Spanish American conferences.

An ominous feature of the Washington conference was the position taken by Argentina. In opening the debate on the proposed customs union, her chief delegate, Roque Sáenz Peña, gave a powerful exposition of his country's policy not only on the subject under discussion, but on the whole question of Latin America's international relations. He stressed the economic ties between the region and Europe, concluding with a personal plea against an exclusively American association: 'Let America be for mankind!'. Since United States policy was concerned basically with limiting the extra-continental ties of the Latin American countries, Argentina, with the closest such ties, was bound to be unco-operative. But Argentina's stand represented a wider Latin American view: opposition to the United States adding economic domination to the political primacy she had already established in the western hemisphere. It is noteworthy that José Martí, the Cuban

---

[9] See above, pp. 95–6.

patriot, writing as correspondent of the Buenos Aires newspaper, *La Nación*, warned that the United States planned to use the conference to further her plans for dominating Latin America.[10]

Before the Second International Conference of American States met in Mexico City (from October 1901 until January 1902)—again on her initiative—there were new and ominous manifestations of United States predominance in the western hemisphere: notably the Venezuelan crisis of 1895, which occasioned Secretary of State Olney's arrogant assertion, and the Spanish American war. The conference achieved little beyond reorganising the Commercial Bureau, now called the International Bureau of the American Republics. Detailed provision was made for its management by a Governing Board consisting of the United States Secretary of State as chairman and the diplomatic representatives of the other American governments accredited to Washington. There was a convention on the rights of aliens which enlarged upon the points contained in the recommendation on 'Claims and Diplomatic Intervention' made at the first conference. The United States did not subscribe to this convention. Agreement on an effective arbitration treaty again proved unattainable. In the interval between the second and third conferences the question of United States intervention in Latin America became a more critical issue through a number of important events, some discussed in the previous chapter. Cuba and Panama had become nominally independent though, in reality, they were United States satellites. As we have seen, in the perpetual treaties signed with both in 1903 the United States obtained the right of intervention in those countries under circumstances which clearly she herself would determine.

In addition to these specific treaty rights, the United States claimed a general right under international law to intervene in any country on behalf of her citizens and their property. In practice, of course, such a right could be exercised effectively only by great powers in relation to smaller, weaker ones. It had been exercised in Latin America (especially in the Caribbean region) many times during the nineteenth century by both the United States and European powers such as Britain and France. The United States had not regarded such interventions by European powers as violations of the Monroe Doctrine as long as there appeared to be no danger that Latin American territory would be

---

[10] Extracts from both Martí's article and the Argentine delegate's speech are contained in Robert N. Burr and Roland D. Hussey, *Documents on Inter-American Cooperation, vol. II, 1881–1948* (Philadelphia, University of Pennsylvania Press, 1955), pp. 37–41, 43–9.

annexed. Even at the beginning of the twentieth century, when United States power in the western hemisphere was so much greater than it had been throughout most of the nineteenth century, the right of European powers to take punitive action against Latin American governments defaulting on their obligations was not challenged in principle by the United States. President Theodore Roosevelt himself stated in his Annual Message to Congress of 3 December 1901: 'We do not guarantee any state against punishment if it misconducts itself, provided that punishment does not take the form of the acquisition of territory by any non-American power.'[11]

It was against this background that Britain—who by now, as we have seen, accepted the Monroe Doctrine—joined with Germany in a blockade of Venezuelan ports in December 1902 to force the Venezuelan government to meet various financial claims presented on behalf of their citizens. Significantly, the European powers had rejected the proposal that a Venezuelan commission should deal with the claims. The British and German governments took the precaution of informing the United States of their intention to impose the blockade. According to the British Ambassador in Washington, Secretary of State John Hay had replied 'that the United States Government, although they regretted that European powers should use force against Central and South American countries, could not object to their taking steps to obtain redress for injuries suffered by their subjects, provided that no acquisition of territory was contemplated'. On this point Professor Perkins has commented: 'Thus, with a degree of definiteness that deserves to be emphasized and reemphasized, the administration at Washington gave its blessing to the coercive measures projected against Venezuela. . . .'[12] However, when the blockade got under way (with Italy joining in) public opinion in the United States was aroused by what seemed a threat to the Monroe Doctrine, and the government had to reconsider its position. The blockade ended in February 1903 when Venezuela agreed to accept arbitration by mixed commissions. Much later Theodore Roosevelt claimed the credit for ending the blockade by issuing a strong warning to Germany, though historians have generally refrained from taking this claim seriously.[13]

---

[11] Perkins, *The Monroe Doctrine, 1867–1907, op. cit.*, p. 322.

[12] *Ibid.*, p. 333.

[13] See, for example, the comments of Dexter Perkins: *ibid.*, pp. 377 ff. But for a more favourable assessment of Roosevelt's claim (and criticism of Perkins's evaluation), see Beale, *Theodore Roosevelt and the Rise of America to World Power, op. cit.*, pp. 342 ff.

The immediate aftermath of the Anglo-German blockade was significant. Luis M. Drago, the Foreign Minister of Argentina, proposed in a note to Secretary of State Hay on 29 December 1902 that the United States should subscribe to the principle that 'public debt gives no place for armed intervention, and less still to the material occupation of the soil of American nations by a European power'. This later came to be known as the Drago Doctrine. In his note Drago referred with approval to the Monroe Doctrine, which he associated with his own principle, and he doubtless expected a warm response in Washington. Such a response was not forthcoming. For not only was the United States determined to retain the unilateral character of the Monroe Doctrine, but she shared in principle a common position with the European powers on the question at issue.

The divergence of interests—and therefore policy—between the United States as a great power and the countries of Latin America as small powers is well illustrated by comparing the Drago Doctrine with the Roosevelt Corollary to the Monroe Doctrine. Like the Argentine Foreign Minister, Theodore Roosevelt pronounced against European intervention in the western hemisphere, but the President did not condemn intervention as such. On the contrary, he claimed for the United States a monopoly of the right (and the assumption of a duty) of intervention in the Americas.[14] In his Annual Message to Congress on 6 December 1904 Theodore Roosevelt made his famous contribution to the Monroe Doctrine:

> Chronic wrongdoing, or an impotence which results in a general loosening of the ties of civilized society, may in America, as elsewhere, ultimately require intervention by some civilized nation, and in the Western Hemisphere the adherence of the United States to the Monroe Doctrine may force the United States, however reluctantly, in flagrant cases of such wrongdoing or impotence, to the exercise of an international police power.[15]

Like the Drago Doctrine, the Roosevelt Corollary was stimulated by the Anglo-German blockade of Venezuela, which had been viewed by

---

[14] In a speech just over two weeks after the President announced his 'corollary', Elihu Root, who had succeeded John Hay as Secretary of State, declared, in words reminiscent of Richard Olney, that the United States was 'sovereign upon this continent' and that 'what we will not permit the great Powers of Europe to do, we will not permit any American republic to make it necessary for the great Powers of Europe to do'. Quoted in Perkins, *The Monroe Doctrine, 1867–1907, op. cit.*, p. 429.

[15] Gantenbein, *The Evolution of Our Latin-American Policy, op. cit.*, p. 362.

public opinion in the United States as a challenge to the Monroe Doctrine.

But the main antecedents of the Roosevelt Corollary are to be found elsewhere. The United States had acquired specific rights of intervention in Cuba and Panama under treaties signed in 1903. In the case of Cuba this, as we saw, involved the Platt Amendment, which had been adopted by the United States Senate in March 1901. It would hardly be surprising to find the United States applying similar measures to other small states lying in the Caribbean region. Elihu Root, the author of the Platt Amendment as Secretary of War, is reported to have described its intervention clause as 'simply an extension of the Monroe Doctrine'.[16] The Dominican Republic was the first Latin American country in which the United States intervened following the enunciation of the Roosevelt Corollary. But this intervention was less a consequence of the Corollary than a factor in stimulating the President's pronouncement.

The decision of the United States government to establish the Dominican customs receivership at the beginning of 1905 was the culmination of a growing involvement in the finances of that small Caribbean country as well as a move to forestall possible intervention by European creditors. The Dominican Republic, like other small Latin American republics, was economically backward and in debt to foreign bankers. In 1893, at the suggestion of the then United States Secretary of State, a North American concern, the San Domingo Improvement Company, became the country's banker. This company inevitably became involved in Dominican politics, and made itself exceedingly unpopular among the Dominicans. In 1901 the Dominican government ended its agreement with the company, and arrangements regarding the latter's indemnity led to dispute. The company refused to submit its accounts for the Dominican government's inspection and insisted upon retaining control of the country's railroads until one-third of the agreed indemnity had been paid. It appealed to the State Department, which urged the Dominican government to submit the question to arbitration. Thus the United States government associated itself with the interests of the San Domingo Improvement Company. But Washington was not well informed of the situation in the Dominican Republic. Not until April 1904 was a Minister appointed in Santo Domingo: before then one man represented the United States in both

---

[16] Perkins, *The Monroe Doctrine, 1867–1907, op. cit.*, p. 404.

Haiti and the Dominican Republic and spent most of his time in Port-au-Prince. This man, a certain William F. Powell, aggressively supported the claims of the San Domingo Improvement Company and other North American companies, and strongly advocated the establishment of a United States protectorate over the Dominican Republic. Powell constantly warned against the machinations of European powers —especially those of Germany, who by this time had replaced Britain as the United States prime suspect among such powers. Theodore Roosevelt later justified his policy by telling Congress that 'there was imminent danger of foreign intervention' in the Dominican Republic and that only the opening of negotiations for a United States customs receivership had 'prevented the seizure of territory in Santo Domingo by a European power.' To describe this as exaggeration would be an understatement. But the Dominican Republic's European creditors were becoming restive, and there were political elements in the country hostile to the United States.

Before an arbitration commission gave its judgement in the case of the San Domingo Improvement Company The Hague Court, a panel of which had been considering the question of claims against the Venezuelan government, pronounced in favour of the European powers which had conducted the blockade, and decreed that they should receive preferential treatment. This could only be viewed in the United States, who had not resorted to force against Venezuela, as an encouragement to European intervention in Latin America. The Hague Court's ruling was given in February 1904. In the following July the arbitration commission gave its decision in the Dominican case: that the compensation due to the Improvement Company should be paid to a financial agent appointed by the United States, with the customs revenues of a number of Dominican ports as security. In the event of default, the financial agent would take over the collection of customs at specified ports. The State Department named an officer of the Improvement Company as financial agent, in spite of the hatred of the company felt by the Dominicans. When the inevitable default took place the company's representative moved into one of the major Dominican ports. Meanwhile the general instability in the Dominican Republic increased the likelihood of United States intervention.

On 30 December 1904 the Minister appointed the previous April, Thomas C. Dawson, was instructed to discuss with the Dominican President 'the disquieting situation' which, according to Secretary of State Hay, arose from recent arbitral awards and the likelihood of some

European powers resorting to an occupation of Dominican customs ports to secure payment of their claims:

> You will ascertain whether the Government of Santo Domingo would be disposed to request the United States to take charge of the collection of duties and effect an equitable distribution of the assigned quotas among the Dominican Government and the several claimants. We have grounds to think that such arrangement would satisfy the other powers, besides serving as a practical guaranty of the peace of Santo Domingo from external influence or internal disturbance.[17]

To assist a favourable conclusion to the ensuing negotiations, two United States warships anchored in Santo Domingo harbour. They remained these to ensure that after negotiation the agreement would be enforced. Specifically, the Secretary of the Navy was told to prevent any revolution against the Dominican government which had signed it. Under the terms of a protocol signed on 7 February 1905, the United States undertook the adjustment of the Dominican Republic's debts, both external and internal, determining the validity of outstanding claims and the amount to be paid to the various creditors. She would collect the customs revenues, from which the Dominican government would receive not less than forty-five per cent of the proceeds for current expenses, the remainder being applied to debt repayment. The United States government, at the request of the Dominican Republic, would 'grant such other assistance as may be in its power to restore the credit, preserve the order, and increase the efficiency of the civil administration, and advance the material progress and the welfare of the Republic'. The United States Senate did not approve the protocol, but Roosevelt went ahead by executive agreement with a proposed *modus vivendi* pending its eventual acceptance.

The Roosevelt Corollary and its immediate application to the Dominican Republic mark the beginning of a distinct phase in relations between the United States and Latin America. For over two decades there were numerous armed interventions by the United States in Latin American countries, and although these took place mainly in the Caribbean region, they importantly affected relations with Latin America as a whole. United States historians traditionally have regarded United States policy towards Latin America during this

---

[17] Munro, *Intervention and Dollar Diplomacy in the Caribbean, 1900–1921, op. cit.,* p. 100.

period as something of an aberration: a phase of imperialism out of character and of limited duration. The Roosevelt Corollary itself has been treated as a perversion of the 'original' Monroe Doctrine. In the final chapter of the third volume of his study of the Doctrine, entitled 'Non-intervention becomes Intervention', Dexter Perkins wrote:

> ... the administration of the customs of Santo Domingo was, very decidedly, a breach with the past; and it required no very great far-sightedness, as history itself was soon to show, to see that the responsibilities thus assumed almost inevitably would lead to further measures of control, and to an active intervention in the affairs of the Dominican republic. The Roosevelt corollary was no inevitable deduction from the language of Monroe; it was, in a sense, *revolutionary*; it transformed a doctrine intended for the protection of the states of the New World against intervention from Europe into a doctrine of intervention by the United States.[18]

At the beginning of the chapter Perkins referred to 'the *evolution* of a doctrine which was intended for the protection of Latin-American states by the United States into one that justified and even sanctified American interference in and control of the affairs of the independent republics of this continent'.[19]

Whether the process was evolutionary or revolutionary, the concept that a doctrine of 'non-intervention' was transformed into a doctrine of 'intervention' does not seem to be valid in the light of either President Monroe's words or the known sentiments of the great men involved in the formulation of the Doctrine. Nor do their actions support such an interpretation.

In his Message, President Monroe himself did not pretend an intention to protect the countries of Latin America, nor even claim to be solicitous for their interests. On two occasions in the passages which constitute the Doctrine[20] he re-affirmed United States neutrality as between Spain and the new Spanish American governments. This was in accordance with United States interests, with which the President understandably and quite frankly was concerned. Non-colonisation, he says in the first paragraph, is asserted 'as a principle in which *the rights*

---

[18] *The Monroe Doctrine, 1867–1907, op. cit.,* p. 433. My italics.
[19] *Ibid.,* p. 396. My italics. Professor Perkins's judgement accords with the claim contained in the Clark *Memorandum on the Monroe Doctrine* which, incidentally, was published during the period in which Perkins was making his extensive study. See below. p. 157.  [20] See above, pp. 61–2.

*and interests of the United States* are involved'. Intervention by the European powers in the Americas would be considered by the United States as 'dangerous to *our* peace and safety'; specifically, any intervention against the newly independent governments of Latin America would be regarded 'as the manifestation of an unfriendly disposition *toward the United States.*'; and, again, 'It is impossible that the allied powers should extend their political system to any portion of either continent without endangering *our*[21] peace and happiness.' This theme runs through the history of the unilateral Monroe Doctrine from 1823 until the present day: extra-continental intervention in the western hemisphere threatens the interests of the United States. If the prevention of such intervention involves the United States herself in intervention in Latin America, there is nothing in such action to violate Monroe's principle. Indeed, given United States acceptance of the right of great powers to intervene in the internal and external affairs of small powers when their interests demand it, then if she should forbid European powers to exercise such a right in Latin America, she must herself intervene to forestall them and ensure that their legitimate grievances are redressed. This is the logic of the Roosevelt Corollary, and its author's claim that he was acting in accordance with President Monroe's dictum and not departing from it must be sustained. 'Non-intervention' did not become 'intervention'. Non-intervention was the Monroe Doctrine's prescription for Europe, not for the United States. The Doctrine is not a self-denying ordinance, but an assertion of United States primacy in the Americas. Her leaders, in making a unilateral declaration of policy, had rejected such an ordinance when Britain had (for her own purposes) proposed it.

The second point concerns not words, but evident intentions. Now, although the phrase 'Manifest Destiny' did not come into popular use until the eighteen-forties, the ideas it expressed, as we have seen, were entertained by United States leaders long before that time. The outstanding men who, in varying degrees, were involved in the formulation of the Monroe Doctrine—Thomas Jefferson, James Madison, James Monroe and John Quincy Adams—all subscribed to such ideas. They looked forward to the day when the United States would be a great power and paramount in the Americas. Even before the Monroe Doctrine was enunciated the United States had intervened in the Floridas to subvert Spanish authority and acquire the territory. The

[21] My italics in all cases.

story of the Monroe Doctrine during the nineteenth century is one not of steady development—internal and external factors checked its growth from time to time. That story, nevertheless, is one of logical growth as United States power was able to make good claims which were either explicit in the Message or which it could be—and was—held to have implied. Theodore Roosevelt was a man of his time: of the new phase of Manifest Destiny in which the United States asserted her now greatly increased strength following the Civil War. But he was also the natural heir of the earlier Presidents who formulated and built upon the Message of 1823.

But whatever the judgements of historians, the Monroe Doctrine henceforth would be associated in Latin American eyes with United States intervention. By the beginning of the twentieth century the Latin Americans had much less reason to fear European intervention than intervention by the United States. Fear of the United States found literary expression in the works of such writers as the Nicaraguan poet, Rubén Darío, and the Uruguayan, José Enrique Rodó. In his well-known article, 'The Triumph of Caliban' (the victory of the United States in the Spanish–American war), Darío recalled the Cuban patriot, José Martí, and wondered 'what that Cuban would say today in seeing that under the cover of aid to the grief-stricken pearl of the Antilles, the "monster" gobbles it up, oyster and all . . .'[22] Similar sentiments were expressed at this time by Rodó in his *Ariel*.[23] Darío also gave vent to his fears in his poem *To Theodore Roosevelt*. Roosevelt, with his belligerent policies and utterances (the 'Big Stick'), his unconcealed sense of Anglo-Saxon superiority and urge to play the policeman of the western hemisphere[24] epitomised what Latin Americans would increasingly come to fear and hate.

Theodore Roosevelt laid the foundations of what has been described as the Panama policy of the United States. His immediate successors, William Howard Taft and Woodrow Wilson, built upon those foundations. Each of these Presidents is often credited with having made a distinctive contribution: Taft is associated with 'Dollar Diplomacy', Wilson with 'Missionary Diplomacy'. Such a distinction is not, however, a meaningful one; nor is it possible to isolate the various aspects of United States policy. The argument over whether promoting the

---

[22] 'Monster' was Martí's word for the United States. Thomas, *Cuba or The Pursuit of Freedom, op. cit.*, p. 417.  [23] See above, p. 2.

[24] Interestingly, Theodore Roosevelt was police commissioner in New York City earlier in his career.

interests of her business concerns or pursuing those of national security
was the main objective of United States policy at this (or any other)
time may be thought of great importance by historians anxious to
defend that policy from charges of imperialism. Otherwise it is irrelevant. United States policy was concerned with promoting security *and*
economic expansion which were intimately linked both in fact and in
the minds of policy makers. If Wilson had a strong sense of mission,
Theodore Roosevelt was hardly lacking in this. If Taft was anxious to
increase United States economic penetration of the Caribbean region,
such penetration increased still further under Wilson. In the words of
Dana Munro, whose study of United States interventions in this region
during the first two decades of the twentieth century seeks to dispel
'the myth of North American imperialism':[25]

> The same purposes inspired the policy of successive administrations from
> Theodore Roosevelt to Woodrow Wilson. The methods used in attempt-
> ing to achieve them varied from one administration to another, but more
> because of accumulating experience and increasing involvement than be-
> cause of any difference in the ultimate goals. Each successive Secretary of
> State took up Caribbean problems where his predecessor had left them, in
> most cases making no abrupt change in the way in which they were being
> handled.[26]

The fact that Wilson was the greatest interventionist of the three reflects the growing United States domination of the region.[27]

There is no doubt that the administrations of Theodore Roosevelt,
Taft and Wilson strongly encouraged United States economic and
financial penetration of the Caribbean region. Whether they exerted
pressure upon reluctant but patriotic United States bankers and businessmen to invest in the region in order to further United States security—
as some United States historians have suggested[28]—may be questioned.
What cannot be questioned is that a very considerable augmentation
of United States investments in the region took place in the first two
decades of the twentieth century. The occupation of Cuba led to a
great increase of the United States economic and financial stake in the

---

[25] Munro, *op. cit.*, p. 530.                    [26] *Ibid.*, p. 531.
[27] It does not, as Munro appears to believe, support his own case that United States
motives for intervention were not economic. See below, pp. 132 ff., for an evaluation of
Wilson's Latin American policy.
[28] E.g. Bemis, *The Latin American Policy of the United States*, p. 166. Munro, *op. cit.*,
pp. 163–4, is less convinced.

island, and the treaty of 1903 facilitated further penetration. The largest investments in neighbouring Hispaniola were those of the San Domingo Improvement Company of New York, 'which for some years had carried on varied and sometimes questionable financial operations in the Dominican Republic'.[29] We have already noted the company's role in events leading up to United States intervention in 1905. Early in the century the National City Bank of New York and its associates began to finance railroad construction in Haiti and bought stock in the Haitian National Bank in 1910, 'almost immediately involving themselves and the American government in controversies with the Haitian government which took on an importance out of all proportion to the amount of money at stake'.[30] In Central America, much the most important North American concern was the United Fruit Company of Boston, Massachusetts, incorporated in 1899. This company came to own not only huge amounts of land in the Central American republics, but also railways and port facilities, including its own ships: a veritable octopus spreading its tentacles over the whole of the region—in the words of its critics. The United Fruit Company possessed considerable political influence in these countries, and did not lack influence in Washington.

United States economic penetration of Central America inevitably led to growing political involvement in the internal affairs of the countries of the region. It was an unfortunate element in the situation that United States diplomatic representatives there were generally of low quality. Almost all chiefs of mission and consuls received their appointments as a reward for political services. As Caribbean posts were relatively unattractive they were given to minor politicians. As for 'career diplomats' in the lower grades, in Munro's words, 'Neither the able nor the incompetent secretaries willingly went to posts in the Caribbean, where living conditions were uncomfortable and the social life was unattractive. Consequently, men were frequently sent to these posts as a punishment for misconduct or inefficiency.'[31] It so happens that Munro himself was later a prominent foreign service officer in the Caribbean region.[32] An indictment of United States diplomacy in the early part of the twentieth century is entertainingly presented by William Sands's account of his experiences in its service in Latin America at that time.[33]

---

[29] Munro, *op. cit.*, p. 17.     [30] *Ibid., loc. cit.*     [31] *Ibid.*, p. 23.
[32] And Head of the Latin American Division of the State Department.
[33] *Our Jungle Diplomacy, op. cit.* See above, p. 14, n. 45.

Although the Roosevelt Corollary had spoken of 'the western hemisphere', its most obvious application was to the small countries of the Caribbean region. Thus, while there was some criticism of the Corollary in the Latin American press, especially in Argentina,[34] the governments of the larger countries of Latin America regarded it officially with equanimity. In his Annual Message to Congress a year later Theodore Roosevelt spoke in reassuring terms for their benefit. United States relations with these countries varied at the beginning of the twentieth century. We shall consider the case of Mexico in some detail presently. Argentina we saw as the most pronounced opponent of an exclusively American system at the First International Conference of American States. Her economic links were predominantly with Europe, especially Britain, and her great economic progress in the latter part of the nineteenth century had encouraged her to aspire to leadership among the Spanish American nations, even of South America as a whole. However, relations between the United States and Argentina generally were limited rather than unfriendly at the beginning of the twentieth century.

United States relations with Chile were rather less limited. They were also cooler. We noted some occasions of friction.[35] To these was added at the start of the twentieth century another, over a claim by the stockholders of a North American company (Alsop) arising out of the War of the Pacific.[36] Mining concessions granted to the company by Bolivia were not recognised by Chile when, as a consequence of the war, she acquired the territory in which they were located. The Chileans maintained that the United States government, which vigorously pursued the matter, was not rightly a party to it. After threats by the United States to sever diplomatic relations, Chile agreed to submit the issue to arbitration by the King of England. The arbitral award proved favourable to the United States interests concerned. Moreover, Chile's contention that the claim was a domestic matter and therefore should not have been the subject of diplomatic intervention was rejected.

It is of interest that Brazil had mediated in the Alsop affair and helped bring about the agreement to name King Edward VII as arbiter.

---

[34] The Argentine newspaper *La Prensa* (8 December 1904) described the Roosevelt Corollary as 'the most serious and menacing declaration against South American integrity which has come out of Washington'. Quoted in Thomas F. McGann, *Argentina, the United States, and the Inter-American System, 1880–1914* (Cambridge, Mass., Harvard University Press, 1957), p. 223.

[35] See above, p. 96.                    [36] See above, pp. 95–6.

For United States relations with Brazil were becoming more intimate and friendly at the beginning of the twentieth century. The overthrow of the Brazilian empire in 1889 marks the start of the friendship which developed between the two countries. The main responsibility for its development lies in several factors. Brazil had a number of territorial claims against her Spanish American neighbours, including Argentina, and desired United States moral support. Moreover, in Professor Burns's judgement, 'In identifying themselves with the United States for purposes of national aggrandizement, Brazilians liked to think of themselves as the South American counterpart of the United States. Explicit in the analogy was a pretension to a moral hegemony over South America similar to that exercised by the United States over the Caribbean.'[37] Specifically, Brazil's rivalry with Argentina for diplomatic leadership in South America encouraged friendship with the United States.[38] Moreover, the latter provided the best market for Brazil's principal exports. From the United States viewpoint, the friendship of the largest Latin American state was important in the pursuit of her overall objectives in the region, especially in view of Argentina's attitude towards the developing inter-American system. Brazil did not feel threatened, as did some of the Spanish American states, by United States ambitions and policies. For most of the first decade of the century Brazil's Foreign Minister was Baron Rio-Branco, a strong exponent of friendship with the United States. His Ambassador in Washington, Jaoquim Nabuco, was very strongly pro-United States in sympathy.[39] Both Rio-Branco and Nabuco supported the Roosevelt Corollary and Pan Americanism.[40]

Rio de Janeiro was the seat of the Third International Conference of American States, held from 23 July until 27 August 1906. Although controversial matters generally were kept off the agenda, the question of pecuniary claims and the forcible collection of debts was prominent. The United States delegates reported that the extent to which force was admissible for the collection of public debts overshadowed in interest all other topics before the conference.[41] Eventually it was decided (as

---

[37] E. Bradford Burns, *The Unwritten Alliance: Rio-Branco and Brazilian–American Relations* (New York and London, Columbia University Press, 1966), p. 172.

[38] Brazil's role in the Alsop affair was something of a diplomatic triumph over Argentina.

[39] Nabuco once described himself as 'an ardent "Monroist," and for that reason a partisan of the ever increasing harmony between Brazil and the United States': Carolina Nabuco, *The Life of Joaquim Nabuco* (Stanford, Stanford University Press, 1950), p. 308.

[40] The Corollary received a good press in Brazil (Burns, *op. cit.*, p. 151).

[41] Connell-Smith, *The Inter-American System, op. cit.*, p. 50.

the United States wanted) to invite the Second Hague Peace Conference to examine the question of the compulsory collection of public debts. A resolution of the Third Conference continued the International Union of American Republics and the Bureau for a further period of ten years. The purposes, organisation and functions of the Bureau were reformulated and new regulations laid down for its administration. The Governing Board of the Bureau was authorised to designate the place at which, within the following five years, the Fourth International Conference should convene, and to provide for the drafting of the programme and regulations.

Before the Fourth Conference met, the Second Hague Peace Conference was held. At The Hague the Latin Americans sought in vain to have the Drago Doctrine accepted as international law. The United States, on the other hand, was successful in securing the adoption of her own proposal that the renunciation of force for the collection of public debts should be contingent upon the acceptance of arbitration. This was a blow for the Latin Americans, since it actually recognised the use of armed force, and, although most of them signed the convention embodying the United States proposal, ten did so with reservations. Few ratified it.

The Fourth International Conference of American States met in Buenos Aires from 12 July until 30 August 1910. The atmosphere of the conference was on the whole harmonious, but very little was achieved. Careful preparation of the programme and exclusion of controversial matters were again largely responsible. Relations between the United States and Latin America were not improving. An attempt by the Brazilian delegation to introduce a motion praising the Monroe Doctrine had to be withdrawn because it aroused criticism of recent encroachments by the United States.[42] Latin American concern was expressed over United States domination of the Governing Board of the Bureau. At the Fourth Conference the 'International Union of American Republics' was renamed the 'Union of American Republics' and the International (formerly Commercial) Bureau became the 'Pan American Union'. The latter now had its seat in the Building of the American Republics in Washington, erected largely through funds provided by Andrew Carnegie, the industrialist, who, incidentally, had been a United States delegate to the First Conference. The exis-

---

[42] Connell-Smith, *The Inter-American System*, p. 52. The motion had been the idea of Nabuco who, but for his death prior to the conference, would have presented it as head of the Brazilian delegation.

tence of the Pan American Union was continued for another period of ten years by resolution of the conference. The Fifth International Conference was provided for along the same lines as the two previous ones; but in the event it was not held until 1923. Meanwhile, relations between the United States and Latin America were importantly affected by the First World War.

At the outbreak of the war Pan Americanism had not achieved a great deal. Four International Conferences had been held (as well as a much larger number of special and technical ones) and many resolutions and recommendations had been passed at them. But few of these agreements had been ratified and those, on the whole, were the less important ones. Little progress had been made towards establishing effective machinery for the peaceful settlement of inter-American disputes, a major purpose of Pan Americanism. At the same time, it is of interest that efforts in this field were linked with the wider conferences at The Hague. When hostilities began in Europe there existed no inter-American machinery for dealing with possible external aggression. No such threat had arisen since the First International Conference, and the United States, powerful enough to sustain the unilateral Monroe Doctrine, had no reason to enter into defence commitments with the countries of Latin America. Nor by now did the Latin American countries want the United States to make such a commitment. For them, fear of United States intervention had already replaced fear of extra-continental aggression. Their main objective was to restrain their powerful neighbour, who was in the process of making the Caribbean her exclusive preserve, and the countries in the region her satellites.

The Latin Americans had not found Pan Americanism much help in restraining the United States. They had failed at the outset to persuade her to accept the Calvo Doctrine, which would have placed her nationals in their territories on the same footing as natives. The United States claimed the right of diplomatic intervention on behalf of her citizens and of using armed force to collect public debts if arbitration were refused. Moreover, the International Conferences were not allowed to become vehicles for criticising United States policies. Management of the conferences was helped by United States domination of what was now the Pan American Union. As we have seen, not only was the United States Secretary of State chairman of the Governing Board, but the other members were diplomatic representatives whose main function was to cultivate good relations with the host nation. The Latin American countries obviously occupied a subordinate position in an organisation which so often proclaimed the absolute equality of its members. The Latin Americans were beginning to demand changes.

Clearly Pan Americanism was of much greater value to the United States. 'According to the Latin-American view', it has been said, 'the United States ministered Pan American good-will in order to allay the ill-will engendered by its practices of intervention'.[43] Certainly the United States was anxious to present her own national policy of excluding unwelcome European influence from the western hemisphere as being that of 'Pan America.' It was in her interests to propagate the 'Western Hemisphere Idea' and to portray relations between herself and the countries of Latin America as being fundamentally different from those between ambitious great powers and vulnerable small ones in other regions of the world. But the façade of harmony was beginning to crack in the face of the realities of international relations in the hemisphere. It seemed to many Latin Americans that behind Pan Americanism lay 'Yankee Imperialism'.

For by the outbreak of the First World War the policy initiated with the Platt Amendment and the Roosevelt Corollary had led to numerous interventions in the Caribbean region. A pattern of intervention was developing whereby the United States eventually added control over the Dominican Republic, Nicaragua and Haiti to her control over Cuba and Panama. During these years there were also a number of interventions in the latter countries, as provided for in the treaties with them. We noted how the Roosevelt Corollary was first applied to the Dominican Republic in 1905, when United States agents took over the customs receiverships by an executive agreement after the Senate had failed to approve the relevant protocol.[44] This arrangement was embodied in a treaty two years later. Under its terms the Dominican government was prohibited from increasing its public debt until it had met its foreign obligations in full. The United States objective was not only to remove any cause for external intervention, but also to promote internal stability.

The United States was also concerned at this time with promoting internal stability in Central America, whose strategic importance had been greatly enhanced by the firm prospect of an isthmian canal after 1903. This region was traditionally turbulent, partly because historical links between the Central American states encouraged intervention in

---

[43] Mecham, *The United States and Inter-American Security, 1889–1960, op. cit.*, p. 72.
[44] See above, p. 118.

one another's affairs. Dictators in one country often attempted to extend their rule into others, and there were frequent accusations of encouragement being given to revolutionary movements in neighbouring territories. Guatemala's Manuel Estrada Cabrera and Nicaragua's José Santos Zelaya were outstanding among such dictators at the beginning of the twentieth century. In 1907, at a time when Zelaya was believed to be the main disturber of the peace in Central America, the United States, with the collaboration of the Mexican dictator, Porfirio Díaz, called a conference of all five republics in Washington.

At the Washington Conference the Central American republics signed a series of treaties generally aimed at promoting not only peace but also co-operation in various fields between them. The most important was the General Treaty of Peace and Amity, under which they agreed to submit all future disputes between them to a Permanent Central American Court of Justice. They also undertook to prevent the use of their territory as a base for revolutionary movements against other states, and to restrict the political activities of refugees from such states. Under another article Honduras was declared to be permanently neutral. Her weakness and central position in the region made control of her government a prime objective in conflicts between her stronger neighbours. In an additional convention to the General Treaty the signatories agreed that they would not recognise any government coming to power through revolution in any one of their countries 'so long as the freely elected representatives of the people thereof have not constitutionally reorganized the country'. 'This provision', Dana Munro observed, 'seemed somewhat unrealistic, for in 1907 there had hardly ever been a free election in any Central American state except Costa Rica....'[45] Neither sponsor of the conference was a party to the treaty, but the United States henceforth followed the non-recognition convention in relation to the signatories. This came to be known as the Tobar Doctrine, after Dr. Carlos Tobar, an Ecuadoran diplomat, who first proposed it. Later its application by the United States was strongly criticised as a form of intervention. In effect, by sponsoring the Central American treaties, the United States was discouraging intervention among the five republics and reserving the right of intervention for herself.

It was Nicaragua that became the main objective of United States intervention in Central America at this time, initially during the

---

[45] *Intervention and Dollar Diplomacy in the Caribbean, 1900–1921, op. cit.,* p. 153.

administration of William Howard Taft. Taft, who became President in 1909, had experience of Caribbean problems before coming to the presidency, but his Secretary of State, Philander C. Knox, a former corporation lawyer, had little knowledge of or sympathy with Latin Americans. The policy of the Taft administration was basically the same as that of its predecessor, but it placed more emphasis upon loans and customs receiverships: it pursued what was described—not only by its critics—as 'Dollar Diplomacy'. The main executor of this policy was the Assistant Secretary of State, Huntington Wilson, who shared Knox's ignorance of Latin America and lack of sympathy with its peoples. The *rationale* of Dollar Diplomacy was well described in an editorial published in the *Washington Post* in January 1911, entitled 'Dollars vs. Bullets':

> ... when an American republic is on the brink of bankruptcy, no friendlier or politically wiser action could be taken by the United States than to seek, through the instrumentalities of American capital, by one stroke to remove all question of European intervention, and at the same time to start the country concerned upon the road to progress, peace and prosperity.[46]

This is the policy, above all, which historians such as Bemis, Munro and Perkins have been so anxious to defend from charges of being motivated by a design to aid United States bankers and businessmen in exploiting the countries to which it was applied. One such country was Nicaragua, where President Zelaya's policies threatened not only the stability of Central America but also specific United States investments. These last included the principal United States company in the country, a mining concern operating the United States–Nicaragua Concession.

In October 1909 there was a revolt against Zelaya which was assisted financially by North American and other foreign interests in Nicaragua and given what Mecham calls 'no little encouragement from the United States government'.[47] The latter abandoned its formal neutrality in the Nicaraguan civil war when two United States citizens fighting on the rebels' side were shot by Zelaya's forces. The State Department, in Munro's words, 'was not disposed to tolerate the murder of American citizens, even though it frowned on their participation

---

[46] Quoted in Peter Calvert, *The Mexican Revolution, 1910–1914: The Diplomacy of Anglo-American Conflict* (Cambridge, Cambridge University Press, 1968), p. 36.
[47] *A Survey of United States–Latin American Relations, op. cit.*, p. 325.

in the revolt and knew that . . . [one of them], at least, was a ne'er-do-well who had been involved in other Central American revolutions'.[48] The decisive point of the civil war came when the government (Liberal) forces were prevented from taking the port of Bluefields (the most important city in Conservative hands) by United States naval forces.[49] With this help the Conservatives went on to gain power. The United States then became involved in the internal struggle for the Nicaraguan presidency. She eventually gave her support to Adolfo Díaz, who had been secretary of the United States–Nicaraguan Concession. Díaz was recognised by the United States as constitutional president, and a treaty was signed with him comparable with the treaty of 1907 with the Dominican Republic.[50] On these events Professor Lieuwen has commented:

> Washington withheld recognition from several successor governments, but in May, 1911, it got the kind of President it wanted—Adolfo Díaz, a stanchly pro-United States employee of the Los Angeles Mining Company in Nicaragua. Díaz was perfectly willing to compromise his nation's sovereignty and allow the United States broad powers of intervention and control in return for the privilege of enjoying apparent political leadership.[51]

When Díaz's position was threatened later that year some two thousand United States marines were landed in his support. After the opposition had been suppressed a small detachment remained as a 'legation guard' to serve as a stabilising factor in Nicaraguan politics. 'The real function of the Marines', declares Lieuwen, 'was to deter the opposition Liberals, and for the next thirteen years there was relative political calm in Nicaragua, which had a succession of Washington-backed Conservative governments headed by Díaz and others of his ilk.'[52]

United States intervention in Nicaragua was thus more far-reaching

---

[48] *Op. cit.*, p. 176.

[49] United States action was taken ostensibly for the protection of foreign nationals and their property. But, 'The method was the same as in Panama in 1903: American naval interposition prevented Nicaraguan governmental forces from suppressing the revolution when it was weak.' Theodore P. Wright, Jr., *American Support of Free Elections Abroad* (Washington, D.C., 1964), p. 38.

[50] See above, p. 128.

[51] Edwin Lieuwen, *U.S. Policy in Latin America: A Short History* (New York, 1965), p. 44.      [52] *Ibid.*, p. 45.

than her action in the Dominican Republic during the previous administration. But it was a logical extension of Theodore Roosevelt's
policy: achieving stability as a corollary to furthering United States
economic and strategic interests in Central America. The facts that
Secretary of State Knox had once been counsel to the corporation which
owned the United States–Nicaragua Concession, and that Adolfo
Díaz was a former secretary of the company,[53] led to allegations that
the United States government was actually involved in bringing about
the revolt against Zelaya. Moreover, American officials on the spot
were friendly to the dictator's enemies, and Huntington Wilson 'openly
sympathized with the revolution from the start'. According to Dana
Munro, however, 'A careful study of the files . . . makes it seem doubtful that the State Department at Washington had any connection with
the revolution in its earlier stages.'[54] But the United States government
made no secret of its general support of its citizens and their property
in situations of this kind, and actions such as the interposition of
warships in a civil conflict threatening both were commonplace among
great powers in their dealings with small—especially non-European—
ones. What is unchallengeable is that the United States intervened in
Nicaragua to maintain in power a government which did not enjoy the
support of the Nicaraguan people. The Liberals were the acknowledged
majority party, and the United States had bent her efforts to keeping
them out of office. Munro himself has observed: 'In Nicaragua, the
continued presence of the legation guard was interpreted to mean that
no revolution would be tolerated. This meant that the conservatives
would stay in power, though everyone, including the State Department, knew that they were a minority party.'[55] The maintenance of a
minority, puppet, government was inconsistent with the principles
professed by the United States in her Caribbean policy. But it was
perfectly consistent with the pursuit of her interests as she saw them,
both in the Caribbean region and in Latin America as a whole.

    Nowhere in the history of United States policy towards Latin
America is the gap between professed principles and actual performance
more pronounced than during the administrations of Woodrow
Wilson; nowhere is what Professor Van Alstyne called 'a strong
pharisaical flavour about American diplomacy'[56] so clearly in evidence.
Wilson was much given to pious statements about promoting con-

---

[53] Bemis, *The Latin American Policy of the United States, op. cit.,* pp. 162–3.
[54] *Op. cit.,* p. 174.          [55] *Ibid., p.* 216.          [56] See above, p. 9.

stitutional government and curbing economic exploitation in Latin America, especially during the early part of his presidency. In his famous speech at Mobile, Alabama, on 27 October 1913, for example, Wilson declared that:

> The future ... is going to be very different for this hemisphere from the past ... the Latin American States ... have had harder bargains driven with them in the matter of loans than any other peoples in the world. Interest has been exacted of them that was not exacted of anybody else, because the risk was said to be greater; and then securities were taken that destroyed the risk—an admirable arrangement for those who were forcing the terms! I rejoice in nothing so much as in the prospect that they will now be emancipated from these conditions, and we ought to be the first to take part in assisting in that emancipation... We must show ourselves friends by comprehending their interest whether it squares with our own interest or not.[57]

Like other United States leaders before him, Wilson said the United States 'will never again seek one additional foot of territory by conquest'.

But, as a British political scientist has observed, Wilson 'had all the customary notions of his day about patriotism, racial superiority, and the duty of the great powers to act as policemen which in recent times historians have, rather unfairly, attempted to shuffle off onto Theodore Roosevelt'.[58] And 'In his desire for a moral world, with the United States in the van of the army of morality, Wilson was indeed not so far removed from Taft as he liked to think.'[59] The truth is that Wilson's policies were based upon the same assumptions as were those of his predecessors, for all his denunciation of them. It is revealing that, in an unpublished paper written in 1907, Wilson had declared:

> Since trade ignores national boundaries and the manufacturer insists on having the world as a market, the flag of his nation must follow him, and the doors of the nations which are closed against him must be battered down. Concessions obtained by financiers must be safeguarded by ministers of state, even if the sovereignty of unwilling nations be outraged in the process. Colonies must be obtained or planted, in order that no useful corner of the world may be overlooked or left unused....[60]

---

[57] Gantenbein, *The Evolution of our Latin-American Policy, op. cit.*, pp. 97–8.
[58] Calvert, *op. cit.*, p. 298.   [59] *Ibid.*, p. 303.
[60] Van Alstyne, *The Rising American Empire, op. cit.*, p. 201.

These were the sentiments of the apostles of American expansion at the end of the nineteenth century, and are, in part, suggestive of Calvin Coolidge's famous remarks in 1927.[61] Woodrow Wilson's policies towards Latin America conformed more closely to the sentiments expressed in this paper than those professed in his Mobile speech. In any case, as we shall see, the practical result of those policies was a considerable strengthening of United States control of the Caribbean region in terms of both her strategic interests and her investments; and not freedom from economic exploitation nor a greater enjoyment of constitutional government for the Latin Americans.

When he took office in March 1913 President Wilson's most immediate problem in Latin America was the situation in Mexico. The dictatorship of Porfirio Díaz had been overthrown two years earlier, and the revolutionary struggle was still under way. Díaz had given lavish concessions to United States citizens and other foreigners, and had maintained a degree of stability in Mexico which had won him high praise in Washington. Secretary of State Elihu Root once said of Díaz:

> If I were a poet I should write eulogies; if I were a musician I should compose triumphal marches; if I were a Mexican I should feel that the steadfast loyalty of a lifetime would not be too much to give in return for the blessings he has brought to my country. But as I am neither poet, musician, nor Mexican, but only an American who loves justice and liberty, and hopes to see their reign among mankind progress and strengthen and become perpetual, I look to Porfirio Díaz, the President of Mexico, as one of the great men to be held up for the hero worship of mankind![62]

As Professor Bemis observed, 'This was laying it on a bit thick.'[63] But there was no doubt that Díaz's dictatorship for long served the interests of the United States. By the same token it did not serve the interests of the mass of Mexican people. At the time of the revolution, as we noted earlier,[64] nearly one-half of Mexico's total national wealth was owned by foreigners, and vast numbers of Mexicans were landless. In the last years of his rule, however, Díaz became concerned over the extent to which United States economic and financial interests dominated Mexico, and pursued a less favourable policy towards them.

---

[61] See below, p. 149.

[62] Quoted in Lesley Bird Simpson, *Many Mexicos* (revised, paperback edn., Berkeley and Los Angeles, University of California Press, 1967), p. 292.

[63] *The Latin American Policy of the United States, op. cit.*, p. 170.

[64] See above, p. 33.

Relations with the United States became cooler, and the dictator's enemies began to plot more freely against him on North American soil.

Porfirio Díaz was overthrown by Francisco Madero in 1911, but that was only the beginning of the struggle for power among the Mexican revolutionaries. The Taft administration recognised Madero in November of that year, but the United States Ambassador in Mexico, Henry Lane Wilson, 'a strong-minded, aggressive representative of American business',[65] developed a strong personal antipathy towards the new President and went to extreme lengths to discredit him and his government. In Howard Cline's words, 'Carried away by his own feelings, Wilson apparently ventured into murkier corners of Mexican politics to achieve his end. It was a personal vendetta rather than a national policy that he was pursuing, as the documents reveal.'[66] Wilson's role caused a great deal of bitterness in Mexico and controversy in the United States. 'Every United States ambassador since his day', says Cline, 'has lived in the shadow of Wilson's actions during the first stages of the Revolution.'[67] Madero had troubles enough even without the United States Ambassador's personal vendetta. His essentially political programme was no answer to Mexico's urgent economic and social problems: no answer to people crying out for land and bread. He was also faced with the mounting claims of foreigners for damages caused in the general strife. But Henry Lane Wilson did his best to undermine Madero's position. When Victoriano Huerta, his commanding general, treacherously captured the President and took office himself, Wilson at once lobbied the other foreign diplomats in Mexico City to give him their support. To round off his considerable part in the affair, Wilson had the gall to refuse to intercede with Huerta for Madero's life when Sra. Madero begged him to do so—on the grounds that this would be meddling in Mexico's internal affairs.[68] Madero was duly murdered: 'shot inadvertently during an attempt to rescue him'.

Ambassador Wilson strongly urged immediate United States recognition of Huerta, but President Taft had not accorded this before he left office in March 1913. Thus the problem was left for Woodrow

---

[65] Howard F. Cline, *The United States and Mexico* (revised, paperback edn., New York, 1963), p. 130. Henry Lane Wilson had connections with the Guggenheim copper interests, which a few years earlier had been in conflict with those of the Madero family; Huntington Wilson, the Assistant Secretary of State, also had such connections. See Calvert, *op. cit.*, pp. 38–40.  [66] Cline, *loc. cit.*

[67] *Ibid., loc. cit.*  [68] *Ibid.*, p. 133.

Wilson. The new President, in the first flush of moral fervour (to teach Latin Americans to elect good men), decided that he would not recognise Huerta and was determined to bring about his downfall. Woodrow Wilson's attitude bears interesting comparison with Henry Lane Wilson's personal animus towards Madero. In view of his warm support of the man the President was seeking to overthrow, Henry Lane Wilson had to be replaced. Meanwhile, Woodrow Wilson sent several personal emissaries to Mexico to report on the situation; their ignorance of Mexico sometimes matched the President's own. Woodrow Wilson tried to get the support of interested European powers in bringing pressure to bear upon Huerta to resign, but this did not achieve the desired result. He therefore decided to facilitate the passage of arms supplies to Huerta's opponents, the Constitutionalists, led by Venustiano Carranza and Pancho Villa. United States warships patrolled the Mexican coast ready to impose a blockade. Then there occurred the incident which led to United States armed intervention.

In April 1914 some sailors from a United States warship who had gone ashore at the Mexican port of Tampico were arrested by members of Huerta's forces. Although they were soon released, the United States Admiral Mayo demanded a formal apology and salute to his country's flag. These demands, Huerta refused—not surprisingly in view of the trivial nature of the incident and the humiliation (both national and personal) which compliance would have involved. President Wilson strongly supported Admiral Mayo and asked Congress to approve the use of force to secure respect for the United States and her rights. To the United States President it was an affair of honour as well as a good opportunity to strike at Huerta. There was delay in obtaining congressional approval because opponents of the President's policy in the Senate wanted to use force on a wider basis to protect the lives and property of United States citizens. In the event, Woodrow Wilson went ahead without congressional approval, which was eventually given to a *fait accompli*. He decided to occupy Vera Cruz rather than Tampico, on the grounds that there was an arms shipment for Huerta's forces shortly to be unloaded there. On 21 April 1914 Vera Cruz was shelled and occupied. This action has been described by Professor Mecham as 'an arrogant and brutal exercise of power, its evils compounded because it all seemed directed to no clear-cut objective'.[69] Wilson claimed to be directing this action

---

[69] *A Survey of United States–Latin American Relations, op. cit.,* p. 358.

against Huerta and not the Mexican people, and professed to be shocked at the heavy casualties. If he really believed the Mexican people would offer no resistance and even welcome United States forces he must have been either excessively naive and ill-informed or a master of self-deception. In the preface to his study of the affair, Robert Quirk comments on Mexican feeling over the Vera Cruz intervention as compared with the war of 1846:

> To the Mexicans, Manifest Destiny was a harsh policy, but one which sprang from realistic and understandable motives. Wilson, however, clothed American aggression with the sanctimonious raiment of idealism. In insisting upon the morality of his acts, he aroused both the hatred and the scorn of the Mexicans—hatred over the invasion but a deep scorn for what they saw as his hypocrisy.[70]

The occupation of Vera Cruz was only the first phase of Wilson's involvement in Mexico.

Huerta was not initially weakened by the occupation. On the contrary, he gained support as the defender of Mexican independence against United States aggression. So Wilson was glad to accept an offer of mediation from Argentina, Brazil and Chile which led to a conference being held at Niagara Falls, Ontario, in May–June 1914. Wilson's acceptance of Latin American co-operation on this occasion is described by Bemis as 'an unchallengeable earnest of Wilson's sincerity. It was a further long step toward the Pan American peace structure of our own days.'[71] But Wilson was seeking an endorsement of his own policies, which he had no intention of changing. As Howard Cline comments, 'The Conference was a successful propaganda device: it seemingly showed the world that Wilson was willing to listen to reason and to consult Latin America, but in fact he kept control and would not compromise.' As for the place of the conference in the development of Pan Americanism, Cline declares: 'Those who glibly write about Wilson's fathering of the Pan-American movement at the Niagara Conference have not looked at the record.'[72] It must be observed, however, that from the United States point of view this has been precisely the main purpose of Pan Americanism: to secure

---

[70] Robert E. Quirk, *An Affair of Honor: Woodrow Wilson and the Occupation of Veracruz* (Lexington, University of Kentucky Press, 1962), pp. v–vi.
[71] *The Latin American Policy of the United States, op. cit.*, p. 179.
[72] *The United States and Mexico, op. cit.*, pp. 161–2.

hemispheric support for her own policies. Although the Niagara conference did not resolve the Mexican situation, Huerta's position was now weakening. United States control of the customs at Vera Cruz was a significant factor in bringing this about. Huerta resigned and left the country in July 1914. In August Mexico City surrendered to the Constitutionalists, and in the following November the United States withdrew from Vera Cruz.

The fall of Huerta was followed by conflict between Carranza and Villa, with Emiliano Zapata, the peasant leader, also opposing Carranza in the southern part of the country. Pancho Villa, angered by Wilson's recognition of Carranza in October 1915, committed a number of outrages against United States citizens first in northern Mexico and then across the frontier on United States territory. Wilson was under great domestic pressure to intervene in Mexico to punish Villa. A large expeditionary force was assembled under General John Pershing, but Wilson wanted to obtain Carranza's agreement to its entering Mexican territory. A protocol was signed, formally giving to each country the right to pursue bandits in the other's territory. However, it had not been ratified before the Punitive Expedition crossed into Mexico in March 1916, and the scale of the operation alarmed Carranza. In less than a month General Pershing's troops were three hundred miles into Mexican territory without capturing Villa. Carranza had never agreed to the expedition, and Mexican opinion was so hostile to it that his position would be undermined if he did not compel its withdrawal. At the same time, Wilson, for comparable domestic reasons in a presidential election year, could not withdraw Pershing's forces. There were a number of clashes between United States and Mexican forces which almost brought war. Fortunately, this was averted: an important factor in preventing it was the deteriorating situation in Europe, where the First World War was in progress and in relation to which United States neutrality was becoming increasingly precarious. When Carranza suggested negotiations to end tensions between the two countries Wilson welcomed it and a Joint High Commission was set up. The main problem was that the Mexicans demanded immediate withdrawal of the expeditionary force while the United States insisted upon certain guarantees. When a protocol was signed for conditional withdrawal Carranza rejected it. But the holding of negotiations had cooled the situation and averted war; for Wilson they had blunted the criticism of his opponents in the election campaign. With United States involvement in the European war imminent her troops began to withdraw from Mexico at the end of January 1917. A month later the famous Zimmermann telegram came to light, with its proposal of a Mexican alliance with Germany and Japan to regain the territories taken from Mexico by the United States. It caused momentary embarrassment. But vastly more important for future relations between Mexico and the United States was the promulgation of a new Mexican constitution in February 1917—as we shall see in the next chapter.

By the time Wilson had extricated the United States from Mexico he had already intervened in a number of Caribbean countries, extending previous interventions in the Dominican Republic and Nicaragua, and initiating a third, in Haiti. In the case of the Dominican Republic the treaty of 1907 had not produced stability, and in 1911 the President was assassinated. In 1914 Woodrow Wilson, who believed the United States possessed the right to ensure orderly, constitutional government in the Dominican Republic, sent commissioners to Santo Domingo to supervise elections. When his administration tried to extend its controls over the country's financial affairs there was strong opposition from the Dominican Congress, and the new President's position became untenable. Although the latter did not request such action, United States marines were sent in to his assistance in May 1916; whereupon he resigned and left the country. When a new provisional President was elected by the Dominican Congress, the United States made recognition contingent upon his acceptance of a treaty embodying the enlarged financial controls and also the establishment of a Dominican constabulary under United States officers. And when the President would not accept these demands in full, the United States stopped payment of all revenues to the Dominican government, which meant that no government salaries could be paid.

It is noteworthy that until May 1915 the United States was represented in Santo Domingo by a minister, James M. Sullivan (a political appointee), who, long before his dismissal, was shown to be unfit for a diplomatic post.[73] A subsequent investigation not only confirmed this:

It also showed that his appointment had been brought about by persons who had interests in the Dominican Republic and that these persons had

---

[73] Professor Link has described this as 'one of the most disgraceful chapters in the history of the American foreign service'. (Arthur S. Link, *Woodrow Wilson and the Progressive Era, 1910–1917*, New York, 1954, p. 97.)

profited financially by their relationship to him. There was no clear evidence that Sullivan himself had taken graft, but he had attempted in improper ways to use his official position to help friends and relatives, and his relations with the Banco Nacional, which he often used as a downtown office, had given rise to deserved criticism.

In Dana Munro's judgement, 'It is extraordinary that the American government should have attempted for several months to deal with so potentially dangerous a situation through a representative who was completely discredited.'[74] But Sullivan was only one of a number of unfortunate appointments to the Caribbean area at this time.[75]

The crisis in Santo Domingo came to a head in November 1916 when the Dominican President called for congressional elections. Convinced that such elections would result in an anti-United States, pro-German government, the Wilson administration ordered a military occupation. It was accompanied by an immediate censorship 'considered necessary not only to prevent the newspapers from inciting the public to resistance but also to check the activities of the recently formed National Press Association, which was endeavoring to present the Dominican point of view in other Latin American countries'.[76] The United States Minister in Santo Domingo (Sullivan's successor) reported in December 1916 that the occupation had been generally accepted except by 'disappointed petty politicians'. He recommended the continuation of military government for at least a year while needed reforms were formulated with the help of 'patriotic Dominicans'. Then there should be a period of control by a junta made up of the 'best native element' to prepare for elections. The State Department concurred generally with the Minister's views.[77] But the occupation was to last very much longer than a year and 'patriotic Dominicans' willing to collaborate with the occupying forces were not forthcoming. Nevertheless, in Professor Bemis's view the occupation was a success:

> The material and moral benefit resulting to the Dominicans from this encroachment upon their sovereignty ... was indubitable. ... It would seem that the long occupation, and the educational and economic improvement flowing from it without any exploitation of the island by the

[74] *Intervention and Dollar Diplomacy in the Caribbean, 1900–1921,. op cit.,* p. 301.
[75] See above, p. 123.
[76] Munro, *op. cit.,* p. 315.                          [77] *Ibid.*

United States and its nationals, has had a certain proven therapeutic effect on political stability. In recent years, after this timely tutelage, the Dominican Republic has been 'running on its own' very successfully.[78]

In fact, of course, the United States occupation led to the establishment of one of the worst dictatorships in the history of Latin America: that of Trujillo, from which the Dominican Republic has not yet recovered.[79]

In Nicaragua, as we saw, United States intervention during the Taft administration had effectively prevented the majority (Liberal) party from coming to power. Woodrow Wilson not only continued to support a blatantly unrepresentative government in Nicaragua. His administration concluded a new treaty with it, tightening the United States grip upon the country and infringing the rights of Nicaragua's small neighbours. This was the Bryan–Chamorro treaty of 1914 (named after Wilson's first Secretary of State, William Jennings Bryan, and the Nicaraguan Minister in Washington, Emiliano Chamorro). Under its terms the United States received perpetual and exclusive rights to construct a canal through Nicaraguan territory; and ninety-nine year leases (renewable for a further ninety-nine years) on the Great and Little Corn Islands in the Caribbean, and on a site for a naval base on the Gulf of Fonseca.[80] Unlike a similar treaty signed during the last months of the Taft administration, the Bryan–Chamorro Treaty was eventually ratified by the Senate. Costa Rica and El Salvador complained to the Central American Court of Justice[81] that their rights had been violated by this treaty. The Court found in their favour: that the rights of Costa Rica in the San Juan River boundary had been violated; and that the establishment of a United States base in the Gulf of Fonseca would threaten the security of El Salvador and violate her rights of condominium in the Gulf. Nicaragua, with the support of the Wilson administration, refused to accept the Court's decision. The Court did not long survive this

---

[78] *The Latin American Policy of the United States, op. cit.*, p. 191.

[79] Bemis makes no reference to Trujillo in his work cited above. At least I have found none, and Trujillo's name does not appear in the index. Nor is there an entry for the Nicaraguan dictator, Anastasio Somoza, whose rise to power was also a consequence of United States occupation and the establishment of a national guard. Bemis, typically, does condemn Sandino, however. See below, p. 151, n. 6.

[80] The Bryan–Chamorro Treaty was terminated in 1971.

[81] This court was established by the General Treaty of Peace and Amity signed by the Central American republics at the Washington conference in 1907. See above, p. 129.

set-back; it was dissolved in 1918. Wilson's concern with United States strategic interests was also shown by his purchase of the Danish West Indies (the Virgin Islands) in 1916 under threat of seizure.[82] In that year, with United States support, Chamorro was elected President of Nicaragua.

Haiti was the next Caribbean country to experience United States intervention. She had long been unstable and in financial difficulties. When in 1914 Germany and France proposed international control of Haiti's affairs, the United States pressed the Haitian government to accept a treaty with her comparable with the Platt Amendment. This Haiti refused to do. When disorders broke out in 1915 United States marines were sent in to establish order: this involved the latter's killing nearly two thousand Haitians.[83] A recent study has judged that 'the Marines probably caused more devastation and loss of life than had ten prior civil wars . . .'[84] Against this background, a treaty was concluded giving the United States full control of Haiti's affairs. A new constitution was imposed upon the Haitians, the authorship of which was claimed by Wilson's Assistant Secretary of the Navy, Franklin D. Roosevelt.[85] Among its provisions was the removal of the prohibition against foreign land ownership.[86] The concern which Wilson had expressed in his Mobile speech over economic exploitation in Latin America proved in practice to mean concern over European economic influence in the region. His administrations vigorously supported United States economic penetration, especially in the Caribbean region. In Haiti, as in the Dominican Republic and Nicaragua—as well as in Cuba and Panama—there was little in the occupation policy to encourage 'the election of good men': rather the reverse. What the United States wanted was compliant men who would collaborate in promoting her interests. In Haiti, especially, racial prejudice on the part of the occupying forces aggravated the resentment aroused by the occupation.[87]

Thus, when the United States entered the First World War her

---

[82] See above, p. 21.

[83] Whitaker, *The Western Hemisphere Idea, op. cit.*, p. 127.

[84] Robert I. Rotberg, *Haiti: The Politics of Squalor* (Boston, Mass., 1971), pp. 122–3.

[85] Rotberg dismisses Roosevelt's claim as 'exaggerated': *ibid.*, p. 124, n. 27.

[86] See above, p. 111. n. 8.

[87] But in Bemis's judgement the United States occupation of Haiti was a success. For he writes (*The Latin American Policy of the States, op. cit.*, p. 193): 'Of the military occupation, which did not end until 1934, and the protectorate the same may be said as that of the Dominican Republic.' See above, p. 140–1.

relations with Latin America had not been transformed as President Wilson's early speeches had promised. There had been the occupation of Vera Cruz, the Pershing expedition against Pancho Villa, and the occupations of the Dominican Republic, Nicaragua and Haiti by United States marines. Latin American participation in the war was very limited. Eight countries declared war on Germany, but only Brazil and Cuba played anything approaching an active part. Although five others severed diplomatic relations with Germany, the remaining neutrals included such important countries as Argentina, Chile and Mexico. It is perhaps worth noting that there was held in Washington in May 1915 the First Pan American Financial Conference, attended by representatives of all the American republics except Mexico and Haiti. Called by the government of the United States, its main purpose was to discuss economic and financial problems arising out of the state of war then existing in Europe.

In consequence of the First World War the position of Latin America relative to the United States was even further weakened. Hitherto, although United States economic penetration of the Caribbean region had been very considerable, South America's foreign trade was still largely with Great Britain and Germany. The First World War and the post-war depression in Europe enabled the United States to change this situation so that she acquired economic as well as political ascendancy over Latin America. Thus whatever benefit the South American countries had derived from the division of influence over them between Europe and the United States was now lost. Truly, 'At the end of World War I, the United States found itself in an unprecedented position in its relations with the twenty countries of Latin America.'[88] This obviously would exacerbate the essentially 'great power–small powers' relationship between the United States and Latin America.

The division between them was underlined by the emergence from the First World War of the League of Nations. For all the Latin American countries were at some time members of the League, while the United States declined to join. By their adherence to the League the Latin American countries were registering a protest against the United States conception of an exclusive inter-American system supporting the Monroe Doctrine. Moreover, membership of the League of Nations enhanced the stature of Latin American countries

---

[88] Wood, *The Making of the Good Neighbor Policy, op. cit.,* p. 3.

F

in international affairs and made them less ready to accept United
States tutelage. Within the League the Latin Americans felt less
inferior than in the United States-dominated inter-American conferences. They even entertained hopes that the League might offer some
leverage against the United States which hitherto they had lacked.
At the same time—and quite naturally—the very reasons which made
the League attractive to Latin Americans aroused hostility among
influential elements in the United States. The latter were opposed to
both increased United States involvement in Europe and any limita-
tion of the Monroe Doctrine as assuring United States hegemony in
the western hemisphere.

In a vain attempt to make it acceptable to these elements, Article 21
was written into the League Covenant: 'Nothing in this Covenant
shall be deemed to affect the validity of international engagements
such as treaties of arbitration or regional understandings like the
Monroe Doctrine, for securing the maintenance of peace.' This
reference to the Doctrine is highly ambiguous, for the Monroe
Doctrine was not a 'regional understanding', whatever that term might
mean. It is not surprising that the United States Senate proposed the
following very specific reservation to Article 21:

> The United States will not submit to arbitration or to inquiry by the
> assembly or by the Council of the League of Nations, provided for in said
> treaty of peace, any questions which in the judgment of the United
> States depend upon or relate to its long established policy commonly
> known as the Monroe Doctrine; said doctrine is to be interpreted by the
> United States alone and is hereby declared to be wholly outside the juris-
> diction of said League of Nations and entirely unaffected by any provision
> contained in the said treaty of peace with Germany.

If Article 21 proved unsatisfactory to the United States Senate, it was
profoundly disturbing to Latin America. Argentina and Mexico
stated in adhering to the League of Nations Covenant that they did
not recognise the Monroe Doctrine as a regional understanding. El
Salvador sent a note to the State Department on 14 December 1919
pointing out that Article 21 had 'awakened warm discussions throughout the whole American Continent, due no doubt to its brevity and
lack of clearness', and requesting 'the authentic interpretation of the
Monroe Doctrine as it is understood in the present historical moment
and in its future application by the Government of the United States'.
The reply was far from satisfactory. Obviously, the League of Nations

offered little by way of a counterpoise to the United States in the western hemisphere.

So, after the First World War, the United States enjoyed an unprecedented position of strength relative to her Latin American neighbours. No non-American power nor the newly formed League of Nations could challenge the Monroe Doctrine. How would this affect United States policy towards the countries of Latin America? From the time of President Monroe's Message of 1823 onwards United States leaders had always claimed fear of extra-continental intervention as justification of their own interventions: had affirmed that they were acting to forestall the machinations of non-American powers. In recent years the Wilson administration, which had intervened more frequently than had any of its predecessors in the Caribbean region, had justified its interventions, above all, in terms of the need to frustrate German designs. Now that the United States possessed a commanding position in the western hemisphere a policy euphemistically described as 'protective imperialism' could not seriously be justified in such terms. Latin Americans, for whom fear of extra-continental intervention had already been replaced by fear of the United States and her claims under the Monroe Doctrine, were likely to grow more restive in the face of continued United States intervention. There would be growing demands for United States acceptance of non-intervention as a principle of her relations with Latin America.

# 5 Good Neighbours and Wartime Partners

The First World War, as we noted at the end of the previous chapter, confirmed and extended United States hegemony in Latin America: her position relative to her neighbours was unprecedentedly strong, and she was unchallenged by any external power. The United States could therefore afford to modify her Latin American policy, especially since its main proclaimed objective had been to prevent extra-continental intervention in the western hemisphere. Certainly, there was no longer any justification for employing the marines to forestall European interventions in the Caribbean region. Yet it was some years before the United States began seriously to contemplate changing her policy. In this chapter we will consider the factors that brought about a reappraisal and the extent to which it transformed relations between the United States and Latin America. How far did the American states become genuinely good neighbours and—in due course—effective wartime partners?

It is not difficult to understand United States complacency in her relations with Latin America. Although she always gave prominence to the argument that her security was threatened, this was not the only justification for the use of force against her small neighbours. Her interventions were justified in terms of treaty obligations (for she enjoyed rights of intervention by treaty in certain cases), a duty to protect the lives and property of her citizens, to maintain order, and to promote good government. Moreover, especially in the previous decade, the marines had been used so frequently as to seem, to the United States, part of the natural order of things. As Bryce Wood has well expressed it:

> It should not be surprising that a certain sense of the normality, and even the propriety of calling on the Marines, should have persisted beyond 1920, independently of the nature of the formal justification for such action;

it was an habitual, nearly automatic response to 'disturbed conditions' or 'utter chaos' in a Caribbean country.[1]

What apparently did not seem 'normal' to United States leaders was that these interventions should cause deep and increasing resentment among the peoples whose territories were being violated. They even persuaded themselves that the 'best elements' in these countries welcomed United States intervention. Even in the cases of prolonged occupation these would be temporary and the results beneficial to the peoples concerned.

The self-image of the United States, so deeply involved in her attitude towards Latin America, was to be severely challenged by developments both within and outside the hemisphere in the coming decades. The most immediate challenge came from the Mexican revolution, in which, as we saw, Woodrow Wilson had been much involved, especially during his first administration. In 1917 Mexico received a new constitution which had very far-reaching implications for United States interests in the country. Especially ominous was article 27, stating that ownership of surface lands did not convey the right to subsoil resources, which were vested in the state and could be exploited only through specific concessions. Mexican citizens and companies alone should acquire ownership of lands and waters or obtain concessions to exploit mines or petroleum deposits. Aliens might be exempted from this restriction if they undertook not to seek diplomatic protection from their own governments (the Calvo Clause[2]); but under no circumstances could they acquire ownership of lands or waters within a zone extending one hundred kilometres from Mexico's frontiers or within fifty kilometres from her coasts. There would be land redistribution involving the division of the large landed estates. Article 27 was to be the main source of dispute between Mexico and the United States. But article 123 dealing with labour legislation importantly affected alien employers; and articles 3 and 130, concerned with religious and educational reforms, aroused Catholic hostility in the United States.

Robert Lansing (who succeeded Bryan as Wilson's Secretary of State in 1915) protested against article 27 and asked for assurances that it would not be applied retroactively against United States oil

---

[1] *The Making of the Good Neighbor Policy, op. cit.*, p. 5.
[2] See above, p. 111.

companies. Carranza gave the United States Ambassador private assurances which did not prove satisfactory and in any case the Constitutionalist President's own position was weakening rapidly. In 1920 Carranza was overthrown by General Alvaro Obregón, and later shot while trying to flee the country. After a short interim period Obregón was elected President by an overwhelming vote. He was not recognised by the United States for over two years, however, because he refused to sign, as a condition of such recognition, a treaty guaranteeing North American property rights acquired in Mexico prior to the new constitution. The United States also demanded other guarantees in respect of her citizens' claims against the Mexican government. Eventually, Obregón, still refusing to sign a formal treaty on the main issue, concluded what came to be called the Bucareli Agreements under which, broadly speaking, the United States companies were exempted from retroactive application of article 27. On the strength of these agreements Obregón was granted recognition by the United States in August 1923.

Obregón had not been recognised, however, when the Fifth International Conference of American States met in Santiago de Chile from 25 March until 3 May 1923. Mexico, therefore, refused to participate because, her government not being recognised by the United States, she had been deprived of representation on the Governing Board of the Pan American Union, which had approved the conference's programme. The programme contained a large number of political items, indicating that the Latin Americans were no longer content to confine the agenda to innocuous subjects upon which harmony was assured. During the conference a bitter attack on the Monroe Doctrine was made by Colombia, and a number of other delegates took the opportunity to ask for it to be defined. They were rewarded only with a statement by the head of the United States delegation that his country regarded it as 'original and essentially national'. The unilateral character of the Doctrine and United States determination not to 'Pan Americanise' it were strongly underlined later in the same year by Secretary of State Charles Evans Hughes when he said: 'as the policy embodied in the Monroe Doctrine is distinctively the policy of the United States, the government of the United States reserves to itself its definition, interpretation, and application'.

The Latin Americans had some success in modifying the organisation of the Pan American Union. With its seat in Washington, its membership limited to their diplomatic representatives there, and its chairman the Secretary of State, the Governing Board of the Pan American Union did indeed resemble a colonial office—as its critics have so often labelled it. It was agreed that henceforth any American state whose government was not recognised by the United States, and who therefore had no Ambassador in Washington, should make a special appointment to the Governing Board. For 'the Governments of the American Republics enjoy, as of right, representation at the International Conferences of American States and in the Pan American Union'. The chairmanship of the Board would henceforth in principle be elective; but invariably the Secretary of State was formally elected to that position. A noteworthy achievement of the Fifth International Conference was the Treaty to Avoid or Prevent Conflicts between the American States, usually known as the Gondra Treaty,[3] which marks a first, though limited, step towards setting up effective inter-American peace machinery.

By the time that the Sixth International Conference was held in 1928 the intervention issue had become much more bitter. Under the aegis of the Monroe Doctrine the United States was using her political hegemony to safeguard and augment her growing economic interests in the western hemisphere, and her economic power to promote political ends. The political instability of the countries of the Caribbean region, together with their economic and strategic importance and geographical proximity to the United States, made them particularly vulnerable to 'protective imperialism'. In the absence of any real external threat to the security of the hemisphere it was only too clearly the interests of the United States which were to be protected—against any unfavourable circumstances arising within the Latin American countries. On 25 April 1927 President Calvin Coolidge made the speech in which he declared: 'it is . . . well established that our Government has certain rights over and certain duties toward our own citizens and their property, wherever they may be located. The person and property of a citizen are a part of the general domain of the nation, even when abroad.' The insistence of the United States on what she maintained was her right of intervention under international law—a right possessed equally by the European powers, but which she forbade them to exercise in the western hemisphere—and

---

[3] Named after Dr. Manuel Gondra, head of the Paraguayan delegation, who proposed it.

her only too frequent exercise of this 'right' in the Caribbean region caused increasing resentment. The Latin Americans began to press her to relinquish this right and accept the principle of non-intervention in her relations with them.

United States intervention in Nicaragua in 1926 was instrumental in bringing the issue to a head. As we saw in the previous chapter, the United States had occupied Nicaragua during the Taft and Wilson administrations to maintain in power unrepresentative Conservative governments serving her interests. The Coolidge administration, believing the situation to be stabilised, decided to withdraw the marines and this was effected by August 1925. But civil conflict broke out again, and once more the marines were sent in. It seemed almost a routine affair, but proved to be far otherwise. This new intervention possessed certain features which produced a deep crisis where others had not done so. In the first place, United States motives for intervening were only too obviously political; secondly, although the intervention was confined to Nicaragua, the involvement was intimately related to a quarrel with Mexico; thirdly, the difficulties experienced by the United States in carrying out her wider objectives prolonged the period of intervention. This in turn brought mounting criticism in the United States and, significantly, concern to the State Department, for there were international repercussions outside the hemisphere.

When civil conflict broke out in Nicaragua in 1926 relations between the United States and Mexico were already strained because of the Mexican government's plans to expropriate foreign-owned land. These plans, and a campaign to restrict the activities of the Mexican clergy, aroused strong feelings in the United States. Moreover, Mexican support for the Liberals in Nicaragua was interpreted as part of a plan to dominate Central America. United States accusations of Mexican designs in Nicaragua may not have been unfounded, but, from Mexico's point of view, she had as much right to be interested in that country as had the United States. It must be noted that but for the latter, Central America would have fallen into Mexico's sphere of influence. As we have seen, it had been a part of Iturbide's empire.[4] We saw that Porfirio Díaz co-operated with the United States in calling the Washington conference on Central America in 1907.[5]

---

4 See above, p. 55, n. 25.
5 See above, p. 129.

Mexican co-operation broke down, however, when it became evident that the United States was bent upon controlling the region.

North American interests affected by the Mexican revolutionary government's policies denounced these as 'Bolshevism', and early in 1927 the United States government joined in the denunciation. Secretary of State Frank Kellogg presented a memorandum to the Senate Committee on Foreign Relations entitled 'Bolshevist Aims and Policies in Mexico and Latin America'. For a short time war with Mexico seemed possible, but this possibility provoked such concern in the United States that the Coolidge administration was compelled to adopt a less threatening attitude. In the autumn Dwight Morrow, a corporation lawyer, was sent as Ambassador to Mexico with a conciliatory brief. However, the civil war continued in Nicaragua, where United States prestige demanded that the Conservative government should not be overthrown by the Liberals (favoured by Mexico). President Coolidge sent Henry L. Stimson as his special representative to Nicaragua for the purpose of obtaining a settlement satisfactory to the United States. Such a settlement involved defeating Augusto C. Sandino, labelled by the United States a 'bandit', but widely regarded in Latin America (and elsewhere in the world) as a patriot.[6] In the light of more recent events, Sandino has been credited with having 'opened a new chapter in inter-American relations by taking to the hills and successfully eluding his United States pursuers for several years, thus becoming the first in a long line of Latin American revolutionary guerrilla leaders stretching all the way to "Che" Guevara and beyond'.[7] Sandino was eventually murdered. According to the United States Minister in Nicaragua at the time, the man responsible was Anastasio Somoza, commander of the National Guard which the United States had trained to keep order when the marines

---

[6] In Bemis's judgement (*The Latin American Policy of the United States, op. cit.*, p. 213), 'Sandino, a curse to the common man of Nicaragua, became a mythical hero to anti-Yankee polemicists in Latin America and Europe, and even to some anti-imperialist writers in the United States.' But see Joseph O. Baylen, 'Sandino: Patriot or Bandit?', *The Hispanic American Historical Review*, vol. xxxi, no. 3 (August 1951), pp. 394–419. The same author's 'American Intervention in Nicaragua, 1909–33: An Appraisal of Objectives and Results', *The Southwestern Social Science Quarterly*, vol. xxxv (September 1954), pp. 128–54, contains a wealth of bibliographical material in its footnotes as well as a useful analysis of its subject.

[7] David Green, *The Containment of Latin America: a history of the myths and realities of the Good Neighbor Policy* (Chicago, 1971), pp. 9–10.

were withdrawn.[8] Thus did the United States intervention pave the way for the Somoza dictatorship.[9]

The long and unsatisfactory involvement in Nicaragua provoked increasing criticism in the United States and questioning of the various motives which the government put forward to explain and justify it. Intervention became occupation; supervision of elections proved vastly more difficult than anticipated; guerrilla operations against alleged bandits were costly and frustrating; and protection of the lives and property of United States citizens was jeopardised by the hostility aroused by the presence of the marines. Finally, Stimson, who had become Secretary of State in the Hoover administration, announced that the marines would be withdrawn immediately after the presidential election in 1932. Meanwhile, a new element had entered into the situation. At an early stage there had been criticism in Europe and Latin America of what was described as United States imperialism. By the autumn of 1931 Stimson, opposing Japanese intervention in Manchuria, was embarrassed by the continued presence of United States marines in Nicaragua. As for landing forces in the larger Latin American countries, Stimson declared: 'If we landed a single soldier among those South Americans now . . . it would put me in absolutely wrong in China, where Japan has done all of this monstrous work under the guise of protecting her nationals with a landing force.'[10] Later on, when the United States became more involved in world affairs generally, her relations with Latin America were to be affected increasingly by broader considerations of foreign policy.

It was against a background of mounting criticism of the United States intervention in Nicaragua that the Sixth International Conference of American States was held in Havana from 16 January until 20 February 1928, with all twenty-one republics represented. The

---

[8] Wood, *The Making of the Good Neighbor Policy, op. cit.*, pp. 140–1. See below, p. 278.

[9] Educated in the United States, Somoza owed his appointment as constabulary chief at least partly to the American Minister in Managua (predecessor of the one who accused him of responsibility for Sandino's murder). According to William Kamman, *A Search for Stability: United States Diplomacy Toward Nicaragua, 1925–1933* (Notre Dame, University of Notre Dame Press, 1968), p. 210, 'he impressed Stimson; and his personality attracted Minister Hanna and his wife, the latter apparently charmed by Somoza's dancing. . . . A few weeks prior to Somoza's appointment, Hanna said of him: "I look upon him as the best man in the country for the position. I know no one who will labor as intelligently and conscientiously to maintain the non-partisan character of the Guardia, or will be as efficient in all matters connected with the administration and command of the Force." '

[10] Wood, *The Making of the Good Neighbor Policy, op. cit.*, p. 45.

United States expected trouble. In his instructions to her delegates the Secretary of State warned them that:

> The past year has seen the development of a vigorous anti-American propaganda throughout Latin America based on charges of 'imperialism and characterized by violent criticism of the relations existing between the United States and Mexico and the American policy in Nicaragua ... it is not improbable that ... certain delegates may attack the policy of the United States Government towards Latin America with special reference to its relations with Mexico, Nicaragua, Panama and Haiti.[11]

Yet on the delicate subject of intervention they were told: 'This Government could not, of course, undertake to limit or bind its action in future unknown contingencies regarding the measure of protection which it might deem it incumbent upon it to exert on behalf of American citizens and property endangered by revolution or other civil turmoil in a foreign country.'

The instructions show also that the United States feared the issue of the Monroe Doctrine was likely to be raised again, even though 'In the view of this Government, that Doctrine has no place in the discussions of the Conference as it is essentially a national policy of the United States'. They reaffirmed the quite untenable position to which the United States persisted in clinging, that the Monroe Doctrine was not incompatible with the national sovereignty of the Latin American countries. But the United States delegates were advised in relation to the Doctrine's interpretation: 'It may be observed that the United States is uninfluenced even by the willingness or desire of any American State to yield any transfer of its territory or to submit to any form of political control or influence of a non-American State.'[12] Another revealing passage reads:

> Recent efforts, which there is no occasion to criticize so long as they are kept within their proper sphere, to bring Latin American States into closer contact with non-American Powers make it important that there should be no sacrifice through such endeavors of essential American interests. There should be no yielding to the suggestion of the control or

---

[11] U.S. Dept. of State, *Papers relating to the Foreign Relations of the United States, 1928*, vol. 1 (U.S.G.P.O. Washington, 1942), pp. 534–85.

[12] This makes explicit what was implicit in President Polk's statement on the Yucatán situation in 1848. See above, pp. 80–1.

influence of non-American Powers in the settlement of political questions of a distinctively American nature, or of the establishment by non-American Powers of territorial or political rights over American territory.

With all these thorny topics apparently in the offing, the United States delegates were reminded, as their predecessors had been, that:

> It should be borne in mind that the function of these Pan American Conferences is to deal so far as possible with non-controversial subjects of general interest, upon which free and full discussion may be had with the purpose and probability of arriving at agreement and cooperation . . . you will bear in mind that the present Conference has not been called to sit in judgment on the conduct of any nation, or to attempt to redress alleged wrongs.

The United States was well aware, then, of increasing Latin American resentment and expected serious opposition at the Sixth International Conference. Therefore the Coolidge administration took steps to strengthen its position. The President himself, accompanied by Secretary of State Kellogg, journeyed to Havana to give an inaugural address; the United States fielded an impressive delegation headed by the distinguished former Secretary of State Charles Evans Hughes; and she reverted to her traditional policy of opposing the inclusion of 'political' subjects on the agenda. In the event the United States was unable to prevent discussion of controversial aspects of her Latin American policy, but Hughes and his colleagues found the opposition less formidable than they had anticipated. A basic weakness of the Latin American position was, of course, that the countries were divided among themselves and so did not present a united front. This point was made by Hughes two months after the Havana conference, when he declared there was not 'an entity known as Latin America on the one side, dealing with an entity known as the United States on the other . . . There is, properly speaking, no concert of Latin American States'.[13]

While common fear of the United States was still not strong enough to cause the Latin American republics to co-operate effectively and continuously with one another, there were individual reasons for weakness at Havana. Most of the countries of the Caribbean region were either occupied by the United States marines (Haiti and

---

[13] Toynbee, *Survey of International Affairs, 1927, op. cit.,* pp. 429–30.

Nicaragua) or enduring some form of client status which made firm opposition impossible. Cuba was negotiating for the repeal of the Platt Amendment and a reduction in the United States tariff on sugar. Chile and Peru were anxious not to offend the arbitrator of their dispute over Tacna and Arica.[14] The fact that Argentina was the leading spokesman for Latin American freedom from United States domination must have deterred Brazil and Chile, resentful of Argentine pretensions to South American leadership, from supporting the cause with warmth.

However, the issue of intervention was raised, and the debate over it has been described as 'so productive of ill feeling and bad language that the minutes of the meeting had to be re-written'.[15] During it Hughes made his well-known defence of the United States position:

> Let us face the facts. The difficulty, if there is any, in any one of the American Republics, is not of any external aggression. It is an internal difficulty, if it exists at all. From time to time there arises a situation most deplorable and regrettable in which sovereignty is not at work, in which for a time in certain areas there is no government at all. . . . What are we to do when government breaks down and American citizens are in danger of their lives? Are we to stand by and see them killed because a government in circumstances which it cannot control and for which it may not be responsible can no longer afford reasonable protection? . . . Now it is a principle of international law that in such a case a government is fully justified in taking action—I would call it interposition of a temporary character—for the purpose of protecting the lives and property of its nationals. I could say that that is not intervention. One can read in text books that that is not intervention. . . . Of course the United States cannot forego its right to protect its citizens. International law cannot be changed by the resolutions of this Conference. . . . The rights of nations remain, but nations have duties as well as rights.[16]

As Hughes presented it, the United States case was virtually unanswerable. Yet in that presentation, with its emphasis upon legal principle, the most important aspects of the intervention issue were glossed over or ignored. First, the issue was only secondarily a matter of rights under international law: primarily it was a matter of

[14] This dispute was a legacy of the War of the Pacific (see above, pp. 95–6). It had been submitted to arbitration by the President of the United States.
[15] S. G. Inman, *Building an Inter-American Neighborhood* (New York, 1937), p. 9.
[16] Quoted in Connell-Smith ,*The Inter-American System* ,*op. cit.*, p. 69.

power, for the United States alone in the western hemisphere was in a position to enjoy such rights. Secondly, it was not a simple matter of the breakdown of government; the United States had on occasion intervened either without such breakdown having taken place or with the purpose of overthrowing a government of which she did not approve. Thirdly, her 'interpositions' had not always been of a truly 'temporary character'. However, although in general Latin Americans were strongly opposed to intervention, only thirteen delegations stood out unreservedly for a specific proposal which would have prohibited it. In any case the United States was determined not to accept the proposal. With no agreement possible, therefore, it was decided to refer the matter to the Seventh International Conference. It was an immediate triumph for Hughes and the United States policy he was defending.

But by the time the Seventh Conference met Franklin Roosevelt was President and the Good Neighbour policy had been launched. The phrase 'good neighbour' was not new. On the contrary, it was a familiar cliché in international relations. Even the Treaty of Guadelupe Hidalgo, by which Mexico lost so much of her national territory to the United States, spoke of future negotiations between the two countries being conducted 'in the spirit of peace and *good neighbourship*'. Nevertheless, the phrase 'Good Neighbour policy' within the context of United States relations with Latin America is associated with Franklin Roosevelt. Since, however, it is widely considered to have been a highly successful policy—perhaps the most successful ever pursued by the United States towards Latin America— both major political parties have been anxious to claim credit for implementing it. We must therefore consider how far Roosevelt was building upon the work of his Republican predecessors.

There are a number of relevant events. The first was the conclusion by the Harding administration of a treaty of conciliation with Colombia which came into force on 1 March 1922. Woodrow Wilson had tried to conclude such a treaty, but Theodore Roosevelt's friends in the Senate had prevented its ratification on the grounds that it appeared to be an apology for an act of aggression. In 1922 Theodore Roosevelt was dead and the treaty, providing for $25 millions by way of compensation to Colombia, omitted Wilson's proposed expression of 'sincere regret'. Moreover, a major factor now was the eagerness of United States oil companies to secure concessions to exploit newly discovered oil fields in Colombia. A large majority in the Senate voted for ratification: 'Enough commercially-minded Republicans and conscious-stricken [*sic*] Democrats were mustered to defeat the Roosevelt-worshipping Republicans and the anti-Wall Street Democrats.'[17] When Colombia accepted this belated and muted act of repentance United States investments in that country rapidly multiplied. It has been said that President Coolidge's appointment of Dwight Morrow as Ambassador to Mexico marks the real beginning of the Good Neighbour policy.[18] But Herbert Hoover is generally credited with having made a much more substantial contribution.[19] While President-elect he embarked on a goodwill tour which took him to ten of the Latin American countries at the end of 1928. During his tour he stressed the good neighbour concept and repudiated that of 'big brother'. In office, Hoover took a number of steps to make good his promise.

The Hoover administration was more reluctant than its predecessors to champion the cause of private citizens with grievances against Latin American governments, and limited its action to protect them in cases of civil disturbance. Woodrow Wilson's recognition policy was abandoned as far as it had applied to Latin America as a whole, though Central America was still treated as a special case. In 1930 came the publication of the *Memorandum on the Monroe Doctrine*, which had been drawn up near the end of the Coolidge administration by Under-Secretary of State J. Reuben Clark. This document was, in effect, a repudiation of the Roosevelt Corollary, of which it declared: 'it is not believed that this corollary is justified by the terms of the Monroe Doctrine, however much it may be justified by the application of the doctrine of self-preservation'. Thus the Clark Memorandum renounced only intervention under the aegis of the Monroe Doctrine, not intervention as such. It did not make the Doctrine acceptable to its Latin American critics, who rejected the claim contained in it that 'So far as Latin America is concerned, the Doctrine is now, and always has been, not an instrument of violence and oppression, but

[17] E. Taylor Parks, *Colombia and the United States, 1765–1934* (Durham, N.C., Duke University Press, 1935: Reprint, New York, 1968), p. 456.

[18] Herbert L. Matthews (ed.), *The United States and Latin America* (2nd edn., Englewood Cliffs, N.J., 1963), p. 130. See above, p. 151.

[19] In Robert H. Ferrell's judgement, *American Diplomacy in the Great Depression: Hoover-Stimson Foreign Policy, 1929–1933* (New Haven, Yale University Press, 1957), p. 215, Latin America was Hoover's 'one area of achievement'. For a detailed analysis see Alexander DeConde, *Herbert Hoover's Latin-American Policy* (Stanford University Press 1951).

an unbought, freely bestowed, and wholly effective guaranty of their
freedom, independence, and territorial integrity against the imperialistic designs of Europe'.[20] In spite of political upheavals brought on
by unstable economic conditions, however, Hoover undertook no
new interventions in the sensitive Caribbean region. The marines
were withdrawn from Nicaragua in 1932 and plans were made in the
same year to evacuate Haiti.

But the intervention issue was not the only major cause of friction
between the United States and Latin America. More far-reaching was
the growing dissatisfaction of the Latin American countries with their
economic relationship to the United States. The world economic
depression underlined their dependence upon the export of agricultural and mineral raw materials and the extent to which their economies
were controlled by foreign (in many cases, United States) enterprises.
Economic nationalism would represent a growing challenge to the
United States. The Hoover administration did nothing positive to
alleviate Latin American distress caused by the world economic
depression. On the contrary, it presented the Latin Americans with a
new grievance in the Smoot–Hawley Act which raised the United
States tariff to the highest level in its history. The political effect of
this tariff far exceeded its impact on trade relations between the
United States and Latin America as a whole, although certain countries
were particularly affected by it. At all events, the changes which took
place in United States Latin American policy during the Hoover
administration did not evoke much sympathy south of the Rio Grande.
Only bolder, more imaginative action would persuade Latin Americans
there was a real change of attitude towards them in Washington.

Franklin D. Roosevelt eventually succeeded in convincing the
Latin Americans that such a change had taken place. Ironically, his
main experience of Latin America before becoming President was
an active part in two of Wilson's interventions.[21] However, during
the 1928 election campaign, when he ran for Governor of New York
State, Franklin Roosevelt wrote an article for *Foreign Affairs* in
which he criticised United States interventions in the Caribbean

20 Gantenbein, *The Evolution of Our Latin-American Policy, op. cit.*, pp. 406–7.

21 As Assistant Secretary of the Navy, Franklin Roosevelt had been involved in the
occupation of Vera Cruz and claimed to have written a new constitution for Haiti when
she was occupied. See above, p. 142. Roosevelt much later claimed that the Good Neighbour policy sprang from regret over the Vera Cruz affair: Wood, *The Making of the Good
Neighbor Policy, op. cit.*, p. 130.

region and demanded the renunciation 'for all time' of 'arbitrary intervention in the home affairs of our neighbours'. A passage in the article is worth quoting for the suggestion it makes of 'collective intervention':

> It is possible that in the days to come one of our sister nations may fall upon evil days; disorder and bad government may require that a helping hand be given her citizens as a matter of temporary necessity to bring back order and stability. In that event it is not the right or the duty of the United States to intervene alone. It is rather the duty of the United States to associate with itself other American Republics, to give intelligent joint study to the problem, and, if the conditions warrant, to offer the helping hand or hands in the name of the Americas. Single-handed intervention by us in the internal affairs of other nations must end; with the cooperation of others we shall have more order in this hemisphere and less dislike.[22]

Both tone and content are in striking contrast to the Roosevelt Corollary and Hughes's speech at Havana in the very year that this article was published.[23]

During the 1932 presidential campaign Roosevelt denounced the Hoover administration's tariff policy, and his subsequent appointment of Cordell Hull, a leading supporter of lower tariffs, as Secretary of State, seemed to lend substance to Latin America's hopes that it, too, might have a 'new deal'. In his inaugural address on 4 March 1933 the new President pledged the United States to pursue the policy of a good neighbour in her international relations. Roosevelt specifically applied the good neighbour concept to Latin America in a speech made during the celebration of Pan American Day on the following 12 April:

> The essential qualities of a true Pan Americanism must be the same as those which constitute a good neighbor, namely, mutual understanding and, through such understanding, a sympathetic appreciation of the other's point of view. It is only in this manner that we can hope to build up a system of which confidence, friendship, and good will are the cornerstones.[24]

But much more than fine words was necessary to convince Latin Americans that this really was the beginning of a new relationship

---

[22] Quoted in Connell-Smith, *The Inter-American System*, *op. cit.*, p. 80.
[23] See above, pp. 115, 155.                   [24] Gantenbein, *op. cit.*, p. 160.

between them and the United States. The marines were still in Haiti, although arrangements had been made for their evacuation in 1934; Haiti, the Dominican Republic and Nicaragua were still financial protectorates; the independence of Cuba and Panama was restricted by treaties in favour of the United States; the latter's recognition policy denied the Central American republics the right of revolution (though the United States did not always enforce this policy); the United States continued to insist upon the unilateral character of the Monroe Doctrine; and she still claimed the 'right of intervention' even while limiting her exercise of such a right. To these long-standing causes of grievance had been added a high tariff policy in circumstances of world economic depression. How far was the Good Neighbour prepared to go in accommodating these grievances—and the developing challenge of economic nationalism—and thus in transforming the traditional Latin American policy of the United States?

The Roosevelt administration was at once faced with something of a test case in Cuba. As we have already noted,[25] Cuba was effectively a protectorate of the United States from the moment she became nominally independent. She rapidly became an economic colony. The possibility of United States intervention—feared by some Cuban politicians, solicited by others—was an ever-present factor in Cuban politics, inhibiting the free development of parties and institutions. There had been a number of such interventions in accordance with the provisions of the Platt Amendment. When Franklin Roosevelt took office the President of Cuba was Gerardo Machado, a dictator whose policies were provoking increasing opposition. The Hoover administration, although it had feared there might be a revolution, had not intervened, thus leaving the problem for its successor. Himself anxious not to intervene openly, Roosevelt sent his Assistant Secretary of State as Ambassador to Havana to bring pressure to bear upon Machado to resign. He was Sumner Welles, generally regarded as a major architect of the Good Neighbour policy, which makes what Bryce Wood has called 'the Cuban experience'[26] the more revealing.

When Welles went to Havana in May 1933 he was recognised by all Cuban politicians as the arbiter of their situation. Machado was duly despatched into exile in August and a new President sponsored by Welles, Carlos Manuel de Céspedes, took office. But in less than

---

25 See above, pp. 102–3.
26 *The Making of the Good Neighbor Policy, op. cit.*, chs. 2 and 3.

a month Céspedes was overthrown by an army mutiny led by Sergeant Stenographer Fulgencio Batista, and Dr. Ramón Grau San Martín, a university professor, was appointed provisional President. This turn of events was a severe blow to Welles's prestige, and he was determined to bring about Grau's downfall. Soon he was urging Roosevelt to land United States troops in Cuba. Welles wanted these troops, not to protect the lives and property of his fellow-country-men, but to sustain a counter-revolution. He called this 'limited intervention' to avoid the necessity of 'full intervention'. He declared:

> The disadvantages of this policy as I see them lie solely in the fact that we will incur the violent animosity of the extreme radical and communist groups in Cuba who will be vociferous in stating that we have supported the Céspedes Government because that Government was prepared to give protection to American interests in Cuba and that our policy is solely due to mercenary motives.[27]

Welles and Adolf A. Berle, Jr., then serving temporarily under him in Havana, emphasised the instability of the Grau government and its lack of popular support; also that its continuance was prejudicial to United States commercial interests.

Although United States troops were not landed in response to Welles's requests,[28] some thirty warships of various kinds were sent to the island and its vicinity. The Roosevelt administration did not recognise the Grau government on the grounds that it had not yet proved itself representative of the will of the people and capable of maintaining law and order throughout the island. Meanwhile, Welles was conducting what he himself described as an 'anomalous' relation-ship with Batista,[29] 'that extraordinarily brilliant and able figure' as he later characterised him,[30] and encouraging him to bring to power a new government to replace Grau. Jefferson Caffery, who succeeded Welles in Havana in December, concurred with his predecessor 'as to the inefficiency, ineptitude, and unpopularity with all the better classes in the country of the *de facto* government. It is supported only by the army and ignorant masses who have been misled by utopian

---

[27] *Foreign Relations, U.S., 1933*, vol. v (U.S.G.P.O., Washington, 1952), p. 398.
[28] In his book, *The Time for Decision* (London, 1945), p. 154, Welles refers to 'innumer-able demands for American armed intervention, especially from certain people represent-ing commercial interests', but makes no mention of his own.
[29] *Foreign Relations, U.S., 1933*, vol. v, *op. cit.*, p. 472.
[30] *The Time for Decision*, *op. cit.*, *loc. cit.*

promises'.[31] The President echoed these sentiments when he referred derisively to Grau at his press conference.[32] United States non-recognition, in Cuba as elsewhere, was an invitation to opponents of the regime from which recognition was withheld. In this case, the invitation was addressed to Batista. When the latter withdrew his support in January 1934 Grau was overthrown. His replacement, Carlos Mendieta, was recognised as President by the United States within five days of his appointment. In view of the Roosevelt administration's stated reasons for not recognising Grau, this was unseemly haste. Obviously, those reasons were disingenuous.

United States action in Cuba in 1933 could hardly be called that of a Good Neighbour. Non-intervention had been practised only in the narrowest sense of not actually landing troops. There had been a considerable show—and therefore threat—of force; there had been interference in the domestic affairs of Cuba to an extent that had made a mockery of that country's national sovereignty; non-recognition had been employed as an effective weapon to subvert a government of which the United States did not approve, The United States had feared a social revolution threatening her interests, and was determined to prevent it. She was successful in so doing, but by frustrating Cuban nationalism and insistent pressures for social change she was storing up trouble for the future. In Hugh Thomas's judgement:

> The events of 1933 finally created a revolutionary generation which, despite some real achievements, regarded itself as thwarted, and its appetite whetted for both power and social change, carried on its desires and its methods, particularly the use of weapons, into the succeeding years; for the revolutionary organizations which helped to overthrow Machado never properly disbanded or laid down their arms.[33]

In that of Bryce Wood, 'the combination of the Cuban political situation and the policy followed by the United States provided not merely an opportunity but positive encouragement for the assertion by Batista of decisive political influence at a critical point in Cuban history.[34]

Before the 'Cuban experience' was over the Seventh International

---

[31] Wood, *The Making of the Good Neighbor Policy, op. cit.*, pp. 84–5.
[32] *Ibid.*, p. 86.
[33] *Cuba or The Pursuit of Freedom, op. cit.*, p. 688.
[34] *The Making of the Good Neighbor Policy, op. cit.*, pp. 110–11.

Conference of American States took place at Montevideo (3 to 26 December 1933). The Cuban delegation represented the Grau government. From Mexico, where sympathy for that government was strong, the United States Ambassador, Josephus Daniels, sent Washington a translation of a memorandum by the Foreign Minister proposing that the Monroe Doctrine be modified so as to prohibit American as well as European intervention in the affairs of the members of the inter-American system.[35] Daniels, who had been encouraging Roosevelt and Secretary of State Hull to refuse Welles's requests to intervene in Cuba, shared the Mexican government's sympathy with Grau and its view that the Monroe Doctrine should be 'Pan Americanised'. He warned Hull against exaggerated reports of communism in Cuba and argued in favour of converting the Doctrine into a general hemispheric policy.[36] But the Secretary of State accepted Welles's advice against recognising the 'radical' Grau government and was opposed to any discussion of the Monroe Doctrine at the Seventh Conference.

The most important matter to be discussed at Montevideo was a draft proposal on the Rights and Duties of States, which contained an article prohibiting intervention in the internal and external affairs of states. As we saw, this matter was outstanding from the Sixth Conference. The instructions of the United States delegates to the Seventh Conference reveal the State Department's objections to this proposal, which, 'without some qualification, would strike directly at the Platt Amendment and our Conventions with Haiti and Santo Domingo. It would also prevent the landing of troops in any country for the protection of American nationals during the frequent revolutions in Latin American countries'.[37] It is evident from these instructions that when they were drafted the United States government had no intention of adhering to the proposed Convention on the Rights and Duties of States unless it were greatly modified.

Apart from United States involvement in Cuba, there were two serious disputes between Latin American countries at the time the Seventh Conference met: the Leticia issue between Colombia and Peru, and the Chaco War between Bolivia and Paraguay. These two disputes revealed only too clearly the inadequacy of the inter-American

---

[35] *Foreign Relations, U.S., 1933*, vol. iv (U.S.G.P.O., Washington, 1950), pp. 20–7.
[36] E. David Cronon, *Josephus Daniels in Mexico* (Madison, University of Wisconsin Press, 1960), pp. 70–3.
[37] *Foreign Relations, U.S., 1933*, vol. iv, *op. cit.*, p. 67.

peace machinery, and, as a consequence, involved the League of Nations in 'American questions'. In neither case had both parties ratified the appropriate inter-American agreements, while all four had subscribed to the League of Nations Covenant. So after *ad hoc* attempts at mediation by fellow members of the inter-American system had failed,[38] the League of Nations assumed jurisdiction over the disputes. The United States, not without some misgiving about setting precedents prejudicial to the Monroe Doctrine, acquiesced in this; the problems were intractable, and neither concerned the Caribbean region, where she was particularly sensitive to extra-continental 'interference'. Incidentally, the League played only a limited role in the solution of the disputes.

The most significant result of the Seventh International Conference was the adoption of the Convention on the Rights and Duties of States. We have already seen how crucial the intervention issue had become in relations between the United States and Latin America, and how the United States was beginning to modify her position even as Charles Evans Hughes was defending it at Havana.[39] But, as the instructions to her delegates confirm, the United States was not prepared to relinquish the right of intervention she claimed to enjoy under international law, even though she had become more reluctant to send her armed forces into the territories of her small neighbours. She would have liked to convince the Latin Americans of her good intentions without giving up the freedom to act when she felt her vital interests demanded it. She discovered at Montevideo how strongly the Latin Americans wanted a firm 'non-intervention' commitment. In spite of her experience at Havana, the strength of Latin American feeling on this issue seems to have surprised the Secretary of State and his fellow delegates. Hull recorded that one of the latter 'almost exploded' when criticism of the United States became violent, while, for himself, it was one of the most uncomfortable and disagreeable experiences he had ever had at a public meeting.[40]

A most critical speech was made—not surprisingly—by the Cuban delegation. One delegate, Professor Herminio Portell Vilá, a distinguished historian of his country's relations with the United States,

---

[38] For United States efforts to mediate in these disputes see Bryce Wood, *The United States and Latin American Wars, 1932–1942* (New York, Columbia University Press 1966).

[39] And even Hughes called it 'interposition of a temporary character'.

[40] Cordell Hull, *The Memoirs of Cordell Hull* (London, 1948, 2 vols.), vol. i, p. 334.

spoke of his research in the State Department archives in Washington which, he said, had led to his discovering from the private papers of Senator Platt that the famous Amendment was meant to be a substitute for annexation, 'because there was a "foolish joint resolution" which kept the United States from annexing Cuba'.[41] Portell Vilá also denounced Sumner Welles's activities and the pressures being exerted by the United States against the Grau government. Interestingly, among Portell Vilá's pupils at Havana University in the middle nineteen-forties was Fidel Castro. Many years later Portell Vilá told Hugh Thomas that he had tried to dissuade Castro from making his attack on the Moncada Barracks in July 1953 when the latter mentioned the plan to him in a Havana bar.[42] Portell Vilá eventually went into exile in the United States, where he actively campaigned for action to bring about Castro's overthrow.[43] At Montevideo in 1933, however, he was a bitter critic of United States intervention in Cuba. The Mexican and Haitian delegates were prominent among those criticising the Monroe Doctrine during the debate.

Cordell Hull decided to accept the Convention on the Rights and Duties of States, though he did so with a reservation which referred to statements and policies of the Roosevelt administration and 'the law of nations as generally recognized and accepted'. The most important article of the convention was the one affirming that 'no state has the right to intervene in the internal or external affairs of another'. In a telegram to the Acting Secretary of State in Washington, informing him that he had voted for the convention (with reservation), Hull declared: 'The demand for unanimous affirmative vote was very vociferous and more or less wild and unreasonable.'[44] The acceptance of this convention was a milestone in the history of relations between the United States and Latin America; but Hull's reservations were important. After all, it was under 'the law of nations as generally recognized and accepted' that the United States had always claimed the right of intervention and rejected the Calvo Doctrine, now virtually included as Article 9 of the Convention. Again, United States treaty rights to intervene were safeguarded by Article 12: 'The present Convention shall not affect obligations

---

[41] Connell-Smith, *The Inter-American System, op. cit.,* p. 88.

[42] *Cuba or The Pursuit of Freedom, op. cit.,* p. 803.

[43] John Plank, 'We Should Start Talking with Castro', in Gray (ed.), *Latin America and the United States in the 1970's op. cit.,* p. 244.

[44] *Foreign Relations, U.S., 1933,* vol. iv, *op. cit.,* p. 201.

previously entered into by the High Contracting Parties by virtue of international agreements.'

We have already seen that the Roosevelt administration's interpretation of 'intervention' was, at this stage, a very narrow one: the actual employment of armed force. Only on the basis of such a narrow definition could it have protested that it was not intervening in Cuba in 1933. Two days after the Montevideo conference ended, President Roosevelt declared that 'the definite policy of the United States from now on is one opposed to *armed*[45] intervention'. In the same speech he said:

> The maintenance of law and of the orderly processes of government in this hemisphere is the concern of each individual Nation within its own borders first of all. It is only if and when the failure of orderly processes affects the other Nations of the continent that it becomes their concern; and the point to stress is that in such an event it becomes the joint concern of a whole continent in which we are all neighbors.[46]

Once again, Roosevelt seemed to be visualising some form of collective intervention, another aspect of the question which was to become of greater significance later on. It is noteworthy that Article 8 of the Convention on the Rights and Duties of States forbids 'any state' to intervene. Not until fifteen years later was 'or group of states' added to this most important of all inter-American principles. Indeed, at Buenos Aires in 1936, 'any state' became 'any one' state.

Between the Montevideo and Buenos Aires conferences the United States relinquished some of her 'treaty rights' of intervention. The Platt Amendment was abrogated in 1934 in this respect, though the United States retained her naval base on leased territory at Guantánamo Bay and strengthened her economic domination of the island. 'To sophisticated diplomatists, particularly to those of the Old World,' the abrogation of the Platt Amendment, wrote Professor Bemis, 'was an incredible self-denial in a vitally strategic island full of property owned by United States nationals.'[47] But in another judgement it was 'an inexpensive gesture to Cuban nationalism, and the events of the preceding months had shown that American interests

---

[45] My italics.
[46] Samuel I. Rosenman (compiler and collator), *The Public Papers and Addresses of Franklin D. Roosevelt, with a special introduction and explanatory notes by President Roosevelt, vol. 2, The Year of Crisis, 1933* (New York, 1938), pp. 545–6.
[47] *The Latin American Policy of the United States, op. cit.,* p. 282.

could be protected by more subtle tactics'.[48] Other such gestures characterised the Good Neighbour policy at this time. The last detachments of marines were withdrawn from Haiti in August 1934, over three months in advance of the date agreed the previous year. Negotiations were also begun on the subject of United States financial control, and in July 1935 agreement was reached for the Haitian government to purchase the National Bank of Haiti from the National City Bank of New York. It was not, incidentally, until some years later that the United States relinquished her remaining special rights in Haiti and the Dominican Republic. Meanwhile a new treaty was signed with Panama (2 March 1936) which specifically ended the right of intervention hitherto enjoyed by the United States. However, the United States Senate delayed ratification until 1939, when an exchange of notes provided that emergency military action could be taken in Panama without prior consultation with the Panamanian government. In January 1934 the special recognition policy applied by the United States to the five Central American republics since 1907 was abandoned. This came about as a result of a coup in El Salvador in 1931 when the new government was eventually recognised by all the other Central American countries and the United States.

There was a further development of the Good Neighbour policy at the Inter-American Conference for the Maintenance of Peace, held at Buenos Aires from 1 to 23 December 1936. On Mexico's initiative, the conference adopted the Additional Protocol Relative to Non-Intervention. In its first article, this reads: 'The High Contracting Parties declare inadmissible the intervention of any one of them, directly or indirectly, and for whatever reason, in the internal or external affairs of any other of the Parties.' United States acceptance of this article meant that she was concurring in a broader interpretation of the principle of non-intervention without the reservations she had made at Montevideo. But the Additional Protocol was no mere repetition of the Montevideo pledge with some elaboration and no United States reservation. Reference has already been made to the phrase 'any one' state, which does not exclude collective action of some kind.

Indeed, the Additional Protocol has to be viewed in conjunction with another document jointly proposed with it and likewise adopted

---

[48] Robert F. Smith, *The United States and Cuba: Business and Diplomacy, 1917–1960* (New Haven, Conn., 1960), p. 157.

at Buenos Aires: the Convention for the Maintenance, Preservation and Reestablishment of Peace. This document embodies the principle of consultation in matters affecting the peace and security of the American states. It was the particular concern of the United States who was exercised over the deteriorating situation in Europe.[49] In its first article the convention calls for consultation 'for the purpose of finding and adopting methods of peaceful cooperation' should the peace of the American republics be menaced. Article 2 calls for consultation without delay to seek 'a method of peaceful collaboration' in the case of war or a virtual state of war between American states; while:

> ... in the event of an international war outside America which might menace the peace of the American Republics, such consultation shall also take place to determine the proper time and manner in which the signatory states, if they so desire, may eventually cooperate in some action tending to preserve the peace of the American Continent.

While the principle had thus been established, no machinery of consultation was provided; nor were the signatories committed to take any subsequent action. As regards the first deficiency, the United States delegation had proposed the creation of a Permanent Inter-American Consultative Committee composed of the Foreign Ministers of the twenty-one republics. Argentina, in particular, opposed this as leading towards the political organisation of the hemisphere and conflicting with the obligations of Latin American members of the League of Nations. For similar reasons the United States was unsuccessful in persuading the other American republics to adopt her own neutrality policy.

Nevertheless, the principle of consultation had been adopted and was importantly linked with that of non-intervention. Together they introduced the concept of 'collective responsibility' on the part of all the American republics in situations which previously would have led to intervention by any one of them. Certainly the United States assumed an essential element of reciprocity in the Additional Protocol and interrelated convention: that is to say, she agreed to the principle

---

[49] In the autumn of 1935 Italy had invaded Ethiopia; in the following March Hitler announced the remilitarisation of the Rhineland and Germany's repudiation of the Locarno Treaty; civil war broke out in Spain a few months later. Moreover, the western hemisphere was beginning to feel the effects of Axis trade and cultural penetration.

of non-intervention on the understanding that the Latin Americans accepted the principle of collective responsibility. As we shall see, the latter did not acknowledge any obligation of reciprocity. In abstaining from interventions which had been affronts to their sovereignty the United States was only behaving as the Good Neighbour she professed to be. Collective responsibility, in the Latin American view, was only too likely to mean 'collective intervention'.

By the time the Eighth International Conference of American States met at Lima (9–27 December 1938) the general world situation had further deteriorated and the United States was anxious to foster hemispheric solidarity. But the Declaration of Lima, the most important achievement of the conference, was hardly testimony to her success. Once again, Argentina took the lead in diluting United States proposals for closer co-operation to meet threats from outside the hemisphere. Her Foreign Minister, stressing the ties of the River Plate countries with Europe, recalled with approval Sáenz Peña's speech on similar lines at the First International Conference of American States.[50] He objected to the Declaration being directed only against 'non-American' threats, and the offending phrase was changed to 'foreign' in deference to Argentina's wishes. Thus, although the signatories reaffirmed their continental solidarity and declared their intention to consult whenever the peace, security or territorial integrity of any of them should be threatened by foreign intervention, it was 'understood that the Governments of the American Republics will act independently in their individual capacity, recognizing fully their juridical equality as sovereign states'. It was agreed that consultation should be through *ad hoc* meetings of Foreign Ministers.

Acceptance of the principle of non-intervention was the core of the Good Neighbour policy. And, as we have seen, this meant essentially that the United States henceforth would not send her armed forces into the territory of her neighbours. The Latin Americans regarded their securing this pledge as a substantial achievement. But there was another, more far-reaching restriction upon their independence: the extent to which their key economic sectors—and, above all, the control and even ownership of their natural resources—were in the hands of United States corporations. It was United States policy as far as possible to limit European economic and financial interests in Latin America and thus to gain control of the region's resources. The

---

[50] See above, p. 112.

policies of Theodore Roosevelt, Taft and Wilson, aided by the First World War, had made great progress in that direction. Following the world economic depression, however, the United States was faced with growing economic nationalism in the Latin American countries. Even before that the Mexican revolution, as we have seen, presented a strong challenge to United States interests and policy.

The Good Neighbour policy was linked with the New Deal, whose first objective was the economic recovery of the United States. Latin America had an important role to play in Roosevelt's programme, since it supplied raw materials, markets for United States heavy industry exports and a profitable field for United States capital investments. Economic nationalism in Latin America was a challenge to the Roosevelt administration as to any other United States government concerned with strengthening United States economic and financial control of the region. Roosevelt's action in Cuba was intended essentially to protect the existing social and economic structure of that country against the threat of revolutionary nationalist change. With the abrogation of the Platt Amendment a new agreement was signed with Cuba further tightening United States control of the island's economy. In Robert F. Smith's judgement: 'In many respects Cuba was the testing ground for the "Good Neighbor" policy, and administration officials repeatedly cited Cuban affairs as evidence of the dollars and cents value of this policy.' Indeed:

> In an address in 1935, Sumner Welles described in glowing terms the increase in exports to Cuba and the revival in value of investments in Cuba, and stated: 'The policy of your Government toward Cuba has been for the past 2 years, in the best sense of the word, the policy of the "good neighbor".'[51]

Professor Smith also points out the business connections of members of Roosevelt's administration and his 'brains trust' with Cuba. Even Secretary of State Hull had worked with the Cuban sugar lobby in 1929 and 1930.[52] Cuba was the first Latin American country to whom the United States applied the Reciprocal Trade Agreements Act of 1934, and it was for financing trade to the island that the (second)

---

[51] *The United States and Cuba: Business and Diplomacy, 1917–1960, op. cit.,* p. 142.

[52] *Ibid.,* pp. 142–3. Professor Smith also mentions the association of Adolf A. Berle, Jr. (whom we noted as supporting Welles's anti-Grau policy in Havana: see above, p. 161) with the American Molasses Company—a firm with Cuban properties.

Export-Import Bank was created in the same year. But Cuba aside, neither of these measures to promote United States trade and investments in Latin America had a great deal of effect in the region generally before the outbreak of war in Europe.

Meanwhile, the Good Neighbour policy was challenged by the expropriation of United States oil companies, first in Bolivia and then in Mexico. Here was a new variant of the perennial question of protecting United States capital in Latin America. In 1935 Sumner Welles as Assistant Secretary of State had declared his belief 'that American capital invested abroad, in fact as well as in theory, be subordinate to the authority of the people of the country where it is located'.[53] But it must be noted that Welles was speaking about the problem of protecting United States interests, not from expropriation, but from domestic violence. In the following year the United States had subscribed to the Additional Protocol Relative to Non-Intervention. Undoubtedly, her delegates at Buenos Aires interpreted 'intervention' to mean the use of armed force; 'internal' affairs to be purely domestic politics; and 'directly or indirectly' to mean the landing of forces or threat of such action. The United States did not believe that acceptance of the Additional Protocol meant she was giving up her legal right to make diplomatic representations on behalf of her nationals in Latin America: a right she had exercised so often in the past. In other words she did not regard diplomatic representation as a form of intervention.

On 13 March 1937 the Bolivian government annulled the petroleum concession of the Standard Oil Company of Bolivia (a subsidiary of Standard Oil of New Jersey) and confiscated its properties. It alleged tax avoidance and illegal export of oil. There were other factors in the situation. Bolivia claimed that the company had been unco-operative during the Chaco War (1932–5);[54] she now wanted to cultivate the friendship of Argentina, who had assisted Paraguay in the war, by granting the oil concession to her. Aware that it faced a serious challenge to its Good Neighbour policy, the Roosevelt administration acted cautiously. Secretary of State Hull, in a 'personal message' rather than a formal protest, said: 'the Government of the United States, in accordance with its consistent efforts to practice the policy of the good neighbor to the fullest extent, does not at any time or in

---

[53] Edward O. Guerrant, *Roosevelt's Good Neighbor Policy* (Albuquerque, University of New Mexico Press, 1950), p. 106.

[54] In which Bolivia was defeated by Paraguay.

any instance contemplate support for one of its nationals who seeks to exploit the government of another country or the nationals of such government, or who pursues methods or practices inherently unfair or unwarranted'. Hull hoped that Bolivia would at an early date offer compensation to the company or arbitration or adjudication as a means of settlement. The Bolivian Foreign Minister replied that he would 'cooperate fully toward whatever adjustment may be feasible which, without entering into the legality of the measures adopted, would demonstrate that in Bolivia foreign capital is guaranteed and protected'.[55] But Bolivia insisted that the matter be dealt with in her courts, and the State Department decided that, tactically, it would be best for the company to exhaust all local remedies before diplomatic representations were made on its behalf. Incidentally, the company's contract contained the customary Calvo Clause.

Meanwhile, the Bolivian oil dispute was overshadowed by the much more significant Mexican expropriation. The Bolivian confiscation could be considered a special case—as the Bolivian government maintained it was—and Bolivia was a relatively unimportant country. But the action of the Cárdenas administration was a vital step in the fulfilment of the Mexican revolution, which presented the most formidable challenge of economic nationalism in Latin America. In David Green's words:

> What gave the Mexican government such prestige in Latin America was precisely what also made it so dangerous to United States interests. That is, the Cárdenas administration stood at the head of the most powerful revolutionary nationalist movement in Latin America. And, in contrast to the situations in both Cuba and Bolivia, the government in Mexico was constitutionally elected and represented a revolutionary tradition going back over twenty years.[56]

We noted how, over a decade earlier, relations between the United States and Mexico had deteriorated to a point when war seemed possible, and how President Coolidge had sent Dwight Morrow as Ambassador to cool the situation.[57] Morrow was successful in reaching a compromise on basic issues between the two countries, but it was only a temporary one. During his stay in Mexico the impetus of the revolution slowed down; when it gathered momentum again under

---

[55] Green, *The Containment of Latin America, op. cit.*, p. 26.
[56] *Ibid.*, p. 28.                          [57] See above, p. 151.

Cárdenas a confrontation with the United States became inevitable. The United States Ambassador in Mexico now was Josephus Daniels, who had been Secretary of the Navy at the time of the occupation of Vera Cruz. It was owing to his having thus been Franklin Roosevelt's former chief and recent political supporter that he received the Mexico City post, which he had requested. Daniels's appointment at first shocked the Mexicans, but he eventually became very popular and played an important role in the oil expropriations case. His friendship with Roosevelt gave him a special opportunity to circumvent the State Department and use his influence in favour of an accommodation with Mexico.

President Cárdenas expropriated the property of the oil companies —British, Dutch and United States—on 18 March 1938 in response to their refusal fully to abide by a ruling of the Mexican Board of Conciliation and Arbitration in a two-year-old labour dispute. Undoubtedly the oil companies' refusal was made in the expectation that they would receive strong backing from the United States government. This proved eventually to be less strong than they anticipated. Once the Roosevelt administration found that the expropriation decree was not to be rescinded, it accepted Mexico's right to expropriate; but it firmly supported the companies' claims for compensation. Doubts arose, however, about the form that support should take, and here the role of Josephus Daniels was important: for he was much more sympathetic towards the Mexican government —and much more critical of the oil companies[58]—than were his superiors in Washington. There was no serious question of using armed force in the view of the United States government, though such a course had its advocates in the country—the major oil company involved conducted a vigorous—even scurrilous—campaign of propaganda to that end.[59] But strong diplomatic representations, coercive economic measures and insistence upon arbitration were used in turn—and eventually abandoned. The Roosevelt administration faced a serious dilemma. It was anxious to maintain the Good Neighbour image, but the Mexican challenge had far-reaching implications for the United States position in Latin America. If United States interests were deprived of their ownership of vital resources in

---

[58] Interestingly, as Secretary of the Navy, Daniels had urged the oil companies' case when they had first been threatened by the 1917 constitution.
[59] Daniels, *Shirt-Sleeve Diplomat, op. cit.*, pp. 255 ff.

one important Latin American country, other countries might follow this example. Again, if Mexico, and subsequently other Latin American countries, took over United States properties and could not operate them, there was a strong likelihood that they would turn to non-American powers to do so. Such powers that came to mind in 1938 were Germany, Italy and Japan. Thus there was a double threat: to United States economic prosperity and to her security. The threat was by no means imaginary. For when the oil companies announced a boycott on the shipping and marketing of Mexican oil ('stolen oil' as they regarded it) Mexico, in self-defence, turned to the Axis countries.

At first, the United States took a hard line. Daniels was ordered to deliver a harshly worded protest and return to Washington for consultations. But the Ambassador did not deliver the note formally, and he remained at his post. The Secretary of the Treasury, Henry Morgenthau, whose view of the situation approximated rather to that of Daniels than to that of the State Department, did not use curtailment of silver purchases from Mexico as a serious reprisal, though these were suspended for a short while during 1938.[60] At one point President Roosevelt (speaking 'off-the-record') expressed himself as far from sympathetic to the inflated claims of the oil companies.[61] Even so, the positions of the two governments were diametrically opposed to each other. The United States emphasised the violation of the rights of her citizens under international law; Mexico insisted that the economic and social objectives of her government took precedence over the legal rights of the oil companies. Thus, while the United States demanded that the issue go to arbitration, the Mexican government refused to accede to this and maintained the issue was a domestic one. Meanwhile, the North American oil companies declared their properties to be worth $450 millions, and they demanded either cash compensation or their return. Neither of these alternatives was acceptable to the Mexican government (or even possible politically for it to accept) and the dispute dragged on during the remainder of Cárdenas's term of office. But something of a breakthrough occurred when one of the oil companies, Sinclair, decided to make a separate settlement—which proved to be relatively better than the others

---

[60] But this policy was by no means entirely altruistic. Seventy per cent of the silver producers in Mexico were North Americans and the silver lobby in Washington was a powerful one.

[61] Cronon, *Josephus Daniels in Mexico, op. cit.,* p. 201.

eventually achieved. The new Mexican President, Manuel Avila Camacho, who took office in December 1940, was more conservative, and conciliatory towards the United States, than his predecessor had been. By this time the European war and the possibility of American involvement made the United States more anxious for a settlement. She had not been able to prevent Mexico from selling oil to the Axis powers, helped in this enterprise, incidentally, by a North American oil man and promoter.[62] Now she was anxious to secure Mexico's co-operation in furnishing air and naval bases. Thus the broader security interests of the United States took precedence over the narrower interests of the oil companies. The United States government accepted the Mexican position that the amount of compensation should be determined by a mixed, two-man commission. This eventually awarded compensation of just under $24 millions—a fraction of what the companies had originally claimed, but not far short of an estimate made by the Department of the Interior for the State Department, which all along had been supporting the grossly inflated amount. Agreements were also reached between the United States and Mexico on agrarian and other claims, the purchase of Mexican silver by the United States Treasury, the provision of credits to Mexico by the Export-Import Bank, and for a stabilisation of the Mexican currency. These agreements were signed less than three weeks before the Japanese attack upon Pearl Harbour.

The Mexican experience might suggest that the outbreak of war in Europe forced the United States to make greater concessions to Latin American economic nationalism. In fact, the war substantially increased United States leverage in her relations with Latin America and her control over the region's resources. As we saw, the Roosevelt administration aimed to stimulate United States exports to Latin America as an essential feature of the country's economic recovery and to take government action to this end. At a press gathering in January 1940 President Roosevelt talked about 'a new approach . . . to these South American things. Give them a share. They think they are just as good as we are and many of them are'.[63] But the essence of the Good Neighbour policy in economic matters, as in the case of

---

[62] Wood, *The Making of the Good Neighbor Policy. op cit.*, pp. 228–9. Mexico complained that the Standard Oil Company (one of those involved in the dispute) was selling oil to the Axis powers at this time with the consent of the United States government.

[63] *Ibid.*, p. 359.

United States acceptance of the principle of non-intervention, was reciprocity. Aid for Latin American economic development was granted in return for such measures as the lowering of tariffs and easing of exchange controls which furthered United States economic penetration of the region. As Latin America became increasingly dependent upon the United States the granting or withholding of economic assistance became a comparably important instrument of the latter's policy. A settlement of the Bolivian oil dispute, for example, was eventually facilitated by Bolivia's desire to obtain economic assistance from the United States. Mexico had received no loans from government lending agencies in the United States during the period of the oil dispute.

With the outbreak of war in Europe the United States made greater efforts to promote continental solidarity under her leadership. A Meeting of Consultation of Foreign Ministers (as provided for under the Buenos Aires and Lima resolutions) met at Panama City from 23 September until 3 October 1939. Its two main objectives were the maintenance of neutrality and the formulation of measures to deal with the economic dislocation which would inevitably follow the war. As regards the first, the delegates claimed 'as of inherent right' that the waters for a distance of approximately three hundred miles from their shores should be 'free from the commission of any hostile act by any non-American belligerent nation, whether such hostile act be attempted or made from land, sea or air'.[64] As regards the second, the Panama meeting resolved to create an Inter-American Financial and Economic Advisory Committee to study ways of reducing the economic consequences of the war for the American states and of increasing inter-American economic co-operation. It also recommended that all the American governments should take measures to combat subversive ideologies in the western hemisphere.

A Second Meeting of Consultation was held at Havana from 21 to 30 July 1940. By then the international situation had become much more threatening for Germany had occupied Denmark, Norway, Belgium, Luxembourg, the Netherlands and much of France. This made more urgent a question already raised at Panama: the possible transfer of colonies in the western hemisphere belonging to countries overrun by the Germans. In response to this situation the United States, in effect, reiterated one of the oldest principles of her foreign

---

[64] It was violated by the famous Battle of the River Plate in December 1939.

policy: the no-transfer rule of 1811.[65] A joint resolution of Congress, passed on 17–18 June 1940, stated:

> That the United States would not recognise any transfer, and would not acquiesce in any attempt to transfer, any geographic region of this hemisphere from one non-American power to another non-American power; and . . .
>
> That if such transfer or attempt to transfer should appear likely, the United States shall, *in addition to other measures*,[66] immediately consult with the other American republics to determine upon the steps which should be taken to safeguard their common interests.

At Havana the United States secured the passage of a resolution which endorsed her position, although there was opposition from some Latin American countries on the grounds that it threatened their neutrality and should have dealt with the whole question of colonies in the hemisphere.[67] Also at Havana the American Foreign Ministers agreed to the principle of collective security: '. . . any attempt on the part of a non-American State against the integrity or inviolability of the territory, the sovereignty or the political independence of an American State shall be considered as an act of aggression against the States which sign this declaration'. But there was no firm commitment to action, only to consultation upon possible action.

From the outbreak of war in Europe, the United States had been more and more concerned with problems of hemisphere defence. She neither anticipated nor even desired any sizeable military contribution by the Latin American countries, but she did want base facilities and also co-operation against subversive activities by Axis agents and sympathisers in Latin America. On security grounds—but with important economic and financial implications—the United States campaigned successfully to replace Axis commercial interests in Latin America with her own. An outstanding example was the case of commercial aviation, especially in the Andean countries where German

---

[65] See above, p. 46.

[66] My italics. The United States would act unilaterally if necessary.

[67] Argentina and Guatemala had territorial claims against Britain. Argentina demanded the return of the Falkland Islands (Malvinas) which (as we saw above, p. 69) Britain occupied in 1833; and Guatemala, British Honduras or Belize (see above, p. 87). Incidentally, Mexico claims part of Belize. She is not pressing her claim, but will do so if the territory's status is changed. Venezuela claims part of the former British Guiana (now the independent state of Guyana). See above, pp. 96 ff.

interests were deemed to constitute a possible threat to the security of the Panama canal. The United States increased the number of her service missions in Latin America, eventually replacing those previously furnished by European countries, and extended the provision of facilities for training Latin American officers in her own military academies and training schools.[68]

The United States did not find it easy to obtain the facilities she sought, for two main reasons. First, the Latin Americans were apprehensive over the growing United States involvement in the war, which threatened their neutrality; secondly, there were considerations of national sovereignty. They were reluctant—understandably so in the light of their experience—to permit United States armed forces on their soil. In Brazil, for example, whose north-eastern 'bulge' was the most vulnerable region of South America, three years of delicate discussions preceded permission to station United States forces. The United States encountered considerable opposition in Panama to her plans for constructing bases outside the Canal Zone. The negotiations have been described as 'certainly among the least edifying in the history of the Good Neighbor Policy'.[69] While they were in progress the Panamanian government was overthrown, though the United States denied responsibility for this. Even so, they dragged on well into 1942 with Panama seeking new concessions and firm assurances that United States troops would be withdrawn at the end of the war in Europe. In the case of Mexico, as we have seen, there was the additional complication of the unsettled oil question. A long-standing boundary dispute between Ecuador and Peru, which flared up again in the spring of 1941, not only threatened the peace of the hemisphere; it delayed United States efforts to secure the use of the strategically important (Ecuadoran) Galápagos Islands. The most co-operative Latin American government was, significantly, that of the Dominican Republic. For that country was under the dictatorship of Rafael Leonidas Trujillo who, like Somoza in Nicaragua, had come to power as head of a national constabulary trained by the United States occupation forces. Incidentally, both Somoza and Trujillo were feted as 'good neighbours' by President Roosevelt in Washington in

---

[68] Edwin Lieuwen, *Arms and Politics in Latin America* (revised, paperback edn., New York, 1961), pp. 190 ff.

[69] William L. Langer and S. Everett Gleason, *The Undeclared War, 1940–1941* (New York, Council on Foreign Relations, 1953), p. 615.

1939.[70] Trujillo's offer of 4 December 1939 has been described as 'virtually a blank check for the forces of the United States to make use of the territory of the Dominican Republic as they saw fit'.[71]

Economic co-operation, though the subject of general agreements reached at Panama and Havana, depended in practice, as did defence measures, on initiatives taken by the United States. Broadly speaking, the Roosevelt administration wanted to strengthen the economies of the Latin American countries (as well, of course, as that of the United States) and to undermine the economic position hitherto enjoyed south of the Rio Grande by the Axis powers. These objectives involved procuring strategic raw materials, needed in increasing quantities by the United States and comparably difficult for the Latin American producers to sell elsewhere; ensuring the Latin Americans a supply of manufactured goods at reasonable prices; and developing 'new lines of Latin American production for which a new or complementary market can be found in the United States or in other republics of the Western Hemisphere'. For the latter purpose, the Financial and Economic Advisory Committee set up in June 1940 an Inter-American Development Commission. Other inter-American agencies were established for such purposes as the stabilisation of the coffee market. There were numerous bilateral agreements between the United States and individual Latin American countries which included the granting of credits, provided almost entirely at this stage by the Export-Import Bank. An attempt to create an inter-American bank as a truly multilateral instrument for promoting Latin American economic development failed because of opposition from both United States private banking and industrial interests and from Latin American governments. A major project which the Export-Import Bank helped to finance was the Volta Redonda Steel Plant in Brazil.

In August 1940 the Roosevelt administration set up the Office for Coordination of Commercial and Cultural Relations between the American Republics, later called the Office of the Coordinator of Inter-American Affairs (CIAA). Its object was to promote 'hemisphere defense, with particular reference to the commercial and cultural aspects of the problem'. The co-ordinator was Nelson A. Rockefeller. The work of the CIAA covered a wide range of activities, including economic development, technical assistance, transportation, education,

---

[70] See below, p. 278.  [71] Guerrant, *Roosevelt's Good Neighbor Policy, op. cit.*, p. 155.

sanitation and public health, as well as cultural exchanges. Opinions of its achievements vary. The money it cost the United States has been described as representing 'a phenomenally large investment in goodwill'.[72] The value of the investment in those terms is debatable, but there is no doubt the United States was anxious to limit Axis influence in Latin America and increase goodwill towards herself. For Latin Americans had become apprehensive over the shift of United States policy away from strict neutrality towards co-belligerency and increasing support of the enemies of the Axis powers, and resentful of her pressures to align them with her. On the eve of Pearl Harbour the United States had not achieved the degree of cooperation from Latin America for which she could have hoped.

The Third Meeting of Consultation of American Foreign Ministers met at Rio de Janeiro from 15 to 28 January 1942. By then, in addition to the United States, the nine Central American and Caribbean countries (Costa Rica, Cuba, the Dominican Republic, El Salvador, Guatemala, Haiti, Honduras, Nicaragua and Panama) had declared war on the Axis powers, while Colombia, Mexico and Venezuela had severed diplomatic relations with them. The remaining Latin American countries had proclaimed their non-belligerency and affirmed their faith in the principle of continental solidarity. However, it is important to note that ten American states were at war while eleven were not. Moreover, the ten belligerents had signed the Declaration of the United Nations on 1–2 January 1942, two weeks before the Rio meeting opened—without any reference to the inter-American system.

The most important United States objective at Rio de Janeiro was the adoption of a resolution by which all the American republics would sever relations with the Axis powers. This proved impossible to achieve, for Argentina and Chile refused to subscribe to such a document. For the sake of unanimity a weaker resolution, merely recommending breaking off relations, was adopted. In his *Memoirs*, Cordell Hull recorded his anger that Sumner Welles, who headed the United States delegation, had accepted this formula which, in the Secretary of State's view, was 'the equivalent of a surrender to Argentina'.[73] Chile's unwillingness to break off relations with the

---

[72] Dozer, *Are We Good Neighbors?: Three Decades of Inter-American Relations, 1930–1960 op. cit.*, p. 116.

[73] Hull, *Memoirs, op. cit.*, vol. ii, p. 1149. Welles answers Hull's criticism in his *Seven Major Decisions* (London, 1951), pp. 101–25. He calls his decision to accept the weaker resolution 'The Decision that saved New World Unity'.

Axis powers was not unreasonable in view of her long and vulnerable coastline; she made an unsuccessful attempt to obtain economic and military aid from the United States as a condition of making the break. Argentina's policy was consistent with her traditional attitude and position, now reinforced by the pro-Nazi sympathies of her government. By the end of the Rio meeting all the Latin American republics except Argentina and Chile had severed diplomatic relations with the Axis powers. The meeting resolved to establish an Inter-American Defense Board and an Emergency Advisory Committee for Political Defense.

Although strongly desiring the Latin American countries to sever diplomatic and commercial relations with the Axis powers, the United States did not press the remaining non-belligerents to make declarations of war. The Inter-American Defense Board was established for political rather than military reasons: to give the Latin Americans a sense of participation in a joint effort to ensure the security of the hemisphere. The work of the Board would in any case be limited by the different degrees to which its members were involved in the war. Brazil and Mexico declared war later in 1942, thus bringing the total number of belligerents to twelve; while Bolivia and Colombia did so the following year. But for most of the war period the remaining South American countries went no further than severing diplomatic relations; Chile did not do even this until a later stage, and Argentina remained neutral much longer. For this reason, and because of the dominant role necessarily played by the United States, military co-operation was conducted essentially on a bilateral basis.

Even before the Inter-American Defense Board was set up in Washington the United States had established joint defence commissions with Mexico and Brazil, and further negotiations with Latin American countries, including Lend-Lease arrangements, were conducted bilaterally. Although there was some co-operation in air and naval patrolling against Axis submarines, the United States bore by far the main burden of hemisphere defence. According to an official statement more than one hundred thousand United States troops were stationed in Latin America during the Second World War.[74] Only Brazil and Mexico sent armed forces overseas, though it must be stated that the United States discouraged a number of offers to do so by other Latin American countries because of the difficulties

---

[74] *Dept. of State Bulletin*, xxviii/718 (1953), p. 466.

involved in administering small contingents. Truly 'inter-American' military co-operation was thus very limited. Lend-Lease aid was furnished to eighteen Latin American countries,[75] totalling some $475 millions, of which over seventy per cent went to Brazil, who contributed an expeditionary force and provided special facilities for air transport. Otherwise the main purpose of Lend-Lease was to strengthen co-operative governments and foster the goodwill of the military.

The Emergency Advisory Committee for Political Defense was much more active than the Defense Board. For while the United States did not seek active military support from her southern neighbours, she was anxious for their co-operation in combating Axis activities in the hemisphere. The Emergency Advisory Committee comprised seven members, nominated by the governments of Argentina, Brazil, Chile, Mexico, the United States, Uruguay and Venezuela. In theory, the members represented the American nations as a whole; in practice they inevitably consulted their own governments and received advice from them. Most of the American states co-operated with the committee in taking measures to control pro-Axis subversion within their own frontiers. The committee's publication of reports (submitted to it by the United States) on widespread Nazi espionage activities in Chile and Argentina had important repercussions. In the case of Chile, it helped bring about a severance of diplomatic relations with the Axis powers in January 1943. In the case of Argentina, the committee's persistent denunciations—and the anomaly of her serving on it—caused her withdrawal just after the termination of her membership had been recommended by that body.

The main objectives of United States economic policy towards Latin America had been formulated between the outbreak of war in Europe and the Rio Meeting of Consultation. After Pearl Harbour they remained fundamentally the same: to ensure an increasing supply of strategic raw materials; to strengthen the economies of the Latin American countries in the interests of the war effort; and to eliminate Axis concerns in the western hemisphere. Financial assistance was given to Latin American countries mainly through the Export-Import Bank, and technical assistance through the Institute of Inter-American Affairs, a subsidiary of the Office of the Coordinator of Inter-

---

[75] Argentina and Panama (who was given aid under special provisions for the protection of the Panama Canal Zone) did not receive Lend-Lease funds.

American Affairs. Created in March 1942, this institute promoted technical programmes as well as projects for health, sanitation and food supply. The United States also took steps to improve transport facilities, including an abortive attempt to complete the Inter-American Highway from the Mexican–Guatemalan border to Panama City. She was successful in bringing about the elimination of Axis-owned airlines in Latin America. But she was unable to supply the Latin Americans with sufficient manufactured goods during the war period, and no civilian supplies were furnished under Lend-Lease. The needs of Latin America in this respect were increasingly subordinated to the United States war effort.

The problem of Argentina continued to strain the wartime partnership, and at the end of 1943 there arose a crisis, not unconnected with it. The government of Bolivia was overthrown on 20 December by a group of young army officers in collaboration with a party called the National Revolutionary Movement (MNR), whose most prominent spokesman was Victor Paz Estenssoro. The United States was determined not to recognise the new Bolivian government, which she said had come to power with Argentina's backing. Above all, she was opposed to the 'revolutionary nationalism' of the MNR, which she saw as a serious challenge to herself. Therefore, she used the Emergency Advisory Committee for Political Defense to obtain agreement on a joint policy of non-recognition. She opposed a consultative meeting which might have produced criticism of this policy as a form of intervention. Argentina denounced the committee's recommendation and recognised the Bolivian government. The United States and the other Latin American countries did not do so until changes had been made in that government (primarily the removal of MNR members) and it had taken certain steps in furtherance of what were declared to be its obligations to hemisphere security and the United Nations. As one of those steps the Bolivian government 'turned over to the United States, for secret deportation, eighty-seven persons selected by United States intelligence agencies as the most dangerous Axis agents in the country'.[76] The Bolivian affair did not improve United States relations with Latin America, for she had virtually forced upon the other countries of the region (except Argentina) a

---

[76] Laurence Duggan, *The Americas: the Search for Hemisphere Security* (New York 1949), p. 107. Duggan, as Head of the Latin American Division in the State Department, was one of the main architects of the Good Neighbour policy.

policy of non-recognition, while paying lip-service to the principle of consultation.

Relations between the United States and Argentina soon deteriorated still further, even though the latter belatedly severed diplomatic relations with the Axis powers at the end of January 1944. When her President Pedro Ramírez was overthrown and replaced by General Edelmiro Farrell in the following month, the United States refused to recognise the new government. Most of the other Latin American countries followed suit. The United States wanted to take much stronger action against the rulers of Argentina, amongst whom Colonel Juan Perón was becoming the outstanding—and, from her point of view, most provocative—figure. President Roosevelt himself condemned the Argentine government for repudiating 'solemn inter-American obligations'. He accused it of being under Nazi-Fascist influence and using Nazi-Fascist methods. There was considerable domestic pressure in the United States for strong action against Argentina. In the event, the Roosevelt administration's fulminations did not prove the prelude to serious economic sanctions—still less to something more drastic. For, by comparison with her neighbours, Argentina was in a much stronger position to resist United States pressure. In particular, effective sanctions would have required the co-operation of Britain, who was not willing, for reasons of trade and investments in Argentina, to give it. Nor did the other Latin American countries support the United States government's threatening attitude towards Argentina. Moreover, there was growing resentment of United States pressure to get them into line through bilateral diplomatic channels instead of calling a Meeting of Consultation as some Latin American governments wanted. But the matter was seen as essentially a quarrel between the United States and Argentina in which the other Latin American countries would have preferred not to have to take sides. The United States was embarrassed by a request made by Argentina to the Governing Board of the Pan American Union for a Meeting of American Foreign Ministers to consider the issue.

The problems of Bolivia and Argentina were symptomatic of a general weakening of the wartime partnership now becoming increasingly evident. But a deterioration in relations between the United States and Latin America was inherent in the partnership itself. For while the Good Neighbour had limited his intervention in the affairs of the Latin Americans, the wartime partner was more and more involved in them. The military bases, the FBI agents searching for subversives,[77] the corps of administrators and businessmen directing all kinds of co-operation: these represented massive intervention. During the war Latin America became ever more conscious of United States economic power which, whether applied in the form of aid or of sanctions, gave the policy of partnership the character of dollar diplomacy. The truth was that United States control of Latin American economic development was strengthened still further by the Second World War. It is not surprising that the considerable increase in United States activity in Latin America, even when it was of a beneficent nature, failed to engender Latin American affection for her.

Another important factor influencing inter-American relations was the disappearance of the threat to the security of the western hemisphere. For while the United States was still engaged in a great war in other parts of the world, the Latin Americans were becoming more concerned over post-war problems. Most important were those relating to their economies, which had been distorted by the war. The United States procurement programmes had increased the already heavy dependence of Latin American countries on the production of a few key raw materials, for which demand inevitably would fall when the war was over. Even when new production lines had been developed these would not be competitive in peacetime conditions. Some Latin American countries had accumulated substantial dollar reserves because the United States had been unable to supply the goods they wanted to purchase. They were anxious about the availability and prices of these things when wartime controls were lifted, and the United States was unwilling to commit herself to post-war planning in this field. Soon the Latin Americans were complaining of the sacrifices they had made to supply the United States with war materials at low prices.

If the Latin Americans feared the United States would neglect their economic problems they had a different apprehension over the military bases built during the war years. They began to suspect the United States of seeking to retain them when the war was over, and such a course did have its advocates in the United States Congress. As early as 1943 a subcommittee of the House of Representatives had

---

[77] During the war about one thousand aliens were deported from Latin America to custody in the United States (Mecham, *The United States and Inter-American Security, op. cit.*, p. 233).

recommended that steps should be taken to obtain the use after the war of the air bases the United States had built in Latin America. This aroused vigorous protests from Ecuador, for the Galápagos Islands were specifically mentioned. Brazil likewise made plain her opposition to the continued use of bases on her soil, and there were acrimonious exchanges between the United States and Panama over bases outside the Canal Zone.

The Latin Americans were also greatly exercised about their overall relationship with the United States in the post-war world. It was evident long before hostilities ended that the United States would henceforth be playing a far greater role in world affairs than hitherto. What did this mean for her relations with Latin America? There was the particular matter of the new world organisation which the United States was planning with her major allies. The publication of the Dumbarton Oaks proposals in October 1944 increased their anxieties, for these cast doubts upon the future of the inter-American system. How could a system so closely linked with the concept of isolationism be reconciled with a world system of which the United States would be a leading member? There was no doubt the post-war world would bring new problems for relations between the United States and Latin America. It also seemed likely to exacerbate old ones.

# 6 The United States and Latin America in the Post-War World I:

## Up to the Cuban Revolution

In the previous chapter we saw how the United States and Latin America became first good neighbours and then wartime partners. We noted that Franklin Roosevelt's policy has generally been regarded as the most successful pursued by the United States towards Latin America; with inter-American co-operation during the Second World War cited as demonstrating its success. But there has been a tendency among historians as well as men in public life to exaggerate the degree of cordiality achieved during Roosevelt's administrations. In any case, the change—in retrospect a rapid change—from good neighbours to wartime partners did not augur well for inter-American relations. If United States acceptance of the principle of non-intervention had mitigated the essentially great power–small powers relationship in the western hemisphere, the wartime partnership exacerbated it. For the United States only too clearly was the senior partner, and growing ever stronger relative to Latin America as the war progressed. The degree to which the economy of Latin America was in the hands of the United States was even greater than before. The Latin Americans were increasingly concerned about the policies the United States would pursue towards them when the war was over.

They therefore pressed for a meeting at which outstanding questions could be discussed. They wanted specifically to consider the Dumbarton Oaks proposals for the world organisation and their implications for the inter-American system; the issue of Argentina; and, above all, their economic problems. The United States was not eager for such a meeting. Certainly she wanted to avoid a formal inter-American conference from which Argentina could not be excluded. She therefore proposed a meeting confined to those American states who had co-operated in the war effort. To make this procedure acceptable to the Latin Americans the United States agreed to consider the problem of Argentina after the main topics had been dealt with. These were the continuance of wartime co-operation; the world organisation and the co-ordination of the inter-American system with it; and the economic and social problems of the Americas. The Inter-American Conference on Problems of War and Peace was held in Mexico City from 21 February until 8 March 1945.[1]

The Latin American countries were much more interested in post-war problems than in the continued war effort. They had a great deal to say about the Dumbarton Oaks proposals. Among a number of criticisms, they objected to the dominant role the great powers had arrogated to themselves, and pressed for adequate representation in the Security Council. They were also greatly exercised over the future of the inter-American system. This concern for their association with the United States requires an explanation. One often put forward is a growing fear of the Soviet Union among Latin American governments at this time, especially the more right-wing ones.[2] But there were other factors. Latin American hopes of using the inter-American system as an instrument for restraining the United States in the exercise of her enormous power had been encouraged by her acceptance of the principle of non-intervention. There were also hopes of securing economic assistance from her, and these were complemented by fears that such expectations would be prejudiced should the United States adopt a 'universalist' rather than a 'regional' policy in the post-war world.

As one of the sponsors of the Dumbarton Oaks proposals the United States would not associate herself with Latin American criticisms of them. Nor was she prepared to commit herself in advance of the United Nations conference at San Francisco to a declaration favouring autonomy for the inter-American system. The Latin Americans therefore drew up a list of points regarding the world organisation which were subsequently transmitted to the United Nations conference and to individual governments attending it as representing a consensus among the states represented at Mexico City 'that did not participate in the Dumbarton Oaks conversations'. The Mexico City conference also considered plans for reorganising and strengthening the inter-American system, which would now be importantly affected by the existence of the world organization.

---

[1] Strictly speaking, a diplomatic conference of allies outside the inter-American system, it has been classified as a 'special' inter-American conference—like the Buenos Aires conference of 1936. See above, pp. 167 ff.

[2] E.g. Duggan, *The Americas: the Search for Hemisphere Security, op. cit.*, p. 117.

Relations between the two organisations needed to be defined. Hitherto the inter-American system, now over half a century old, had not been based upon a treaty or convention. Its existence had been continued by resolutions adopted at successive International Conferences of American States. It was now decided to give the system an 'organic pact' or charter. Important changes in its structure were proposed. The Governing Board of the Pan American Union was charged with preparing a draft document and submitting it to the American governments by the end of the year. It would be discussed at the next International Conference scheduled for Bogotá in 1946.

Meanwhile, the Mexico City conference adopted a resolution entitled 'Reciprocal Assistance and American Solidarity', better known as the 'Act of Chapultepec'.[3] This resolution contained important innovations in the field of inter-American peace and security. It declared that: 'The security and solidarity of the Continent are affected to the same extent by an act of aggression against any of the American States by a non-American State, as by an act of aggression of an American State against one or more American States.' Such aggression against one or more of them would be considered aggression against them all. This was an advance upon the resolution on collective security adopted at the Havana meeting in 1940, which had been limited to aggression by a non-American state against an American state.[4] Moreover, the Act of Chapultepec provided for sanctions (including the use of armed force) in principle, though without laying down any procedure through which they would be adopted. The pledge to apply sanctions was restricted to the duration of the war,[5] but the Act of Chapultepec looked forward to the conclusion of a treaty embodying these obligations in permanent form. On the insistence of the United States delegation, the Act of Chapultepec contained the proviso that:

> The above Declaration and Recommendation constitute a regional arrangement for dealing with such matters relating to the maintenance of international peace and security as are appropriate for regional action in this Hemisphere. The said arrangement, and the pertinent activities and procedures, shall be consistent with the purposes and principles of the general international organization, when established.

---

[3] After the castle in Mexico City where it was signed.          [4] See above, p. 177.
[5] The United States administration was able to undertake these obligations in wartime under the President's executive powers. The treaty which was adumbrated for the postwar period would, of course, require 'the advice and consent' of the Senate.

Ho Hum

Since under the Dumbarton Oaks proposals no enforcement action might be taken by regional agencies without authorisation by the Security Council of the world organisation, a crucial issue was involved here for the inter-American system.

Economic and social problems aroused most interest among the Latin American delegations. They hoped to receive from the United States concrete assurances of assistance to carry them over the difficult period of transition from war to peacetime conditions. They were disappointed. What they received was primarily advice—and unwelcome advice at that. They should discard tariffs, encourage private capital and ban state enterprises: measures which would facilitate United States trade and investments. In Professor Whitaker's words, Assistant Secretary Clayton gave them:

> general (rather too general) assurances of aid from the United States. . . . On the other hand, they were specifically urged to lower their trade barriers—which to them meant placing their newly developed industries in competition with the older, larger, and more efficient industries of the United States. The net result of the address and the discussion that followed it was to stress the essentially bilateral character of 'inter-American' economic relations and the dichotomy between economically 'colonial' Latin America and the economically mature United States.[6]

Professor Mecham, also a generally sympathetic interpreter of United States policies, likewise affirms that 'with respect to meeting Latin America's need for long-range economic development, we can only record that, at the Mexico City conference the United States lent its voice to glowing generalities, but withheld its support of concrete programs.'[7] The Economic Charter of the Americas contributed little towards a solution of Latin America's economic and social problems. But it underlined the basic divergence of interests between the United States and Latin America in the economic field.

The other important item at Mexico City was the matter of Argentina. By now the United States had decided to make her peace with the Buenos Aires government before the United Nations conference was held at San Francisco. The delegates therefore expressed their 'hopes that the Argentine Nation will cooperate with

---

[6] Arthur P. Whitaker (ed.), *Inter-American Affairs: An Annual Survey, 1945* (New York, Columbia University Press, 1946), pp. 12–13.

[7] *A Survey of United States–Latin American Relations, op. cit.*, p. 162.

the other American Nations, identifying itself with the common policy these nations are pursuing, and orienting its own policy so that it may achieve its incorporation into the United Nations as a signatory to the Joint Declaration entered into by them'. Argentina was invited to adhere to the agreements of the Mexico City conference embodied in its 'Final Act'. The Argentine government accepted the invitation. It declared war on the Axis powers and agreed to take immediate steps to eliminate Axis influence in the country. Thus was the immediate problem of Argentina settled. But the fundamental differences between the United States administration and the Argentine government had not been removed, and it was only a matter of time before the problem arose again in an acute form.

The United Nations conference, held at San Francisco from 25 April until 26 June 1945, must be regarded as a significant occasion in the history of relations between the United States and Latin America. For it marks the beginning of a new period of much more extensive participation by the American states in world affairs and therefore of one in which extra-continental developments have exerted far greater influence than hitherto upon inter-American relations. In particular, the San Francisco conference underlined the difference in power status between the United States and Latin America, and provided a foretaste of the problems the Cold War would bring to relations between them.

It was evident at once that within the United Nations the United States and the countries of Latin America belonged to different groups of nations with conflicting interests. One group consisted of the great powers, determined to have a preponderant voice in the new world organisation, and the other of the small powers, anxious to impose limits upon great power domination. This dichotomy was particularly evident in the opposition of Latin American countries, along with other small powers, to the proposed veto in the Security Council. The United States naturally joined the other great powers in preventing any significant modification of the veto provision. She therefore opposed also the Latin American demand for recognition in the United Nations Charter of the juridical equality of states, now one of the basic principles of the inter-American system. For this principle was incompatible with the privileged position held by the five permanent members of the Security Council; so the vaguer term 'sovereign equality' was adopted. The United States likewise joined the other great powers in resisting any enlargement of the authority of the General Assembly at the expense of the Security Council, a change also supported by many Latin American countries. For reasons deriving from her status as a great power (and her relations with other great powers, especially the Soviet Union), the United States opposed a permanent seat on the Security Council for Latin America. The latter had to be content with two non-permanent seats.

The Latin Americans were more successful in their endeavours on behalf of the inter-American system. The United States administration (which, between the Mexico City and San Francisco conferences, had been changed by the death of Franklin Roosevelt and the succession of Harry S. Truman to the presidency) was divided on the issue of regionalism. The United States wanted essentially to maintain her hegemony over Latin America, but to prevent her own exclusion from other regions of the world through the establishment of comparable spheres of interest by rival powers: she sought, in David Green's words, 'a closed hemisphere in an open world'.[8] Senator Arthur Vandenberg, as chairman of the Senate Foreign Relations Committee a very influential member of the United States delegation, put it rather differently. He wanted to find a formula which would safeguard what he described as 'legitimate regional arrangements' without inviting 'the formation of a lot of dangerous new "regional spheres of influence" '.[9] In particular, the United States wished to avoid giving the Soviet Union any justification for building a sphere of influence in eastern Europe and a 'bloc' in the United Nations. But she was well aware of Soviet economic weakness and inability to challenge her in the western hemisphere. The United States therefore had less reason to press the case for the inter-American system at San Francisco. At Mexico City, however, she had joined with the other members of the system in agreeing in principle to strengthen their regional organisation and to sign a collective security pact. So eventually, with Latin American support, the United States made a proposal which emerged as Article 51 of the United Nations Charter: 'Nothing in the present Charter shall impair the inherent right of individual or collective self-defence if an armed attack occurs against a Member of the United Nations, until the Security Council has taken measures necessary to maintain international peace and

---

[8] *The Containment of Latin America, op. cit.*, p. 255.
[9] Arthur H. Vandenberg, Jr. (ed.), *The Private Papers of Senator Vandenberg* (Boston, Mass., 1952), p. 187.

security. . . .' The Inter-American Treaty of Reciprocal Assistance was to be the first defence pact having this article as its juridical basis.

At the same time, the Dumbarton Oaks proposals on regional arrangements were incorporated as Chapter VIII of the Charter. While encouraging the peaceful settlement of disputes by such means, this stipulates that 'no enforcement action shall be taken under regional arrangements or by regional agencies without the authorization of the Security Council' (Article 53), and that 'the Security Council shall at all times be kept fully informed of activities undertaken or in contemplation under regional arrangements or by regional agencies for the maintenance of international peace and security' (Article 54). Thus, while the right of individual or collective self-defence may be exercised without authorisation of the Security Council (and continued until the Council takes over), this applies only in cases of *armed attack*. Otherwise, enforcement action may be taken only with the authorisation of the Security Council. This distinction was to be a contentious issue for the inter-American system.

With the adoption of the United Nations Charter at San Francisco the American states could proceed with the plans agreed at Mexico City: to conclude a defence pact and draft a charter for the inter-American system, taking into account, in both cases, the obligations they had all undertaken as members of the new world body. The first plan was for a defence treaty, to negotiate which a conference was arranged for the following October at Rio de Janeiro. But just over two weeks before it was due to convene the United States requested a postponement. The problem of Argentina, which had been glossed over because of the San Francisco conference, was again exercising the United States. The Truman administration accused the Argentine government of repudiating its international obligations, and declared that the United States would not associate itself with the 'present Argentine régime' in the treaty of military assistance to be negotiated at Rio. The militant nationalism of the Argentine government was seen in Washington as a serious challenge to the United States position in the hemisphere, especially since Argentina's comparative economic strength made her less susceptible to pressure than the rest of Latin America. Moreover, the United States feared she would not get the support of the other American republics if she took up the Argentine question at the conference. Therefore she proposed the treaty should be negotiated through diplomatic channels, which would have meant a series of bilateral consultations between the United States and each of the Latin American countries. There were understandably strong objections to this.

Meanwhile, United States relations with Argentina were worsening. The United States Ambassador in Buenos Aires until August 1945 had been Spruille Braden, described by Dean Acheson in his *Memoirs* as a 'bull in a good-neighbor shop'.[10] Extremely vocal in his denunciations of the Argentine government, Braden had thereby intervened most blatantly in the country's domestic affairs. In August 1945 he was appointed Assistant Secretary of State. The Secretary of State (James F. Byrnes) said of Braden's appointment:

> It is particularly a recognition of his accurate interpretation of the policies of this Government in its relations with the present Government of the Argentine. As Assistant Secretary in charge of Latin American affairs, it will be his duty to see that the policies which he has so courageously sponsored in the Argentine are continued with unremitting vigor.[11]

Therefore the United States government was fully—even provocatively—endorsing the speeches and other activities of Braden in Argentina which could only be interpreted as advocating a change of government there. Incidentally, on his way home from Buenos Aires Braden conferred with the United States Ambassador in Rio de Janeiro, Adolf A. Berle, Jr., whom we saw occupying a temporary post in Havana in 1933.[12] In late September 1945 Berle made a speech in which he indicated that the United States would like to see a change of government in Brazil. In the following month President Vargas of Brazil was forced to resign, and Berle's speech became a subject of controversy over many years.

Against the background of deteriorating relations between the United States and Argentina the Foreign Minister of Uruguay, Dr. Eduardo Rodríguez Larreta, proposed to the other American governments a policy of collective action against any member of the inter-American system repeatedly violating the essential rights of man and failing to fulfil its international obligations. Rodríguez Larreta argued that peace and democracy were inter-dependent and, in effect, that the very existence of an anti-democratic government in the

---

[10] Dean Acheson, *Present at the Creation: My Years in the State Department* (London, 1970), p. 187.

[11] *Dept. of State Bulletin*, xiii/322 (1945), p. 291.

[12] See above, p. 161. Since then Berle had spent a period as Assistant Secretary of State.

western hemisphere was a danger to the other members of the inter-American system. Obviously, Uruguay had more reason than most to fear the Argentine government against which Rodríguez Larreta's Note was directed, and, as one of the most democratic countries in the western hemisphere, little reason to fear such collective action against herself. But there was suspicion that the Uruguayan proposal had been instigated by the United States. This was alleged by Sumner Welles, who had resigned from his position as Assistant Secretary of State in August 1943 and had since been extremely critical of United States handling of the Argentine problem. Whatever the truth in Welles's allegation—which was denied—Secretary of State Byrnes was quick to give his government's 'unqualified adherence to the principles enunciated by the distinguished Uruguayan Foreign Minister'.[13]

The other Latin American countries soon showed their disagreement. Collective action could only too easily mean United States intervention with such Latin American support as she could muster given all the means of exerting pressure she commanded. They had not struggled so long to make non-intervention the cornerstone of the inter-American system, and the system itself an instrument of restraint upon their powerful neighbour, to compromise these achievements just when the United States was blatantly interfering in Argentina's domestic affairs. It is significant that some of the most anti-fascist and democratic governments in Latin America were among those strongly opposed to the Rodríguez Larreta proposal. The warm reception given to the Uruguayan Foreign Minister's note by the United States administration (regardless of the suspicion that the latter had inspired it) increased the general Latin American coolness towards it. Only a small minority supported the proposal. The Latin Americans felt, not without justification, that United States policy towards Argentina stemmed not from any special regard for democracy, but from the fact that her government was unco-operative. Moreover, there was the persistent feeling that the issue was not hemispheric but bilateral, concerning the United States and Argentina; and the natural reaction, in spite of distrust for the Argentine government, was to sympathise with the fellow Latin American country. The United States enhanced this feeling by publishing the 'Blue Book'.

---

[13] *Dept. of State Bulletin*, xiii/336 (1945), p. 892.

The State Department's *Consultation among the American Republics with Respect to the Argentine Situation*, published in February 1946, contained an indictment of the Farrell–Perón government. The indictment itself was by no means unjustified. But its publication, about two weeks before a presidential election was due to take place in Argentina, proved a major blunder. To begin with, the title was an irritant to the Latin Americans, who resented the form the 'consultation' had taken.[14] Moreover, it seemed that publication was timed to influence the Argentine election. It probably did so, but not in the way the United States administration had hoped,[15] for Perón was able to assert that the voters' choice lay between him and Braden. In what was judged by impartial observers to be a fair election, Perón won the presidency and the United States suffered a humiliating moral defeat. The other Latin American countries, when approached once more, made it clear they did not share the United States view of the Argentine problem and were anxious for reconciliation with Perón.[16]

Therefore, the United States had little alternative but to retreat from her position and proceed with arrangements for the Rio conference. This was finally fixed for 15 August 1947. By that time the Cold War was getting under way. In the previous March President Truman had announced United States support for western European countries who felt themselves threatened by the Soviet Union: the genesis of the Truman Doctrine or policy of containment. In June George Marshall, who had succeeded Byrnes as Secretary of State, made at Harvard University the speech which adumbrated the European Recovery Programme.[17] Such was the background to the signing of the Inter-American Treaty of Reciprocal Assistance (generally called the Rio Treaty). In the event, it was the first of the 'Cold War pacts' and the forerunner of the North Atlantic Treaty and others.

The Rio Treaty provides for collective defence against both armed attack and 'an aggression which is not an armed attack', whether

---

[14] Welles, *Where are We Heading?* *op. cit.*, p. 230, says that the 'consultation' took the form of the State Department's summoning Latin American Ambassadors in Washington to hand them copies of the 'Blue Book' twelve hours before it was published. The book's main author was reputed to be Spruille Braden.

[15] That the United States government should have entertained such a hope indicates an inability to appreciate the realities of its relations with Latin America.

[16] This is apparent in the 'U.S. Memorandum to American Republics on Argentine Situation', *Dept. of State Bulletin*, xiv/355 (1946), pp. 666–7.

[17] Gordon Connell-Smith, *Pattern of the Post-War World* (Harmondsworth, 1957), pp. 65 ff.

originating from within or outside the Americas. Thus it has a dual character. It provides for collective defence against armed attack in harmony with Article 51 of the United Nations Charter; and it constitutes a regional arrangement under Chapter VIII of the same document in the event of any other act or threat of aggression.[18] In the first case, as we have noted, the signatories of the Rio Treaty may defend themselves until the Security Council takes 'the measures necessary to maintain international peace and security'; in the second, they cannot take 'enforcement action' without the Council's authorisation.[19] In both cases measures to be taken will be determined by an 'Organ of Consultation' which will be the Meeting of American Foreign Ministers.[20] This body takes its decisions by a vote of two-thirds of the ratifying states, excepting the parties involved in the case of a dispute between American states. All ratifying signatories are bound by decisions to apply measures to meet aggression 'with the sole exception that no State shall be required to use armed force without its consent'. The Governing Board of the Pan American Union[21] may act provisionally as an organ of consultation until a Meeting of American Foreign Ministers can take place. Sanctions which the Organ of Consultation may apply to an aggressor range from the recall of chiefs of diplomatic missions to the use of armed force. The region to which the Rio Treaty applies is defined and includes Canada and the European dependencies in the western hemisphere. The rights and obligations of the signatories under the United Nations Charter are reaffirmed.

The Rio Treaty came into effect on 3 December 1948, when the fourteenth signatory (Costa Rica) deposited its ratification. It was eventually ratified by all the signatories. Thus did responsibility for the defence of the western hemisphere devolve formally upon Latin America as well as the United States. In practice, of course, the latter

---

[18] It is noteworthy that while the Rio Treaty contains specific reference to Article 51 there is no mention of Chapter VIII. For, as we have seen (above, p. 189), at Mexico City in 1945 the United States had insisted that the Act of Chapultepec constituted such a regional arrangement. By now, however, she wanted to minimise this aspect of the Rio Treaty. In the coming years she would press for the virtual autonomy of the inter-American system and use her influence to minimise United Nations involvement with important 'American' questions.

[19] See above, p. 193.

[20] As we saw in the previous chapter, there were three Meetings of Consultation between 1939 and the end of the Second World War.

[21] The OAS Council under the Charter. See below, p. 202.

would still provide an overwhelmingly large proportion of the military power which would make the Rio Treaty effective. And her influence would give her the 'decisive voice in identifying 'an aggression which is not an armed attack'. Moreover, there remained *in the background*[22] the Monroe Doctrine embodying the 'inherent right' of individual self-defence as well as the claim of the United States to determine for herself when her security was threatened in the hemisphere.

Although the adoption of the defence treaty was the only item on the agenda of the special Inter-American Conference for the Maintenance of Continental Peace and Security (15 August to 2 September 1947) it was not the only subject discussed. A number of Latin American delegations demanded consideration of their economic problems. Fears expressed at Mexico City had proved only too well founded. With the lifting of wartime price controls in the United States Latin Americans, who had sold during the war in a controlled market, now had to buy in a free one. The value of their accumulated foreign exchange was, therefore, considerably diminished. But, in addition to being more expensive, the industrial equipment needed by Latin American countries was still difficult to obtain, even though the United States greatly increased her shipments between 1945 and 1947. This situation grew worse for Latin America as the United States concentrated mainly upon meeting Europe's needs. At the same time, United States imports from Latin America declined, especially in the case of those goods produced by Latin American industries developed during the war period. Nor, in view of their depressed economic condition, could Latin America do much, for the moment, to revive its pre-war markets in other regions. Economic dependence upon the United States was greater than ever before.

Secretary of State Marshall, addressing the conference as head of the United States delegation, endeavoured to show both the greater

---

[22] Since the development of the Good Neighbour policy United States leaders publicly have emphasised 'hemispheric solidarity' and 'inter-American agreements' rather than the unilateral Monroe Doctrine. The United States has not, of course, abandoned the Doctrine, which remains fundamental to her Latin American policy. But, as Dexter Perkins recommended in 1955: 'A prudent statemanship [*sic*] will talk more and more of common action and less and less of the message of 1823.' And he went on, 'It is unfortunate that in the recent imbroglio with regard to Guatemala Secretary Dulles described the situation as "a direct challenge to the Monroe Doctrine" and declared that "no member of the Rio pact gives up what the Charter of the United Nations calls the inherent right of self-defense; that right is reserved."' (*A History of the Monroe Doctrine, op. cit.*, p. 392.) For Mr. Dulles's references to the Monroe Doctrine during the Guatemalan crisis, see below, p. 213, nn. 66, 67.

plight of Europe and that the latter's rehabilitation was vital to the economy of the western hemisphere. Moreover, he asserted that long-term economic development in Latin America required 'a type of collaboration in which a much greater role falls to private citizens and groups than is the case in a program designed to aid European countries to recover from the destruction of war'.[23] In other words, there would be no Marshall Plan for Latin America. President Truman likewise stressed the urgent needs of Europe in his own address to the Rio conference just before it closed, though he promised his administration would tackle vigorously the economic problems of Latin America. Moreover, on the eve of the conference he had dismissed the notion of a Marshall Plan for Latin America, saying there had been one in the western hemisphere for over a century: the Monroe Doctrine.[24] Mr. Truman's statement is of some significance in interpreting his administration's policy towards Europe at that time and also reveals a lack of sensitivity towards Latin American feelings. At all events, the Latin Americans received no satisfaction on economic matters at Rio.

Latin America's dissatisfaction with United States policy towards its economic problems was underlined, during the interval between the Rio meeting and the Ninth International Conference of American States, by the establishment of the United Nations Economic Commission for Latin America (ECLA). In August 1947, at the Fifth Session of the United Nations Economic and Social Council, Chile had proposed that such a commission should be appointed. All the other Latin American countries expressed support for this proposal, but the United States did not favour it. An Inter-American Economic and Social Council had been functioning provisionally since the Mexico City conference created it in 1945, and the United States considered there would be a duplication of effort between this organ of the inter-American system and the proposed commission. Moreover, the United States representative thought the question should be discussed first at the Ninth International Conference. However, the Latin Americans, who were to be in frequent opposition to the United States on economic issues in the United Nations, had their way. Membership of ECLA, which came into being in February 1948,

---

[23] Dozer, *Are We Good Neighbors?*, op. cit., p. 242.

[24] *Public Papers of the Presidents of the United States, Harry S. Truman, Containing the Public Messages, Speeches, and Statements of the President, January 1 to December 31, 1947* (United States Government Printing Office, Washington, 1963), pp. 383-4.

consisted of the United States, Great Britain, France and the Nether-lands,[25] in addition to the twenty Latin American republics. Its headquarters, appropriately, were established in Santiago, Chile's capital.

The most important outcome of the Ninth International Conference of American States, which met in Bogotá from 30 March to 2 May 1948, was the adoption of the Charter of the Organization of American States (OAS), giving the inter-American system at last a constituent document. The OAS is described in the first chapter of its charter as being 'within the United Nations . . . a regional agency' and there is reference to its 'regional obligations under the Charter of the United Nations'. Membership is open to all American states, but no procedure is provided for admission of new, or for expulsion of present members. The OAS Charter reaffirms principles already proclaimed as ideals of the inter-American system. Article 5(d), for example, asserts that 'The solidarity of the American States and the high aims which are sought through it require the political organization of those States on the basis of the effective exercise of representative democracy'. An attempt to include a definition of democracy, made at the suggestion of the Brazilian and Uruguayan delegations, was, however, abandoned in the face of the difficulties involved. Of interest is paragraph (e) of Article 5: 'The American States condemn war of aggression: victory does not give rights'. The Argentine delegation vigorously proposed that the phrase 'victory does not give rights' should be included. But the United States insisted that it was properly applicable only to a victorious aggressor. As a result, the Argentine proposal was linked to the condemnation of war of aggression. This argument recalls the debate on 'the right of conquest' at the First International Conference of American States when the United States had taken the same position.[26] Another historic source of discord between the United States and Latin America reflected in the OAS Charter concerns the treatment of aliens and the right of diplomatic representation. A compromise wording was achieved in the relevant article (12), hiding the deep division of viewpoint on this issue.

Predictably, the principle of non-intervention is affirmed in the broadest terms. Article 15 declares:

---

[25] Countries with dependencies in the western hemisphere.
[26] See above, p. 112.

No State or group of States has the right to intervene, directly or indirectly, for any reason whatever, in the internal or external affairs of any other State. The foregoing principle prohibits not only armed force but also any other form of interference or attempted threat against the personality of the State or against its political, economic and cultural elements.

and Article 17:

The territory of a State is inviolable; it may not be the object, even temporarily, of military occupation or of other measures of force taken by another State, directly or indirectly, on any grounds whatever. No territorial acquisitions or special advantages obtained either by force or by other means of coercion shall be recognized.

Article 15 represents an expansion of the provisions of the Additional Protocol of Buenos Aires. For while the latter spoke only of intervention by any one state, Article 15 applies also to any group of states. This expansion reflects Latin American fear of 'collective intervention': fear which had recently been heightened by the Rodríguez Larreta proposal.

Whether the term 'group of states' in this context could be applied to the OAS itself was to give cause for future debate. Meanwhile, the principle of non-intervention had to be reconciled with that of collective security, especially since the American states had signed the Rio Treaty and the United Nations Charter. Article 19, therefore, declares that 'Measures adopted for the maintenance of peace and security in accordance with existing treaties do not constitute a violation of the principles set forth in Articles 15 and 17.' A further extension to the principle of non-intervention is to be found in Article 16, which affirms that no state may use or encourage the use of coercive measures of an *economic*[27] or political character in order to force the sovereign will of another state and obtain from it advantages of any kind. The Cuban delegation, which had raised this matter unsuccessfully at the Rio de Janeiro conference the previous year, was the foremost supporter of a move to condemn 'economic aggression'. Cuba had been much put out by the United States Sugar Act of 1947; over a decade later 'economic aggression' was to be of much greater significance in relations between the two countries.

---

[27] My italics.

The Charter describes the principal organs of the OAS. The International Conference of American States, 'the supreme organ', is renamed the Inter-American Conference and is required to meet every five years.[28] The Meeting of Consultation of Ministers of Foreign Affairs is to be held 'in order to consider problems of an urgent nature and of common interest to the American States, and to serve as the Organ of Consultation' (Article 39).[29] The Governing Board of the Pan American Union becomes the OAS Council, responsible for the proper discharge by the Pan American Union of the duties assigned to it, and empowered to act provisionally as Organ of Consultation.[30] The OAS Council has three subsidiary organs, of which the most important is the Inter-American Economic and Social Council. Strong Latin American opposition, in which Mexico played a prominent part, prevented the inclusion of a Defence Council in the structure of the OAS. The Inter-American Defense Board was continued in existence by a separate resolution of the Ninth International Conference. An Advisory Defense Committee is provided for to assist the Organ of Consultation, but it has never been formed. The other principal organs of the OAS are the Pan American Union (the Secretariat), the Specialized Conferences and the Specialized Organizations.

The third major document of the inter-American system (after the Rio Treaty and the OAS Charter) is the American Treaty on Pacific Settlement or Pact of Bogotá. The pacific settlement of disputes between American states had been a major objective of the inter-American system from the outset. But although the principle that all inter-American disputes should be settled by peaceful means has long been accepted, its embodiment in acceptable treaty form has proved elusive. When the Ninth International Conference opened none of the many agreements reached between the American states had been ratified by all of them. Nor did the Pact of Bogotá prove any more successful. There were numerous reservations, some very far-reaching, and ratification was slow and only partial.

Mention has already been made of links between the OAS and the United Nations. Both the Rio Treaty and the OAS Charter contain

---

[28] In the event no Inter-American Conference took place after the Tenth in 1954 (see below, pp. 212 ff.). Under the OAS Amended Charter the Inter-American Conference has been replaced as 'the supreme organ' by the annual General Assembly. See below, p. 262, n. 75.

[29] See above, p. 197.                                          [30] *Ibid.*

articles declaring that none of their provisions shall be construed as impairing the rights and obligations of the signatories under the Charter of the United Nations. The relationship of the regional to the world body was not too clearly defined, however, and there was ample room for argument over the issue of competence between them, especially in the field of international peace and security. In all three major OAS documents the signatories pledged themselves to use inter-American peace procedures before referring their disputes to the United Nations, but there were bound to be cases where OAS members would prefer to have recourse to the world body. In the field of economic and social co-operation the Latin American countries had already shown their dissatisfaction with the Inter-American Economic and Social Council by insisting upon the establishment of ECLA. The OAS and the United Nations were to prove competitors in key fields of international co-operation.

Latin American dissatisfaction was confirmed by the content and fate of the Economic Agreement of Bogotá. After heated discussion, this document was signed with so many reservations that it would have been virtually useless even if it had been ratified. Two points in the document may suffice to illustrate the basic differences between the United States and Latin America. Over raw materials, the Latin Americans were understandably concerned about the fall in prices they had so recently experienced. On their insistence, it was resolved that 'as a general policy, there should be taken into account the need to compensate for the disparity that is frequently noted between the prices of raw materials and the prices of manufactured products, by establishing the necessary balance between them' (Article 3). The United States delegation entered a formal reservation against this. On the other hand, Article 25 was included on United States insistence:

> The States shall take no discriminatory action against investments by virtue of which foreign enterprises or capital may be deprived of legally acquired property rights, for reasons or under conditions different from those that the Constitution or laws of each country provide for the expropriation of national property. Any expropriation shall be accompanied by payment of fair compensation in a prompt, adequate and effective manner.

A number of Latin American countries, including Argentina and Mexico, made reservations to this article, reaffirming the primacy of their national constitutions and laws, and demonstrating once more

that the Calvo Doctrine and the old problem of diplomatic intervention were still alive. But all the reservations proved superfluous, since
the Economic Agreement of Bogotá failed for want of ratification.

More eloquent than the discussions at the conference was the
outbreak of rioting in Bogotá during its proceedings, touched off by
the assassination of the Colombian Liberal leader, Jorge Eliecer
Gaitán. This rioting, called the *Bogotaƶo*, was described by the
Colombian authorities and the United States delegation as communist-
inspired. It is of interest that the presence in Bogotá at the time of the
young Fidel Castro was subsequently cited as showing both the
communist character of the rioting and that Castro was a communist
even then. In this connection Professor Mecham is worth quoting.
In a work published in 1961 and written before Castro either declared
himself to be, or was widely accused of being, a communist, Mecham
declared, supporting the official United States position, that 'international Communism had resorted to direct action in Bogotá to
break up and discredit the great conference of American states'.[31]
Four years later he wrote, 'many Communists from other countries,
including Fidel Castro of Cuba, had foregathered to discredit or
disrupt the conference'.[32] Others, however, interpreted the *Bogotaƶo*
differently. Willard L. Beaulac, United States Ambassador in Bogotá
at the time, has written many years later that he did not hold the
communists responsible for the uprising, though (like Mecham) he
declares that they took prompt advantage of it: 'The reaction of
Colombians to Gaitan's assassination was spontaneous and massive.'
Indeed, he says, 'There may have been a revolution of frustrated
expectations in Colombia in 1948. The Colombian masses that year
had well-founded reasons to complain about the conditions in which
they lived, and against the privileged classes who controlled the
country's economy.'[33] And in Laurence Duggan's judgement,
'Bogotá showed dramatically the necessity for combining with
measures for inter-American solidarity on the official level, measures
which will solve the deep-rooted problems of Latin America—low
productivity and its corollaries: ignorance, disease, hunger, and
political instability.'[34]

---

[31] *The United States and Inter-American Security, op. cit.,* p. 301.
[32] *A Survey of United States–Latin American Relations, op. cit.,* p. 211.
[33] *A Diplomat Looks at Aid to Latin America* (Carbondale and Edwardsville, Southern
Illinois University Press, 1970), pp. 64–5.
[34] *The Americas: The Search for Hemisphere Security, op. cit.,* pp. 1–2.

Against the background of the Bogotá rioting the Ninth International Conference passed a resolution entitled 'The Preservation and Defense of Democracy in America'. This has often been called the first anti-communist resolution adopted by the inter-American system. Mecham describes it as 'a resounding anti-Communist hemisphere resolution' adopted with 'unanimous approval'.[35] But, in fact, it was softened, as such, by the condemnation—to meet Latin American wishes—of 'any other totalitarian doctrine'. There was a similar outcome to subsequent attempts by the United States to obtain stronger measures than many Latin Americans were prepared to accept against what she denounced as communist intervention.

Thus the pattern of United States relations with Latin America in the post-war world was already emerging when the Bogotá conference ended. The United States was concentrating upon her wider interests —especially in Europe and the Far East—and giving Latin America very low priority. She saw no reason to change her traditional policy towards her southern neighbours: emphasis remained upon stability and the strong encouragement of private enterprise. The Latin Americans resented what they considered United States 'neglect' and policies aimed at increasing her control of their economies rather than assisting their development. They wanted governmental aid. But, as Secretary of State Dean Acheson (Marshall's successor) declared: 'In providing assistance for economic development, it would be contrary to our traditions to place our government's public funds in direct and wasteful competition with private funds.'[36] And, in Professor Donald Dozer's words, 'The Truman administration . . . began forthwith to push with increased aggressiveness a program to foster private United States capital investment in Latin America'.[37] It is significant that a high proportion of such investment was in the extractive industries, especially petroleum.

A fundamental aspect of the problem was underlined when Edward G. Miller, Jr., Assistant Secretary of State for Inter-American Affairs, declared it to be a 'misconception' that 'the United States because of its size and prosperity is responsible for solving the problems of the other American Republics and that when they have difficulties the United States is to blame'.[38] But Miller ignored two basic factors in

---

[35] *The United States and Inter-American Security*, *op. cit.*, p. 429.
[36] Quoted in Connell-Smith, *The Inter-American System*, *op. cit.*, p. 156.
[37] *Are We Good Neighbors?*, *op. cit.*, p. 244.
[38] *Dept. of State Bulletin*, xxii/561 (1950), p. 521.

the situation. In the first place, by her policy of economic penetration and control of Latin America, aggressively pursued under successive administrations—with its corollary of excluding European influence as far as possible—the United States could not escape a considerable measure of responsibility for the region's economic and social problems. And secondly, in the furtherance of her hegemony she had fostered the idea of a special relationship with Latin America which naturally encouraged demands for special treatment—and this she was not prepared to grant.

The other major influence upon United States relations with Latin America at this time was the developing Cold War. Her confrontation with the Soviet Union increased United States concentration upon other areas of the world and confirmed Latin America as a low priority area. But, at the same time, Latin American political support for the United States position in the Cold War was not unimportant, especially in the United Nations General Assembly, where the twenty Latin American votes at first comprised two-fifths of the total. The Korean war enhanced the importance of the General Assembly after the Soviet Union returned to the Security Council, which she had been boycotting when hostilities began.[39] On 28 June 1950, three days after the outbreak of the Korean war, the OAS Council declared its 'firm adherence to the decisions of the competent organs of the United Nations' and solemnly reaffirmed 'the pledges of continental solidarity which unite the American States'. But only the Colombian government (that of the dictator, Laureano Gómez) sent troops to Korea.[40]

In connection with the Korean war, which had taken a new turn with the intervention of China, the Fourth Meeting of Consultation of American Foreign Ministers was held in Washington from 26 March until 7 April 1951. Called at the request of the United States 'to consider problems of an urgent nature and of common interest to the American States', the Meeting revealed once again the divergence of objectives between Latin America and herself. The United States was concerned to strengthen hemispheric security; the Latin Americans

---

[39] The Soviet boycott had been in protest against the Security Council's refusal to seat the People's Republic of China. It was during Russia's absence that the initial resolutions on the Korean war were adopted. Following her return to the Security Council the Korean situation was dealt with by the General Assembly on the basis of the 'Acheson Plan' or 'Uniting for Peace' resolution.

[40] For comments on the Colombian government's motives for sending troops to Korea see Germán Arciniegas, *The State of Latin America* (New York, 1952), pp. 187–95.

were anxious to strengthen their economies. The Brazilian delegate reportedly said bluntly that the only nation in the hemisphere actually threatened by external aggression was the United States;[41] several others urged that the best way to prevent the spread of communism in Latin America would be to raise the living standards of the masses for which United States financial assistance was needed. But they received no concrete assurances of such aid. Even before the Meeting took place, the Latin Americans had reason to fear that favourable terms of trade resulting from the Korean war were about to be reversed 'as the United States moved to limit the prices it paid for raw materials but failed, meanwhile, to halt the advancing price of its own manufactures'.[42] In the following months their fears were realised.

The Fourth Meeting of Consultation called for co-operation, in conformity with the Rio Treaty, to strengthen collective defence. Later in 1951 the United States Congress passed the Mutual Security Act and under its provisions Mutual Defense Assistance Agreements were eventually signed with twelve Latin American countries, beginning with Ecuador in January 1952. Under the terms of this first pact the United States government agreed to 'make available . . . equipment, materials, services, and other military assistance designed to promote the defense and maintain the peace of the Western Hemisphere'. In return, Ecuador promised to make effective and exclusive use of this assistance for implementing defence plans, to build up and maintain her own defensive capacities, 'to facilitate the production and transfer . . . of . . . strategic materials required by the United States', and to co-operate with the United States in limiting her trade with the Soviet group of nations.[43] But United States motives for associating the Latin American countries with the defence of the continent against external military threats were, as always, primarily political. Before long she would be calling for co-operation in measures to meet the threat of subversion: in practical terms a more significant matter than possible armed aggression. This would lead the United States to emphasise the training of Latin American officers in 'counter-insurgency' and generally to strengthen the military as the strongest anti-communist group in Latin America.

Relations between the United States and Latin America did not

[41] *The Times* (London), 4 April 1951.
[42] Richard P. Stebbins, *The United States in World Affairs, 1951* (New York, Council on Foreign Relations, 1952), p. 314.
[43] Lieuwen, *Arms and Politics in Latin America, op. cit.*, p. 201.

improve during the remaining period of the Truman administration and were, indeed, at a low ebb when President Eisenhower took office in January 1953. Eisenhower's Secretary of State was John Foster Dulles, one of the most influential holders of that office. Moralistic and devious, like Woodrow Wilson, Dulles added to these traits the background of a corporation lawyer, comparable with, for example, that of Philander C. Knox, William Howard Taft's Secretary of State. Professing to see the Cold War as a moral crusade—for example, he criticised India's neutralism as immoral—Dulles held up Marcos Pérez Jiménez's dictatorship in Venezuela as a model for Latin America:

> Venezuela is a country which has adopted the kind of policies which we think that the other countries of South America should adopt. Namely, they have adopted policies which provide in Venezuela a climate which is attractive to foreign capital to come in.

According to Robert F. Smith, Dulles 'concluded by saying that if all Latin American countries followed the example of Venezuela, the danger of Communism and social disorder would disappear'.[44]

John Foster Dulles combined a strong commitment to United States economic penetration of Latin America with a fanatical determination to oppose Soviet influence in the region. As early as 1947 he warned: 'Soviet policy in South America subjects the Monroe Doctrine to its severest test. There is a highly organized effort to extend to the South American countries the Soviet system of proletariat dictatorship. It ignores the declaration of President Monroe, made to Russia and others in 1823, that "to extend their system to any portions of this Hemisphere is dangerous to our peace and security".'[45] Six years later, Dulles declared he saw a parallel between existing conditions in Latin America and those in China in the nineteen-thirties, when the communist movement was just beginning. And, he went on, 'the time to deal with this rising menace in South America is now'.[46]

As evidence of his concern for an improvement in relations with

---

[44] *The United States and Cuba, op. cit.*, p. 184.

[45] Quoted in Green, *The Containment of Latin America, op. cit.*, p. 263.

[46] George Pendle, 'Latin America', in Peter Calvocoressi, *Survey of International Affairs, 1953* (London, Oxford University Press for the Royal Institute of International Affairs, 1956), p. 366.

Latin America, the new President, early in April 1953, sent his brother, Dr. Milton Eisenhower, as his special representative to the countries of South America to consider what changes in United States policy might achieve this. After a five-week tour, Dr. Eisenhower submitted a report to the President in November 1953.[47] In it he stated that 'economic cooperation is without question the key to better relations between the United States and the nations to the South'. In his opinion, the United States should pursue stable trade policies with Latin America, with a minimum of mechanisms permitting the imposition of increased tariffs or quotas, and a long-range policy on basic materials providing for stock-piling of Latin American imperishable materials when prices were declining. There should be substantial public loans (mainly by the International Bank for Reconstruction and Development) for sound economic development projects for which private financing was not available; and the United States programme of technical co-operation should be expanded. Dr. Eisenhower believed the Latin Americans misunderstood the United States position and policies. Moreover, they would have to realise 'the value to the community of private competitive enterprise and private profit'. Latin American governments would have to adopt sound budgetary, fiscal, and credit policies; bring about conditions of political and economic stability; and give assurances of fair and equitable treatment in order to attract United States capital. In spite of some new suggestions, the basic recommendations of the report differed little from the policy of the Truman administration. It was hardly likely that the Eisenhower administration would place less emphasis upon the role of private capital than had its predecessor. In his Message to Congress on 7 January 1954 President Eisenhower declared that: 'Military assistance must be continued. Technical assistance must be maintained. Economic assistance can be reduced.' There would be exceptions to such reductions (notably in the case of Korea), but in this connection Latin America was not mentioned.[48]

Yet the Eisenhower administration was already engaged upon a programme of large-scale economic aid and technical assistance to Bolivia. It has been estimated that between 1952 and 1964 the United States furnished more *per capita* economic assistance to Bolivia than

---

[47] M. S. Eisenhower, 'United States–Latin American Relations: Report to the President', *Dept. of State Bulletin*, xxix/752 (1953), pp. 695–717.

[48] *Ibid.*, xxx/760 (1954), p. 76.

to any other Latin American country.[49] This is of particular interest because in 1952 a revolution had occurred in Bolivia bringing to power Victor Paz Estenssoro of the National Revolutionary Movement (MNR), who had been opposed by the United States in 1943.[50] Moreover, the new Bolivian government, under strong popular pressure, embarked upon a policy of nationalising the tin mines and redistributing land. Juan Lechín, leader of the militant tin-miners, became Minister of Mines and Petroleum. Nevertheless, the United States government decided to recognise Paz and give him aid. In the words of a Senate document:

> The Department of State, which constantly appraises political, social, and economic developments, has concluded that the Bolivian Government is now Marxist rather than Communist and has advocated United States support of this regime on the same premise that it advocated support of the preceding military junta—to prevent displacement by more radical elements. . . .[51]

United States policy was influenced by the fact that Bolivia is far removed from the sensitive Caribbean region and her economic interests there were not considerable. The Bolivian government gave assurances in respect of United States companies, and Dr. Eisenhower, who visited the country during his South American tour in 1953, strongly supported the aid programme. The President's brother was convinced that this was the best way to ensure peaceful change and avoid communism in Bolivia.[52] Thus United States policy was to encourage the more conservative elements in the Bolivian government, and in this she was successful. She insisted, as a condition of receiving economic assistance, that the Bolivian government should reach an agreement with the former owners of the tin mines in respect of compensation.[53] In 1955 Lechín resigned as minister of mines, reputedly a condition of further United States aid.[54] Thus United States policy of assistance to the Bolivian revolution conformed,

---

[49] See, for example, Cole Blasier, 'The United States and the Revolution', in James M. Malloy and Richard S. Thorn (eds.), *Beyond the Revolution: Bolivia since 1952* (Pittsburgh, University of Pittsburgh Press, 1971). p. 53.          [50] See above, p. 183.

[51] Quoted in Richard W. Patch, 'Bolivia: U.S. Assistance in a Revolutionary Setting', in Richard N. Adams *et al.*, *Social Change in Latin America Today: Its Implications for United States Policy* (paperback edn., New York, 1961), p. 130.

[52] Milton S. Eisenhower, *The Wine is Bitter: The United States and Latin America* (New York, 1963), *passim*.

[53] Blasier, *op. cit.*, p. 75.          [54] Patch, *op. cit.*, p. 133.

paradoxically, to her overall anti-communist, counter-revolutionary strategy.

The situation in Latin America causing the Eisenhower administration most concern in its early years of office was that obtaining in the Central American republic of Guatemala. The Ubico dictatorship had been overthrown in 1944 and Juan José Arévalo[55] was subsequently elected President. Arévalo began a reform programme which was continued by his successor, Jacobo Arbenz. In 1952 the Arbenz government initiated a comprehensive land reform programme: a much needed measure, but by no means a drastic one.[56] However, it involved the expropriation of 160,000 hectares of uncultivated land belonging to the powerful United Fruit Company of Boston.[57] The company argued that it needed the lands as banana-growing reserves, and contested both the valuation put upon them and the proposed method of compensation. The valuation had been based upon the company's tax returns, and compensation was to be by way of bonds. This situation is reminiscent of the expropriation of the oil companies in Mexico in 1938. In Professor Ronning's words:

> All the social and economic injustices of the Mexican scene were present in Guatemala. The United Fruit Company (UFCO) in Guatemala represented the same challenge to the country's independence that the oil companies had presented in Mexico. Its importance in the Guatemalan economy made it relatively even more powerful than the Mexican oil companies had ever been.[58]

The dominant position of the United Fruit Company in Guatemala aroused widespread resentment, the more so because of the circumstances in which it had been secured: 'There was general agreement in Guatemala, even among those most opposed to the Arbenz regime (elected in 1951), that UFCO contracts negotiated with General Ubico, the most detestable of dictators in Guatemalan history, had been negotiated at the expense of the country and were in need of drastic revision.'[59]

---

[55] Later author of the anti-United States polemic, *The Shark and the Sardines.* See above, p. 2.

[56] See, for example, Thomas F. Carroll, 'The Land Reform Issue in Latin America', in Albert O. Hirschman (ed.), *Latin American Issues: Essays and Comments* (New York, The Twentieth Century Fund, 1961), pp. 178–80.

[57] See above, p. 123.

[58] *Law and Politics in Inter-American Diplomacy, op. cit.,* p. 42.

[59] *Ibid.*

The United States government made strong diplomatic representations on behalf of the company, denouncing the compensation offered as not conforming with the minimum standards prescribed by international law. It applied economic and political pressures against Guatemala. The Arbenz administration was denounced as being communist-dominated, and as providing 'international communism' with a bridgehead in the Americas. Arbenz, an elected President, undoubtedly had communist support, though the extent of communist influence in his government was debatable.[60] However genuine United States fears of international communism in the Guatemalan situation, the State Department's protestation that it had not been importantly influenced by the expropriation of United Fruit lands carried little conviction—and carried even less in the light of information that important figures in the Eisenhower administration had close links with the company. Apparently the Secretary of State himself had been a member of the law firm which drew up the company's agreements with the Ubico government, and his brother, Allen Dulles, who, as head of the Central Intelligence Agency, was to play a key role in subsequent events, had once been president of United Fruit. John Moors Cabot, Assistant Secretary of State for Inter-American Affairs, was cited as a shareholder; and Spruille Braden, another important figure in United States relations with Latin America,[61] as head of United Fruit public relations.[62] But the Eisenhower administration did not need the incentive of such interests in shaping its policy towards Arbenz.

The United States sought Latin American support for her position *vis-à-vis* Guatemala at the Tenth Inter-American Conference, held at Caracas from 1 to 28 March 1954. It was perhaps appropriate that Secretary of State Dulles's call for concerted action against international communism should have been made in the capital of the Pérez Jiménez dictatorship which he had declared to be an ideal bulwark against it.[63] Dulles took to Caracas a draft anti-communist resolution which was virtually his only interest in the proceedings. In Professor Alexander's judgement, Dulles's conduct at Caracas:

... shocked many seasoned observers of Latin American developments. Not only did Dulles use the full weight of the United States Government

---

[60] For an assessment of the degree of communist influence, see Ronald M. Schneider, *Communism in Guatemala, 1944–1954* (New York, 1959).

[61] See above, pp. 194–6.

[62] Gerassi, *The Great Fear in Latin America, op. cit.*, p. 241.          [63] See above, p. 208.

to induce the Conference to take a position uncongenial to the majority of the Latin American countries, he did it in a manner likely to lose friends and alienate the peoples of the southern part of the hemisphere.

Concerned with almost nothing but the 'Anti-Communist Resolutions' aimed at Guatemala, Dulles seemed to the Latin Americans indifferent to their feelings, their fears of 'Yankee Intervention', and the concentration of their interest on entirely different problems. He stayed at the Conference only long enough to see adoption of the Resolution. Then he took a plane home the very day the Resolution was passed, leaving his subordinates to deal with the economic and social questions which were the primary concern of the Latin American delegations.[64]

However, Dulles had been by no means wholly successful.

The core of the United States draft was contained in a passage declaring:

That the domination or control of the political institutions of any American State by the international communist movement, extending to this Hemisphere the political system of an extra-continental power, would constitute a threat the sovereignty and political independence of the American States, endangering the peace of America, and would call for appropriate action in accordance with existing treaties.[65]

This was, in effect, an endorsement of the Monroe Doctrine,[66] which would be challenged by the mere existence of a communist government in the western hemisphere.[67] The Latin Americans were not prepared to support this, for it would reopen the door to intervention against any government the United States might denounce as being under the control of international communism. They knew that, specifically, the United States wanted their approval in overthrowing the Arbenz government of Guatemala, regarding whose communist character many of them had serious reservations.

In view of Latin American objections, the key passage was amended

---

[64] Robert J. Alexander, *Communism in Latin America* (New Brunswick, N.J., Rutgers University Press, 1957), p. 400.

[65] U.S. Dept. of State, *Tenth Inter-American Conference, Report of the U.S. Delegation* (1955), p. 8.

[66] At a news conference after his return from Caracas, Dulles gave the impression that he regarded the anti-communist resolution eventually adopted as such. U.S. Dept. of State, *Intervention of International Communism in Guatemala* (1954), pp. 10–11.

[67] In a radio and television address on 30 June 1954 Dulles declared of the Guatemalan crisis: 'This intrusion of Soviet despotism was, of course, a direct challenge to our Monroe Doctrine, the first and most fundamental of our foreign policies.' *Ibid.*, p. 30.

so that the last phrase read: 'and would call for a Meeting of Consultation to consider the adoption of appropriate action in accordance with existing treaties'. And further to allay Latin American fears of intervention in their internal affairs, the following paragraph was added to the resolution:

> This declaration of foreign policy made by the American republics in relation to dangers originating outside this Hemisphere is designed to protect and not to impair the inalienable right of each American State freely to choose its own form of government and economic system and to live its own social and cultural life.[68]

Even so, Mexico and Argentina abstained in the vote on this resolution and, of course, Guatemala, against whom it was directed, opposed it. Among those delegations which supported Dulles's resolution, only certain dictatorships did so without misgivings.[69] John C. Dreier who, as United States Ambassador to the OAS was present at the conference, wrote some years later:

> ... the Resolution, duly approved by more than a sufficient majority of governments, has turned out to be largely ineffectual because, in the last analysis, the Latin American countries have generally been more concerned with its potential danger as a basis for intervention led by the United States than with the danger of Communist intervention in their own affairs.[70]

This is hardly surprising. For the traditional justification of United States interventions in Latin America had been the alleged necessity to forestall interventions by 'foreign' powers. In this century the question of extra-continental intervention had been predominantly an academic one, while that of United States intervention had been

---

[68] This paragraph offered little reassurance to the Latin Americans, however, since their freedom to choose did not apparently include the choice of a government which the United States considered to be 'communist-dominated'. After all, Arbenz had been elected.

[69] Connell-Smith, *The Inter-American System*, *op. cit.*, p. 231.

[70] *The Organization of American States and the Hemisphere Crisis* (New York, Council on Foreign Relations, 1962), p. 53. It is of interest, however, that in his memoirs President Eisenhower described this resolution as forming 'a charter for the anti-Communist counterattack that followed' and cited it as justification for his administration's action against the Arbenz government: '... it seemed to me that to refuse to cooperate in providing indirect support to a strictly anti-Communist faction in this struggle would be contrary to the letter and spirit of the Caracas resolution'. Dwight D. Eisenhower, *The White House Years*, vol. 1, *Mandate for Change, 1953–1956* (London, 1963), pp. 424–6.

the reality in the international relations of Latin America. This was to be the key factor in limiting Latin American support for United States policies to meet the challenge of international communism in the hemisphere.

Mr. Dulles argued that by its opposition to the anti-communist resolution the Guatemalan government had demonstrated its communist character, and he reportedly said on leaving Caracas, 'Now of course, we shall have the task of assuring that the enemies of freedom do not move into the breach which has been disclosed within our ranks.'[71] The United States expressed great concern in May 1954 when the Arbenz government received a shipment of arms originating in Czechoslovakia, and she requested (with limited success) the consent of other members of the North Atlantic Treaty Organization to search their merchant ships on the high seas for further arms shipments to Guatemala.[72] She concluded Mutual Security Treaties with Guatemala's neighbours, Nicaragua (in April) and Honduras (in May), and sent war materials to them. But, ominously, the United States did not request a Meeting of Consultation of American Foreign Ministers to consider the situation.

On 19 June Guatemala was invaded from Honduras by troops led by an exiled officer, Colonel Carlos Castillo Armas. The Guatemalan government complained to the Security Council of the United Nations of 'open aggression ... perpetrated by the Governments of Honduras and Nicaragua at the instigation of certain foreign monopolies'. It also appealed on the same day to the Inter-American Peace Committee,[73] but subsequently withdrew its request to the regional body in order that its case should be dealt with exclusively by the Security Council. The Security Council, of which the United States representative, Mr. Henry Cabot Lodge, was president at the time, met on 20 June to hear Guatemala's case; Honduras and Nicaragua were also represented at the meeting. Guatemala alleged that she was the victim of aggression and requested the Security Council to call upon Honduras and Nicaragua to intern the insurgent forces operating from their territory. She also asked the Council to send an observation com-

---

[71] Pendle, '*Latin America*', *op. cit.*, p. 374.

[72] It is debatable whether this was a serious request or part of the 'build-up' to United States action to overthrow Arbenz.

[73] This body, provided for during the Second World War but not established until afterwards, was utilised to help resolve disputes between members of the OAS because of the ineffectiveness of the Pact of Bogotá. See above, p. 202.

mission to Guatemala. The two accused countries denied the charges, which they said should be dealt with by the OAS. This last was also the strongly expressed contention of the United States. Cabot Lodge vigorously denounced the Soviet Union's support of Guatemala's request as interference in the affairs of the western hemisphere. Brazil and Colombia (the Latin American members of the Security Council) proposed a resolution referring the matter to the OAS, which, slightly amended, was supported by ten members of the Council but vetoed by the Soviet Union. Finally, an ineffective resolution proposed by France was adopted under which the Council called for 'the immediate termination of any action likely to cause bloodshed and [requested] all Members of the United Nations to abstain, in the spirit of the Charter, from giving assistance to any such action'.

Honduras and Nicaragua then asked the Inter-American Peace Committee to appoint a special investigating subcommittee to visit them and Guatemala. But Guatemala refused to co-operate in this proposal and, supported by the Soviet Union, requested a further meeting of the Security Council. The United States strongly opposed the adoption of a provisional agenda containing the Guatemalan complaint, going so far as to threaten that the future of the whole system of peace and security created by the United Nations Charter was at stake. Cabot Lodge contended that the Guatemalan crisis was a local dispute which Chapter VIII declared should be dealt with through regional arrangements where these existed. The OAS was such an arrangement 'which through its regularly constituted agencies is dealing actively with the problem now'. The Soviet representative (Guatemala was not invited to attend pending the adoption of the agenda) argued that the Security Council should consider the Guatemalan complaint, both because it was already seized of it and in view of its primary responsibility in the field of international peace and security. But the provisional agenda was not adopted. Four nations voted in favour, five (including the three American republics) voted against, and two (France and Great Britain) abstained. The effective consequence was to leave the matter to the OAS.

Having thus failed to obtain any satisfaction from the Security Council, the Guatemalan government decided to co-operate with the Inter-American Peace Committee, which then arranged to send an investigating team to the three countries immediately involved on 28 June. Two days before that date ten members of the OAS, including the United States, called for a Meeting of Consultation in view of what they described as 'the demonstrated intervention of the international communist movement in the Republic of Guatemala and the danger which this involves for the peace and security of the Continent'. A special session of the OAS Council, held on 28 June, convoked a meeting of the Organ of Consultation[74] for 7 July at Rio de Janeiro. It is again revealing that the OAS Council did not follow what had become the usual procedure of constituting itself provisional Organ of Consultation and acting on the matter, for by this time the overthrow of the Arbenz government was virtually assured. The United States Ambassador, John E. Peurifoy, was playing a leading—indeed a flamboyant—part in arranging a new government in Guatemala acceptable to Washington.[75] With the installation of the new government the case ceased to exist. The Peace Committee's investigating team got no farther on its journey than Mexico City. On 2 July the OAS Council, meeting in special session, adopted a resolution, presented by Honduras and seconded by the United States, postponing *sine die* the Meeting of Consultation. Argentina, however, believed the affair should be investigated, implying that the countries accused by Guatemala would welcome the opportunity to have the truth of their denials of complicity confirmed. But this proved not to be the case, for the matter was not pursued. The documents relating to the OAS action were sent to the United Nations. The case was now officially closed, but the matter was not ended.

In so far as it involved the issue of competence between the inter-American system and the United Nations, the Guatemalan case, among other things, underlined the difficulty of distinguishing between a dispute and an act of aggression, as well as that of reconciling the rights and obligations of members under the United Nations and OAS Charters in the field of international peace and security. Guatemala contended that she was the victim of aggression and therefore entitled to have her case dealt with by the Security Council, even though the Arbenz government twice appealed to the Inter-American Peace Committee. The United States asserted in the Security Council that this was a local dispute which *had to be* dealt with by the OAS. She was, in effect, seeking to establish the autonomy of the inter-American system in dealing with disputes among its members.

---

[74] See above, p. 197.
[75] See, for example, David Wise and Thomas B. Ross, *The Invisible Government* (London, 1965), pp. 165–83.

But, in reality, the issue of competence was irrelevant in the Guatemalan affair, for the two organisations were presented with quite different cases. It is apparent that the United States used the 'regional' argument primarily in order to prevent any United Nations action prejudicial to the success of the operations against Arbenz in which she was engaged: for, as became known later, the Central Intelligence Agency was the instigator of the invasion. In the OAS, to which (in the Security Council) she so strongly urged Guatemala should take her complaint, the Arbenz government would have been not the plaintiff but the defendant, against charges by the United States and other American republics. The record indicates, however, that the convocation of a Meeting of Consultation was no more than a smoke screen; that the United States had no wish to have the affair discussed in the OAS either. Her policy ensured that neither the inter-American system nor the United Nations was able to assist the Arbenz government. Mr. Dulles claimed in a broadcast to the people of the United States on 30 June: 'The events of recent months and days add a new and glorious chapter to the already great tradition of the American States.'[76] For Latin Americans, however, these events represented another chapter in the tradition of United States intervention in their internal and external affairs which had been broken only partially by the Good Neighbour policy.

Nor were the Latin American countries alone in their misgivings. There was a wider feeling among members of the United Nations that Guatemala should have had a proper hearing by the Security Council, and it is significant that two major allies of the United States, France and Great Britain, abstained in the vote to have the Guatemalan case put on the agenda for the second time, thereby not supporting United States opposition to its inclusion. In his first report to the General Assembly following the affair, the Secretary General of the United Nations declared that: ' . . . a policy giving full scope to the proper role of regional agencies can and should at the same time fully preserve the right of a Member nation to a hearing under the Charter'.[77]

The implications of the Guatemalan case for the countries of Latin America were serious. The United States had claimed not only that the Guatemalan government had no right to take its complaint to

---

[76] US Dept. of State, *Intervention of International Communism in Guatemala op. cit.*, p. 33.

[77] United Nations, General Assembly, *Official Records*, Ninth Session, Suppl. 1 (A/2663), p. xi.

the United Nations, but that its doing so, and thereby invoking the support of the Soviet Union, had substantiated the case against it: that it was dominated by international communism and therefore constituted a threat to the hemisphere. Regardless of their feelings towards the Arbenz government, the other Latin American countries felt it important that their right of appeal to the world organisation should be confirmed, even though United States influence in the United Nations—as the Guatemalan case had underlined—was so great as severely to limit the value of this right. A number of them denied in a subsequent General Assembly debate that membership in the OAS restricted their right to have immediate recourse to the United Nations. Even Brazil, who had supported the United States in the Security Council, denied that she had thereby implied that the latter could not deal with the case.[78]

Thus the Guatemalan affair was a very significant event in United States relations with Latin America since the end of the Second World War. It was reminiscent of earlier interventions in the Caribbean region, and it helped to set the stage for the later Cuban crisis. It had certain lessons to teach the Cuban leaders. Castro undoubtedly was influenced by events in Guatemala in making preparations to ensure that the Central Intelligence Agency did not repeat its 'success' against him. The CIA, on the other hand, appears to have thought it could so so in the very different Cuban circumstances.[79] Incidentally, Che Guevara was in Guatemala for a short while during the crisis, and the experience was not lost upon him, nor upon other Latin American revolutionaries.[80] In Latin America as a whole, it re-awakened and reinforced fears of United States intervention, both collective and unilateral. Nor did subsequent developments in Guatemala support United States claims to be defending the freedom of the Americas; rather did they confirm the essentially counter-revolutionary character of her Latin American policy. After what Mecham calls 'the restoration of popular government' in Guatemala[81]

---

[78] Inis L. Claude, Jr., 'The OAS, the UN, and the United States', *International Concili-ation*, No. 547 (March 1964), pp. 33–34.     [79] See below, p. 231, n. 10.

[80] Richard Gott, *Rural Guerrillas in Latin America* (revised, paperback edn., Harmonds-worth 1973), p. 61, calls the overthrow of Arbenz 'this cardinal event' in the history of the guerrilla movements in Latin America.

[81] *A Survey of United States–Latin American Relations, op. cit.*, p. 193. In his account of the Guatemalan crisis Mecham glosses over the role of the United States. He writes of her 'alleged giving of indirect aid to the rebels (which aid, incidentally, did not prove to be necessary)'. *Ibid.*, p. 219.

labour unions and all political parties were suppressed. And, although limited agrarian reform continued, the United Fruit Company received back most of its lands. The social revolution initiated by Arévalo was halted. Guatemala entered another period of dictatorship and increasing violence. Castillo Armas himself was assassinated in 1957. In the following year, General Miguel Ydígoras Fuentes, who had served under Ubico before 1944, became President.

It had been clear at the Tenth Inter-American Conference that Latin American hopes of receiving United States economic aid were an important consideration in discouraging more open support for Guatemala. But these hopes were disappointed: full discussion of economic problems was shelved until a meeting of American finance ministers at Rio de Janeiro (22 November until 2 December 1954). At Rio, however, the United States promised little beyond more substantial and speedier loans, with increased lending authority for the Export-Import Bank. What the Latin Americans wanted was higher and more stable prices for their raw materials; larger credits for the industrialisation of their countries; United States participation in a new international bank concerned exclusively with their economic development; and encouragement in their plans for establishing a Latin American common market. These wishes were not met at the Rio conference; nor did a special committee, established after a Meeting of the Heads of State of the American Republics had been held at Panama City in July 1956, accomplish anything important. No less disappointing was the long-awaited Economic Conference of the Organization of American States held at Buenos Aires in August–September 1957. The Economic Declaration of Buenos Aires was nothing more than a statement of principles. The United States continued to maintain that existing institutions were adequate to finance 'sound' projects.

However, the Buenos Aires conference did accept in principle the economic integration of Latin America and recommended co-operation with the United Nations Economic Commission for Latin America (ECLA) in studying it. ECLA, concerned with the subject since the previous year, had submitted to the conference a study entitled 'ECLA Activities Relating to Payments and a Regional Market in Latin America'. It is significant—but not surprising—that the movement towards regional markets in Latin America received impetus from the United Nations body and not the OAS. This was owing primarily to the attitude of the United States, who viewed the economic integration of Latin America with suspicion linked with general dislike of ECLA. Of course, the movement towards economic integration was an expression of Pan Latin Americanism rather than Pan Americanism. According to a prominent writer on the subject:

> Official United States documents and the writings of leading United States experts in Hemispheric affairs abound in circumstantial evidence that until the middle of 1960 the United States looked upon integration efforts with a mixture of ideological disapproval and deep distrust. These attitudes were closely related to a general distrust of ECLA. Over a decade, many influential people in the United States—both in the government and in the private sector—considered ECLA an intruder in Hemispheric economic relations, a defender of dangerous statist and 'socialistic' tendencies, and a competitor of the OAS. Any proposals coming from or sponsored by ECLA were viewed as a continuous incitement to Latin American countries to 'gang up' against the United States in order to force economic and other concessions. These attitudes were further strengthened by the thinly disguised fear of some United States foreign trade interests that expansion of intra-regional trade in Latin America—the United States' second largest market—would be detrimental to United States exporters.[82]

Regional economic integration in Latin America was encouraged by developments in western Europe; and the presence of observers from a large number of extra-continental nations at Buenos Aires reflected an awareness that Latin America's economic problems could not be solved within a purely hemispheric framework.

As we have seen, relations between United States and Latin America had become more responsive to the general world situation since the end of the Second World War; they had been influenced especially by the establishment of the United Nations (with full American participation) and the development of the Cold War. In the middle nineteen-fifties there occurred new developments in the world situation of significance for inter-American relations. In 1955 (two years after the death of Stalin) Mr. Khrushchev emerged as the leader of the Soviet Union, with his proclaimed policy of 'peaceful coexistence'. In December of the same year a 'package deal' over the admission of new members began the process of enlarging the United Nations and greatly increasing the size of the Afro-Asian group of countries

---

[82] Miguel S. Wionczek, 'Latin American Free Trade Association', *International Conciliation*, No. 551 (January 1965), pp. 24–5.

within it. The General Assembly could no longer be counted upon to provide the necessary majority for anti-communist measures; it became progressively more neutralist, and, above all, 'anti-colonial' in sentiment. In this last respect the Latin American countries were generally sympathetic towards the Afro-Asian nations.[83] Most ominously, for all these countries—African, Asian and Latin American —the problems of economic development were (and are) vastly more important than any threat from international communism, and the division of the world into rich and poor nations more meaningful than one between 'Free' and 'Communist'. However, this is to look ahead. In April 1955 fewer than thirty African and Asian countries attended the first major conference of non-aligned nations held at Bandung in Indonesia.

But the idea of a 'Third Position' in the world—a middle way between capitalism and communism—had a prominent advocate in Latin America for several years before the Bandung conference: Juan Perón, the President of Argentina. We have already seen Perón as the *bête-noire* of the United States in the nineteen-forties,[84] and have noted Argentina's traditional coolness towards Pan Americanism. Perón was also following traditional policy in seeking to extend Argentina's influence over her Spanish American neighbours, who formerly were part of the Viceroyalty of the Rio de la Plata.[85] But he claimed a new philosophy in *justicialismo*, which embraced, in respect of foreign policy, the concept of a Third Position in world affairs, aligned with neither the United States nor the Soviet Union. Nationalism was a strong ingredient in Perón's policies, both foreign and domestic. But Perón could not sustain a non-aligned position. Faced with mounting economic difficulties and opposition to his dictatorial rule, he turned for financial assistance to the United States, where the Eisenhower administration decided belatedly to adopt a more conciliatory policy towards him. The Argentine ruler agreed to grant oil concessions to North American companies. This in its turn offended

---

[83] Some Latin American countries (notably Argentina, Guatemala and Venezuela) themselves had 'anti-colonial' claims to British dependencies in the western hemisphere. See above, p. 177, n. 67. These claims remain (at the end of 1973) unsatisfied.

[84] See above, pp. 184, 193, ff.

[85] I.e. Bolivia, Paraguay and Uruguay. The latter, however, had been an area of rivalry between the Spanish and Portuguese empires during the colonial period: a rivalry which was continued by Argentina and Brazil. As we saw above (p. 69), Britain forced these countries to accept Uruguay as an independent buffer state between them in 1828. Rivalry for influence over Uruguay did not cease, however. See below, p. 260.

Argentine nationalism, and lost Perón further support.[86] He was overthrown by the armed forces in September 1955. Thus had the United States contributed to both Perón's rise to power and his downfall. Her opposition had helped to secure his election in 1946;[87] her support was a not insignificant factor in his overthrow nine years later.

Relations between the United States and Latin America became more difficult during the later nineteen-fifties. Latin Americans were increasingly dissatisfied with the United States response to their economic problems and her only too apparent predilection for dictators who co-operated with her. The fact that these years witnessed the downfall of a number of such dictators added to United States embarrassment rather than otherwise. As one writer pointed out: 'This progressive restriction of the area of authoritarian government in Latin America had been accomplished by the people of the countries concerned with no particular encouragement, still less any active help, from the United States.'[88] And although the United States maintained that her policy towards dictators was based on the principle of non-intervention, her sincerity was questionable after her intervention in Guatemala to overthrow a government of which she did not approve.[89] In 1958 the United States was made forcibly aware of Latin American resentment by the treatment meted out to Vice-President Nixon during his 'goodwill' tour.

In the spring of 1958, when Mr. Nixon set out on a tour which took him to seven Latin American countries,[90] unwarranted complacency prevailed in Washington over the state of inter-American relations. The violent demonstrations against the Vice-President came as a great shock to the government and public opinion alike. For although the visit provoked disorders in only two countries, Peru and Venezuela, and the immediate reaction was to blame them upon communist agitators, the United States came to realise that they were symptomatic of much wider discontent. There were particular

---

[86] Harold F. Peterson, *Argentina and the United States, 1810–1960* (New York, State University of New York, 1964), pp. 492–3.

[87] See above, p. 196.

[88] Richard P. Stebbins, *The United States in World Affairs, 1958* (New York, Council on Foreign Relations, 1959), p. 353.

[89] The extent to which the Arbenz government was under communist influence is debatable. There is no doubt about United States disapproval and determination to overthrow it.

[90] Uruguay, Argentina, Paraguay, Bolivia, Peru, Colombia and Venezuela.

economic grievances as well as the general ones already mentioned. These included United States restrictions and tariffs on certain basic agricultural commodities exported by Peru; restrictions on imports of Venezuelan oil; and the knowledge that the United States was contemplating quota restrictions on imports of zinc and lead—a blow to Mexico and Peru. There was also widespread criticism of United States friendship with dictators, several of whom, including Pérez Jiménez of Venezuela (overthrown the previous January), and former President Odría of Peru, had received high decorations from the United States government. Mr. and Mrs. Nixon were the targets of pent-up Latin American resentment. President Eisenhower despatched troops to the Caribbean region in case they were needed in order to ensure their safety. Fortunately, the troops were not needed, although the Vice-President and his wife had some unpleasant moments.[91]

In spite of Mr. Nixon's experience, the Eisenhower administration was slow to take action to improve its relations with Latin America. It was President Juscelino Kubitschek of Brazil who took the initiative. He wrote to President Eisenhower proposing an 'Operation Pan America' designed to revitalise the inter-American system through new measures of political and economic co-operation. Eisenhower's reply was non-committal, and contained the following revealing sentence: 'There is a wide range of subjects to be discussed and explored, including, for example, the problem of implementing more fully the Declaration of Solidarity of the Tenth Inter-American Conference held at Caracas in 1954.'[92] This was the anti-communist resolution.[93] In August 1958, however, the United States government announced that it was now prepared to consider the establishment of an inter-American bank. After an informal meeting of American Foreign Ministers in the following month, the OAS Council was asked to set up a 'Special Committee to Study the Formulation of New Measures for Economic Cooperation', subsequently known as the 'Committee of Twenty-One'. At its first meeting (Washington,

---

[91] But it must be observed that Nixon courted some of these by his evident desire for the maximum publicity in order to further his political ambitions. Willard Beaulac, for example, who was United States Ambassador in Buenos Aires at the time, speaks (*A Diplomat Looks at Aid to Latin America*, *op. cit.*, p. 7) of 'the imprudence of a youthful and ambitious vice-president'.

[92] *Dept. of State Bulletin*, xxxviii/992 (1958), p. 1090.

[93] See above, pp. 212 ff.

17 November until 12 December 1958) this committee agreed to the establishment of an inter-American development bank. But President Kubitschek's 'Operation Pan America' was accepted only in principle —and shelved.[94] In the following month, Dr. Milton Eisenhower made a second report (after a visit, this time, to Central America), confirming his earlier one and describing the situation as even more serious than in 1953.[95]

When the Committee of Twenty-One held its second meeting, at Buenos Aires from 27 April until 8 May 1959, there had occurred an event marking the beginning of a new phase in United States relations with Latin America, and the central character in that event made a dramatic appearance at its proceedings. Dr. Fidel Castro had overthrown the Cuban dictator, Fulgencio Batista, at the end of 1958. He now proposed a $30,000 million Marshall Plan for Latin America over a ten-year period. Castro declared that 'what we need can be obtained only from the United States, and only by means of public financing'.[96] The committee as a whole did not take this proposal very seriously. But both the substance of the proposal, and the challenge to the United States of which it was a part, would have to be treated with increasing seriousness in the coming years.

---

[94] But subsequent measures of inter-American economic and social co-operation (The Act of Bogotá and the Alliance for Progress) purported to be 'within the framework of Operation Pan America'. See below, pp. 232–3.

[95] M. S. Eisenhower, 'United States–Latin American Relations, 1953–1958: Report to the President', *Dept. of State Bulletin*, xl/1021 (1959), pp. 89–105.

[96] Quoted in Connell-Smith, *The Inter-American System, op. cit.*, p. 168.

# 7 The United States and Latin America in the Post-War World II:

## Since the Cuban Revolution

This chapter covers one of the most crucial periods in the history of relations between the United States and Latin America. The Cuban revolution was followed by a series of events which challenged United States hegemony in the western hemisphere to an unprecedented degree. The revolutionary Cuban government's alignment with the Soviet Union, and its subsequent exclusion from the inter-American system, made United States relations with the island a matter of global and not merely hemispheric significance. The Cuban missile crisis of October 1962 was perhaps the most immediately dangerous international event of the post-war world. The nineteen-sixties brought a growing identification of Latin America with the 'Third' or 'developing' world. They witnessed new efforts by the countries of Latin America to lessen their economic dependence upon the United States, both by forming a common front in negotiating with her, and by widening their commercial relations outside the hemisphere. These developments were linked with the fortunes of the Alliance for Progress, whose birth and virtual demise fell within this decade. Towards the end of the decade there was evidence of greatly increasing (anti-United States) nationalism in Latin America, and a new phenomenon emerged of social revolution led by military governments in Peru and (for a while) Bolivia. In the early nineteen-seventies further developments occurred which could prove of comparable significance with the Cuban revolution in the history of inter-American relations: the election of a Marxist President in Chile and his overthrow by military coup after three critical years in office.

It was nothing new for Cuba to play an important role in relations between the United States and Latin America as a whole. We have already seen the island's significance at various key stages in the history of inter-American relations. We noted the part played by United States concern over the future of Cuba in the formulation of the Monroe

Doctrine, and Cuba's place in the expansionist plans of the proponents of Manifest Destiny (including the latter's fears of an 'Africanisation' of the island). We saw how importantly Cuba figured in the emergence of the United States as a world power at the end of the nineteenth century. We noted how the treaty of 1903 gave to the United States the specific right of intervention in the internal and external affairs of Cuba which she soon was to claim in general terms (in the Roosevelt Corollary to the Monroe Doctrine) over the whole region, and which was to be the central issue in inter-American relations during the early decades of the twentieth century. We observed Cuba's significant role in the formulation of the Good Neighbour policy, illustrating both United States opposition to social revolution in the region and the limits of 'non-intervention'. United States support for Fulgencio Batista seemed to many Latin Americans typical of a general policy of preferring such dictatorships which co-operated with her to democractic governments which might initiate changes inimical to her interests.

The Cuban situation of the nineteen-sixties had its roots deep in the history of the island's relations with the United States. United States power—and presence—weighed particularly heavily upon Cuba. The latter's economy was tied to that of her great neighbour, who also secured the lease in perpetuity of Cuban territory as part of the price of granting her nominal independence. The historical experience of Cuba well illustrates how United States hegemony followed upon the exclusion of extra-continental power from the hemisphere. For Cuba passed at once from being a European possession to becoming a United States satellite. It is not surprising that Cuban nationalism should be directed against the United States; nor was racial prejudice an insignificant factor in the attitude of North Americans towards the Cubans. The Cuban revolution involved an assertion of Cuba's nationhood and the dignity of Cubans after over half a century of client status, and a total rejection of the United States self-image as the island's liberator and benefactor. Both as a nationalist and as a revolutionary—indeed as a national revolutionary—Fidel Castro represented a most serious challenge to the United States.

There has been considerable—but inconclusive—debate over Dr. Castro's communist sympathies in the early stages of his revolution. There is no doubt of his determination to bring about a revolution which would end the privileged position hitherto enjoyed by the United States in the island's affairs. This being the case, it is difficult to envisage any politically feasible course whereby a United States administration could have averted the clash that in fact ensued. And in this inevitable struggle with the United States, Castro could hope to survive only with Soviet support. Thus there came about the situation which historically it had been the major objective of United States Latin American policy to prevent. The Monroe Doctrine proclaimed that the United States could not view the extension of an extra-continental system to any part of the western hemisphere otherwise than as endangering her peace and security. The alignment of Cuba with the Soviet Union was the clearest possible violation of the Doctrine.

But this is to move ahead of events. Following Batista's defeat, the Eisenhower administration proceeded cautiously. It almost immediately recognised the new Cuban government. It is difficult to escape the conclusion that American leaders were importantly influenced by a conviction—apparently well justified by historical experience as well as by current circumstances—that once in power Castro would be forced by the facts of Cuba's position *vis-à-vis* the United States drastically to modify his revolutionary proposals. Only gradually did the Eisenhower administration come to realise that it had misread the situation.[1] As the Cuban government moved to expropriate United States properties and to conclude trade agreements with the Soviet Union and other communist countries, relations with its powerful neighbour grew dangerously worse. In July 1960—after showing no little restraint in the face of provocation—the Eisenhower administration virtually ended Cuba's sugar quota in the United States market. This action was denounced by Castro as 'economic aggression' in a complaint to the Security Council of the United Nations. In the same month Mr. Khrushchev, in a speech strongly supporting the Cuban leader, was quoted as saying: 'Figuratively speaking, Soviet artillerists, in the event of necessity, can with their rocket firepower support the Cuban people if the aggressive forces in the Pentagon dare begin intervention against Cuba.' On the same day President Eisenhower, citing Khrushchev's speech as showing a 'clear intention to establish Cuba in a role serving Soviet purposes in this hemisphere', warned that the

---

[1] Complacency was a characteristic of the Eisenhower administration in its dealings with Latin America. On his return from a goodwill tour of South American countries in February–March 1960, the President declared in a broadcast that 'our relationships with our sister Republics have, with notable—but very few—exceptions, reached an alltime high': Richard P. Stebbins, *The United States in World Affairs, 1960* (New York, Council on Foreign Relations, 1961), p. 301. Not long after making that statement, however, Eisenhower ordered the training of Cuban exiles in Guatemala (see below, p. 230, n. 6).

United States would not 'in conformity with its treaty obligations, permit the establishment of a regime dominated by international communism in the Western Hemisphere'. Commenting on the President's statement at a news conference three days later, Khrushchev contended that the Monroe Doctrine had lost its validity; it was dead and should be buried.

The Russian leader's assertion roused the State Department to affirm that 'the principles of the Monroe Doctrine are as valid today as they were in 1823 when the Doctrine was proclaimed'. It described the Doctrine as 'supported by the inter-American security system through the Organization of American States'. But was this really so? The Guatemalan experience of 1954 suggested otherwise. Already the advent of Castro had added to the international tensions prevalent in the traditionally turbulent Caribbean region; in particular, there was mounting antagonism between the Cuban leader and Trujillo, the right-wing Dominican dictator. With his outspoken admirers in the United States Congress,[2] Trujillo—even more than Batista in Cuba— was the very archetype of Latin American dictator Washington appeared to favour. Castro, on the other hand, represented something new in Latin America, and his very hostility towards the United States was bound to win him supporters. The denunciation of Castro by the United States seemed to many Latin Americans in striking contrast to her long-standing support of Trujillo.[3] While the United States infinitely preferred Trujillo to Castro, the feelings of many Latin Americans were exactly the opposite. When the Fifth Meeting of Consultation of American Foreign Ministers was held at Santiago de Chile in August 1959 to consider the Caribbean situation, the United States found herself the champion of non-intervention in the face of strong demands for measures to bring about the downfall of the Dominican dictator.

A year later, the Sixth and Seventh Meetings of Consultation, held at San José, Costa Rica, dealt respectively with situations involving

[2] See below, pp. 277–8.
[3] For example, horror expressed in the United States at the trial and execution of people accused of committing atrocities during the Batista regime was regarded as hypocritical when contrasted with the lack of comparable reaction in Washington to the massacre of a large number of Haitian civilians for which the Trujillo dictatorship was responsible (see below, p. 278). Nor had there been comparable condemnation of atrocities committed by the Batista regime itself, while the brutalities of numerous other Latin American dictatorships enjoying United States support in the past had largely been overlooked.

the Dominican Republic and Cuba. But, while the Sixth Meeting considered specific charges brought by Venezuela under the Rio Treaty against Trujillo of aggression culminating in an assassination attempt against her President, the Seventh debated only the general question of communist intervention in the western hemisphere. The Sixth Meeting, having found the Trujillo regime guilty of Venezuela's charges, resolved that the other American states should break diplomatic relations and partially interrupt economic relations with the Dominican Republic. This was the first time in the history of the inter-American system that sanctions had been imposed upon one of its members. Whether the OAS, in its capacity as a 'regional agency' under the United Nations Charter,[4] could impose such measures without the authorisation of the Security Council was the subject of subsequent debate in the latter body. The Soviet Union argued that, since the OAS measures clearly constituted 'enforcement action', they needed Security Council approval. But the United States, supported by a majority of the Council, contended that the term 'enforcement action' applied only to the use of armed force. The Security Council therefore merely 'took note of' OAS action against the Dominican Republic. Thus the United States achieved a significant success for her policy of restricting United Nations involvement in 'American' questions. The precedent would later be cited in the case of Cuba. But at this point it was not relevant. For a declaration of the Seventh Meeting against 'Sino-Soviet' intervention in the Americas did not mention Cuba by name and provided no basis for action to bring about Castro's overthrow. Neither United States support for sanctions against Trujillo, nor a promise of additional economic aid made on the eve of the San José meetings, persuaded the Latin American delegations to accept a stronger resolution.[5]

For some months now (since March 1960) the Central Intelligence Agency had been planning an invasion of Cuba by Cuban exiles.[6] The

---

[4] Since the Dominican Republic had not committed an armed attack upon Venezuela Article 51 of the United Nations Charter did not apply. See above, pp. 192–3.

[5] It is of interest that the Mexican delegation insisted upon appending a 'Statement' to the Final Act of the Seventh Meeting affirming the general character of the resolution and 'that in no way is it a condemnation or a threat against Cuba, whose aspirations for economic improvement and social justice have the fullest support of the Government and the people of Mexico'.

[6] According to his memoirs, *The White House Years, vol. 2: Waging Peace, 1956–1961* (London, 1966), p. 533, President Eisenhower ordered the CIA to organise the training of Cuban exiles, mainly in Guatemala, on 17 March 1960. In the following December he suggested to the State Department the formation of a Cuban government in exile and its recognition by the United States (*ibid.*, pp. 613–14).

urge to do something drastic was very strong. In the United States view Cuba had become a Soviet satellite in the western hemisphere, thereby flouting the Monroe Doctrine to a degree that could not be tolerated. Unwilling openly to invade Cuba in order to effect Castro's downfall, the United States government chose the course of sponsoring an invasion by Cuban exiles which, it presumed,[7] would give the signal for a popular uprising within the island. But, in the event, this plan was not put into operation by the Eisenhower administration. In the autumn of 1960 a presidential election campaign was in progress. Senator John F. Kennedy, the Democractic candidate, attacked the Republican administration for allowing a communist base to be established only ninety miles from the shores of the United States[8] and called for action seemingly along the lines already being planned by the CIA.[9] Vice-President Nixon, his Republican opponent, who, of course, was privy to the invasion project—and indeed strongly supported it—denounced Kennedy's proposal as irresponsible.[10] When he assumed the presidency, Mr. Kennedy inherited the invasion plan and, because of his campaign position on the Cuban issue, he had a moral commitment to it. Moreover, he was concerned about public criticism should he abandon a plan to overthrow the Cuban leader, and apparently was influenced also by 'his own deep feeling against Castro (unusual for him)'.[11] In April 1961 the new President authorised the CIA plan to be put into effect, but he was determined to minimise the role played by United States forces in the actual military operations. Under these circumstances, the invasion in the Bay of Pigs failed.

---

[7] The plan's only hope of success lay in such an uprising. The United States government had no reliable evidence that this was likely to take place, and was very much a victim of its own propaganda in assessing the situation in Cuba at this time.

[8] This was political opportunism on Kennedy's part. Earlier he had criticised the Eisenhower administration for not dealing with Castro more sympathetically. On this point, see the comments of Philip W. Bonsal, *Cuba, Castro, and the United States* (University of Pittsburgh Press, 1971), pp. 181 ff. Bonsal was the last United States Ambassador to Cuba.

[9] Nixon later asserted that Kennedy had been briefed on the project; Kennedy denied that this had been the case.

[10] Nixon declared in reply that the United States should 'quarantine' Castro as she had done Arbenz in 1954! In fact, the CIA-planned invasion of Cuba was in essence an attempt to repeat the successful subversion of the Guatemalan government seven years earlier. As we have noted, the Cuban exiles, ironically, were trained in Guatemala. Both the presidential candidates were, of course, fully aware of the role of the CIA in the Guatemalan crisis of 1954. See above, p. 218.

[11] Sorensen, *Kennedy, op. cit.*, p. 341.

This episode weakened the United States position in a number of ways. On the eve of the invasion the State Department issued a White Paper claiming that the United States initially had welcomed Castro's revolution, and became concerned only after he had 'betrayed' it. Whatever credence this might otherwise have enjoyed was virtually destroyed by the ominous predilection shown by those organising the invasion for former supporters of Batista and their distinct suspicion of Cuban exiles who had at first supported Castro but later defected from him. At the United Nations only her powerful influence prevented the United States from being condemned for aggression against Cuba, whose delegation had for some time been protesting that such an invasion was being planned—in the face of scornful denials by the American delegation. President Kennedy subsequently assumed complete responsibility for the abortive invasion, but warned the Latin American governments that, if necessary, the United States would act unilaterally to safeguard her security. Certainly, the Bay of Pigs invasion would make it more difficult for these governments to support the United States in what many Latin Americans regarded as *her* quarrel with Castro.

The invasion plan was not the only significant legacy in the field of inter-American relations bequeathed to President Kennedy by his predecessor. We have already noted that, on the eve of the San José Meetings of Foreign Ministers, the Eisenhower administration had promised increased economic aid to Latin America. In the following September, at the third and final meeting of the Committee of Twenty-One, held at Bogotá, the United States undertook to make available an additional $500 millions for 'projects designed to contribute to opportunities for a better way of life for the individual citizens of the countries of Latin America'. This pledge was contained in a document designated the 'Act of Bogotá, Measures for Social Improvement and Economic Development within the Framework of Operation Pan America'.[12] United States support for these measures represented a further shift in the position of the Eisenhower administration in response to events in Latin America. The Act of Bogotá thus paved the way for Kennedy's Alliance for Progress much as President Hoover's initiation of the policy of non-intervention had done for Franklin Roosevelt's Good Neighbour policy.[13] But shortly after winning the election Kennedy asked Adolf Berle, Jr., who, as we have seen, had

---

[12] See above, pp. 224–5.                    [13] See above, pp. 157–8.

considerable experience of inter-American affairs, to head a task force on Latin America to work on a new United States initiative.

The Alliance for Progress, outlined by President Kennedy in a speech to Latin American diplomats at the White House in March 1961 was inaugurated on the following 17 August with the adoption of 'The Charter of Punta del Este,[14] Establishing an Alliance for Progress within the Framework of Operation Pan America'. It was also to be within the framework of representative democracy. In subscribing to this charter the United States promised to provide the major share of 'a supply of capital from all external sources during the coming ten years of at least 20 billion[15] dollars', the greater part of which sum 'should be in public funds'. For their part, the Latin American governments pledged themselves to carry out *inter alia* 'the social reforms necessary to permit a fair distribution of the fruits of economic and social progress'. Each country was to formulate its own national development programme for which external assistance would be forthcoming. A minimum target was set for every country of a 2·5 per cent *per capita* annual increase in economic growth. Economic integration in Latin America, steps towards which had been taken[16] in spite of United States lukewarmness in the past,[17] was recognised in the Charter of Punta del Este as necessary to accelerate the process of economic development in the hemisphere. Cuba, although represented at Punta del Este, did not sign the charter, and the United States made it clear in any case that she would provide no funds for the island as long as its government retained its ties with the Soviet Union. Che Guevara, who headed the Cuban delegation, warned the other Latin American delegates that 'this meeting is in some way tied to a foreign ministers' meeting at which the case of Cuba is to be discussed. We understand that many steps have been taken in this direction, to search for affirmative votes for the meeting'.[18] As we shall see, such a meeting was in fact held at Punta del Este itself in the following January.

---

[14] Named after the Uruguayan seaside resort where it was signed.

[15] I.e. US billion, equal to 1,000 millions.

[16] The Treaty establishing a Free Trade Area and instituting the Latin American Free Trade Association was signed at Montevideo on 18 February 1960 by representatives of Argentina, Brazil, Chile, Mexico, Paraguay, Peru and Uruguay, with provision for Bolivia's adherence. Colombia, Ecuador and Venezuela subsequently adhered to the Montevideo Treaty. In December 1960 El Salvador, Guatemala, Honduras and Nicaragua signed the General Treaty of Central American Economic Integration. Costa Rica adhered later.

[17] See above, pp. 220–1.

[18] Gerassi (ed.), *Venceremos!*, *op. cit.*, p. 186.

The close association of the Alliance for Progress with the United States anti-communist policy in Latin America gravely prejudiced the fulfilment of the programme. For those governments most firmly supporting measures against Castro tended to be the least inclined to carry out the reforms upon which the success of the Alliance depended. There were other built-in contradictions. A significant one was pointed out by David Huelin:

> The centre and right-wing parties that come within the U.S. definition of 'democratic' can probably be relied on to preserve attractive investment climates and to respect all the rights of private, including foreign, investors, but they are unlikely to undertake the agrarian and other reforms that the Alliance for Progress demands. The populist movements are largely committed to precisely these reforms, but also to others that would involve the expropriation of foreign investments and would be most distasteful to U.S. opinion.[19]

As we have already noted, the Hickenlooper Amendment to the Foreign Assistance Act, passed a year later, called for the suspension of aid to any country that expropriated United States-owned property without providing prompt and equitable compensation.[20] In any case, the United States was determined to foster stability in Latin America, while far-reaching reforms, in the short term, tend to cause instability. Moreover, in spite of being formulated as a co-operative enterprise, the Alliance was widely regarded as a United States rather than an authentic inter-American programme; it was unhappily described as 'A New Deal for Latin America'. And, although an Inter-American Committee on the Alliance for Progress was subsequently created, the United States continued to make the crucial decisions on allocating the funds she furnished—virtually the whole of which in the event had to be spent on goods produced by her.[21] These decisions derived from rivalries between the different government departments and agencies concerned, as well as from conflicts between the Executive and the Congress.[22]

---

[19] 'Latin America's development crisis', *The World Today*, vol. 19, no. 9 (September 1963), p. 409.

[20] See above, p. 17.

[21] The United States Congress stipulated in the Foreign Assistance Act of 1962 that appropriated funds must be spent in the United States unless the president found this stipulation to be inconsistent with the national interest in special cases.

[22] See above, p. 13, n. 39.

Meanwhile, with the Alliance for Progress getting under way, the Cuban question came once more before the OAS. We have already seen the links between United States policies towards Castro and Trujillo. We noted that sanctions were imposed upon the Dominican Republic by the Sixth Meeting of Consultation in August 1960. The United States, who (after initially proposing free elections in the Dominican Republic as an alternative) supported these sanctions, had by now come to regard Trujillo as a liability in her relations with Latin America. Therefore she was pursuing a policy towards the Dominican dictator which could later be directed against Castro. This was evident in January 1961 when she unilaterally imposed further economic sanctions against Trujillo: a measure which encouraged his opponents within the country to hope for United States support against him. Abraham Lowenthal has asserted that:

> American officials in Santo Domingo identified and encouraged a group of anti-Trujillo Dominicans, assuring them that the United States govern-ment would cooperate with them should they gain power. According to some reports, U.S. agents may even have materially aided the Dominican plot which culminated in Trujillo's assassination on May 30, 1961.[23]

Whatever the truth about her involvement in Trujillo's death, the United States was now embarked upon a policy of intervention in Dominican affairs linked with her policy towards Cuba. In Professor Slater's view, this represented 'its most massive intervention in the internal affairs of a Latin American state since the inauguration of the Good Neighbor policy'.[24] I have previously quoted Lowenthal's judgement that the prevention of a 'second Cuba' shaped United States policy towards the Dominican Republic at every stage after Trujillo's death.[25] A United States naval task force patrolled the Dominican coast from very soon after the latter event. In November 1961 it made a dramatic show of force to discourage members of the Trujillo family from attempting to seize power. Such was the unpopularity of the former dictatorship that the United States action aroused little hostile reaction in Latin America as a whole. However, sensing the danger against himself, Castro complained of United States intervention in the

---

[23] *The Dominican Intervention, op. cit.*, p. 10.
[24] Jerome Slater, *The OAS and United States Foreign Policy* (Ohio State University Press, 1967), p. 185.
[25] See above, p. 20.

Dominican Republic to both the Security Council and the OAS Council, but without success.

This episode increased the already strong domestic pressure upon President Kennedy to take some new action against Dr. Castro, and he was anxious to obtain Latin American support for this. But there was a basic difference of viewpoint between the United States and the majority of Latin Americans on the Cuban question. For the former, the very existence of Castro's government, aligned with the Soviet Union, was a threat to the peace and security of the Americas; but for the latter, sanctions could not be imposed upon Cuba under the Rio Treaty unless she committed a specific act of aggression against another American state. When the OAS—at United States urging—resolved to hold a Meeting of Foreign Ministers to consider the Cuban problem, six member states (in addition to Cuba) did not support the resolution: they were Argentina, Bolivia, Brazil, Chile, Ecuador and Mexico. The six thus included the major countries of the region and much more than half its total population. Brazil's position was especially significant for, as we have seen, she generally has stood closer to the United States than has any other of the larger Latin American countries in this century. But under Presidents Kubitschek, Quadros and (at this time) Goulart she was endeavouring to pursue an 'independent' foreign policy. For a brief period there was an unusual degree of co-operation in this field between Brazil and Argentina. However, the United States hoped that, before the Foreign Ministers met, one or more of the six would change its position; she had particular hopes of Argentina, where the government was weak and the military strongly anti-Castro. But President Frondizi persisted in his opposition, and his inevitable overthrow by the army did not occur until the following March.

The Eighth Meeting of Consultation, held at Punta del Este in January 1962, imposed limited sanctions upon Cuba and excluded its 'present government' from participation in the inter-American system: a formula necessitated by the fact that the OAS Charter makes no provision for the expulsion of a member state. The 'exclusion' of Cuba was not supported by the six;[26] neither did it noticeably weaken Castro's position nor bring nearer the downfall of his government. A special consultative committee established by the Eighth Meeting to combat communist subversion in the hemisphere was weakened by the fear of

---

[26] Thus the decision to exclude Cuba received only the bare two-thirds majority required, even though all delegations (except the Cuban) supported that part of the resolution affirming the incompatibility of Marxism-Leninism with the inter-American system.

many Latin American governments that its activities might lead to intervention in their internal affairs. Bolivia did not support the establishment of this committee because of her experience with the Emergency Advisory Committee for Political Defense during the Second World War.[27] Thus it was demonstrated yet again that the issue was a divisive one in inter-American relations, with Latin American opposition to communism being outweighed by fears of United States intervention.

As the year progressed, the United States government became increasingly concerned at growing military links between Cuba and the the Soviet Union. In September, following a statement by the President, Congress passed a joint resolution, citing the Monroe Doctrine and calling for whatever action might be necessary to prevent in Cuba 'the creation or use of an externally supported military capability endangering the security of the United States'. On 22 October 1962, finally in possession of irrefutable evidence that nuclear missile sites were being installed in Cuba, President Kennedy declared his intention to institute a naval quarantine; to increase aerial surveillance of the island; and to make simultaneous appeals to the OAS Council and the Security Council. This last action was unprecedented in the history of the inter-American system; but the crisis was a global one. Confronted with the grave situation—and aware of United States determination to act unilaterally in any case—the OAS gave her a larger measure of support than in any previous crisis. The Council passed a resolution calling for the removal of the missiles, and authorising the use of armed force if necessary to achieve this. But it is noteworthy that Brazil, Mexico and Bolivia (three of 'the six' at Punta del Este earlier in the year) abstained from voting upon that part of the key resolution which implied support for an armed invasion of Cuba. Moreover, the degree of support the United States obtained was to meet the immediate crisis, not for her general policy towards the Cuban government. The role of the OAS had in any case been minimal,[28] and the crisis was resolved by direct negotiations between the United States and the Soviet Union. None of the former's allies, in Latin America or elsewhere, played a significant role in its resolution.

The outcome of the Cuban missile crisis was a triumph for President

---

[27] See above, p. 183.

[28] Yet the United States set considerable store by the OAS Council resolution, and the quarantine did not come into effect *officially* until after it had been passed. See below, p. 274. There was subsequently participation by some Argentine and Venezuelan warships in the quarantine force.

Kennedy in global terms, but it represented an only limited success within the hemispheric context. Although humiliated by the manner in which the settlement was reached, Castro was strengthened rather than weakened by the outcome.[29] For, when the dust had settled, he was still in power, in defiance of the Monroe Doctrine and the acknowledged desire—and apparent impotence—of his great enemy to overthrow him. Whatever the exact nature of a pledge not to invade Cuba which the United States gave to Russia as part of the settlement,[30] it would henceforth be much less easy to launch such an invasion than it had been before the October crisis. Events during the following year confirmed the limited character of the United States success. It proved difficult to obtain support for further measures to curb Castro's subversive activities, and to persuade the remaining Latin American governments which had not yet done so to sever their diplomatic relations with Cuba. Meanwhile, inter-American relations remained far from satisfactory. Disappointment with the achievements of the Alliance for Progress was widespread; the hoped-for overall economic growth rate had not yet been reached. Latin Americans resented United States control of the disbursement of Alliance funds (and their 'tied' character), while in the United States it was felt that the Latin Americans should do very much more to help themselves. The only too obvious connection between the Alliance for Progress and United States policy towards Castro was a recurring source of frustration and resentment.

Thus, when President Kennedy was assassinated in November 1963, the promise of a new era in inter-American relations associated with him was unfulfilled. Moreover, Latin America was ceasing to be regarded in the United States as 'the most critical area' that the late President had called it. President Johnson did not appear to be as sympathetic towards Latin American aspirations as his predecessor had seemed. However, the shift in policy during Johnson's presidency was more apparent than real. In spite of the emphasis in the Charter of Punta del Este upon economic and social development taking place within a democratic framework, the United States had done little in practice to

---

[29] Castro showed a measure of independence by refusing to allow United Nations inspection of the missile sites (to check the removal of the missiles and installations) which was part of the settlement between the United States and Soviet leaders.

[30] The United States maintained that the pledge had been contingent upon the inspection of the missile sites, but appeared to feel herself bound by it.

encourage democracy in Latin America. Military coups in Argentina and Peru in 1962, and in Guatemala, Ecuador, the Dominican Republic and Honduras in the following year were encouraged by United States policy—under the Kennedy administration—of strengthening the military as the strongest force against communism. Particularly significant was the overthrow of Juan Bosch, the first legally elected President of the Dominican Republic for thirty-eight years.

The Johnson administration was soon faced with a crisis in the Panama Canal Zone. The crisis itself was sparked off by an incident over the unauthorised flying of their national flag by United States students in the grounds of their school. But the dispute was an old one. Panama had long criticised the annual payment she received for the zone as inadequate (it was raised to $1·9 millions in 1955), and complained of racial discrimination against her citizens. More recently, she had been anxious to establish, in principle, her sovereignty over the zone (which, of course, she did not exercise) through flying her flag there; and the right to do so—alongside the flag of the United States—was conceded in 1963. However, Panamanian nationalism is affronted by the United States presence, and a desire to 'nationalise' the Canal is inherent in the situation. Following riots and loss of life in the incident of January 1964 Panama broke off diplomatic relations with the United States and charged her in both the Security Council and the OAS with aggression. Mediation was conducted by the latter body. Although peace was soon restored in the Canal Zone, it proved very difficult to settle the differences between the disputants, since the Panamanian government insisted that the United States should negotiate a revision of the 1903 treaty between the two countries, while the United States government would agree only to 'discuss differences' between them. The fact that 1964 was an election year in both countries hampered efforts to reach a settlement. A formula was eventually found which made possible the re-establishment of diplomatic relations and the initiation of 'talks to seek the prompt elimination of the causes of conflict between the two countries without limitations or preconditions of any kind'. It was announced in December 1964 that negotiations would begin to prepare a new treaty.

Meanwhile, the Cuban problem again came before the OAS. In December 1963 Venezuela charged the Castro government with acts of intervention and aggression: the supply of arms to Venezuelan terrorists. Before the American Foreign Ministers met to consider these charges (having in the meantime appointed a commission to investigate them)

I

a military coup took place in Brazil, giving that country a strongly anti-communist government which soon severed relations with Cuba and reversed the 'independent' foreign policy. The Johnson adminis- tration warmly welcomed this overthrow of constitutional government in the most important country in Latin America. It was convinced that communist influence was becoming a real threat under President Goulart and, to say the least, did nothing to discourage the Brazilian military from deposing him.[31] The change of government in Brazil greatly enhanced the prospects of stronger resolutions being adopted against Dr. Castro at the Ninth Meeting of Consultation held at the Pan American Union in July 1964. Moreover, Cuba was now accused of specific acts of intervention and aggression against another American state; the question had become—at least formally—one of Latin Ameri- can support for Venezuela, and not for the United States. The Ninth Meeting called for the severance of diplomatic relations with Cuba, and a cessation of trade and shipping with the island. However, these mea- sures were not supported by Bolivia, Chile, Mexico and Uruguay— the only countries which, in fact, now maintained such relations. If fully implemented, these sanctions would have isolated still further the Castro government from the rest of the hemisphere; but a resolution asking for the support of friendly non-American states underlined their limited effectiveness. Castro, naturally, denounced the decisions taken by the Ninth Meeting, pointing out—with justification—that the kind of aggressive acts for which he had been condemned had for long been committed on a much larger scale by the United States against himself.[32]

Some two weeks after the Ninth Meeting Chile severed her relations with Cuba, and Bolivia and Uruguay subsequently followed suit. Undoubtedly, considerable pressure had been exerted upon their governments to take this action. But the Mexican government—which had refused to send its Foreign Minister to the Meeting—announced that it would not cut its ties with Cuba. It maintained (as it had done all along) that there was no juridical basis for invoking the Rio Treaty to deal with Venezuela's charges against Cuba. It is of interest that Mexico offered to abide by any decision of the International Court of Justice on this issue—an offer which, not surprisingly, was not taken

---

[31] See above, p. 29.
[32] And, as we have seen, the United States had been subverting governments in Latin America (including Cuba) since long before the Cuban revolution.

up. Mexico's official position on the Cuban issue did not prevent her maintaining good relations with the United States, with whom she concluded a settlement of the long-standing Chamizal problem[33] soon after President Johnson took office. The truth is that the United States derived certain very tangible advantages from having 'one window looking into Cuba'.

Meanwhile, the United States government appeared less concerned than it had been for some time over relations with Latin America. Certainly it was not under the considerable domestic pressure to take stronger action against Castro which had been such an important factor at Punta del Este in January 1962. By now the Cuban problem had become overshadowed by Vietnam. The Johnson administration was soon to derive satisfaction from the outcome of the Chilean elections at the beginning of September 1964: victory for the Christian Democratic presidential candidate, Eduardo Frei, over a rival—Salvador Allende—who had communist support. But the United States was by no means reconciled to the continued existence of the Castro government. At any time the Cuban problem might erupt and present the United States with a strong temptation to settle accounts with Castro. A resolution of the Ninth Meeting had contained the ominous warning that should the government of Cuba 'persist in carrying out acts that possess characteristics of aggression and intervention' the other American states would act against it individually or collectively, if necessary by armed force. Meanwhile, the United States was determined not to allow the establishment of 'a second Cuba' in the hemisphere. President Kennedy had expressed this determination in a speech shortly before his death. The Cuban experience, it could be argued, had demonstrated that the only way to prevent such an occurrence was for the United States to take swift unilateral action should a communist take-over of another Latin American country seem likely (or even possible). Her fellow members in the OAS could not be relied upon to accept United States judgement in identifying such a situation, but her power would ensure a sufficient measure of endorsement by the inter-American system of whatever course she adopted. It fell to President Johnson to give practical application of this argument in the Dominican Republic in the spring of 1965.

The Dominican crisis began on 24 April, when a revolt took place in Santo Domingo against the ruling military junta with the apparent

---

[33] See above, p. 35.

aim of restoring to power the former President Juan Bosch, who had been overthrown by a coup in September 1963. Four days later, United States marines were sent into the Dominican Republic: an action reminiscent of the Roosevelt Corollary and the period of armed interventions that lasted until the adoption of the Good Neighbour policy. Eventually they numbered over twenty thousand. The Johnson administration declared at first that it had acted to protect United States and other foreign citizens,[34] a motive recalling the earlier era; but subsequently demonstrated that its real objective was to forestall the establishment of another Soviet satellite in Latin America. Whatever her motives, by acting unilaterally and without consultation in the OAS, the United States clearly had violated the principle of non-intervention. She reported her action to the United Nations and the OAS. In both the Security Council, which was called at the request of the Soviet Union, and the OAS Council there was criticism by Latin American countries of United States intervention.

The two Latin American members of the Security Council at this time were Bolivia and Uruguay. Bolivia, where a military coup had overthrown the government in the previous November, supported the United States contention that the Dominican crisis should be dealt with by the OAS. But the delegate of Uruguay, one of the most democractic of the Latin American republics, denounced what he called the 'Johnson Doctrine', which was 'a corollary of the Monroe Doctrine', as incompatible with the principles of non-intervention and self-determination, and urged the Security Council to exert its authority in the Dominican situation. Yet although the Security Council remained seized of the matter, and Secretary General U Thant sent a representative to the Dominican Republic, the world body had very limited influence upon events there.

At the Tenth Meeting of Consultation of American Foreign Ministers, convened at the Pan American Union on 1 May, the United States pressed for the formation of an inter-American peace force which would formally multilateralise her intervention. Opponents of this proposal believed it would merely give an OAS label to what would remain essentially a United States operation; that it would sanction 'collective

---

[34] It alleged that it had done so at the request of the 'military authorities' in Santo Domingo. But this 'request' was solicited by the United States Ambassador on instructions from Washington. Moreover, by the time it had been obtained, the marines had been ashore for several hours. See, for example, Lowenthal, *The Dominican Intervention, op. cit.*, p. 104.

intervention' and create a dangerous precedent. There were considerable doubts about the extent to which the Dominican 'constitutionalists'[35] were under communist influence. The United States experienced great difficulty in securing the necessary two-thirds majority support. Chile, Ecuador, Mexico, Peru and Uruguay opposed the resolution, while Venezuela abstained from voting. Chile and Mexico were especially critical of the United States intervention. The fourteen affirmative votes included that of the Dominican Republic, the diplomatic authority of whose delegation was extremely dubious. Nevertheless, an inter-American peace force was eventually formed, with a Brazilian commander. Brazil furnished a sizeable contingent of men, and much smaller contingents came from Costa Rica (in her case, of police, since she possessed no regular army), El Salvador, Honduras, Nicaragua and Paraguay. The United States forces were to be nominally under the Brazilian commander, who had a United States deputy. With the arrival of Latin American units in the Dominican Republic, some of the marines were withdrawn; but United States troops still constituted an overwhelming majority of the inter-American peace force. The key member of an OAS commission sent to Santo Domingo to promote a political settlement was Mr. Ellsworth Bunker, the United States Ambassador to the organisation.[36]

The United States was determined to secure the formation of an anti-communist government in the Dominican Republic. Neither the leader of the insurrection, Colonel Francisco Caamaño Deñó, nor former President Bosch was acceptable to her. In spite of her continued protestations that she was neutral in the struggle and wanted only that the Dominican people should have freedom to choose a new government, her very presence denied them such a choice, and her actions, especially in the crucial early stages, favoured the military junta. Constitutionalist forces frequently were in conflict with those of the United States, which gradually were encroaching upon the area of Santo Domingo controlled by Caamaño. In Professor Slater's judgement, 'the United States used an excessive amount of force against the constitutionalists and, more importantly, failed to use enough force to

---

[35] They claimed to be fighting to restore constitutional government. The United States called them the 'rebels', the 'loyalists' being the supporters of the military junta—and thus of United States intervention.

[36] Mr. Bunker subsequently became United States Ambassador in Saigon, where he played a similar role in bringing about elections.

curb the terrorism of the Dominican police and military'. Of one incident, Slater declares:

> The most completely inexcusable U.S. action during the entire period of the intervention, in my view, was its acquiescence in and probable support of Imbert's May military attack on the constitutionalist sector in northern Santo Domingo, ending in the brutal slaughter of hundreds of constitutionalists and innocent civilians. In large part for narrow political purposes (additional pressures on the constitutionalists in the forthcoming negotiations), American policy makers had demonstrated a shockingly callous willingness to expend other people's lives.[37]

As the position of the constitutionalists weakened, the United States withdrew her support from the more intransigent members of the military junta, including General Imbert (mentioned by Slater above), and a provisional government was formed. Elections were held the following year under OAS auspices; but they had not been preceded by a meaningful political dialogue. The inter-American peace force withdrew from the country by September 1966.

Thus the United States succeeded in preventing the establishment in the Dominican Republic of a government which might have gone the way of the Cuban and certainly would have been one of which she did not approve. She had achieved her objective in intervening. But at what cost? At home, the credibility of the Johnson administration was weakened as a result not so much of its policy in the Dominican crisis, as by its attempts to explain and justify it. Even without the revelations of American journalists, its statements on the Dominican situation were so inconsistent as rapidly to undermine confidence in its veracity. But reputable American journalists on the spot revealed the hollowness of their government's protestations of impartiality in the civil conflict; the flimsy evidence upon which its claims to have thwarted a communist takeover of the insurrection against the junta were based; the gross exaggeration—even fabrication—of atrocities of which the constitutionalists were accused; and the often unscrupulous denigration of

---

[37] Jerome Slater, *Intervention and Negotiation: the United States and the Dominican Revolution* (New York, 1970), pp. 203–4. On this incident, Slater cites Tad Szulc, *Dominican Diary* (New York, 1965), especially p. 240. Szulc, of *The New York Times*, is one of the reputable American journalists cited by Theodore Draper (below, p. 245, n. 31.) With Karl Meyer, another experienced journalist, Szulc had earlier written a graphic account of the Bay of Pigs affair: Tad Szulc and Karl E. Meyer, *The Cuban Invasion: The Chronicle of of a Disaster* (New York, 1962).

both Bosch and Caamaño.[38] Nor were the journalists alone in criticising the Johnson administration. Senator William Fulbright, chairman of the Senate Foreign Relations Committee and the only important figure in American political life to have opposed the launching of the Bay of Pigs invasion, condemned United States action in the Dominican Republic as a 'grievous mistake'. He declared that the United States had intervened for the purpose of preventing the victory of a revolutionary force which it judged to be dominated by communists. His contention, the senator said, was not that there was no communist participation, but that the administration had acted on the arbitrary premise that the revolution was controlled by communists. This it had failed to establish, then or since. Fear of communism, he declared, tended to lead the United States into opposition to all revolutions and hence made her the ally of all the unpopular and corrupt oligarchies of the hemisphere.[39]

There could be no doubt about the adverse effect of the United States intervention in Santo Domingo upon her relations with Latin America as a whole. Her intervention was viewed with anger and dismay throughout the region; anger among the vast majority against yet another manifestation of 'Yankee imperialism', and dismay among Latin American leaders seeking to co-operate with the United States in the face of widespread anti-Americanism. The intervention was a profoundly humiliating experience for Latin Americans, recalling the worst humiliations of the past. It only too clearly confirmed a traditional United States predilection for right-wing dictators as guarantors of stability and guardians of American interests; and her more recent bolstering of the military as the strongest bulwark against communism. In this context, the intervention could hardly have taken place in a more unhappily appropriate country. An earlier United States intervention in the Dominican Republic had paved the way for Trujillo's rise to power. Now it appeared that the United States was intervening once again to support Trujillo's natural successors: a point which the final emergence of Trujillo's former lieutenant, Joaquín Balaguer, as President—even though duly elected—seemed to confirm. Another

---

[38] The evidence of these journalists is well presented in Theodore Draper, 'The Dominican Crisis: A Case Study in American Policy', *Commentary*, vol. 40, no. 6 (December 1965) гр. 33–68.

[39] *The New York Times*, international edn., 20 September 1965, Editorial: 'Fulbright Speaks'. See also Fulbright, *The Arrogance of Power, op. cit.*, pp. 86 ff.

link with the past (fitting only too aptly into the historical pattern
of inter-American relations) was forged by the partisan role of the
United States Ambassador in Santo Domingo, W. Tapley Bennett, Jr.
For Bennett refused to mediate when asked to do so by the constitutionalists at the beginning of the conflict because he believed the
military junta, which he supported, would defeat them. But when
they looked likely to win he called for the United States marines to be
sent in. Of the Ambassador's refusal to mediate at the request of
the constitutionalists, Senator Fulbright has written: 'a great opportunity was lost ... Ambassador Bennett was in a position to bring
possibly decisive mediating power to bear for a democratic solution
but he chose not to do so on the disingenuous ground that the exercise
of his good offices at that point would have constituted 'intervention'.'[40] Bennett's response recalls that given by Henry Lane Wilson
to President Madero's wife in 1913 when she asked him to intercede to
prevent her husband's murder.[41] In justice to Ambassador Bennett,
however, it must be stressed that while Wilson was motivated by
personal animus towards the Mexican President, he was implementing United States policy of supporting the military junta in Santo
Domingo.

The United States intervention in the Dominican Republic dealt a
severe blow to the inter-American system, which was treated in the
crisis as the mere rubber stamp of her policies which its critics have
long held it to be. The United States government had made explicit
once more what had always been implicit in the hemispheric situation:
that she would, in spite of treaty agreements, intervene unilaterally if
circumstances (in her judgement) warranted it. Ironically, the Dominican crisis occurred at a time when measures for strengthening the inter-
American system were under consideration within the organisation.
The United States and some Latin American governments wished to
reinforce the OAS as an instrument for combating the challenge from
international communism. But this was opposed by those governments
which saw such a development as a further threat to the principle of
non-intervention. Both sides were confirmed in their view by the
Dominican experience. On the other hand, all the Latin American
governments wanted to enhance the role of the inter-American system
in the field of economic development: that is to say, to obtain firmer
pledges of aid on more favourable terms from the United States. The

---

[40] *The Arrogance of Power, op. cit.*, p. 90.          [41] See above, p. 135.

latter was unwilling to enter into the commitments they demanded. The difficulties of strengthening the inter-American system against this background were demonstrated at the Second Special Inter-American Conference,[42] held at Rio de Janeiro from 17 to 30 November 1965, after being twice postponed because of the Dominican crisis. There was no question of establishing a permanent inter-American peace force: nor would the United States be bound to specific measures to promote Latin American economic development. After further meetings the OAS Charter was finally amended by a Protocol adopted by the Third Special Inter-American Conference held at Buenos Aires in February 1967.[43] The Amended Charter incorporated the principles of the Alliance for Progress and various institutional changes, but it did not strengthen the security system of the hemisphere.

The truth is that by this time the climate of inter-American relations was becoming ever less favourable to the OAS. Inter-American conferences traditionally had served the purpose of demonstrating some degree of hemispheric solidarity; now they merely confirmed the basic lack of a genuine community of interests shared by the United States and Latin America. The Latin American countries, concerned above all with their economic problems, were coming to identify themselves with the rest of the developing world. In 1964 the first United Nations Trade and Development Conference (UNCTAD) had met at Geneva. Prior to the conference, the Latin American governments had held a meeting at Alta Gracia, Argentina, to discuss the formulation of a common position, and subsequently established a Special Commission for Latin American Coordination (CECLA). In the event, the division between the developed and developing countries was most marked at the Geneva Conference, with the United States and the countries of Latin America, of course, on opposing sides.

But while Latin American governments realised the urgent need to form a common front to strengthen their economic position *vis-à-vis* the United States and the developed countries generally, economic

---

[42] The First Special Inter-American Conference, held at Washington in December 1964, adopted a procedure for the admission of new members. No such procedure had been included in the OAS Charter, and there were now several prospective new members among British Caribbean territories. Trinidad and Tobago, Jamaica and Barbados eventually joined the OAS after achieving independence. For a brief analysis of the main positions taken at the Second Special Conference, see Gordon Connell-Smith, 'Inter-American Relations Today', *Bank of London & South America Limited Quarterly Review*, vol. vi, no. 2 (April 1966), pp. 68–70.

[43] The OAS Amended Charter came into effect in February 1970.

co-operation between them was still very limited. In particular, the process of economic integration in the region was proving slow and difficult. As we noted,[44] two organisations were involved: the Latin American Free Trade Association (LAFTA), eventually embracing all the countries of South America and Mexico, and the Central American Common Market (CACM). Greater progress was achieved in Central America, where there was a much smaller grouping—with less variation in economic levels between the member countries—than in LAFTA. Moreover, while CACM provided for across-the-board tariff reductions, LAFTA involved a series of negotiations to determine the items of existing trade between the signatories which would make up agreed percentages by which tariffs progressively would be reduced. The negotiations became increasingly difficult as the required percentage reductions could not be made without bringing key products within their scope. This position was soon reached. In 1965 President Frei of Chile called for an 'act of political will' to strengthen LAFTA. Chile under Frei was a strong supporter of Latin American integration and often a stern critic of the OAS. When his initiative failed, Frei took a leading part in the formation of a sub-grouping within LAFTA to accelerate the economic integration process: the Andean group.[45]

Yet by the end of 1966 President Johnson was expressing vigorous support for a Latin American Common Market and was known to favour a 'summit' meeting to launch it, as well as to revitalise the Alliance for Progress and improve inter-American relations generally. Such a common market was now favoured by United States corporations operating overseas. These envisaged:

> one large regional market within which the production and sales divisions of their Latin American subsidiaries could operate in essentially the same way as their counterparts in the United States. David Rockefeller, leading the U.S. Business Advisory Council of the Alliance, had been urging a vigorous push by the United States to make Latin America one undivided economic space.[46]

Thus the first Meeting of American Chiefs of State to be held since 1956[47] took place in April 1967 at Punta del Este, where the Alliance for Progress had been inaugurated in August 1961, and the decision to

---

[44] See above, p. 233, n. 16.                    [45] See below, pp. 254-5.
[46] Levinson and de Onís, *The Alliance That Lost Its Way: A Critical Report on the Alliance for Progress, op. cit.,* p. 172.                    [47] See above, p. 220.

exclude Castro's Cuba from the inter-American system was taken in January 1962. It ended with a 'Declaration of the Presidents of America calling for the creation of a Latin American Common Market by 1985, incorporating LAFTA and CACM. The Declaration was accompanied by an 'Action Program' which included strengthening both these organisations. But United States enthusiasm increased Latin American fears of the great North American corporations. The Mexican President declared at the summit meeting: 'The integration of Latin America is (and we should fight to keep it so) an exclusively Latin American process.'[48] Some months earlier, Celso Furtado, the Brazilian economist, had warned that: 'Economic integration will serve the development needs of the region only if it stems from a common policy formulated by really independent national governments and not from the co-ordination of the interests of the great foreign business enterprises operating in Latin America.'[49]

Only a few weeks after the summit meeting the Cuban problem was again before the OAS, and once again at the request of Venezuela. In January 1966 Fidel Castro had played host to the 'First Afro-Asian-Latin American Peoples' Solidarity Conference', more generally referred to as the Tricontinental Conference. Apart from the enormous affront which the mere holding of it offered to the United States and to Latin American governments, the Tricontinental Conference established the Latin American Solidarity Organization (OLAS), with its headquarters in Havana and the objective of promoting revolution in the region. It was decided to hold the First Latin American Peoples' Solidarity Conference in 1967 under OLAS's sponsorship. Venezuela's request for a Meeting of Consultation referred to these developments as well as to actions by the Cuban government against herself. The Twelfth Meeting of Consultation began at the Pan American Union in June 1967; it adjourned while the Venezuelan charges were investigated.

Before it reconvened in the following September, the First Conference of the Organization for Latin American Solidarity took place in Havana. It lasted from 31 July until 10 August 1967. In the previous April the Executive Secretariat of the Tricontinental Organization published a message purportedly from Che Guevara, Castro's former lieutenant, whose whereabouts had been the subject of speculation

---

48 Levinson and de Onís, *op. cit.*, p. 174.
49 'U.S. hegemony and the future of Latin America', *The World Today*, vol. 22, no. 9 (September 1966), p. 385.

since the spring of 1965. The message called for 'two, three, many Vietnams'.[50] This became a slogan for the conference, of which Guevara was named 'President of Honour'. Another interesting feature of the First OLAS Conference was a huge portrait of Simón Bolívar as a symbol of the revolutionary struggle in Latin America.

The Twelfth Meeting held a further session from 22 to 24 September, this time attended by the Foreign Ministers themselves. It achieved little. The position of the principal opponents of more vigorous measures against Cuba had not been changed either by Venezuela's complaints or by the OLAS conference. In any case, few new measures were open to the OAS short of the use of armed force; and this was not under serious consideration, even though Argentina's military government declared its readiness to support it 'when a sufficient number of states feels the proper time has come'. Such a time seemed remote. The United States was unable to get the necessary support for black-listing foreign firms trading with Cuba. Non-American states 'that share the principles of the inter-American system' were requested to restrict their trade and financial operations with Cuba. An appeal was even made to governments friendly to Castro (principally the Soviet Union and East European countries) to refrain from supporting what were denounced as his 'interventionist and aggressive activities'. Once again it was made clear that Cuba was no longer an inter-American problem. The United States economic blockade undoubtedly hurt Cuba considerably, but it would not bring down the Castro government as long as the latter was able to obtain economic assistance and to trade on a substantial scale outside the hemisphere. A new development was a recommendation that member states of the OAS should bring to the attention of the United Nations future Cuban actions which contravened the General Assembly's own resolution on intervention.

The Twelfth Meeting was enlivened when the Foreign Minister of Bolivia produced photographs which he claimed were of Che Guevara in the Bolivian jungle. According to Castro, Guevara had left Cuba voluntarily in April 1965 because 'other lands of the world' claimed his 'modest efforts'. His disappearance had given rise to various rumours until it was definitely established in the autumn of 1967 that he was leading a guerrilla action in Bolivia. The Bolivian government, whose armed forces were trained and supported by the United States, expressed confidence that Guevara soon would be defeated and captured.

---

[50] The message is reproduced in Gerassi (ed.), *Venceremos!*, *op. cit.*, pp. 413–24.

Then, in October, came news of his capture and death. With Guevara's failure the fortunes of the guerrillas in Latin America seemed at a low ebb. Undoubtedly, it confirmed the Soviet leaders' view that their best course to gain influence in Latin America was through developing relations with the governments in the region, whatever their complexion, rather than supporting apparently futile attempts to overthrow them. More importantly, there was the growing possibility of a general rapprochement between Russia and the United States. A visit by the Soviet Prime Minister, Mr. Kosygin, to Havana not long before the OLAS conference was apparently an attempt to reconcile two opposing viewpoints on the feasibility of armed revolution in Latin America.

By the following year the war in Vietnam had come to overshadow all other problems facing the United States, and intense dissatisfaction with his administration's policies in South East Asia forced President Johnson not to stand for re-election. In this situation inter-American relations received comparatively little attention in Washington. When President Nixon took office in January 1969 Latin America was once again a low priority area. The Cuban problem was in a quiescent phase, and the Alliance for Progress, so closely related to it, was thoroughly discredited. Yet, in the previous autumn, an event had taken place which could prove a very significant landmark in the history of inter-American relations: the expropriation of the assets of the United States-owned International Petroleum Company (IPC) by the military junta which seized power in Peru on 3 October 1968.

The Peruvian situation,[51] which began to develop shortly after the military junta led by General Juan Velasco Alvarado took power, had certain significant features. Peru has for long been in urgent need of economic development and drastic social reforms. It is one of the poorest countries of Latin America, with a total gross national product substantially inferior to the gross annual revenue of the Standard Oil Company of New Jersey, of which IPC is a subsidiary. United States interests have occupied a dominant position in the exploitation of Peru's mineral and other resources, and the country has been almost totally dependent upon the United States government and private banks for the refinancing of its large external debt. Peru traditionally has been friendly to United States investment. Her oligarchy is one of the

---

[51] Much useful background information about the situation, as well as judgements upon it, are contained in *United States Relations with Peru. Hearings before the Subcommittee on Western Hemisphere Affairs of the Committee on Foreign Relations, United States Senate, Ninety-First Congress, First Session, April 14, 16, and 17, 1969, op. cit.*

most powerful in Latin America, while she has a large Indian population living, in the greatest poverty, outside the national economy and
society. Democracy has few roots in Peru and, without far-reaching
economic and social reforms, it is difficult to see how it could flourish
there. Certainly the government of Fernando Belaúnde Terry (1963–8)
failed to overcome the entrenched opposition to even modest reforms.
The United States did little to help him, an omission she may since
have regretted.[52] The immediate cause of Belaúnde's downfall was his
failure to resolve—to the satisfaction of Peruvians—a long-standing
dispute with the International Petroleum Company.

The first major act of the Velasco government was to announce the
expropriation of the widely detested IPC. It was not at first clear
whether this was to be the initial step of a government determined to
carry out a social revolution, or merely a popular move providing some
justification for the coup. The government said IPC was a special case
in that it had violated Peruvian laws, but other revolutionary measures
followed. Meanwhile, the United States government indicated that it
expected prompt and adequate compensation to be paid to IPC, and
warned that the Hickenlooper Amendment[53] required the severance of
all economic aid to Peru if this was not forthcoming within six months
of the expropriation. The Peruvian government declared its willingness
to pay compensation (though less than the company claimed its assets
were worth), but put forward a claim for a much larger sum for oil
extracted by the company between 1924 and 1968 under an agreement
which the Peruvian government declared was illegal. Confronted by
much more serious problems in other regions as well as domestic tensions, President Nixon was anxious to pursue a 'low profile' policy in
Latin America. He therefore took no precipitate action, but instead
sent a special envoy to Lima in the hope of eventually bringing about a
settlement satisfactory to the United States.

In order to demonstrate that he did not lack interest in the region
as a whole, Mr. Nixon performed the ritual of sending a high-ranking
mission on a fact-finding tour of the individual Latin American coun-

---

[52] In fact, the United States curtailed economic aid to Peru in order to exert pressure
upon Belaúnde to make a settlement favourable to IPC. According to Richard Goodwin,
former adviser to President Kennedy on Latin American affairs, giving evidence to the
subcommittee, the United States government had not made its own evaluation of IPC's
claim. It had supported the company's own assessment of what sum was due to it (*ibid.*,
p. 90). Cf. the oil dispute with Mexico before the Second World War (see above, pp.
173 ff.).                                          [53] See above, p. 17.

tries. It was headed by his old political rival, Governor Nelson Rockefeller, who, although a prominent landowner and business man in the region, was thought to be acceptable to the Latin Americans.[54] Rockefeller's appointment apparently had been suggested to the President by the OAS Secretary General. It is an interesting commentary upon the changing climate of inter-American relations over the intervening years that the hostile reception accorded to Mr. Rockefeller at various points during his tour (and the fact that some governments declined to accept his visit)[55] caused little of the shock with which the United States had received the news of Mr. Nixon's own experiences in 1958.[56] It is a commentary of another kind that Mr. Rockefeller's visit to Haiti appears to have evoked particular enthusiasm, and that the governor allowed himself to be photographed in a happy pose with President Duvalier, the most notorious dictator in the region. Mr. Rockefeller did not visit Peru.

Early in its dispute with the United States the Peruvian government had taken steps to increase its trade with communist countries, and at the beginning of 1969 agreed to establish diplomatic relations with the Soviet Union for the first time. Peru's Foreign Minister declared that his country was on the road to an 'independent international policy'. There was no serious suggestion, however, that the Velasco government was Marxist. The challenge it offered to the United States was recognised as that of nationalism: an assertion by the Peruvians of control over their internal and external affairs, and thus of independence from United States domination. An important new feature of this expression of nationalism linked with social revolution was its being led by the military, traditionally upholders of the *status quo* and in the nineteen-sixties firm allies of the United States in her anti-communist policy in the hemisphere.

While the IPC question made its way through Peru's administrative procedures the United States found herself engaged in another significant dispute in Latin America. This was over fishing rights and territorial waters, and concerned not only Peru, but also Chile and Ecuador;[57] moreover there was widespread support in the region for their

---

[54] During the Second World War Mr. Rockefeller held the office of Co-ordinator of Inter-American Affairs. See above, p. 179.

[55] Those of Chile, Peru and Venezuela.

[56] See above, p. 223.

[57] In January 1971 the Fourteenth Meeting of Consultation of American Foreign Ministers was held to consider Ecuador's dispute with the United States over this matter.

position. Brazil also was among those Latin American countries claiming jurisdiction over an expanse of sea up to two hundred nautical miles from their coasts. United States and other leading maritime nations did not recognise this claim. Two important issues were involved. First the Latin American countries were anxious to conserve their fishing resources against exploitation by greater maritime powers; in recent years her fishing industry had become especially important to Peru. Secondly, the Latin American countries were attempting to assert their right to change a system of international law which they claimed —justifiably—was created in the main by great powers to further their own interests. Thus the issue highlighted the basic clash of interests between the United States as the most developed country and the Latin American republics as members of the developing world.

In addition to her involvement in the fishing rights dispute, Chile became more closely linked with Peru's challenge to the United States when President Frei announced on 26 June 1969 that an agreement had been made with the United States-owned Anaconda Company to buy out the latter's vast copper mining operations in Chile. It can hardly be doubted that both the Frei administration and the company were influenced by events in Peru. Unlike the Peruvian situation, however, there was no dispute with the United States; but neither did Frei's action arouse comparable enthusiasm among nationalists in Chile—or elsewhere in Latin America. The moderately reforming government of Belaúnde had been overthrown after making an agreement with IPC comparable with Frei's announced plan to buy out Anaconda. Moreover, the new Chilean agreement itself replaced an earlier plan for 'Chileanisation' as an alternative to nationalisation of the United States-owned copper concerns, thus reflecting growing pressure on Dr. Frei to pursue more radical policies. It was by no means certain that the Anaconda agreement would satisfy Chilean nationalist aspirations, and prove an acceptable alternative to the Peruvian course of expropriation.

Meanwhile, the Chilean government continued to be the leading advocate of greater Latin American unity in strengthening the region *vis-à-vis* the United States. We have already noted the prominent part played by Chile in the movement towards Andean economic integration.[58] This movement was crowned with some success when a pact was signed by Bolivia, Chile, Colombia, Ecuador and Peru—but not

---

[58] See above, p. 248.

by Venezuela—in Bogotá in May 1969. Nor is it without significance that Viña del Mar, the Chilean seaside resort, was the site of the conference which produced the 'Consensus' named after it, and that this document was presented to President Nixon on 11 June by the Chilean Foreign Minister, Sr. Gabriel Valdés.

The 'Consensus of Viña del Mar' was adopted at a meeting of the Special Commission for Latin American Coordination (CECLA) held at ministerial level in May 1969. We saw how CECLA had been formed to co-ordinate Latin American views for the first meeting of UNCTAD in 1964.[59] CECLA had held a number of meetings since then, during a period when Latin American disillusionment with the Alliance for Progress and dissatisfaction with the terms of their trade with the United States steadily increased. At Viña del Mar the Latin Americans reiterated that what their situation demanded was not more 'aid', but better terms of trade. The Brazilian delegation produced figures indicating that three-quarters of the current Alliance for Progress budget was being used to pay debts owed by Latin American countries to the United States. Between 1961 and 1966 Latin America received more than $6,000 millions in loans and investments, but over the same period it had to pay out in interest and remitted profits more than $12,000 millions.[60]

The Consensus, affirming 'the distinctive personality of Latin America' in its relations with the other members of the international community, stressed the need for unity if the region was to secure better terms of international trade. Although recognising that they must make greater efforts on their own behalf—both individually and co-operatively —in order to overcome their underdevelopment, the Latin American governments declared that the attainment of their goals 'depends to a large extent on the international community recognizing and assuming their responsibilities, and particularly those countries which now have greatest influence in international decisions'. Of such countries, the United States was, of course, the most important. The Consensus plainly expressed dissatisfaction with the past performance of the United States and other developed countries. The document could not be viewed by the United States otherwise than as a series of demands for concessions on her part in order to facilitate Latin America's economic development.

This was further emphasised in the speech made by the Chilean

---

[59] See above, p. 247.
[60] *Latin America* (London), vol. iii, no. 21 (23 May 1969), p. 162.

Foreign Minister when he presented the Consensus to President Nixon in the presence of the diplomatic representatives of the other signatories. The occasion was a confrontation between Latin America and the United States, with the Consensus intended to convey 'a genuine Latin American position.' The Chilean Foreign Minister declared that, far from receiving real financial assistance, Latin America was helping to finance the development of the United States and other affluent nations. The region now wanted better trading terms—such as tariff preferences and lowering of non-tariff barriers to their trade with the United States; easier terms for debt service; and removal of restrictions on existing aid funds. President Nixon's response to the Consensus was understandably cautious and he subsequently offered only very minor concessions in the matter of 'untying' United States loans. Both traditional United States policy towards Latin America and the current mood of the Congress were unfavourable to concessions such as the Latin Americans were demanding, and the region was no longer regarded as critical and requiring new initiatives. Thus the Latin Americans were able to get little satisfaction from the inter-American economic conferences held in the months following. The Consensus did not bring much in the way of immediate results. But the Latin American governments had demonstrated to the United States the extent of their frustration (the language of the Consensus had been unusually strong) and their determination to form a common front in negotiating with her on economic questions affecting them all. The Consensus was an expression of growing 'continental nationalism'.

There was another expression of nationalism in the region in the following October: the nationalisation of the United States-owned Bolivian Gulf Oil Company by the government of General Alfredo Ovando Candia. The latter, who had come to power by a military coup at the end of September, had been prominent in the campaign that led to the capture and death of Che Guevara two years earlier. Nevertheless, General Ovando soon anounced his intention to carry out a social revolution, and he appeared to be formulating policies comparable with those being implemented by General Velasco's government in Peru. It was another instance of Latin American nationalism and social reform being led by the military, and could have further important repercussions in other parts of the region. Almost at once, the Bolivian government announced the establishment of diplomatic relations with Roumania in order to secure economic and technical agreements to help continue oil production.

In November the report of Governor Rockefeller's mission was published under the title of *Quality of Life in the Americas*. In contrast with the complacency of the administration, Mr. Rockefeller was very pessimistic and anxious to strengthen the 'special relationship' with Latin America, which he declared had deteriorated badly. He made the interesting assertion that 'the political and psychological value of the special relationship cannot be over-estimated'. Warning that communist subversion was still a dangerous threat, Governor Rockefeller proposed new measures to combat it, including the establishment of a western hemisphere security council. In spite of the sympathy of some governments (notably that of Brazil), these proposals were most unlikely to receive wide support in Latin America.[61] On the other hand, Rockefeller's proposals for helping Latin American economic development—such as substantial tariff reductions and the untying of United States aid—were correspondingly unlikely to be acceptable to the United States Congress, even should the President support them. Mr. Rockefeller's advocacy of strengthening the military in Latin America as a bulwark against communism came at a time when this very policy had been under considerable criticism in 'Hearings on United States Military Policies and Programs in Latin America' conducted by the Senate Subcommittee on Western Hemisphere Affairs.[62] When war broke out betweeen El Salvador and Honduras at the end of June 1969, Senator Fulbright declared that the United States bore some responsibility for these hostilities because of such policies and programmes, and called for the withdrawal of all her military missions from Latin America. Regarding the Rockefeller report as a whole, President Nixon described it as 'a major contribution' to the formulation of his administration's policy for the hemisphere. But he continued to pursue the 'low profile' policy.

In September of the following year the policy was put to its sternest test when the Chilean presidential election was won by Dr. Salvador Allende, at the head of a Popular Unity Front which included communists and socialists.[63] This was the first time an avowed Marxist had become Head of State through free elections anywhere in the world.

---

[61] It was confirmed in the OAS the following year, when measures to combat terrorism and kidnappings were discussed, that the Latin American governments as a whole continued to give priority to economic questions and were unwilling to adopt co-operative measures to deal with terrorists which might involve intervention in their affairs.

[62] See below, p. 270, n. 7.

[63] Allende was defeated by Frei in the election of 1964. See above ,p. 241.

The event therefore aroused wide international interest. It was a great blow to the United States, to whom it had always been an article of faith that such a thing was not possible. Moreover, it had occurred in 'her own hemisphere'; and in what traditionally has been regarded as Latin America's most stable and democratic country. The Nixon administration did not conceal its displeasure at Dr. Allende's victory. But the United States proceeded cautiously: this was not Guatemala, and the year was not 1954. Yet Allende's position was very vulnerable. He had not received a majority of the votes (in fact just over thirty-six per cent), and he faced a Congress in which his coalition was in the minority. He could count for support of part of his programme (for example, the nationalisation of the copper companies) from the Christian Democrats, the main opposition party; their votes in the Congress had made possible his taking office. But such support was given in return for a pledge that he would fulfil his election promise to act strictly within the constitution. In carrying out this pledge, Allende faced potential threats from his own extreme supporters as well as from extremist opponents. It was ominous that even before he was confirmed in office the Commander-in-Chief of the Chilean army, General Schneider, who had declared that the armed forces would remain outside politics, was assassinated—apparently by right-wing extremists who wanted military intervention to prevent Allende becoming President. The latter also faced the hostility of powerful North American companies threatened by his programme, and the economic and financial pressures which the United States government was able and likely to exert against him on their behalf. It would later be asserted by a prominent North American columnist that the United States International Telegraph and Telephones (ITT) Company had tried to persuade the CIA and the State Department to prevent Allende's assumption of office.[64]

In spite of his vulnerability, Dr. Allende pressed ahead with his promised programmes both at home and abroad. Almost immediately upon his taking office Chile resumed diplomatic relations with Cuba. Before the end of the year a bill to nationalise copper was placed before the Chilean congress, and shortly afterwards plans were announced to take over the country's private banks. At the beginning of 1971 Chile established diplomatic relations with China, and numerous trade and financial agreements with other communist countries were signed

---

[64] This matter became the subject of congressional hearings in the United States.

during the year. While avoiding confrontation with the Chilean government, as with those of Peru and Bolivia, the United States applied pressure by such actions as restricting credits both directly and through her influence in the leading international financing institutions. In August 1971 the Bolivian government of President Juan José Torres (who had deposed General Ovando in October 1970 and replaced his government by one claiming to be more radical) was overthrown by right-wing army officers. Meanwhile, the Peruvian military was by no means united on the pace and extent of social reforms, after raising considerable expectations among the people. Allende, too, had raised hopes among his supporters beyond what he could fulfil in the immediate future.

The Latin American countries were angered when, in response to the dollar crisis which occurred in the summer of 1971, President Nixon announced a ten per cent surcharge on imported manufactured goods and a ten per cent reduction in foreign aid.[65] At the beginning of September their finance ministers met in Buenos Aires under the auspices of CECLA to protest against these measures. There was little indication that the United States would make significant concessions in response to their protests. The outlook was bleak. For all the brave words of the Consensus of Viña del Mar, economic co-operation between the Latin American countries was still very limited; and the process of economic integration remained on the whole a matter of continuing disappointment. LAFTA, the most widely embracing group in terms of membership, was stagnant. The progress of CACM, which at first was much greater, had long since diminished; the Central American Common Market suffered a severe blow when war broke out between two of its members (El Salvador and Honduras) in 1969. A reconciliation of these two countries—a prerequisite to further progress—was proving extremely difficult to achieve. Even the Andean group, the more ambitious and successful of the two sub-regional groups formed in 1969,[66] was seriously weakened by Venezuela's failure to join it.

The position and policy of Brazil, distinct from the Spanish American countries and closer to the United States, further weakened the

---

[65] The United States subsequently promised that the cut in foreign aid would not apply to Latin America. But the surcharge was the greater grievance.
[66] The other was a grouping of the River Plate countries formed to develop the region's resources.

prospects for unity in Latin America. Although not infrequently opposed to the United States on particular economic issues, and sub-scribing in principle to the concept of a 'Latin American personality' (as presented in the Consensus of Viña del Mar), Brazil's military government firmly supported the overall United States position within the inter-American system. This was in line with Brazil's traditional policy in the twentieth century—charted by Baron Rio-Branco[67]—of cultivating United States friendship as a corollary to seeking the leader-ship of South America: what has been described as a 'subsphere of influence' within the inter-American system.[68] In the early nineteen-seventies, following rapid economic progress, Brazil substantially in-creased her influence in the neighbouring Spanish American countries of Bolivia, Uruguay and Paraguay. The overthrow of the reformist military government of General Torres in Bolivia in 1971 was almost certainly supported by Brazil; Uruguay, for long one of the most demo-cratic countries of Latin America (as we have noted[69]), now had a quasi-military government aligned with Brazil; and the Paraguayan dictator, Alfredo Stroessner, brought his country closer to her. Fear of Brazil's growing power and influence was aroused among the Spanish American countries, but especially in Argentina, her traditional rival for leadership in South America. Argentina was greatly concerned over her own loss of influence in countries in which she has always had a particular interest.[70] Although ideologically closer to Brazil since civilian governments were overthrown in both countries, Argentina's military rulers decided to abandon the concept of 'ideological frontiers' and to improve relations with other Spanish American governments, such as Chile and Peru, where the challenge to the United States was most in evidence.[71] Fear of Brazil and growing identification with the currently increasing 'continental nationalism' were among factors leading to the return of Argentina's former President, Juan Perón. The Argentine military who, ever since the latter's overthrow in 1955, had striven to keep his supporters out of power, eventually acquiesced.

In May 1973 a new, elected Peronist President, pledged to make way for Perón, took office. Almost at once diplomatic relations were re-sumed with Cuba, to whom the Argentine government subsequently

---

[67] See above, p. 125.

[68] Astiz, *Latin American International Politics, op. cit.*, p. 173.

[69] See above, pp. 195, 242.                    [70] See above, p. 222.

[71] General Alejandro Lanusse, the head of Argentina's military government, was the first Latin American leader to meet Dr. Allende after the latter became Chile's President.

offered substantial credits. As we saw earlier, during his years in the presidency (1946–55) Perón had preached a doctrine which he called *justicialismo*: a 'Third Position' between capitalism and communism, and therefore between the United States and the Soviet Union.[72] He had also tried to expand Argentina's influence over her Spanish American neighbours through a number of bilateral agreements. Evidently, Perón now hoped to resume such policies with greater success, affirming their relevance to the contemporary situation. His supporters claimed that his Third Position had anticipated, and was now in harmony with, that of the Third World—with which Latin America was coming increasingly to identify itself. Indeed, Peronists proclaimed their leader's prescience in anticipating world developments. The Peruvian government had for some time claimed to be pursuing an independent international policy, and to be implementing a revolution which was neither capitalist nor communist. Now the Peruvian Prime Minister declared in Buenos Aires that a good deal of common ground existed between the ideology and objectives of Peru's revolution and the basic programme of Argentine *justicialismo*.[73] The situation in the summer of 1973 seemed propitious to Perón, who might hope to harness resentment of the United States and suspicion of Brazil in a new bid for leadership among the Spanish American countries. But Argentina would first have to achieve internal stability: Perón must succeed in this regard where the previous military governments had failed.

Argentina was the third Latin American country to resume diplomatic relations with Cuba in defiance of the OAS resolution of 1964.[74] Peru had become the second to do so (following Chile's example) in July 1972. The Velasco government had meanwhile continued to pursue radical policies, which brought further disputes with North American interests. Although not formally invoking the Hickenlooper Amendment, the Nixon administration retaliated by reducing its own aid and by preventing Peru from obtaining certain loans from international agencies in which the United States was influential. The 'group of 77' (Third World countries) met in Peru prior to the Third United Nations Conference on Trade and Development (UNCTAD), held at Santiago de Chile in the spring of 1972. Peru also played a prominent role at the Third UNCTAD, calling for international monetary

---

[72] See above, p. 222. As we noted, Perón had not been able to maintain such a position in practice.
[73] *Latin America, op. cit.*, vol. vii, no. 22 (1 June 1973), p. 175.
[74] See above, p. 240. Mexico had not broken off relations with Cuba.

reform along lines favourable to the developing countries. It was in Lima, the Peruvian capital, that a Special Committee for the Reorganization of the Inter-American System held its first meetings in June–July 1973. As we have already noted, the OAS Charter was amended in February 1967, and the new charter came into effect three years later.[75] But significant developments in inter-American relations since then had stimulated further dissatisfaction with the OAS and Latin American demands for much more far-reaching changes in the organisation. Not only was there long-standing disillusionment with the OAS as an instrument for obtaining better terms of trade and aid from the United States; there was also a growing feeling that the Inter-American Treaty of Reciprocal Assistance should be terminated as no longer having relevance to the world situation or value for Latin America. Indeed, many Latin Americans maintained that the Rio Treaty had been misused by the United States as an instrument of intervention in their affairs; and there was widespread resentment of United States pressure to keep them in line with her policy towards Cuba. Some countries, Peru and Chile prominent among them, demanded that Cuba should be re-admitted to the OAS, which itself should put into practice the principle of 'ideological pluralism' rather than insist that its members pay lip-service to 'representative democracy'.[76] Argentina now supported the position of Peru and Chile on this issue, and called for radical changes in the inter-American system.

Dr. Castro, who had long since denounced the OAS and denied any intention of returning to it while the United States remained a member, nevertheless derived considerable satisfaction from these developments.[77] He had, of course, warmly applauded the victory of Allende, whom he visited in 1971, and he praised the Peruvian government and others, such as that of Panama, involved in disputes with the United States. The holding of an extraordinary meeting of the United Nations Security Council in Panama in March 1973 gave the Panamanian government an opportunity to air its grievances against the United States on a world stage. In the event, the latter had to use her veto to prevent the adoption by the Council of a resolution on the Canal issue

---

[75] See above, p. 247. Under its terms the quinquennial Inter-American Conference was replaced by an annual General Assembly. It was the OAS Third General Assembly meeting in April 1973 (in Washington), which set up the Special Committee.

[76] 'Ideological pluralism' became something of a slogan at the OAS Third General Assembly, where it was accepted as a general principle.

[77] At this stage there was not a majority of governments favouring Cuba's re-admission to the OAS, however—still less the expulsion of the United States!

which she found unacceptable. While reaffirming his conviction that socialism would eventually be achieved in these and other Latin American countries, Castro declared he would meanwhile co-operate with all Latin American governments pursuing nationalist policies in the face of United States hostility. He mentioned also Venezuela, whose government was taking steps towards the eventual nationalisation of her oil industry.[78] The Venezuelan government was also moving cautiously towards resumption of diplomatic relations with Cuba. As continental nationalism grew in Latin America, so would the isolation of Cuba break down.

But meanwhile President Allende's position was weakening. His own extreme supporters created difficulties for him by taking matters into their own hands, encouraging, for example, the occupation of land and factories. His extreme opponents in their turn resorted to violence. Among his opponents were those who genuinely feared for the future of Chilean democracy, and those so vehemently opposed to his policies that they were prepared to employ extra-constitutional means to overthrow him. Lacking the necessary majority for more controversial measures, Allende resorted to ways of circumventing Congress: for example, by effecting nationalisation through purchasing the shares of the companies concerned. The opposition likewise sought to manipulate the constitution against the President. In October 1972, in the midst of rampant inflation, a strike of lorry drivers and transport owners in protest against threats of nationalisation spread through the country. Supported by the opposition parties, it paralysed commerce, increased food shortages and forced the government to use troops to keep order in the streets of the capital. The strike ended only when, in the following month. Allende brought three senior military officers into his cabinet.

In December the President made a big effort to rally international support. The North American Kennecott Copper Corporation was endeavouring to prevent the sale of Chilean copper on world markets in retaliation for the nationalisation of its properties without what it claimed as adequate and effective compensation.[79] Its action aggravated an already critical shortage of foreign exchange, for Chile was having great difficulty in renegotiating her very considerable foreign debt and securing international credits. During a two-week tour of the Americas

---

[78] Castro's speech on May Day, 1973: *Granma* (weekly English edn.), 13 May 1973.

[79] Allende had not denied the company's right to compensation, but affirmed that this was offset by 'excess profits' over the years.

and Europe (including the Soviet Union) Dr. Allende addressed the
United Nations General Assembly. In his speech he accused the
International Telegraph and Telephones Company of trying to start a
civil war in Chile (which the company subsequently denied); Kennecott
of attempting to deprive Chile of her export earnings; and international
agencies controlled by the United States of instituting a financial
blockade against his country. Chile's economic and financial position
continued to deteriorate. The United States government was not prepared to assist her unless Allende would resolve to its satisfaction the
question of compensation to the nationalised American copper companies. This was politically impossible for Allende. Although the
Chilean government increased its support in Congress as a result of
elections in March 1973, these also brought successes to both political
extremes. Moreover, Allende still lacked a majority in the legislature.
A strike of copper miners, which further aggravated the economic
situation, added to the government's constitutional difficulties; for the
opposition supported the miners. Chile was rapidly becoming un-
governable.

In June 1973 an abortive military coup appeared to strengthen
Allende's position—but only temporarily. There was a growing likelihood of civil war, and Allende opened talks with the Christian
Democrats in an effort to avoid it. Another strike of transport owners
at the end of July produced an even graver situation than the first. Then,
the introduction of senior military officers into the government had
helped to end the crisis. Now, with the armed forces growing increasingly restive, the Commander-in-Chief, General Prats, resigned. As
Minister of Defence, General Prats had been a great source of strength
to the President, and his resignation was a most serious blow. On 11
September the Allende administration was overthrown and the
President met his death in a military coup. The right-wing junta which
now took power at once broke off relations with Cuba, whom it
accused of subversive activities in Chile with Allende's connivance.
Castro, in turn, denounced the junta for a 'fascist coup' inspired by the
United States. As regards the latter accusation, there was no evidence
of direct involvement by the Nixon administration, though the actions
of the transnational companies and the use of economic sanctions by
the United States had contributed significantly to Allende's downfall.
In keeping with his low-profile policy, President Nixon did not give
the new military government of Chile the warm welcome which his
predecessor had accorded those who overthrew President Goulart of

Brazil in 1964.[80] Perhaps he had less reason for satisfaction with the outcome.

The overthrow of Allende was much more dramatic, bloody and full of wider immediate consequence than that of Goulart. Nor was the initial conduct of the Chilean junta such as to sustain the pretence that its coup had meant a return to constitutional government.[81] Its reprisals against the late President's supporters involved executions on a scale which, although impossible to assess accurately, aroused very considerable international concern and protest. Much of the North American press and important sections of the United States Congress expressed strong disapproval of the Chilean junta. Apart from its fierce anti-communism, the latter appeared as yet to have no clear policy to deal with Chile's grave problems. How far it would prove an asset or a liability to the United States in her relations with Latin America remained to be seen. The immediate beneficiary of the coup, apart from its supporters within Chile, was Brazil, with whose rulers the Chilean junta had an obvious ideological affinity. The Chilean coup was a blow to developing Spanish American co-operation to counter Brazil's growing power and influence in South America. It was thus a severe set-back for Juan Perón, who was elected President of Argentina later in September. Perón would have to be circumspect in his relations with Brazil, even while it was more important than ever to try to regain influence among the other Spanish American countries. Argentina's position was the more precarious because of Perón's age (seventy-eight) and poor state of health. With Allende's overthrow, Peru was in a more exposed position in the vanguard of Latin American nationalism and social revolution. The future of the Andean group, which had been strengthened earlier in the year by the eventual adherence of Venezuela, was plunged into doubt. It had recently been making notable progress.

At the end of 1973 the policy of the Nixon administration towards Latin America was uncertain. In November Secretary of State Henry Kissinger was to have met with the Latin American foreign ministers at Bogotá. He had to cancel this engagement because of pressing problems arising mainly out of the renewal of war between the Arabs and Israel. The Latin Americans met without him. They had a number of

---

[80] See above, p. 240.

[81] Secretary of State Dean Rusk had actually congratulated the Brazilian military regime which overthrew Goulart on 'a move to insure the continuity of constitutional government'. (Levinson and de Onís, *The Alliance That Lost its Way, op. cit.*, p. 90.)

issues they wished to take up urgently with the United States. The overthrow of Allende had deepened their concern over the interference of the giant transnational corporations in the politics of the countries in which they had investments, and over the use of economic sanctions by the United States government. The reorganisation of the inter-American system was still under discussion; linked with it was the question of relations with Cuba. Panama had considerable support in pressing her case over the Canal. Although Dr. Kissinger earlier had indicated a willingness to reach an accommodation with Latin America on at least some of these issues, the time was not auspicious. Mr. Nixon's authority as President had weakened considerably during 1973[82] because of the Watergate revelations and other scandals touching the White House. Moreover, there were other problems considered much more urgent by the United States than those troubling the Latin Americans. Above all, there was the energy crisis, which had become more acute at the end of the year with the dramatic increase in the price of oil and the shortages aggravated by the Middle East conflict. Yet the energy crisis may portend the beginning of a crucial readjustment of relations between the producers of vital raw materials and the consumers in the wealthier, industrialised world. If this proves to be the case, such a readjustment has far-reaching implications for relations between the United States and Latin America.

---

[82] This was particularly inauspicious for Panama, whose expectations of a favourable settlement of the Canal issue were raised at the end of 1973. For there has always been strong opposition to such a settlement in the United States Congress.

# 8 Conclusion

As this historical analysis of relations between the United States and Latin America has shown, these have always been between one great power and a number of weak ones. The United States was an established power—and within the hemisphere could even be considered *relatively* a great one—by the time most of the Latin American countries became independent. Already United States leaders entertained an ambition that their country should become the only great power in the western hemisphere: to exclude the European great powers and to establish an *imbalance* of power in the Americas, detached from the European *balance* of power. The Monroe Doctrine was the expression of this ambition: it has been the core of United States Latin American policy from the time it was formulated until the present day. The fulfilment of United States ambition—making good the claim implicit in the words of President Monroe's Message of 1823—has been the dominant theme in the history of relations between the two Americas. In establishing and substantially maintaining her hegemony over Latin America, the United States has displayed the characteristics of a typical dynamic power, expanding territorially as well as economically, politically and culturally.

Yet the United States has been at great pains to portray her relations with Latin America as being different from those traditionally obtaining between great powers and small, weak ones. She has presented the Monroe Doctrine itself—in what is described as its 'original form' at least—as an instrument for protecting Latin America from predatory non-American powers rather than for promoting her own hegemony in the hemisphere. The United States has fostered Pan Americanism in order to propagate the idea of a community of interests shared by Latin America and herself, both of whom would alike be threatened by extra-continental intervention. The inter-American system based upon Pan Americanism is depicted as a unique association of juridically equal states, in self-flattering contrast to the imperialist relationships established in comparable circumstances by traditional great powers. The United States has been particularly concerned to rebut charges that she has pursued imperialist policies towards Latin America. The importance of her self-image and its projection in Latin America and the world at large—and the role cast for the inter-American system in sustaining it—have been stressed in this study.

But the inter-American system is not a unique kind of association as its admirers have claimed; nor can it mask the realities of the power situation. It could be compared, for example, with the *societas leonina* in which a hegemonial dependency was disguised in the Roman empire.[1] And United States relations with Latin America have shown an unmistakable similarity to those between the traditional European powers and their dependencies. The United States began her independent life as heir in the Americas to one great imperial power; she subsequently acquired by conquest a substantial portion of the heritage of another. Her leaders were determined that the United States should be a great empire, though a continental one, not beyond the seas in the manner of European empires. The ideas of the Monroe Doctrine have been described as 'imperialism preached in the grand manner'.[2] When the United States began to assert her hegemony over Latin America at the end of the nineteenth century her leading expansionists saw this as part of her becoming a world power with an overseas empire. Her thrust into the Caribbean was linked with expansion in the Far East. As in the case of the Filipinos, over whom the United States enforced her rule in the manner of a traditional imperial power, an assumption of racial superiority was an important element in her approach to Latin America. For example, Theodore Roosevelt, like many of his fellow citizens, referred contemptuously to Latin Americans as 'dagoes'. In the eyes of the expansionists the United States had a civilising mission in Latin America comparable with that of the European powers in other 'backward' areas of the world. That mission embraced Roosevelt's 'taking the Panama Canal' and the claim, contained in his corollary to the Monroe Doctrine, to a monopoly of intervention in the western hemisphere.

Following the Spanish-American war the United States established

---

[1] Georg Schwarzenberger, *Power Politics: A Study of International Society* (London, 1951), p. 6.                                    [2] See above, p. 86, n. 24.

protectorates over Cuba and Panama. The attitude of the 'pro-consuls' and their successors in the former and the 'zonians' in the latter towards the 'natives' was indistinguishable from that of privileged Europeans in comparable situations. In describing one particular incident in the case of Cuba, for example, Hugh Thomas has declared: 'The dispatch of General Crowder to Havana in 1921 without consultation with the Cuban Government was an act with few parallels even in the history of British imperial relations with the decrepit Moguls of Delhi.'[3] A comparison has already been made between the independence granted by the United States to Cuba and that given by Britain to Egypt: each designed to ensure that the donor's vital interests be safeguarded by restrictions upon the recipient's sovereignty. In other words, the United States and Britain were, in effect, exercising a form of indirect rule in the Caribbean area and the Middle East respectively. The perpetual treaties with Cuba and Panama gave the United States the right of intervention under circumstances to be decided by herself. The policy embodied in them was applied to the Caribbean region generally in the early decades of this century. Economic control and occasional armed occupations characterised the Caribbean or Panama policy of the United States.

United States leaders as well as historians have agreed that this was an imperialist phase of her relations with Latin America, although mitigated by its generally benevolent motivation. In any case, they maintain, it was an aberration and confined almost wholly to the particularly sensitive Caribbean region. However, since the end of the Second World War the United States has been accused more strongly than ever before of imperialism in her Latin American as well as wider policies. The accusation is essentially one of economic imperialism, with the concomitant political domination of those countries whose economies are dependent upon her, their key sectors often largely owned by her giant transnational companies. There can be no doubt of Latin America's high degree of dependence upon the United States for markets and investment capital; nor of the consider-able influence wielded in the region by vast United States economic enterprises. Thus, in varying degrees, the Latin American countries are penetrated systems. Nevertheless, the United States denies that she is an imperialist power, and declares the Soviet Union to be the great imperialist power of the post-war period. In so doing she

---

[3] *Cuba or The Pursuit of Freedom, op. cit.*, p. 1419.

stresses her own interpretation of imperialism as direct political control, whereas her critics—and not only communists—emphasise economic control.

Undoubtedly there are basic similarities between United States relations with Latin America (especially, but by no means exclusively, with the countries of the Caribbean area) and the Soviet system in eastern Europe. Each of these great powers has demonstrated its determination to have friendly governments in areas of proximity and strategic significance to it; and each has interpreted 'friendly governments' to mean governments as far as possible under its control.[4] Interestingly, a United States diplomat wrote during the Second World War: 'There is no essential difference between our desire and determination to have friendly neighbors to the south of us and Comrade Stalin's determination to have friendly neighbors on the Western borders of Russia: for Stalin now feels that he is practically sovereign in Eastern Europe and that there *his* fiat is law.'[5] And much more recently, a liberal United States senator (Frank Church[6]) declared of United States intervention in Latin America to sustain unrepresentative but co-operative governments: 'I must say that it bears a very striking resemblance to the Russian policy, where Soviet intervention clearly serves the purpose of preserving the status quo within the Russian sphere of influence . . . it appears that the preservation of the status quo is the dominant objective sought by both the United States and the Soviet Union in the world today.'[7]

Both the United States and the Soviet Union have deployed armed force to maintain their own system: the former most recently in the Dominican Republic in 1965, and the latter in Czechoslovakia in 1968. In each case the objective of the intervention was to prevent the possible defection of a *second* satellite. For Yugoslavia had left the Soviet system in 1948, and Cuba the inter-American system in 1962. These defections had been possible because Tito and Castro were

---

[4] In the Declaration of Yalta (1945) the United States accepted Russia's right to have friendly governments in eastern Europe, but subsequently denounced Stalin for imposing communist governments in that region.

[5] Sands, *Our Jungle Diplomacy, op. cit.*, p. 236. Sands was making a comparison with, and using the phraseology of, Secretary Olney's famous speech of 1895 asserting a United States 'fiat' in the western hemisphere. See above, p. 97.

[6] See above, p. 17.

[7] *United States Military Policies and Programs in Latin America. Hearings before the Subcommittee on Western Hemisphere Affairs of the Committee on Foreign Relations, United States Senate, June 24 and July 8, 1969* (U.S.G.P.O., Washington, 1969), p. 42.

strong national leaders, not dependent upon the support of the hegemonial power to sustain them in office nor correspondingly vulnerable to subversion. As we saw, the United States sent thousands of her marines into Santo Domingo in order to prevent a 'second Cuba'. As soon as possible after doing so she enlisted the support of her Latin American allies for the establishment of an inter-American peace force to multilateralise her action. In the case of Czechoslovakia, members of the Warsaw Pact participated from the outset in what was a very much larger-scale invasion. In both situations there was a great deal of brutality and no little loss of life. There is another significant analogy. The unacceptability to the Russians of the Czech communist leader, Alexander Dubcek, because of his tolerance of dissenting views, was paralleled by the United States rejection of Juan Bosch as being 'soft on communism'.

Most North Americans would deny the validity of both the general analogy between United States and Soviet policies within their respective spheres of influence, and the particular parallel between the interventions in the Dominican Republic and Czechoslovakia.[8] The United States self-image, in which there is no valid comparison between the inter-American system and the Soviet system (and, therefore, between these two interventions), must be seen in its historical context. For historically the United States, within her overall Latin American policy, has assumed special responsibility for stability and orderly government in the often turbulent Caribbean region. The exercise of this responsibility has sometimes involved the use of armed force and not inconsiderable loss of life. Commenting on an earlier period, when United States armed interventions were regarded as a 'normal' response to crises in the region,[9] Bryce Wood declared:

In Washington ... approval of the use of force by the United States was not seen as inconsistent with condemnation of the use of force by Latin

---

[8] See, for example, Slater, *Intervention and Negotiation: The United States and the Dominican Revolution, op. cit.*, p. 221: 'The U.S. "sphere of influence" in the Caribbean is not to be compared with the tight and repressive Soviet political, military, and economic control of Eastern Europe.' Professor Slater here disregards the repressive dictatorships in the Caribbean which have enjoyed the warm support of the United States. But in any case a comparison between the systems of the two major world powers is not only valid but particularly relevant for a study of contemporary international relations. Nor does Professor Slater's assumption that the United States is *incomparably* more permissive in her sphere of influence appear to be justified by his own account of the Dominican intervention. [9] See above, p. 146.

K

American countries. These two lines of conduct were really part of a single system of thought. The Marines were regarded as being an arm of the law—international law, in this case, as interpreted and upheld by the United States.[10]

President Coolidge, rebutting criticism of his intervention in Nicaragua in the nineteen-twenties, put the same thought in more homely terms: 'We are not making war on Nicaragua any more than a policeman on the streets is making war on a passerby.'[11] The idea of the United States exercising 'an international police power' in the western hemisphere is, as we have seen, associated with Theodore Roosevelt, from whose corollary to the Monroe Doctrine the phrase has been taken.[12] It was part of his view of the United States as the civilised power of the hemisphere, with its significant racial overtones. But Theodore Roosevelt merely gave forceful expression to a view widely held by his fellow countrymen, including Presidents such as Woodrow Wilson. The Monroe Doctrine, of which the corollary was a logical extension, involves an assumption by the United States of certain rights in respect of Latin America which she does not concede to other great powers in respect of smaller countries of comparable significance to them[13]—above all, smaller *European* countries such as Czechoslovakia and Hungary.

This historic United States approach has been strongly and increasingly challenged as she has extended its application in the contemporary world. For, just as in 1956 condemnation of Russia's invasion of Hungary was blunted by the Anglo-French attack upon Egypt—which aroused far greater anger among non-European peoples—so were expressions of outrage in the West against Soviet action in Czechoslovakia twelve years later much weakened by United States military involvement in Vietnam. Critics of her post-war policies have not failed to point out that the United States, and not the Soviet Union, has been engaged in war almost continuously since 1950. And while the United States has been convinced of the rightness of the causes for which she has fought and armed others to fight—at least until grave setbacks induced doubt and self-criticism—others have

---

[10] *The United States and Latin American Wars, 1932–1942, op. cit.*, p. 2.

[11] Quoted in Selig Adler, *The Uncertain Giant: 1921–1941. American Foreign Policy Between the Wars* (paperback edn., New York, 1969), p. 100.

[12] See above, p. 115.

[13] In other words, the United States has sought to maintain 'a closed hemisphere in an open world'. See above, p. 192.

seen, in her bolstering and even creation of corrupt regimes in Asia, the projection on a wider scale of her historic support of repressive dictatorships in her traditional sphere of influence. Indeed, United States foreign policy since the end of the Second World War has been described by many observers—both friendly and unfriendly—as a global application of the Monroe Doctrine. Whatever the rightness or otherwise of her motives, the United States has employed a very great deal of armed force indeed *against non-European peoples*. Justly or unjustly, she has incurred wide international opprobrium in so doing.

Increasing United States involvement in Vietnam in the middle nineteen-sixties had important influence upon her relations with Latin America. On the one hand, for example, it relegated the Cuban problem to the background. This was beneficial since, as we have seen, Cuba has been a divisive issue in inter-American relations. On the other hand, the cost of the Vietnam war adversely affected United States foreign aid programmes, and therefore the Alliance for Progress. Latin America was confirmed as a low priority area and became the subject of a low profile policy. But repercussions of the Vietnam war were only one aspect of increasing influence upon inter-American relations of wider international developments. We have seen how the emergence of the Third World—developing and *non-European*—and growing Latin American identification with it, have called into question the region's special relationship with the United States. Symbolic of changing relationships was the meeting of the United Nations Security Council in Panama in March 1973, at which the future of the Canal was debated. For Panama's very existence as a sovereign state symbolises United States hegemony in Latin America, and Panamanian nationalism, with its racial overtones, is a focal point of the challenge which growing Latin American nationalism poses to the hegemonial power.

The discussion of perhaps the most sensitive 'American' question by the world body, and the critical resolution which the United States felt bound to veto, demonstrate a serious threat to the future of the inter-American system, at least in its traditional form. And this would be a serious setback to the United States. For, in spite of widespread criticism that it is no more than a rubber stamp for her policies, the United States herself sets considerable store by that system as giving the legitimacy of multilateralisation to those policies. This was seen most strikingly in the Cuban missile crisis when, although the

Organization of American States played no apparent role in the making of the vital decisions, the United States based the legality of her 'quarantine' of the island upon the Inter-American Treaty of Reciprocal Assistance. On this point Robert Kennedy wrote:

> It was the vote of the Organization of American States that gave a legal basis for the quarantine. Their willingness to follow the leadership of the United States was a heavy and unexpected blow to Khrushchev. It had a major psychological and practical effect on the Russians and changed our position from that of an outlaw acting in violation of international law into a country acting in accordance with twenty allies legally protecting their position.[14]

The case of Cuba illustrates also another very important function of the inter-American system complementary to its role in organising Latin American support for United States policies. It is the use of the system to give support to what might be called 'non-policies'. When President Kennedy was under pressure to overthrow Dr. Castro, which he did not believe was a viable policy, he found it very useful to point to United States treaty obligations precluding unilateral action and to stress the need to work through the OAS. In Professor Slater's words: 'The endless round of Council meetings and the spate of largely meaningless, ineffectual, and unenforced reports and resolutions on antisubversive and other measures—all ostensibly designed to increase pressure on the Cuban government—have really served to obfuscate the unwillingness of the United States to take the drastic action that would be necessary to overthrow Castro.'[15] Incidentally, when Kennedy had himself called for action to overthrow Castro during the 1960 presidential election campaign, Richard Nixon (who was a warm supporter of the secret plans already under way to launch an invasion of Cuba by Cuban exiles) used the very arguments of treaty obligations, and the need to work through the OAS, against his rival candidate and in defence of what purported to be the Eisenhower administration's policy.

The inter-American system of itself has imposed only limited restraint upon the United States. The significance of the principle of non-intervention, whose adoption has generally been regarded as

---

[14] *13 Days*, op. cit., p. 119. All the points made in this passage are of dubious validity; but it is of considerable interest that Robert Kennedy made them.

[15] *A Revaluation of Collective Security*, op. cit., p. 43.

Latin America's greatest gain from membership, has been much exaggerated. The very fact of United States power makes intervention by her in many forms inevitable: only in the case of its most overt forms can she realistically be expected to exercise restraint. Although the United States subscribed to the broadest interpretation of non-intervention in the OAS Charter,[16] her leaders have made it clear by both word and deed that when she felt her security to be threatened the United States would act unilaterally in spite of her treaty obligations. Her interventions in Guatemala, Cuba and the Dominican Republic since signing the OAS Charter demonstrate a policy of working through the OAS where feasible, but of acting unilaterally when, in her judgement, this was necessary.

The truth is, however, that the United States has consistently pursued a policy involving a great deal of intervention in both the internal and the external affairs[17] of the Latin American countries. The Monroe Doctrine itself places strict limits upon the relations of Latin America with non-American powers: these shall not be allowed to threaten the security of the United States. As we have seen, the United States has intervened with armed force in the internal affairs of a number of Latin American countries, often with the stated purpose of forestalling intervention by extra-continental powers. Her interventions, in their turn, have facilitated economic penetration, leading to economic control and ownership of key resources—and the maintenance or installation in power of governments willing to make these concessions to United States interests in return for the semblance of power and the reality of privilege. Although almost all the armed interventions have taken place in the Caribbean area, even the largest Latin American countries have been penetrated to a considerable degree politically, economically, culturally and militarily by the United States.

Thus the United States has been able to influence—very often decisively—the kind of governments in power in Latin America. Understandably, she has used her influence in favour of co-operative governments: co-operative, that is, in furthering the objectives of United States policy in the region. Such governments, for their part, are representative of groups whose interests are furthered by co-operation with the United States; sometimes that co-operation alone

---

[16] See above, pp. 200–1.
[17] This is the phrase used in the various agreements in which the principle of non-intervention is included. It is, of course, not possible to separate them in practice.

keeps them in power. Given the fragile structures of virtually all the Latin American countries, it is exceedingly difficult for governments in the region to resist United States pressure even when those in power desire to do so. Thus it has been to the advantage of the United States to have there governments which are unrepresentative of the Latin American peoples. Unrepresentative governments generally have proved in Latin America the most co-operative, and certainly the most easily subverted when they pursued unco-operative policies. Professor Silvert, in analysing the question of race and national cohesion in Latin America, contrasted the narrowly based government of Guatemala in 1954 with the much more broadly based Cuban government in 1961, comparing the ease with which the United States was able to overthrow the former with the possibly very heavy cost of a successful operation against Fidel Castro. This last constituted one reason, in Silvert's judgement, why President Kennedy did not follow through the initial Bay of Pigs invasion.[18]

In the cases of both Guatemala and Cuba the United States pursued a counter-revolutionary policy. This was in line with her position in Latin America as a whole as well as in other regions of the world. The United States claim to have favoured the Cuban revolution 'before Castro betrayed it' carries no conviction, for in Cuba as elsewhere real revolution (as opposed to the innumerable coups so characteristic of Latin American politics) could not but be inimical to her interests. Nor can President Kennedy's attempts to portray the United States as an authentic revolutionary nation be taken seriously. The United States is profoundly conservative and counter-revolutionary. The most important feature of both the Mexican and Cuban revolutions (the authentic revolutions of Latin America) has been their essentially nationalist character. They brought to power 'national revolutionary' governments, furthering national integration, a process which included, importantly, regaining for the nation key resources alienated by previous regimes. The policies pursued more recently by the military government in Peru and, for a time, the left-wing coalition in Chile have posed a similar threat to the United States. In Latin America nationalism, and concomitant revolution, are essentially anti-(North) American. The United States is thus threatened by both. Her policy in Latin America must, in principle,

---

18 Kalman H. Silvert, 'Race and National Cohesion in Latin America', in George W. Shepherd, Jr. (ed.), *Racial Influences on American Foreign Policy* (New York, 1970), pp. 140 ff.

be to support those elements which are strongly anti-revolutionary and not strongly nationalistic. And this is the policy she generally has pursued.

What then of the mission to promote democracy in Latin America, so often proclaimed an important objective of United States policy? It is an article of faith among North Americans, including scholars as well as politicians, that the United States supports representative democracy in Latin America. They attribute her obvious lack of success in promoting it to the limitations of her power and influence; thus, at the same time, implying that United States domination of the region is less than critics would have them believe. Clearly, there are limits to United States power and influence, though she has had considerable success in securing her policy objectives in the region. Moreover, it would not be easy to foster democracy in the Latin American environment. However, the record does not support the contention that the United States seriously has tried to do this, in spite of all the rhetoric devoted to proclaiming that she has done so. Historically, as we have seen, she has been the beneficiary of dictatorships in the Americas from Napoleon Bonaparte, the doubtful owner of Louisiana, onwards. And Latin American governments which have endeavoured to deprive her of the benefits she has received from dictatorships in order to improve the lot of their peoples have incurred her strong hostility. United States interventions have led to dictatorships; often they have been deliberately made to bolster up or even put into power dictatorial but co-operative governments. Yet, on occasions, the United States has pleaded the principle of non-intervention as grounds for not intervening *against* dictatorships. However desirable in principle a democratic Latin America may be—and the sincerity of those North Americans subscribing to it need not be questioned—in practice little headway has been made in the face of United States interests which so patently have conflicted with it.

In considering the enormous gap between United States professions and her practice in this matter it is important to remember that in her interpretation democracy is closely identified with private, capitalistic enterprise. Dedication to private enterprise, demonstrated by concessions to her economic and financial interests, is understandably a significant, if not decisive, criterion in securing United States approval for a Latin American government. As a corollary, such a government will be staunchly anti-communist. Thus could a United States congressman note approvingly of Trujillo's dictatorship, 'that the

Dominican Republic was stable and that it enjoyed spiritual and material well-being, supported United States policies, had given the United States territory for military bases and had encouraged American investment'. For another admirer, in the Senate, Trujillo 'was a staunch friend, had provided a base in the guided missile program, was a foe of communism in the Caribbean and represented "stability and good government in an area of turmoil" '.[19] Franklin Roosevelt's 'Good Neighbourhood' included Trujillo, whom he entertained 'only a year and a half after Welles had drawn Roosevelt's attention to a despatch from Minister R. Henry Norweb containing an account of the killing by the Dominican national police and army of at least one thousand Haitian civilians in peculiarly horrible circumstances, following a series of border incidents'. That 'neighbourhood' also included the Nicaraguan dictator, Anastasio Somoza, regarding whom:

> President Roosevelt established a precedent by going to the railroad station to meet Somoza, and an impressive military parade was held in the visitor's honor. Somoza stayed overnight in the White House and thus became the only guest so hospitably entertained after having been officially reported by a United States Minister as having planned and been responsible for a murder.

According to Bryce Wood, 'Such a welcome for a dictator of infamous reputation gave rise to expressions of incredulous indignation in Latin America'.[20] More recently, the United States has supported the military as a supposedly democratic element in Latin American politics, apparently in agreement with Professor Mecham's judgement that: 'if the United States is interested in stability, order, and democratic progress, it behooves [*sic*] this country to continue to give support through the military-assistance program to the professional military in Latin America; they are fair insurance against Communist *coups* in any of the governments'.[21] The equation here is between democracy and anti-communism, which has been a constant feature of United States policy, justifying her support of co-operative dictatorships while she professes concern for representative government.

[19] G. Pope Atkins and Larman C. Wilson, *The United States and the Trujillo Regime* (New Brunswick, N.J., Rutgers University Press, 1972), pp. 72–3.
[20] *The Making of the Good Neighbor Policy*, *op. cit.*, p. 155. The two previous quotations are at the same reference. The murder in question was that of Sandino. See above, p. 151.
[21] *The United States and Inter-American Security*, *1889–1960*, *op. cit.*, p. 340.

Yet the United States has also sought to equate democracy with the holding of elections. But again the matter of elections has been linked with basic objectives, and, above all, with maintaining the *status quo* and preventing revolutions. In his study of this question, Professor Theodore Wright concluded:

> The United States has not deliberately embarked upon a policy of promoting democracy in other countries. It has supported free elections as an answer to certain concrete policy problems which accompanied its rise to world power. The chief of these has been how to prevent or halt revolutions. In practically every case related in this study, political stability was the direct or indirect goal of American electoral intervention.[22]

The United States insisted upon—and sometimes supervised—elections in order to promote stability and justify her support of particular governments. Such elections are hardly meaningful, even when the United States is genuinely disinterested. As Wright observed, 'a technically "free and fair" election can never play the role assigned it by democratic theory—a real test of party strength, as long as American participation influences the minds and ballots of the voters'.[23] This has been demonstrated most recently in the Dominican Republic, where elections were held in 1966 under international observation but in the aftermath of a United States armed intervention. The elections were cited as the ultimate justification for the intervention and hailed as inaugurating a new era of constitutional government in that country. However, developments in the Dominican Republic since then—including the continuance in office of President Balaguer, the former Trujillo lieutenant who won the 1966 and subsequent elections—suggest that the 1965 intervention will prove to have been no more conducive to democracy than previous interventions in the Dominican Republic and other Caribbean countries.[24] At all events, United States criticism of Dr. Castro for not holding elections (and of other members of the Soviet system for the kind of elections they actually do hold) must be viewed against her own support of dictatorships and ready acquiescence in the unrepresentative character of so many governments (and not merely in

---

[22] *American Support of Free Elections Abroad, op. cit.*, p. 137.
[23] *Ibid.*, p. 157.
[24] Incidentally, Colonel Francisco Caamaño, leader of the constitutionalists in the civil war, was killed in February 1973, apparently in a clash with Dominican troops while leading a small guerrilla group.

Latin America) co-operating with her. Elections held under such governments mean little. Ironically, most observers agree that Castro would very easily win elections in Cuba—including fair ones!

Cuba, as this study has shown, provides a significant test-case for United States concern with freedom and democracy in Latin America. Cuba also throws into contrast United States professions with her performance; and her self-image with the image of her which prevails among Latin Americans. Hugh Thomas called his monumental book *Cuba or The Pursuit of Freedom*.[25] In the nineteenth century the United States did not support Cuba's freedom from Spain because it did not accord with her interests to do so; she wanted not freedom for the island, but control of it for herself. This she obtained at the end of the century. In the twentieth century the freedom Cuba has pursued has been freedom from the United States. This, whatever its short-comings, Castro's revolution has achieved. Cuba has attained nation-hood and national dignity if not an impressive gross national product. The achievements of the Cuban revolution are to be measured in values which the United States generally does not appreciate; for it involves a rejection of fundamental North American values as well as of the United States self-image as the island's liberator and benefactor. Professor Langley has well observed: 'It is not Castro's political dictatorship that is so reprehensible as his open denial of the Jacksonian credos of democracy, capitalism, and progress.'[26] Arthur Schlesinger, who wrote the White Paper on Cuba, which was meant to justify in advance United States involvement in the Bay of Pigs invasion,[27] records in *A Thousand Days* how he was appalled at what he calls the debasement of Havana by his fellow-countrymen in pre-Castro days: 'One wondered how any Cuban—on the basis of this evidence—could regard the United States with anything but hatred.'[28] He records also how, when he included in the White Paper an admission that the United States had committed errors in her policy towards Cuba, 'I was told, "we" should not admit error in our dealings with Latin American countries; it was unbecoming, and they would not respect us in the future.'[29]

---

[25] The observations which follow are my own. I have merely taken the phrase 'the pursuit of freedom' from Thomas.

[26] Lester D. Langley, *The Cuban Policy of the United States: A Brief History* (New York, 1968), p. 187.

[27] See above, p. 232.                          [28] *Op. cit.*, p. 151.

[29] *Ibid.*, p. 209. But Schlesinger adds that his document emerged substantially intact.

Cuba has become free of United States domination, but heavily dependent upon the Soviet Union. Her case has been cited as supporting the long-affirmed contention of the United States that Latin American countries cannot maintain an independent existence and that they are better off under her benevolent paramountcy than under the domination of an extra-continental power. But hitherto Cuba's case does not support the assertion that 'the United States is a much more permissive paramount than the Soviet Union'.[30] The Soviet presence does not bear down upon her as did that of the United States before the revolution when, in Raymond Carr's words, 'The presence of the United States was psychologically oppressive in Cuba as in no other country, except possibly Panama'.[31] The Russian presence is far less obtrusive, and bears no comparison with that of the United States in former times as described by Schlesinger and many others. The United States doubtless wants Cuba to be free: but free from the Soviet system and back within her own sphere of influence. Freedom for Latin America has always meant to the United States freedom from extra-continental domination, not from her own.

To contrast United States professions of concern for democracy and freedom with her practice of supporting, and even installing, co-operative dictators is to suggest Machiavellianism and hypocrisy; and, of course, her Latin American policy (and foreign policy generally) display a great deal of both. In other words, the United States has behaved like a great power. Ironically, those aspects of the United States political system which seem to North Americans to make for a more enlightened foreign policy tend to have a contrary effect. In democracies, foreign policy has to appear to be idealistic: to be presented in terms of great principles. The people of the United States have a notable weakness for 'Doctrines'. But, like other peoples, they are strongly motivated by self-interest. In representative democracies, perhaps above all other systems, governments must be seen to be promoting the interests of their peoples. In the case of the United States, as we have noted, the diffusion of power and competing influences within the system aggravate the contradiction between idealism and self-interest, profession and practice. This contradiction has been particularly evident in her policy towards Latin America,

---

[30] Norman A. Bailey, *Latin America in World Politics* (New York, 1967), p. 179.
[31] 'The Cold War in Latin America', in Plank (ed.), *Cuba and the United States: Long-Range Perspectives, op. cit.*, p. 165.

the more so since the United States has been at such pains to propagate the idea—perhaps to convince herself as much as Latin Americans—that there exists a harmony of interests between the two Americas.

Nowhere has this been more apparent than in the case of the Alliance for Progress, in conception the most enlightened policy towards the region ever launched. This was described as 'A New Deal for Latin America', and those responsible for formulating it generally saw it in that light. The Alliance was intended to further economic development and social justice in Latin America, and to strengthen representative democracy. Unfortunately, it was based upon an assumption (following Castro's success) that change in Latin America was inevitable, and that United States policy must be to ensure that such change came about through evolutionary and not revolutionary processes. In other words, the Alliance for Progress was in line with traditional United States policy of seeking stability and preventing revolution in Latin America. This inevitably led to the strengthening of unrepresentative but anti-communist governments and, especially, of the Latin American military. At the same time the economic development of Latin America was not to be allowed to weaken United States economic control of the region; on the contrary, the Alliance for Progress soon developed into an instrument for strengthening it. Moreover there was an important miscalculation in the concept of the Alliance. It was assumed that economic development would increase the stability of Latin America. But the reverse is true: economic development generates instability as expectations rise. Since stability remained a prime objective of her policy, the United States favoured regimes which seemed to promise it. The Alliance as an instrument of change was correspondingly weakened. In any case it only too rapidly degenerated into becoming essentially a programme of loans tied to purchases of United States goods and equipment.

But basically the failure of the Alliance for Progress stems from there being no real community of interests between the United States and Latin America. The Alliance postulated a partnership where there exists only a hegemonial relationship. It called for far-reaching changes when the United States and her most important collaborators in the region wanted, broadly speaking, to maintain the *status quo* through limited concessions. But even the generally modest reforms for which the United States pressed were often resisted by conservative Latin American governments; more far-reaching reforms affecting her own interests incurred the opposition of the United States herself.

There can be no far-reaching economic and social changes in Latin America as long as the region remains so dependent upon the United States: as long as the present imbalance of power persists between the two Americas. This is so in principle. It has been amply demonstrated by Latin American experience.

As we have seen, United States policy has been based upon the premise that Latin America is a region that must be dominated either by her or by some extra-continental power or powers. The Monroe Doctrine made clear that she would not accept the second alternative; it led, therefore, to the first. Nor was it difficult for the United States to convince herself that this was the better alternative for Latin America also; and, indeed, it may have been so. But Latin Americans could hardly be expected to accept either the inevitability of being faced with these alternatives, or having the choice made for them. From their point of view, some redress of the imbalance of power which would lessen their dependence was desirable. Only in the last two decades have opportunities arisen for Latin America to develop closer relations with non-American powers which would offset in significant measure the power of its northern neighbour. As recently as the end of the Second World War United States domination of Latin America was virtually unchallenged.

Since the end of the Second World War relations between the United States and Latin America have been influenced far more than hitherto by events outside the western hemisphere; and the world environment generally has been unfavourable to harmonious inter-American relations. The divergence of interests between the United States as the most powerful nation in the world and the countries of Latin America as weak ones forming her immediate zone of influence has been underlined and widened. At the same time Latin American dissatisfaction with a position of dependence and subordination to the interests of the United States has increased. The latter's policies in the Cold War received only lukewarm support from Latin America, and when the region itself was directly involved inter-American relations were strained by a resurgence in an acute form of the old issue of intervention. Further strains resulted from the refusal of the United States to meet Latin American demands for economic aid of the kind and on the scale of the Marshall Plan for Europe. This divergence of interests was reflected in the inter-American system which became correspondingly ineffective and unsatisfactory to both the United States and Latin America.

But the emergence of the 'Third World' had particularly important influence upon relations between the two Americas. For if Latin Americans were lukewarm allies of the United States when the world appeared to be polarising between the 'Free' and the 'Communist' groups, they were ranged against her when the idea took root that the countries of the world were more meaningfully divided between the industrialised or developed countries and the primary producing or underdeveloped ones.[32] The Third World countries, who are basically 'neutralist' in the Cold War, are the underdeveloped group. They are located in Africa, Asia—and Latin America. There has occurred among them the 'revolution of rising expectations'. Most of them are newly independent countries who have found that political independence has not meant the end of economic domination; for they are dependent upon the industrialised powers for markets and investment capital, while key sectors of their economies often are foreign-owned. In many cases political rule by European powers has been followed by economic control by the United States: this process has been called 'neo-colonialism'. These countries have received 'aid' which has had the effect of increasing their dependence upon the donors, and they have demanded instead more favourable terms of trade. Their demands have been strongly voiced at the United Nations Conferences on Trade and Development (UNCTADs).

It is not difficult to see how Latin America fits into this situation. Most of the Latin American countries have been politically independent for approximately a century and a half. But they have never achieved economic independence, being first dependent primarily upon Britain and other European powers and, in this century, increasingly upon the United States. In the Caribbean region extensive United States economic penetration had already preceded political independence, as in the case of Cuba and, more recently, British Commonwealth countries such as Jamaica. Incidentally, the closer association of newly independent Commonwealth Caribbean countries with Latin America—for example, through membership of the OAS—further identifies the region with the Third World, and not merely in the matter of economic dependence. Not only are the countries of the Third World poor and underdeveloped; their peoples are coloured. And a significant feature of the post-war world has been the increasing

---

[32] 'Underdeveloped' was later changed to the euphemistic but often inaccurate 'developing'. I have generally employed the latter term, however, because of its wide usage.

importance of race in international relations. It has always been an important feature in relations between the United States and Latin America. It is likely to become more so in the future. 'Black power' in the Caribbean, with repercussions and even links with similar movements in the United States herself, may be an ominous pointer.

It is within the Caribbean region, the most sensitive part of Latin America from the United States point of view and the one apparently most securely under her control, that the greatest challenge to her position has developed. Fidel Castro achieved what historically it has been the primary objective of United States Latin American policy to prevent: the introduction of extra-continental power into the western hemisphere to challenge her hegemony. When Castro in effect[33] withdrew Cuba from the inter-American system and introduced the Soviet system into Latin America, the Monroe Doctrine had been successfully breached. And this at a time when the United States had never been more powerful, and when the Doctrine, in practice, had been extended to western Europe and other parts of the world. Although there has been no 'second Cuba' the United States has faced further challenges to her position in Latin America. One such is the Peruvian social revolution under military leadership; another was that from the short-lived Marxist coalition government in Chile, whose consequences may yet prove of considerable significance in inter-American relations. Problems of long-standing, such as the Canal dispute with Panama, have taken on a new dimension in a rapidly changing world. Nationalism has markedly increased in Latin America, bringing the United States into more frequent confrontation with individual governments as well as with the Latin American countries as a group on basic issues.

There have been other important developments. In recent years trade links between Latin America and the Soviet Union have grown, reflecting both the desire of the former to lessen its dependence upon the United States and Russian policy of improving relations with Latin American governments regardless of their political complexion. Interestingly, Brazil received more than half the aid to Latin America from the Soviet group of countries in the period from 1954 until 1970.[34] Brazil, staunch ally of the United States in her anti-communist policies, has had serious disputes with her on economic matters.

---

[33] Formally, his government was 'excluded' from the system. See above p. 236.

[34] *Latin America, op. cit.*, vol. vi, no. 2 (14 January 1972), p. 16. Cuba, of course, is not included in this calculation.

And, of course, if Brazil is to achieve her ambition to be a great power she must become less dependent economically and financially upon the United States.[35] Soviet trade with Latin America today is very limited. But Russia's inability to provide quality goods at competitive prices is largely responsible for this, not Latin America's unwillingness to trade with her. China may well follow a similar policy towards Latin America now that her admission to the United Nations has opened up new possibilities for regular diplomatic contacts with the region. In relative terms the presence of the Soviet Union and China in Latin America has substantially increased during the last decade or so. In absolute terms, however, it remains small.

Meanwhile, there has been a substantial increase in Latin America's economic and financial links with western Europe and Japan. The Japanese have enjoyed the important advantage over the United States of pursuing economic policies uncomplicated by political objectives. Incidentally, the drive of the West Germans to increase trade and investment in Latin America has been affected to some extent by political considerations, notably the question of East Germany, with whom some Latin American countries have traded. The case of Cuba is of particular interest because, as we have already noted, she has achieved economic independence of the United States only to become very heavily dependent upon the Soviet Union. Clearly Dr. Castro would like to develop trade with non-communist powers in order to lessen this dependence; and the United States has been unable to persuade her major allies to cease trading with Cuba. But the latter's dependence upon the Soviet Union remains fundamental to her economic development. The case of Cuba thus continues to support the United States contention that the Latin American countries have only a choice of patrons, not a prospect of independence. At all events it is most unlikely that there will be a 'second Cuba' in the foreseeable future. The United States would not tolerate one, and the Soviet Union shows every sign of not wanting to sponsor one.

Thus, although Latin America has become increasingly aware of the disadvantages of dependence upon the United States and correspondingly anxious to lessen it through closer relations with extracontinental powers, opportunities for so doing—though increasing—remain limited. Latin American resentment at United States domina-

---

[35] The European Economic Community has surpassed the United States as Brazil's most important trading partner.

tion is growing faster than the means of diminishing it. Latin American frustration is likely to grow: perhaps dangerously so. Nevertheless, from a United States point of view the challenge to her traditional position in Latin America is a very real one, both in terms of Latin American nationalism directed against her and of growing economic competition from Europe and Japan. The trend is towards a diminution of United States hegemony over Latin America even if this is long-term. The future of relations between the two Americas will be greatly influenced by the way the United States responds to this trend. This study has shown the ambivalence of her attitude towards Latin America. The latter is at once the United States special sphere of influence and a low priority area in her foreign policy. The history of inter-American relations suggests that these would be greatly improved should the United States reverse her attitude: should she consider Latin America less important to her in theory and give it greater importance in practice. But the vast margin of superiority in power which she still enjoys in the hemisphere induces complacency rather than concern. On the basis of historical experience the outlook is unpromising.

# Index

Aberdeen, Lord, gives British view on Texas, 78
Acheson, Dean, 194, 205
Acheson Plan, 206, n. 39
Act of Bogotá (1960), 225, n. 94, 232
Act of Chapultepec (1945), 189, 197, n. 18
Adams, John Quincy, and Spanish American independence, 49, 52–5, 57–8
    and Canning's proposal to Rush, 59–61
    and Cuba, 59–60
    and Panama Congress, 66
    opposed to acquisition of Texas, 76
Adams–Onís Treaty (1819), 47, 53–4, 72, 75
Additional Protocol Relative to Non-Intervention (1936), 167–8, 201
Advisory Defense Committee, 202
Afro-Asian-Latin American Peoples' Solidarity Conference, 1st (Tricontinental Conference), 249
Agency for International Development (AID), 12–13, 23, 30
Aix-la-Chapelle, Congress of (1818), 58
Allende, Salvador, election and overthrow, 40, 226
    defeat by Frei in 1964 election, 241
    difficulties of his administration, 257–8
    resumes relations with Cuba and establishes them with China and other communist countries, 258–9
    problems with US companies and foreign exchange, weakening position and eventual overthrow, 263–4
Alliance for Progress, 5, 13, 36, 225, n. 94
    described, 233
    built-in contradictions of, 234
    widespread disappointment with, 238
    US Business Advisory Council of, 248
    thoroughly discredited by 1969, 251
    Latin American criticism at Viña del Mar, 255–6
    affected by Vietnam war, 273
    evaluated, 282–3
Alsop claim, 124–5
Alta Gracia Conference (1964), 247
American Finance Ministers Meeting (Rio, 1954), 220

American Treaty on Pacific Settlement (Pact of Bogotá, 1948), 202
    ineffectiveness, 215, n. 73
Anaconda copper company, 254
Andean group, Frei's role in forming, 248
    Bogotá pact (1969), 254–5
    weakened by Venezuela's failure to join, 259
    strengthened by Venezuela's adherence (1973), 265
    overthrow of Allende as set-back, ibid.
Arab-Israel War, 265–6
Arbenz, Jacobo, 211 ff., 223
Arévalo, Juan José, 2, 211, 220
Argentina, 16
    and territorial waters, 34
    rivalry with Brazil, 37–8, 125, 260
    and Panama Congress (1826), 109
    at 1st Conference, 110–12
    and League of Nations Covenant, 144
    opposes US at Buenos Aires Conference (1936), 168
    also 'dilutes' US proposals at 8th Conference, 169
    and Chaco War, 171
    claims Falkland Islands, 177, n. 67
    weakens main resolution at 3rd Meeting, 180
    strained war-time relations with US, 182–4
    accepts Mexico City 'Final Act' (1945), 191
    worsening relations with US, 193–6
    and Guatemalan crisis, 214, 217
    Perón's 'Third Position' and US, 222–3
    one of 'the six' at 8th Meeting, 236
    participates in Cuban quarantine, 237, n. 28
    fear of Brazil in 1970s, 260
    resumes relations with Cuba and offers her credits, 260–1
    Perón's return to power, 260–1, 265
    justicialismo, the Third World and Peru's revolution, 261
    overthrow of Allende as set-back, 265
    see also 'Argentine problem', United Provinces of the Rio de la Plata

'Argentine problem', 180–1, 183–4, 190–1,
    193–6
Arthur, Chester A., 107
Avila Camacho, Manuel, 175
Axis powers, 38
    actions in 1935–6 influencing inter-
    American co-operation, 168, n. 49
    and Mexican oil, 174
    victories in Europe (1940), 176
    agents and sympathisers in Latin America,
    177–8
Ayacucho, Battle of (1824), 2, 55

Balaguer, Joaquín, 245, 279
Balmaceda, José, 96
*Baltimore* affair, *ibid.*
Bandung Conference of non-aligned nations
    (1955), 222
Barbados, joins OAS, 247, n. 42
Batista, Fulgencio, 161–2
    overthrown, 225, 228
    atrocities of regime, 229, n. 3
    supporters among exiles, 232
Battle of River Plate (1939), 176, n. 64
Bay Islands, Britain and, 86–7
Bay of Pigs, 12, 17, 230–2, 276
Belaúnde Terry, Fernando, 252, 254
Belize (British Honduras), 83, 87
    claimed by Guatemala, 177, n. 67
    Mexico's claim, *ibid.*
Bennett, W. Tapley, Jr., 246
Berle, Adolf A. Jr., 15, n. 48
    in Cuba, 161
    business associations with Cuba, 170, n. 52
    Ambassador in Brazil, 194
    heads Kennedy task force, 232–3
Bidlack, Benjamin, 84
Bidlack Treaty, 84–5, 103–5
Blaine, James G., attacks Clayton-Bulwer
    Treaty, 94–5
    concern over War of the Pacific, 95–6
    and Chilean civil war, 96
    advocate of Pan Americanism, 107–8
'Blue Book', US, directed against Argentine
    government, 195–6
*Bogotazo*, 204
Bolívar, Simón, 36
    and Panama Congress, 66–7, 109
    and Pan Americanism, 108
    portrait at OLAS Conference, 250
Bolivia, and War of the Pacific, 95–6
    and Chaco War, 171
    oil dispute with US, 171–2, 176
    and Emergency Advisory Committee for
    Political Defense, 183, 237
    one of 'the six' at 8th Meeting, 236
    and Cuban missile crisis, 237
    position at 9th Meeting, 240
    supports US in Dominican crisis (1965),
    242
    Guevara meets death in, 250–1
    in Andean group, 254–5

nationalisation of Bolivian Gulf Oil Com-
    pany, 256
Brazil's influence in (1970s), 260
    *see also* Bolivian revolution
Bolivian Gulf Oil Company, 256
Bolivian revolution, US aid to, 209–11
Bonaparte, Joseph, 49
Bosch, Juan, overthrown, 239
    and Dominican crisis (1965), 241 ff.
    unacceptable to US, 243
    denigration of by US, 244–5
    compared with Dubcek, 271
Braden, Spruille, 15, n. 48, 194, 196, 212
Brazil, 1, 12, 25, 27
    as 'penetrated system', 29–30
    and territorial waters, 34, 254
    rivalry with Argentina, 37–8, 125, 260
    and Latin American integration, 38
    early US relations with, 48–9
    independence recognised by US (1824), 55
    seeks US alliance following Monroe's
    Message, 64
    and Panama Congress (1826), 109
    origins of friendship with US, 125
    (*see also* Rio-Branco)
    and US bases in 2nd World War, 178, 186
    at 4th Meeting, 207
    and Guatemalan crisis, 219
    'independent' policy on Cuba, 236–7
    reversal following military coup and
    9th Meeting, 240
    strongly supports US Dominican inter-
    vention (1965), 243
    criticises Alliance for Progress at Viña del
    Mar, 255
    growing power and influence, 260
    beneficiary of Allende's overthrow, 265
    recipient of Soviet aid, 285
    European Economic Community most
    important trading partner, 286, n. 35
British Guiana, and Anglo-Venezuelan dis-
    pute (1895), 96–9
    and Venezuela's claim, 177, n. 67
Bryan, William Jennings, 141
Bryan-Chamorro Treaty (1914), *ibid.*
Bucareli Agreements (1923), 148
Buchanan, James, and Cuba, 82
    opposes Clayton-Bulwer Treaty, 86, n. 24
    accepts British Central American treaties, 87
    and Mexico, 89–90
Building of the American Republics
    (Washington), 126
Bunau-Varilla, Philippe, 104–5
Bunker, Ellsworth, 243
Butler, Anthony, United States Minister to
    Mexico, 75
Byrnes, James F., 194, 195, 196

Caamaño Deñó, Francisco, unacceptable to
    US, 243
    denigration of by US, 244–5
    death of, 279, n. 24

Cabot, John Moors, 212
CACM, *see* Central American Common Market
Caffery, Jefferson, 161–2
Calhoun, John C., 80
Calvo, Carlos, 111
Calvo Doctrine (and 'clause'), 111, 127, 165, 172, 204
Canada, 46, 50, 51, 63, 82, 197
Canning, George, proposal to Rush, 56–60
and Polignac Memorandum, 65
and Panama Congress, 67–8
Cárdenas, Lázaro, expropriates oil companies (1938), 172–4
Caribbean region, special significance in inter-American relations, 4, 284–5
US policy towards (Panama policy), 5–6, 121–3
Carnegie, Andrew, 126
Carranza, Venustiano, 136, 138, 148
Castañeda, Jorge, 33
Castillo Armas, Carlos, 215, 220
Castro, Fidel, 2, n. 3, 19, 285, 286
and Portell Vilá, 165
and *Bogotazo*, 204
and Guatemalan crisis, 219
attends 2nd Meeting of 'Committee of 21', 225 (*see* Marshall Plan for Latin America)
communist sympathies, 227
and Trujillo, 229
Pres. Kennedy's feeling against, 231
strengthened by missile crisis, 238
denounces decisions of 9th Meeting, 240
host to Tricontinental Conference, 249
and to OLAS Conference, 249–50
visits Allende, 262
praises Chile, Peru and Panama, 262–3
reference to Venezuela, 263
Tito compared with, 270–1
CECLA, *see* Special Commission for Latin American Coordination
Central America, independence recognised by US, 55
invites US to Panama Congress, 66
dissolves into present five states, 83
British encroachments in region, 83–5
Anglo-US rivalry, 85–7
US filibusters in, 87–8
growing fear of US in region, 88
Central American Common Market (CACM), Treaty establishing, 233, n. 16 (*see also* General Treaty of Central American Economic Integration)
progress of, 248
'Action Program' to strengthen, 249
(*see also* Latin American Common Market)
diminished progress, 259
weakened by El Salvador-Honduras war, *ibid.*

Central American Court of Justice, 35, 129, 141–2
*see also* Washington Conference of Central American States
Central Intelligence Agency (CIA), 12–13, 29, 258
and Guatemala, 212, 218
and Bay of Pigs, 219, 230–1
Céspedes, Carlos Manuel de, 160–1
Chaco War (1932–5), 163, 171
Chamizal dispute, 35, 241
*see also* Mexico
Chamorro, Emiliano, 141–2
Charter of Punta del Este, 233
*see also* Alliance for Progress
Chile, territorial waters and fishing rights, 34, 253–4
early US trade to, 42
Poinsett appointed consul to, 50
independence recognised by US (1823), 55
seeks US alliance following Monroe's Message, 64
and War of the Pacific, 95–6, 112, 124
civil war in and *Baltimore* affair, 96
at 1st Conference, 112
and Alsop claim, 124
at 3rd Meeting, 180–1
and establishment of ECLA, 199
one of 'the six' at 8th Meeting, 236
position at 9th Meeting, 240
elections of 1964, 241
critical of US Dominican intervention (1965), 243
declines Rockefeller mission, 253
in Andean group, 254–5
situation in under Allende, 258–9, 263–4
resumes relations with Cuba, 258
broken again after military coup, 264
*see also* Allende
China, 6, 8, 25, 208
and Korean war, 206
establishes relations with Chile (1971), 258
current limited influence in Latin America, 286
Chincha Islands, seized by Spain from Peru (1864), 91
Church, Frank, critic of US Latin American policy, 17
likens to Soviet policy, 270
CIA, *see* Central Intelligence Agency
Civil War, US, 82, 90–3
Clark, J. Reuben, 157
Clark *Memorandum on the Monroe Doctrine*, 119, n. 19, 157–8
Clay, Henry, and Spanish American independence, 52–5
and an American 'system', 52
and Panama Congress, 66–7, 68, n. 51
Clayton-Bulwer Treaty (1850), 85–6
and the Monroe Doctrine, 86
growing US dissatisfaction with, 94–5

Clayton-Bulwer Treaty—*Cont.*
    replaced by second Hay-Pauncefote
        Treaty (1901), 103
Cleveland, Grover, and Venezuelan crisis
        (1895), 97–9
    and 1st Conference, 108
Cold War, 11, 21, n. 70, 39, 196, 206, 208
Colombia, loss of Panama, 20, 35, 104–5
    part of Gran Colombia, 41, n. 1
    seeks US alliance following Monroe's
        Message, 64
    invites US to Panama Congress, 66
    concern over British encroachments in
        Central America, 83
    concludes Bidlack Treaty with US, 84
    and Panama riots (1856), 88
    attacks Monroe Doctrine at 5th Con-
        ference, 148
    treaty of conciliation with US, 156–7
    sends troops to Korea, 206
    in Andean group, 254–5
Commercial Bureau of the American Re-
        publics, 110
    reorganised as International Bureau, 113
    renamed 'Pan American Union', 126
Committee of Twenty-One, *see* Special
        Committee to Study the Formulation
        of New Measures for Economic Co-
        operation
Commonwealth Caribbean countries and
        Latin America, 4, n. 12, 247, n. 42, 284
Congress of Lima,
    1st (1847–8), 108
    2nd (1864–5), *ibid.*
Consensus of Viña del Mar (1969), 36, 255–6,
        259
    Nixon's response to, 256
Continental Congress (Santiago de Chile,
        1856), 108
Convention for the Maintenance, Preserva-
        tion and Reestablishment of Peace
        (1936), 167–8
Convention on the Rights and Duties of
        States (1933), 165–6
Coolidge, Calvin, 19
    speech concerning US citizens and pro-
        perty abroad, 149
    ¬intervention in Nicaragua (1926), 150–2
    addresses 6th Conference, 154
    contribution to Good Neighbour policy,
        157
    and US as 'policeman', 272
Cosío Villegas, Daniel, 2
Costa Rica, protests at Bryan-Chamorro
        Treaty, 35, 141
    seeks European protection against US
        (1856), 88
    and peace force in Dominican Republic, 243
Crowder, General, 269
Cuba, ch. 1, *passim*
    Jefferson's interest in, 45
    substantial early US trade with, 48

and origins of Monroe Doctrine, 59–60
US opposition to Mexico and Colombia
        liberating (1826), 66–8
and Manifest Destiny, 81–2
and slavery issue in US, 81–2
and the 'Expansionists of 1898', 100 ff.
independence of and Platt Amendment,
        102–3
events of 1933, 160–3
abrogation of Platte Amendment, 166
business connections of Roosevelt's
        'brains trust' in, 170
increased US trade with, 170–1
and condemnation of 'economic aggres-
        sion' in OAS Charter, 201
historical importance of in inter-American
        relations, 226–7
accuses US in UN, 228, 232, 235–6
excluded from inter-American system, 236
relations resumed with Chile, 258
with Argentina and Peru, 261
relations broken off by Chilean military
        junta, 264
Cuba as test-case of US Latin American
        policy, 280–1
*see also* Bay of Pigs, Castro, Cuban exiles
Cuban exiles, 32, 165, 232
    Pres. Eisenhower orders training of, 228,
        n. 1, 230, n. 6
    *see also* Bay of Pigs
Cuban revolution, *see* Castro, Cuba
Czechoslovakia, arms to Guatemala, 215
Russian invasion of (1968) and US
        Dominican intervention (1965) com-
        pared, 270–1

Daniels, Josephus, 14, 163
    and Mexican oil dispute, 173–5
Danish West Indies (Virgin Islands), 21, 142
Darío, Rubén, 121
Dawkins, Edward, 68
Dawson, Thomas C., 117–18
Declaration of Lima (1938), 169
Declaration of the Presidents of America
        (1967), 249
Declaration of Yalta (1945), 270, n. 4
Democracy in Latin America
    *see* Representative democracy in Latin
        America
*Democratic Review*, 81, 99 (*see also* O'Sulli-
        van)
Díaz, Adolfo, 131–2
Díaz, Porfirio, 33–4
    and Washington Conference (1907), 129
    Root's eulogy of, 134
    overthrow of, 134–5
Diplomatic representations (as form of inter-
        vention), 111–12, 113
'Dollar Diplomacy', 121–2, 130
Dominican crisis (1965), 17, 19–20
    account of, 241–4
    significance of, 244–7, 270–1

Dominican Republic, 15, 16, 20, 21, 110, n. 6
  independence recognised by US (1866), 55
  Samaná Bay sought by US, 90
  country reannexed by Spain (1861–5),
    90–1
  Grant tries to annex, 94
  US intervention in (1905), 116 ff.
  Woodrow Wilson intervenes in, 139–41
  OAS sanctions against, 230 (*see also*
    Trujillo)
  US show of force (1961), 235
  elections in (1966), 244 (*see also* Domini-
    can crisis)
  situation since 1966, 279
Drago, Luis M., 115
Drago Doctrine, *ibid.*
Dubcek, Alexander, compared with Bosch,
    271
Dulles, Allen, 212
Dulles, John Foster, 198, n. 22
  appraised, 208
  and Guatemalan crisis, 212–15, 218
Duvalier, François, 253

ECLA, *see* United Nations Economic Com-
    mission for Latin America
Economic Agreement of Bogotá (1948),
    203–4
Economic Charter of the Americas (1945),
    190
Economic Conference of the OAS (Buenos
    Aires, 1957), 220
Economic Declaration of Buenos Aires
    (1957), *ibid.*
Economic integration of Latin America,
    ECLA gives impetus to, US suspicious
    of, 220–1
  US Business later favours, 248
  Johnson supports, 248–9
  *see also* Andean group, CACM, LAFTA
Ecuador, territorial waters and fishing
    rights, 34, 253–4
  part of Gran Colombia, 41, n. 1
  US and Galápagos Islands, 178, 186
  signs defence agreement with US, 207
  one of 'the six' at 8th Meeting, 236
  opposes US on Dominican intervention
    (1965), 243
  calls for 14th Meeting, 253, n. 57
  in Andean group, 254–5
Edward VII, King of England, arbiter in
    Alsop case, 124
Egypt, independence (1922) compared with
    that of Cuba (1903), 102, 269
Eisenhower, Dwight D., 15, n. 49, 24, n. 74,
    208
  sends brother on mission to South
    America, 209
  despatches troops to Caribbean, 224
  response to 'Operation Pan America', *ibid.*
  complacency in respect of Latin America,
    228, n. 1

and Cuba, 228, 230, n. 6
and Act of Bogotá, 232
Eisenhower, Milton, 1st report to President,
    209
  and Bolivia, 210
  2nd report to President, 225
El Salvador, protests at Bryan-Chamorro
    Treaty, 35, 141
  and Monroe Doctrine, 144
  coup in ends US Central American
    recognition policy, 167
  and peace force in Dominican Republic,
    243
  war with Honduras (1969), 257, 259
El Salvador–Honduras (1969), *ibid.*
Emergency Advisory Committee for Poli-
    tical Defense, 181–2
  and Bolivia, 183, 237
Estrada Cabrera, Manuel, 129
European Economic Community, 286, n. 35
European Recovery Programme, 196
'Expansionists of 1898', 99–100
Export-Import Bank, 13, 170–1, 175, 179,
    220

Falkland Islands (Malvinas), occupied by
    Britain (1833), 69
  claimed by Argentina, 177, n. 67
Farrell, Edelmiro, 184
Fish, Hamilton, 94
Flores, Juan José, 108, n. 4
Floridas, the, 42–7
Foreign Assistance Act (1962), 234, n. 21
France, 42–4, *passim*
  invasion of Spain (1823), 58
  Polignac Memorandum, 65
  interventions in Vera Cruz and River
    Plate, 69
  interest of in Texas, 77–8
  and proposed isthmian canal, 83–4
  intervention (by Napoleon III) in Mexico,
    92–3
  proposes international control of Haiti
    (1914), 142
  and Guatemalan crisis, 216, 218
Franklin, Benjamin, 41
Frei, Eduardo, elected Chile's President, 241
  initiative to strengthen LAFTA, 248
  role in forming Andean group, *ibid.*
  and Anaconda copper company, 254
Frelinghuysen, Frederick T., 107
French revolution, 43
Frondizi, Arturo, 236
Fulbright, J. William, and US 'self-image',
    xiii–xiv
  opposes Bay of Pigs invasion, 17, 245
  condemns US Dominican intervention,
    17, 245–6
  declares US partly responsible for El
    Salvador–Honduras war, 257

Gadsden Purchase (1853), 80

Gaitán, Jorge Eliecer, 204
Garfield, James A., 107
General Treaty of Central American
  Economic Integration, 233, n. 16
  *see also* Central American Common
  Market
General Treaty of Peace and Amity (1907),
  129, 141, n. 81
Germany, and Venezuelan blockade, 114
  US suspicion of in Dominican Republic,
  117
  proposes international control of Haiti
  (1914), 142
  West Germany and Latin America, 286
Gómez, Laureano, 206
Gondra, Manuel, 149, n. 3
  *see* Treaty to Avoid or Prevent Conflicts
  between the American States
Good Neighbour policy, x, 5, 9, 16
  origins of, 156 ff.
  the 'Cuban experience', 160 ff.
  and US 'New Deal', 170–1
  appraisal of, 187
Goodwin, Richard, on IPC question, 252,
  n. 52
Goulart, João, overthrow of, 12–13, 29–30,
  264–5
  'independent' policy on Cuba, 236–7
Governing Board of Pan American Union,
  126–7, 149
  under Rio Treaty, 197
  becomes OAS Council under OAS
  Charter, 202
Gran Colombia, independence recognised by
  US (1822), 41, 54
  *see also* Colombia, Ecuador, Venezuela
Grant, Ulysses S., 15 and Monroe Doctrine,
  94
Grau San Martín, Ramon, 22, 161–3
Great Britain, 41–5, *passim*
  war with US (1812), 46–7, 51
  early influence in Brazil, 48–9
  rivalry with US concerning Spanish
  American independence, 56 ff. (*see also*
  Adams, Canning)
  role in creating Uruguay and other interventions, 69
  rivalry with US in Mexico, 74–5
  and in Texas, 77–8
  and in Yucatán, 80
  interests in Central America, 83 ff. (*see
  also* Belize, Mosquito kingdom)
  rivalry with US in Central America, 85–7
  (*see also* Clayton–Bulwer Treaty)
  and Napoleon III's Mexican intervention,
  92
  and War of the Pacific, 95
  and Venezuelan crisis of 1895, 96–9
  accepts abrogation of Clayton–Bulwer
  Treaty, 103
  recognises Monroe Doctrine, 106
  and Venezuelan blockade, 114

refuses sanctions against Argentina, 184
  and Guatemalan crisis, 216, 218
Greytown (San Juan), occupied by British,
  69, 85
  bombarded by US warship, 86–7
  relinquished by Britain, 87
'Group of 77' *see* Third World
Guadalupe Hidalgo, Treaty of (1848), 79–80
  and 'good neighbourship', 156
Guantánamo Bay (Cuba), 6, 22, 166
Guatemala, seeks British and French protection against US (1855), 88
  claim to Belize, 177, n. 67
Guatemalan crisis (1954), 211–20
  situation in 1954 compared with Cuban in
  1961, 276
Guevara, Che, 2, 21, 151
  in Guatemala, 219
  at Punta del Este (1961), 233
  message urging 'many Vietnams', 249–50
  'President of Honour' of OLAS Conference, 250
  in Bolivia, *ibid.*
  capture and death, 251
Guizot, François, gives French view on
  Texas, 78
Guyana, *see* British Guiana

Hague Court of Arbitration, 117
Hague Peace Conference, 126
Haiti, independence recognised by US
  (1862), 55
  at 1st Conference, 111, n. 8
  US intervention in (1915), 142
  US marines withdrawn from, 167
  massacre of Haitians by Trujillo dictator-
  ship (1937), 229, n. 3, 278
  welcomes Rockefeller mission, 253
Hanna, Matthew, 152, n. 9
Harding, Warren, contribution to Good
  Neighbour policy, 156–7
Harrison, Benjamin, and the *Baltimore*
  affair, 96
Hay, John, 103, 114, 115, n. 14, 117–18
Hay–Bunau–Varilla Treaty (1903), 105–6
Hay–Herrán Treaty, rejected by Colombian
  Senate, 104
Hay–Pauncefote Treaties (1900, 1901), 103
Hayes, Rutherford, and an isthmian canal,
  94
Heads of State, Panama Meeting (1956), 220
Heads of State, Punta del Este Meeting
  (1967), 248–9
Herrán, Tomás, 104
Hickenlooper Amendment, 17, 234, 252, 261
Hispaniola, 123
Holy Alliance, 6, 58, 60, 69
Honduras, weakness as source of Central
  American conflict, 129
  and Guatemalan crisis, 215 ff.
  and peace force in Dominican Republic, 243
  war with El Salvador (1969), 257, 259

Hoover, Herbert, contribution to Good Neighbour policy, 157-8, 232
Huerta, Victoriano, 135-8
Hughes, Charles Evans, American people and foreign policy, 18
stresses unilateral character of Monroe Doctrine, 148
on Latin America as entity, 154
defends US interventions at 6th Conference, 154-6
Hull, Cordell, 10, 159
at 7th Conference, 164-6
earlier work with Cuban sugar lobby, 170
and Bolivian oil dispute (1937), 171-2
anger at Welles's 'surrender' to Argentina (1942), 180

Imbert, General, 244
Inter-American Committee on the Alliance for Progress, 28, 234
Inter-American Conference, *see* International Conferences of American States
Inter-American Conference for the Maintenance of Continental Peace and Security (Rio de Janeiro, 1947), 196-9
Inter-American Conference for the Maintenance of Peace (Buenos Aires, 1936), 167-9
Inter-American Conference on Problems of War and Peace (Mexico City, 1945), reorganisation of inter-American system, 188-90
Act of Chapultepec, 189-90
Latin American dissatisfaction over economic and social matters, 190
the problem of Argentina, 190-1
Inter-American Defense Board, 21, 181-2, 202
Inter-American Defense College, 21
Inter-American Development Bank, 28, 225
Inter-American Development Commission, 179
Inter-American Economic and Social Council, 199, 202
Inter-American Financial and Economic Advisory Committee, 176, 179
Inter-American Peace Committee, 215, n. 73, 216-17
Inter-American peace force (*ad hoc*), 243-4
no question of permanent force, 247
Inter-American System, 5, 24-8, 39-40, 267-8
reorganisation discussed at Mexico City (1945), 188-90
post-war reorganisation, 196-204
imposes sanctions on Dominican Republic, 230
Cuba excluded from, 236
weakened by US Dominican intervention (1965), 246
steps to strengthen, 246-7

call for radical changes in, 262
compared with Soviet system, 270-2
value of to US, 273-4
*see also* Organization of American States (OAS), Pan Americanism
Inter-American Treaty of Reciprocal Assistance (Rio Treaty, 1947), 7, 28
described, 196-8
comes into effect, 197
Monroe Doctrine and, 198
value to Latin America questioned, 262
as legal basis of US Cuban 'quarantine', 274
International Bank for Reconstruction and Development, 209
International Bureau of the American Republics, *see* Commercial Bureau of the American Republics
International Conferences of American States
1st (1889-90), 110-13
2nd (1901-2), 113
3rd (1906), 125-6
4th (1910), 126-7
5th (1923), 148-9
6th (1928), 152-6
7th (1933), 162-6
8th (1938), 169
9th (1948), 200-2
10th (1954), 212-15
International Court of Justice, 240-1
International law invoked by United States, 22-3, 33-4
Latin America and, 33-5
International Petroleum Company (IPC), expropriation, 251 ff.
International Telegraph and Telephones Company (ITT), 258, 264
International Union of American Republics, 27, 110
renamed 'Union of American Republics', 126
Intervention, as issue in inter-American relations, 32-3
'non-recognition' (US) as intervention, 22
diplomatic representations (US) as intervention, 111-12
*see also* Non-intervention
IPC, *see* International Petroleum Company
Iturbide, Augustín de, 27, 55, 73

Jackson, Andrew, and East Florida, 47
and Texas, 75-7
Jamaica, joins OAS, 247, n. 42
US economic penetration, 284
Japan, trade and investment in Latin America, 40, 286
Jefferson, Thomas, 44, 47, 49
and Cuba, 45
consulted by Monroe, 59
Johnson, Lyndon B., and Latin America, 238-9

Johnson Lyndon B.—*Cont.*
and Panama Canal Zone crisis, 239
welcomes Goulart's overthrow, 240
and preventing 'a second Cuba', 241
and Dominican crisis, 241 ff.
credibility weakened, 244
supports Latin American Common
Market, 248–9
does not stand for re-election, 251
'Johnson Doctrine', 242
Juárez, Benito, 89, 91–3
*Justicialismo*, 222, 261

Kellogg, Frank, and 'Bolshevism' in
Mexico, 151
accompanies Coolidge to 6th Conference,
154
Kennecott Copper Corporation, 263–4
Kennedy, John F., 5, 14, 18, n. 57, 29, n. 86
interest in counter-insurgency, 7, n. 22
and Bay of Pigs, 231–2, 276
domestic pressure over Cuba, 236
and Cuban missile crisis, 237–8
assassination, 238
encourages Latin American military, 239
'no second Cuba', 241
Kennedy, Robert F., 13, 18, n. 57, 24, 274
Khrushchev, Nikita S., and peaceful coexistence, 221
and Cuban revolution, 228–9
declares Monroe Doctrine 'dead', 229
and Cuban missile crisis, 274
Kissinger, Henry, xvii, 265–6
Knox, Philander C., 130
J. F. Dulles compared with, 208
Korean War, 16
OAS Council and, 206
Colombia sends troops, *ibid.*
and Latin American trade, 207
Kosygin, Alexei, visits Havana before
OLAS Conference, 251
Kubitschek, Juscelino, and Operation Pan
America, 224–5
and 'independent' foreign policy, 236

LAFTA, *see* Latin American Free Trade
Association
Lansing, Robert, 147
Lanusse, Alejandro, 260, n. 71
Latin America as entity, 1–2
Hughes's comments on, 154
Latin American Common Market, to be
established by 1985, 249
Latin American Free Trade Association
(LAFTA), Treaty establishing, 233, n.
16 (*see also* Montevideo Treaty)
difficulties, 248
'Action Program' to strengthen, 249 (*see
also* Latin American Common Market)
stagnant, 259
Latin American integration, obstacles to,
37–8

*see also* Economic integration of Latin
America
Latin American military, US policy of
strengthening, 21, 239, 278
social revolution led by, 226, 253
Latin American nationalism (anti-US), 8,
31, 226, 276–7, 285
'continental nationalism', 256, 260
*see also* 'Latin American personality'
Latin American Peoples' Solidarity Con-
ference, 1st (1967), 249–50
'Latin American personality', affirmed in
Consensus of Viña del Mar, 255, 260
Latin American Solidarity Organization
(OLAS), 249
'Latin Americanism', 25
economic integration as, 221
Law of the Sea Conference, Caracas (1974),
34, n. 100
League of Nations, 38, 143–5, 168
and inter-American disputes, 164
Lechín, Juan, 210
Lend-Lease, 181–2
Lesseps, Ferdinand de, 94, 103–4
Leticia dispute, 163
Lincoln, Abraham, and the Mexican war, 79
Lodge, Henry Cabot ('expansionist of
1898'), 100
Lodge, Henry Cabot, US representative in
Security Council (1950), 215–16
Louisiana Purchase, 42–5, 277

Machado, Gerardo, 160
McKinley, William, and Spanish-American
war, 100
and an isthmian canal, 103
and Pan Americanism, 108
McLane–Ocampo Treaty (1859), 89
Madero, Francisco, 33, n. 96, 135–6
Madison, James, and the Floridas, 45–6
and Spanish American insurgents, 49–51
consulted by Monroe, 59
Mahan, Alfred Thayer, 95
*Maine*, sinking of, 100
Manifest Destiny, 3, 20
main elements of, 71–2
Mexico and, 72 ff
Cuba and, 81 ff. (*see also* O'Sullivan)
new phase of, 99 ff. (*see also* 'Expan-
sionists of 1898')
Vera Cruz occupation compared with, 137
Marshall, George C., 196, 198–9, 205
Marshall Plan for Latin America, rejected by
US, 199
proposed by Castro, 225
Martí, José, 102, 112–13, 121
Martín García, occupied by France (1838),
69
Maximilian, Archduke, Emperor of Mexico,
27, 92–3
Mayo, Admiral, 136
Meeting of Consultation of American

Foreign Ministers, under Rio Treaty 197
under OAS Charter, 202
Meetings of Consultation
  1st (1939), 176
  2nd (1940), 176–7
  3rd (1942), 180–1
  4th (1951), 206–7
  5th (1959), 229
  6th (1960), 229–30
  7th (1960), 229–30
  8th (1962), 236–7
  9th (1964), 240
  10th (1965), 242–3
  12th (1967), 249–50
  14th (1971), 253, n. 57
Mexican revolution, 33–4, 135–9, 147–8, 172 ff.
Mexican war with US, 9, n. 28, 20, 79–80
Mexico, significance in inter-American relations, ix–x
  as 'penetrated system', 30
  'revolutionary sympathy' for Cuba, *ibid.*
  1917 constitution and US concern, 34, 147–8
  oil dispute with US, 34, 173–5
  Chamizal question, 35, 241
  early US interest in, 44, 48
  recognised by US (1822), 41, 54–5
  seeks US pledge following Monroe's Message, 64
  invites US to Panama Congress, 66
  early relations with US, 72 ff.
  loss of Texas, 76–7 (*see also* Mexican war with US, Guadalupe Hidalgo, Treaty of)
  Gadsden Purchase, 80
  Buchanan and, 88–90
  'The Reform' and Maximilian's empire, 91–3
  Woodrow Wilson and, 134–9 (*see also* Pershing, Vera Cruz)
  and League of Nations Covenant, 144
  and Central America, 150–1
  Kellogg and 'Bolshevism' in, 151
  Morrow as US Ambassador in, *ibid.*
  and 'Pan Americanising' Monroe Doctrine, 163
  at 10th Conference, 214
  and US quota restrictions, 224
  Statement on Cuba at 7th Meeting, 230, n. 5
  and Cuban missile crisis, 237
  and decisions of 9th Meeting, 240–1 (*see also* International Court of Justice)
  critical of US Dominican intervention (1965), 243
  and Latin American integration, 249
Middle East, compared with Caribbean area, 269
Miller, Edward G. Jr., 205–6
Monroe, James, 6, 49, 51–2

and recognition of Spanish American governments, 41, 53–5
and Canning's proposal to Rush, 59–61
his Message to Congress (2 December, 1823), 61–5
Monroe Doctrine, 2–6, 9, 11, 18, 32, 38
  Monroe's Message analysed, 61–5
  the Message and the Panama Congress, 66
  disregarded by British and French interventions, 69
  link with Manifest Destiny, 70
  'period of quiescence', 71
  Polk and, 77–81
  and Clayton–Bulwer Treaty, 86
  association with US intervention, 88, n. 30, 121
  and Spain's reannexation of Dominican Republic, 90–1
  and Napoleon III's challenge in Mexico, 91–3
  and no-transfer principle, 94
  and Venezuelan crisis (1895), 96–9
  receives Britain's 'unwavering support', 106
  and Venezuelan blockade (1902), 114–15
  Platt Amendment as extension of, 116
  relationship of Roosevelt Corollary to 'original' analysed, 119–21
  and League of Nations Covenant, 144
  attacked by Colombia at 5th Conference, 148
  Hughes stresses unilateral character of, *ibid.*
  and sovereignty of Latin American countries, 153–4
  Mexican proposal for 'Pan Americanising', 163
  criticised at 7th Conference, 165
  and Rio Treaty, 198
  Truman describes as Marshall Plan for Latin America, 199
  Dulles declares tested by Soviet policy (1947), 208
  Caracas anti-communist resolution as endorsement of, 213–14
  Cuban revolution and, 228, 238
  Khrushchev declares dead, 229
  State Department reaffirms, *ibid.*
  'Johnson Doctrine' as corollary of, 242
  in US self-image, 267
  as imperialism, 268
  global application of since 1945, 273
  *see also* Clark Memorandum, Roosevelt Corollary
Montevideo Treaty (1960), 233, n. 16
Morgenthau, Henry, 174
Morrow, Dwight, sent as US Ambassador to Mexico, 151, 157, 172
Mosquito kingdom, British protection of, 83, 85, 87
Mutual Defense Assistance Agreements, 21, 207

Nabuco, Jaoquim, 125, 126, n. 42
Napoleon I, and Louisiana, 43–4, 277
  invasion of Iberian peninsula (1807–8),
    44–7
  US 'associate in 1812 war', 51
Napoleon III, intervention in Mexico, 92–3
National Aeronautic and Space Adminis-
    tration (NASA), 6–7
National City Bank of New York, 123, 167
Nationalism (Latin American), *see* Latin
    American nationalism
New Granada, *see* Colombia
New Orleans, 43–4
Niagara Falls Conference (1914), 137–8
Nicaragua, 19, 35
  and British encroachments, *see* Greytown,
    Mosquito kingdom
  Walker's filibustering and fears of US,
    87–8
  seeks European protection, 88
  and an isthmian canal route, 103–4
  —US intervention in (1909), 129 ff.
  and Woodrow Wilson, 141–2
  and Guatemalan crisis, 215 ff.
  and peace force in Dominican Republic,
    243
Nixon, Richard M., 7, 16, 36
  'goodwill' tour of South America (1958),
    223–4
  and Bay of Pigs, 231
  becomes President, 251
  pursues 'low profile' policy, 252
  sends Nelson Rockefeller to Latin America,
    252–3
  and Rockefeller report, 257
  economic measures (1971) anger Latin
    America, 259
  measures against Peru, 261
  and overthrow of Allende, 264–5
  and US treaty obligations, 274
Non-intervention, adopted (with US res-
    ervations) at 7th Conference, 165–6
  (*see also* Convention on the Rights and
    Duties of States)
  Additional Protocol at Buenos Aires, 1936
    (*see* Additional Protocol Relative to
    Non-Intervention)
  clauses in OAS Charter, 200–1
  *see also* Intervention
North Atlantic Treaty Organization
    (NATO), 7, 196, 215
Norweb, R. Henry, 278
No-transfer principle, resolution of Con-
    gress (1811), 46
  part of Monroe Doctrine, 94
  reiterated in 1940, 176–7

OAS, *see* Organization of American States
OAS Amended Charter, 28, 202, n. 28, 247
OAS Charter, centrepiece of inter-American
    system, 28
  relationship to UN, 200, 202–3, 217 ff, 230

  and representative democracy, 200
  non-intervention clauses, 200–1
  principal organs, 202
OAS General Assembly, replaces Inter-
    American Conference, 202, n. 28, 262,
    n. 75
  3rd (1973), 262, n. 75
Obregón, Alvaro, 22, 34, 148
Odría, Manuel A., decorated by US, 224
Office for Coordination of Commercial and
    Cultural Relations between the Ameri-
    can Republics, *see* Office of the Co-
    ordinator of Inter-American Affairs
Office of the Coordinator of Inter-American
    Affairs (CIAA), 179–80
OLAS, *see* Latin American Solidarity
    Organization
Olney, Richard, 97–9, 115, n. 14, 270, n. 5
Onís, Luis de, 47, n. 7
Operation Pan America, 224–5
  and Act of Bogotá, 225, n. 94, 232
  and Alliance for Progress, 225, n. 94,
    233
Organization of American States (OAS),
  and Guatemalan crisis, 216–17
  relations with UN, 202–3, 217–19, 230
  and Cuba, 229–30, 236–7
  *see also* Inter-American System
'Ostend Manifesto', 21, n. 67, 82, 88
O'Sullivan, John L., coins phrase 'Manifest
    Destiny', 81
  and Cuba, 81–2
  death of, 99
Ovando Candia, Alfredo, 256, 259

Pact of Bogotá, *see* American Treaty on
    Pacific Settlement
Panama, a flashpoint of racial friction, 4
  US installations in and around Canal
    Zone, 6
  strong anti-US nationalism, 31
  UN Security Council meeting in (1973),
    38, n. 108, 262–3, 273
  Hay–Bunau–Varilla Treaty, 105–6
  US signs new treaty with (1936), 167
  opposition to US bases outside Canal
    Zone, 178, 186
  1964 dispute with US, 239
  as symbol of US hegemony, 273
  *see also* Colombia
Panama, Congress of (1826), 64, 66–8,
    108–9
Panama policy, *see* Caribbean region
Pan American Financial Conference, 1st
    (1915), 143
Pan American policy (US), 5, 14
Pan Americanism, 25–7, 33, 107–8, 267
  limited achievement by 1st World War,
    127–8
  Niagara Falls Conference (1914) and, 137
  *see also* Inter-American System
Paraguay, and Chaco War, 171

and peace force in Dominican Republic, 243
Brazil's influence in (1970s), 260
Paraguayan War (1864–70), 109
Paris, Treaty of (1898), 103
Paz Estenssoro, Victor, 183, 210
Peace Corps, 13
'Pentagon', 12
Pérez Jiménez, Marcos, dictatorship praised by Dulles, 208, 212
decorated by US, 224
Perón, Juan, 184
elected President of Argentina (1946), 196
and 'Third Position', 222
overthrown (1955), 223
return to power, 260–1, 265
Pershing, John, and punitive expedition, 138
Peru, territorial waters and fishing rights, 34, 35, 253–4
Poinsett appointed consul to, 50
independence recognised by US (1826), 55
and hostilities with Spain over Chincha Islands, 91
and War of the Pacific, 95–6
and Nixon visit (1958), 223–4
opposes US on Dominican intervention (1965), 243
policies of Velasco government, 251 ff.
declines Rockefeller mission, 253
in Andean group, 254–5
resumes relations with Cuba, 261
host to 'group of 77', *ibid.*
role at 3rd UNCTAD, 261–2
exposed position following Allende's overthrow, 265
Peurifoy, John E., 217
Philippines, 9, n. 28, 268
Pierce, Franklin, tries to buy Cuba, 82
attempts to obtain Samaná Bay, 90
Pinckney Treaty (1795), 43
Platt Amendment, imposed upon Cuba, 102
as extension of Monroe Doctrine, 116
interventions under, 160
Portell Vilá denounces at 7th Conference, 164–5
abrogated (1934), 166
Poinsett, Joel, US agent in South America, 50–1
Josephus Daniels's judgement of, 74, n. 7
Minister in Mexico, 74–5
Polignac Memorandum, 65, 74
Polk, James K., and the Monroe Doctrine, 77–81
and Texas, 79–80
and war with Mexico, *ibid.* (*see also* Guadalupe Hidalgo, Treaty of)
tries to purchase Cuba, 82
and Bidlack Treaty, 84–5
Portell Vilá, Herminio, 164–5
Porter, Charles O., 16
Powell, William F., 117
Prats, General, 264

Puerto Rico, 9, n. 28, 20, 67
Roosevelt Roads base in, 6
Punta del Este, Alliance for Progress launched at, 233
8th Meeting held at, 236–7
Meeting of American Presidents at, 248–9

Quadros, Jânio, and 'independent' Brazilian foreign policy, 236
*Quality of Life in the Americas*, 257

Race, as factor in inter-American relations, x, 4, 268, 284–5
Panama a 'flashpoint of racial friction', 4
in US occupation of Haiti, 142
Ramírez, Pedro, 184
Reciprocal Trade Agreements Act (1934), 170
Representative democracy in Latin America, in OAS Charter, 200
and Alliance for Progress, 233
and US policy, 277 ff.
'Right of conquest', 112, 200
Rio-Branco, Baron of, 125, 260
Rio de la Plata, blockaded by Britain and France (1845), 69
Rockefeller, David, and Latin American Common Market, 248
Rockefeller, Nelson, Coordinator of Inter-American Affairs, 179
mission to Latin America (1969), 252–3
report on his mission, *Quality of Life in the Americas*, 257
Rodó, José Enrique, 2, 121
Rodríguez Larreta, Eduardo, 194–5
Rodríguez Larreta proposal, 194–5, 201
Roosevelt, Franklin D., x, 5, 14, 16
and Haitian constitution, 142
*Foreign Affairs* article, 158–9
Pan American Day speech (1933), 159
and Grau San Martín, 162
interpretation of 'intervention' (1933), 166
'off-the-record' remarks about oil dispute, 174
'Give them a share' speech, 175–6
condemns Argentine government, 184
death of, 192
Roosevelt, Theodore, 4, 9, n. 28, 14
'the Chilean volunteer', 96, n. 44
expansionist in 1898, 100
attitude towards Cubans, 103
and isthmian canal, 103 ff.
'I took the Canal', 105
and Venezuelan blockade, 114
and US Panama policy, 121–2
attitude towards Latin Americans, 268
*see also* Roosevelt Corollary
Roosevelt Corollary, 4, 20–1, 115–16, 242
application to Dominican Republic (1905), 116 ff.
significance analysed, 118–21

Roosevelt Corollary—*Cont.*
  reception in Argentina, 124
  reception in Brazil, 125
Root, Elihu, 115, n. 14
  and Platt Amendment, 102, 116
  eulogy of Porfirio Díaz, 134
Ruatan, occupied by Britain (1839), 69, 83
  relinquished (1860), 87
Rush, Richard, 58–9, 60, 65
Rusk, Dean, 265, n. 81
Russia, 61, 67, 208
  *see also* Soviet system, Soviet Union
Sáenz Peña, Roque, speech at 1st Conference, 112
  recalled at 8th, 169
Saint Domingue, 43
Salazar, José Maria, 64
Salisbury, Lord, 69, 98
Samaná Bay, 90
Sandino, Augusto C., 141, n. 79, 151–2
San Domingo Improvement Company, 116–17, 123
San Francisco Conference (1945), different power status between US and Latin America, 191–2
  collective defence and regional arrangements, 192–3
Santa Anna, Antonio López de, 73, 76, 80, 91
Santana, Pedro, 90
Schneider, General, 258
Scruggs, William Lindsay, 97
Seward, William, and Spain, 91
  and Napoleon III, 92–3
Sinclair Oil Company, 174–5
Smith, Earl, 29, n. 86
Smoot–Hawley Act, 158
*societas leonina*, 268
Somoza, Anastasio, 141, n. 79, 151–2
  entertained by Franklin Roosevelt, 278
Soviet system, compared with US in Latin America, 11, 25, 30, 270–2
Soviet Union, 6, 8, 25, 40, 192
  Latin American governments' fear of in 1945, 188
  and onset of Cold War, 196
  and Korean War, 206
  and Guatemala, 216
  and Cuban revolution, 228 ff.
  and application of sanctions by OAS (1960), 230
  and Cuban missile crisis, 237
  and Dominican crisis (1965), 242
  appeal to by 12th Meeting, 250
  discourages more revolutions in Latin America, 251 (*see also* Kosygin)
  current policy towards Latin America, 285–6
  limits of influence in the region, 286
Spain, ch. 2, *passim* (*see* Pinckney Treaty, Adams-Onís Treaty), 80
  reannexes Dominican Republic (1861–5), 90–1
  seizes Chincha Islands (1864), 91

and Napoleon's Mexican intervention, 92
  *see also* Spanish America, Spanish-American War
Spanish America, early North American trade with, 41–2
  US territorial ambitions in, 42 ff.
  wars of independence, 49–56
Spanish-American War (1898), 9, n. 28, 18–19, 20, 100 ff.
Special Commission for Latin American Coordination (CECLA), Viña del Mar meeting, 36, 255–6
  established, 255
  Buenos Aires meeting (1971), 259
Special Committee for the Reorganization of the Inter-American System, 262
Special Committee to Study the Formulation of New Measures for Economic Co-operation (Committee of Twenty-One)
  1st Meeting (Washington, 1958), 224–5
  2nd Meeting (Buenos Aires, 1959), 225
  3rd Meeting (Bogotá, 1960), 232
Special Consultative Committee on Security against the Subversive Action of International Communism, 23, 236–7
Special Inter-American Conferences
  1st (1964), 247, n. 42
  2nd (1965), 247
  3rd (1967), *ibid.*
Stalin, Joseph, 221, 270
Standard Oil Company, 171, 175, n. 62, 251
Stimson, Henry L., and Nicaragua, 151–2
  concern at international repercussions of Nicaraguan intervention, 152
  impressed by Somoza, 152, n. 9
Stroessner, Alfredo, 260
Sullivan, James M., 139–40

Taft, William Howard, 14, 121–2, 130
Taylor, Zachary, 79
Tehuantepec, Isthmus of, 80, 89
Teller Amendment, 101–2
Terrorism and kidnappings, measures to combat discussed in OAS, 257, n. 61
Texas, 43–7, 72, 75 ff.
  independence of, 76
  annexation by United States, 77
  Britain and France and, 77–8
Third World, Latin American identification with, 5, n. 13, 39, 273
  origins of, 221–2
  and Perón's 'Third Position', 222, 261
  'group of 77', 261
  significance for inter-American relations, 284
Tito, Marshal, compared with Castro, 270–1
Tobar, Carlos, 129
Tobar Doctrine, *ibid.*
Torres, Juan José, 259, 260
Treaty to Avoid or Prevent Conflicts between the American States (Gondra Treaty, 1923), 149

Tricontinental Conference, *see* Afro–Asian–
Latin American Peoples' Solidarity
Conference
Trinidad and Tobago joins OAS, 247, n. 42
Trujillo, Rafael, support in US Congress,
16, 229, 277–8
  US occupation leads to his dictatorship, 141
  wartime co-operation with US, 178–9
  and Castro, 229
  and massacre of Haitian civilians (1937),
  229, n. 3, 278
  attempted assassination of Venezuelan
  President, 230
  death of, 235
  entertained by Franklin Roosevelt, 278
Truman, Harry S., 35, 192, 193, 196, 199,
205, 208, 209
Truman Doctrine, 9, 196
*Tupamaros*, 23, n. 73
Tyler, John, 77

Ubico, Jorge, 211–12, 220
United Fruit Company, 123, 211–12, 220
United Nations, 25, 38
  Declaration of, 180
  Dumbarton Oaks proposals, 186–8, 190
  Charter of, 192–3 (*see also* San Francisco
  Conference)
  OAS relationship to, 200, 202–3, 217 ff.,
  230
  and Korean War, 206
  enlarged membership, 221–2
United Nations General Assembly, Latin
American support for US in, 8, 206
  Guatemalan case discussed in, 218–9
  addressed by Allende, 264
United Nations Security Council, extra-
ordinary meeting in Panama, 38, n. 108,
262–3, 273
  and Guatemalan crisis, 215–19
  Cuban complaints against US in, 228,
  235–6
  and OAS sanctions against Dominican
  Republic, 230
  and Cuban missile crisis, 237
  and US-Panama dispute (1964), 239
  and Dominican crisis (1965), 242
United Nations Conference on Trade and
Development (UNCTAD)
  1st (1964), 247
  3rd (1972), 261–2
  Third World demands at UNCTADs, 284
United Nations Economic Commission for
Latin America (ECLA)
  established (1948), 199–200
  and Latin American economic integration,
  220–1
  US distrust of, *ibid*.
United Provinces of the Rio de la Plata,
  Poinsett appointed consul to, 50
  seek recognition by US, 52

independence so recognised (1823), 55
  seek US pledge following Monroe's
  Message, 64
  *see also* Argentina
United States, self-image, xii–xiv, 8–12, 25,
101, 147, 267–8, 280
  Latin American policy objectives, 6 ff.
  a counter-revolutionary power, 8, 276–7
  policy formulation, 12–20
  instruments of policy, 20–5
  economic aid to Latin America, 23–4 (*see
  also* Act of Bogotá, Alliance for Progress, Consensus of Viña del Mar)
  as imperialist power, 268–70
  policy compared with Soviet system, 270–3
  value to of inter-American system, 273–4
  intervention in Latin America, 275–6
  beneficiary of dictatorships, 277–8
  and holding of elections, 279–80
  Cuba as test-case of her professions,
  280 ff.
  new challenges to her hegemony, 283 ff.
  *see also* Destiny Manifest Monroe Doctrine
  and other specific headings
United States Congress, role in foreign
policy, 15–17
  Trujillo's supporters in, 16, 229, 277–8
  passes no-transfer resolution, 46
  and recognition of new Spanish American
  nations, 52–4
  and Panama Congress (1826), 64, 66
  votes annexation of Texas, 77
  and War of the Pacific, 96
  and *Baltimore* affair, *ibid*.
  resolution on Cuba (1898), 100–1
  determines status of Cuba, 103
  considers Nicaraguan canal route, 104
  and 1st Conference, 108
  resolution reiterating no-transfer principle (1940), 176–7
  and retention of bases in Latin America,
  185–6
  and Foreign Assistance Act of 1962, 234,
  n. 21
  disapproval of Chilean junta (1973), 265
  opposition to revision of Panama Canal
  treaty, 266, n. 82
  *see also* United States Senate
United States Senate, role in foreign policy,
  15–16
  and Bidlack Treaty, 84–5
  rejects McLane–Ocampo Treaty, 89
  rejects Grant's treaty to annex Dominican
  Republic, 94
  and Dominican protocol (1905), 118, 128
  action on Vera Cruz occupation, 136
  rejects League of Nations, 143–4
  Foreign Relations Committee is given
  Kellogg memorandum on 'Bolshevism',
  151
  and conciliation treaty with Colombia,
  156–7

United States Senate—*Cont.*
  delays ratification of new Panama treaty
    (1936), 167
  Subcommittee Hearings on US military
    policies and programmes in Latin
    America, 257
  *see also* United States Congress
United States Information Agency (USIA),
    13, 24
United States–Nicaragua Concession, 130–
    132
United States Sugar Act of 1947, Cuba and,
    201
Uruguay, *Tupamaros* in, 23, n. 73
  created, 69
  and decisions of 9th Meeting, 240
  denounces 'Johnson Doctrine' (US
    Dominican intervention, 1965), 242–3
  Brazil's influence in (1970s), 260
U Thant, 242


Valdés, Gabriel, 255
Vandenberg, Arthur, 192
Vanderbilt, Cornelius, and William Walker,
    87
Vargas, Getúlio, 194
Vaughan, Charles, 68, n. 51
Velasco Alvarado, Juan, 251–2, 256, 261
Venezuela, part of Gran Colombia, 41, n. 1
  dispute with Britain over British Guiana,
    96–9, 177, n. 67
  Anglo-German blockade of (1902), 114
  and Nixon visit (1958), 223–4
  charges against Dominican Republic in
    OAS, 230
  participates in Cuban quarantine, 237,
    n. 28
  charges against Cuba in OAS (1963),
    239–40
  does not support US in Dominican
    crisis, 243
  further charges against Cuba (1967), 249–
    50
  declines Rockefeller mission, 253
  not at first in Andean group, 254–5
  eventual oil nationalisation planned, 263
  adheres to Andean pact (1973), 265
Vera Cruz, occupied by France (1838), 69
  and Napoleon III's intervention in
    Mexico, 92
  occupied by US (1914), 136–7
  Josephus Daniels's role, 173
Vietnam War, 16, 19
  overshadows Cuban problem, 241
  overshadows all other problems, 251
  weakens West's position on Czecho-
    slovakia (1968), 272
  influence on inter-American relations,
    273
Villa, Pancho, 136, 138
Volta Redonda Steel Plant, 179

Walker, William, filibustering in Central
    America, 87–8, 108
Walters, Vernon, 29, n. 89
War of the Pacific (1879–83), 95–6, 109,
    112
  and Alsop claim, 124
Warsaw Pact (1955), 271
Washington, George, 64
Washington Conference of Central Ameri-
    can States (1907), 129
Watergate, 29, n. 89, 266
Welles, Sumner, 14–15
  in Cuba, 160–1, 165
  relations with Batista, 161
  sees Cuba as example of Good Neighbour
    policy, 170
  at 3rd Meeting, 180
  alleges US instigated Rodríguez Larreta
    proposal, 195
  criticises US handling of *Blue Book*, 196,
    n. 14
  and massacre of Haitians in Dominican
    Republic (1937), 278
Western Europe,
  trade and investment in Latin America, 40
'Western Hemisphere Idea', 25–7, 128
Wilson, Henry Lane, personal vendetta
    against Madero, 135
  removed by Woodrow Wilson, 136
Wilson, Huntington, 130, 132, 135, n. 65
Wilson, Woodrow, 5, 10, 14, 21, 35, 121–2
  appraisal of his Latin American policy,
    132–4
  and Mexico, 134 ff.
  intervention in Dominican Republic, 139–
    41
  and Nicaragua, 141–2
  and Haiti, 142
  and treaty of conciliation with Colombia,
    156
  J. F. Dulles compared with, 208
1st World War, Latin American participa-
    tion in, 143
  US relative position strengthened as con-
    sequence of, 143–5
2nd World War, hemisphere defence, 177–9,
    181–2
  economic co-operation, 179, 182–3
  the 'Argentine problem', 180–1, 183–4
  weakening partnership, 184–6
  post-war planning, 188 ff.


Ydígoras Fuentes, Miguel, 220
Yucatán, 80–1
Yugoslavia, situation compared with Cuba,
    270–1


Zapata, Emiliano, 138
Zea, Leopoldo, 2, 8, n. 24
Zelaya, José Santos, 129–32
Zimmermann telegram, 139

DATE DUE

I

NO